KW-179-380

THE LIMITS OF REGIONALISM

The International Political Economy of New Regionalisms Series

The International Political Economy of New Regionalisms Series presents innovative analyses of a range of novel regional relations and institutions. Going beyond established, formal, interstate economic organizations, this essential series provides informed interdisciplinary and international research and debate about myriad heterogeneous intermediate level interactions.

Reflective of its cosmopolitan and creative orientation, this series is developed by an international editorial team of established and emerging scholars in both the South and North. It reinforces ongoing networks of analysts in both academia and think-tanks as well as international agencies concerned with micro-, meso- and macro-level regionalisms.

Editorial Board

Timothy M. Shaw, University of London, UK
Isidro Morales, Universidad de las Américas, Puebla, Mexico
Maria Nzomo, Embassy of Kenya, Zimbabwe
Nicola Phillips, University of Manchester, UK
Johan Saravanamuttu, Science University of Malaysia, Malaysia
Fredrik Söderbaum, Göteborgs Universitet, Sweden

Recent Titles in the Series

Latin America's Quest for Globalization
Edited by Félix E. Martín and Pablo Toral

Exchange Rate Crises in Developing Countries
Michael G. Hall

Globalization and Antiglobalization
Edited by Henry Veltmeyer

Asia Pacific and Human Rights
Paul Close and David Askew

Twisting Arms and Flexing Muscles
Edited by Natalie Mychajlyszyn and Timothy M. Shaw

The Limits of Regionalism
NAFTA's Labour Accord

ROBERT G. FINBOW,
Dalhousie University, Canada

ASHGATE

© Robert G. Finbow 2006

All rights reserved. No part of this publication may be reproduced, stored in a retrieval system or transmitted in any form or by any means, electronic, mechanical, photocopying, recording or otherwise without the prior permission of the publisher.

Robert G. Finbow has asserted his moral right under the Copyright, Designs and Patents Act, 1988, to be identified as the author of this work.

Published by
Ashgate Publishing Limited
Gower House
Croft Road
Aldershot
Hampshire GU11 3HR
England

Ashgate Publishing Company
Suite 420
101 Cherry Street
Burlington, VT 05401-4405
USA

Ashgate website: http://www.ashgate.com

British Library Cataloguing in Publication Data
Finbow, Robert G.
The limits of regionalism: NAFTA's labour accord. – (The
international political economy of the new regionalisms series)
1. Labor market – United States 2. Labor market – Mexico
3. Labor market – Canada 4. Labor supply – North America
5. Free trade – North America 6. Regionalism (International
organization) 7. North America – Economic Integration –
Social aspects
I. Title
331.1'2'097

Library of Congress Cataloging-in-Publication Data
Finbow, Robert G., 1956–
   The limits of regionalism: NAFTA's labour accord / by Robert G. Finbow.
        p. cm. -- (The international political economy of new regionalisms
series)
   Includes bibliographical references and index.
   ISBN-13: 978-0-7546-3337-2
   ISBN-10: 0-7546-3337-3
 1. Canada. Treaties, etc. 1993 Sept. 14. 2. Labor laws and legislation--North
America. 3. Free trade--North America. I. Title.

   KDZ432.A41993F56 2006
   344.701--dc22

2006018447

ISBN-10: 0 7546 3337 3
ISBN-13: 978-0-7546-3337-2

Printed and bound in Great Britain by MPG Books Ltd. Bodmin, Cornwall.

UNIVERSITY OF PLYMOUTH

9007760753

90 0776075 3

WITHDRAWN
FROM
UNIVERSITY OF PLYMOUTH
LIBRARY SERVICES

Contents

This book is dedicated to my loving wife, Katherine, who inspired my interest in Mexico, assisted with translation and acculturation, and showed endless patience with this interminable distraction from our young family. It is also dedicated to my two boys, Gregory and Bobby, who also shared in the time sacrifice and who embody the hope of transnational harmony.

List of Figures and Tables

Preface

This study originated in the author's comparative research on social policy in Canada and the United States, which employed neo-institutional perspectives to account for policy variations in industrial relations and social policy. It was natural to expand this research to North America as a whole with the advent of free trade. My extensive travels in Mexico with my wife inspired a search for ways of promoting mutually beneficial exchange as economic integration proceeded. It was difficult to accept portrayals of the NAFTA as a zero-sum game where Mexican labour would benefit at the expense of Canadian and American workers, or to perceive North American critics of NAFTA as entirely altruistic in their motives. But on the other hand, witnessing the common negative effects of liberalization on working people and the unemployed in all three countries, it became clear that the rosy predictions of benefits from trade and investment liberalization were either unintentionally exaggerated or manipulatively misleading. So an assessment of the effectiveness of social elements of the NAFTA became imperative.

Mexico's desire to benefit from comparative advantages in labour costs conflicts with Canadian and American workers desire to avoid further weakening of unionism and the welfare states, with the progression of transnational integration and technological changes towards a post-Fordist flexible production paradigm. It is difficult to balance the benefits of free commerce with the needs of working people, to develop freer trade which is also socially equitable. NAFTA is a unique case study of the new regionalism across the North South divide, where divisions over labour rights are even more pronounced. As a scholar sympathetic to workers' welfare and with a family rooted on both sides of the continental divide, it was important to seek answers to these dilemmas, to discover means of encouraging free trade to proceed in ways which redounded broadly to citizen's welfare, not solely to corporate profit and elite enrichment. As the project unfolded, the prospects for finding such positive solutions appeared disappointingly minimal, especially given competition from China and post-9-11 disruptions to transborder regionalization. Above all, there is no easy compromise between Mexican concerns over protectionism and market access, and North American fears of social dumping.

At the same time, the North American Agreement on Labour Cooperation created a unique opportunity to assess the impact of new regional, transnational institutions on trinational social constituencies. While social links across borders were too weak to challenge the multinational consensus in favour of free trade and investment flows, the NAFTA labour accord created a new opportunity for labor and allied groups to connect across the North-South divide. However, these new institutions were used slowly, and I felt unable to provide a firm assessment for some years, after enough submissions and cooperative activities produced a 'critical mass'. While research materials mounted and conference papers grew stale, administrative tasks at Dalhousie and our new family provided additional diversions, so I made too few intermediate contributions to the debate over the NAALC. However, I amassed an empirical record which will be useful to those interested in the NAALC experiment. The melding of neo-institutional and new regionalism literatures with the debates on labour rights and trade hopefully provides a useful synthesis and depiction of NAALCs accomplishment, limits and prospects.

The publishers at Ashgate were exceedingly patient with the longs delays on this manuscript, which now has the advantage of a dozen years of experience with the NAALC. Hopefully this elapsed time permits a more complete assessment of the weakness of the social dimension in North American regionalism, NAALC's performance over time, and the potential institutional effects on social movements and labour organizations across these very different societies. I hope it illuminates potential bridges between North and South, between free trade and fair trade, and between worker rights and economic integration.

Robert G. Finbow
Halifax, NS
March 2006

Acknowledgements

The author wishes to acknowledge the support of the Canada-United States Fulbright Program. In particular, Victor Konrad generously allowed me to make the study genuinely trinational, by granting permission to conduct research in Mexico. The Social Sciences and Humanities Research Council and Dalhousie University's Research Development Fund also contributed support to later research. I have received great cooperation from the NAALC Secretariat both in Dallas under John McKennirey and Lance Compa and in Washington, from Alfonso Onate, Anthony Giles, Tequila Brooks and Marcelle Saint-Arnaud. The US Department of Labor's International Labor Affairs Bureau also assisted generously, especially Irasema Garza, her replacement Louis Karesh, and their researchers. Special thanks go to John Mondejar, who guided me through their library resources, and provided immense assistance in supplying documents and keeping me up to date on changing cases. The Canadian NAO under May Morpaw and Kenneth Banks, with assistance from Marc Renaud, has also been supportive in providing information and documents as needed. Mexico's NAO under Miguel Orozco Deza and his successors was also helpful; special thanks there go to Claudia Anel Valencia Carmona.

In academia, my hosts Clint Smith at the North American Forum at Stanford University, Monica Gambrill at the North American research Centre at UNAM in Mexico City, Raphael Fernandez de Castro at ITAM and Victor and Maria Urquidi at El Colegio de Mexico also contributed strong support. My research assistant, Alfonso Motta Allen, contributed his knowledge of Mexican practices and institutions and did valuable research for the project. Earlier researchers at Dalhousie, such as Fred Deveaux and Christine Arab, also contributed. The excellent electronic research collection at Dalhousie University's Killam Library was indispensable, especially such databases as Proquest, JSTOR, ABI Inform, Newscan and others. Timothy M. Shaw showed patience, perseverance and generosity in supporting and encouraging this publication. Finally, my wife helped me to digest Spanish language materials and arranged many interviews during our research trips to her country.

List of Abbreviations

ACLU – American Civil Liberties Union
AFL-CIO – American Federal of Labor – Congress of Industrial
  Organisations
AFA – Association of Flights Attendants (AFL-CIO)
AIFLD – American Institute for Free Labor Development (AFL-CIO)
ANAD – Asociación Nacional de Abogados Democraticos (Association of
  Democratic Lawyers)
ASEAN – Association of South East Asian Nations
ASSA – Asociacion Sindical de Sobrecargos de Aviacion
CAB – Conciliation and Arbitration Board
CAFTA – Central American Free Trade Agreement
CALL – Canadian Association of Labour Lawyers
CANICINTRA – Cámara Nacional de la Industria de Transformación
CAT – Centro de Apoyo al Trabajador
CAW – Canadian Auto Workers
CCALC – Canada Chile Agreement on Labour Cooperation
CCRALC – Canada Costa-Rica Agreement on Labour Cooperation
CEP – Communication, Energy and Paperworkers Union of Canada
CETLAC – Centro de Estudios y Taller Laboral, A.C.
CJM – Coalition for Justice in the Maquiladoras
CLC – Canadian Labour Congress
COMPARMEX – Confederación Patronal de la República Mexicana
CONCAMIN – Confederación de Cámaras Industriales
CROC – Confederacíon Revolucionario de Obreros y Campasinos
CROM – Confederacíon Revolucionario de Obreros Mexicanos
CSN – Confédération des syndicates nationaux (Quebec)
CT Congresso de Trabajo
CTM – Confederacion de Trabajadores Mexicanos (Confederation of
  Mexican Workers)
CUPW – Canadian Union of Postal Workers
CWA – Communication Workers of America
DOL – US Department of Labor
ECE – Evaluation Committee of Experts
EEOC – Equal Employment Opportunities Commission
EU – European Union

FAT – Frente Autentico de Trabajo
FCAT(B) – Federal Conciliation and Arbitration Tribunal (or Board)
FESEBES – Federation of Goods and Services Workers of Mexico
FLSA – US Fair Labor Standards Act
FTAA – Free Trade Area of the Americas
FTSTE – Federation of Labour Unions of Workers Representing the State
FTTQ – Federation des travailleurs et travailleuses du Québec
GATT – General Agreement on Tariffs and Trade
GE – General Electric
GSP – General System of Preferences
HRW/A – Human Rights Watch/Americas
HRW/WP – Human Rights Watch Women's Project
IBT – International Brotherhood of Teamsters
ICFTU – International Confederation of Free Trade Unions
ILRF – International Labor Rights Fund
ILO – International Labour Organization
INS – Immigration and Naturalization Service
ISI – Import Substitution Industrialization
LCF – La Conexion Familiar
LPA – Labor Policy Association
MHSSN – Maquiladora Health and Safety Support Network
MOU – Memorandum of Understanding
MWPA – Migrant and Seasonal Agricultural Worker Protection Act
NAALC – North American Agreement on Labour Cooperation
NACEC – North American Commission for Environmental Cooperation
NACLC – North American Commission for Labor Cooperation
NAFTA – North American Free Trade Agreement
NAO – National Administrative Office
NELP – National Employment Law Project
NGOs – non-governmental organizations
NLRA – US National Labor Relations Act
NLRB – US National Labor Relations Board
NMASS – National Mobilization Against SweatShops
OECD – Organization for Economic Cooperation and Development
OSHA – US Occupational Health and Safety Administration
PAN – Partido de Accion Nacionale (National Action Party)
PRD – Partido Revolucionario Populare (Popular Revolutionary Party)
PRI – Partido Revolucionario Institucional (Institutional Revolutionary Party)
RFSHS – Federal Regulation on Workplace Health, Safety and Environment
SCMW – Support Committee for Maquiladora Workers
SEMARNAP – Mexican Ministry of Environment, Natural Resources, and Fishing

SITEMAG – Matamoros Garment Workers Union

SNTSMARNAP – Ministry of Environment, Natural Resources, and Fishing Union

STIMAHCS – Independent Metal Workers Union

STPS – Secretario del Trabajo y Prevision Social, Mexico

STRM – Sindicato de Telefonistas de la Republica Mexicana (Telephone Workers' Union).

STTZTRRCGMH – Sonora Maquiladora, Shoe, Clothing and Dry Cleaning Workers' Union

SUITTAR – Tarrant Independent Union

SUSTP – Fisheries Department Union

TEAM – Teamwork for Employers and Managers Act

UAW – United Automobile, Aerospace, and Agricultural Implement Workers

UE – United Electrical, Radio and Machine Workers of America

UFW – United Farm Workers

UNT – Union Nacional de Trabajadores (National Union of Workers)

UNITE – Union of Needletrades, Industrial and Textile Employees

UNCTAD – UN Conference on Trade and Development

UPIU – United Paperworkers International Union

USAS – United Students Against Sweatshops

USCIB – US Council on International Business

USTR – United States Trade Representative

USWA – United Steel Workers of America

WCB – Workers' Compensation Board

WTO – World Trade Organization

PART I
Balancing Trade and Labour Rights
in North America

Introduction: Labour, Trade and Regionalism

Regionalism, Labour Relations and NAFTA

Regionalism, a predominant trend in the global economy, creates economic, political and moral challenges for nations. While many states have entered into regional free trade arrangements to liberalize the flow of goods, services and investments, few have seriously grappled with the extensive environmental and social fallout brought on by such integration. Transnationalism has proven particularly problematic for labour relations and working conditions in various parts of the globe. While corporate investors and intellectual property holders have flourished in this new regionalism, individual workers have faced severe adjustment costs. Pressures for diminished wages, less generous benefits, onerous practices and dangerous workplaces have multiplied, with devastating effects on many workers. This is evidenced by the spread of sweatshops, child labour, gender discrimination, occupational illnesses and injuries, and migrant poverty as employers press the costs of global competition onto their employees. At the same time, many states have withheld or diminished rights to union organization and collective bargaining, essential to offset such pressures. These trends have deepened as transnational trade flows and regional regimes increasingly cross the North-South divide. There is a fundamental disjuncture between the economic needs, policy traditions and social climate in developed and developing nations which makes it difficult to find mechanisms to facilitate valuable commerce and protect vulnerable workers in both hemispheres.

These dilemmas and pressures are exemplified by the new regionalism in North America, spanning the global divide of rich and poor states along the Rio Grande. It has been twelve years since the North American Free Trade Agreement (NAFTA) came into force, reducing trade and investment barriers between Canada, the United States and Mexico. The NAFTA, adopted after acrimonious debates, secured approval only after negotiation of side agreements on labour and the environment. Adopted to meet domestic political needs in the American context, the North American Agreement on Labour Cooperation (NAALC) proposed an innovative regime, explicitly linking trade liberalization and labour rights in a comprehensive fashion. It is appropriate to assess how fruitful this innovation has been and what contribution it has made to the augmentation of labour rights in the process of integration. More broadly, in the context of regionalization of the global economy, it is important to consider what the NAALC experiment indicates about the prospects and limits of regionalization processes in North America and beyond.

NAFTA's labour accord was heralded by supporters as a seminal departure from prior trading regimes, as a means of bridging the troublesome link between trade liberalization and labour adjustment. It was viewed as a positive instance of the 'new regionalism', taking transnational integration to new levels, facilitating a mutually beneficial integration across the North-South divide. While not constituting a complete social charter, NAALC created a means for review of domestic labour law enforcement.[1] Herzenberg hoped that, despite its limits, the NAALC could promote 'equitable, productive and socially sustainable continental development' providing a genuine 'alternative to neo-liberalism'.[2] While all three countries have serious limitations in labour standards, Mexico's laws are often superior while their implementation is limited by lack of development and excess labour supply; the NAFTA labour accord allows for joint efforts to combat adverse effects of integration and improve labour standards.[3] Vanderbush argued that while NAFTA could attract investment to Mexico based on weak worker rights, the NAALC created a means to defend the economically weak; the impact of NAFTA would depend on the use of the accord by labour.[4]

Critics were generally dismissive of NAALC's potential, and viewed it cynically as a paper tiger designed to assuage political pressures rather than encourage effective enforcement of labour laws and rights. Guerra and Torriente alleged that the labour accord is a weak vehicle designed 'to publicly denounce the violation of labor laws [and] to sensitize public opinion regarding these violations and their impact'[5], with insufficient enforcement powers. Pomeroy argued that political opposition from business and sovereignty concerns in Canada and Mexico limited the side agreement's powers to penalize violations of labour standards or to provide redress for aggrieved workers. She called for sanctions, including monetary penalties, to encourage Mexico to enforce labour laws.[6] Labour and human rights organizations decried the inadequate side agreement and felt the first NAALC submissions

1   Lance Compa, NAFTA's Labor Side Accord: A Thee-Year Accounting' *NAFTA: Law and Business Review of the Americas* 3 (1997), 7.

2   Stephen Herzenberg, 'Calling Maggie's Bluff: The NAFTA Labor Agreement and the Development of an Alternative to Neoliberalism' *Canadian American Public Policy* 28 (1996), 1–2.

3   Stephen F. Befort and Virgina E. Cornett, 'Beyond the Rhetoric of the NAFTA Treaty Debate: A Comparative Analysis of Labor and Employment Law in Mexico and the United States' *Comparative Labor Law Journal*, 17 (1996), 269–313.

4   Walt Vanderbush 'Mexican Labor in the Era of Economic Restructuring and NAFTA: Working to create a Favorable Investment Climate,' *Labor Studies Journal* 20 (1996), 58.

5   Maria Teresa Guerra and Anna L. Torriente, 'The NAALC and the Labor Laws of Mexico and the United States' *Arizona Journal of International and Comparative Law* 14 (1997), 511–12.

6   Laura Okin Pomeroy, 'The Labor Side Agreement under the NAFTA: Analysis of its Failure to Include Strong Enforcement Provisions and Recommendations for Future Labor Agreements Negotiated with Developing Countries' *George Washington Journal of International Law and Economics* 29, (1996), 769–800.

demonstrated its weaknesses.[7] Many saw the European Union model as preferable to the 'toothless' NAALC.[8]

While NAFTA is part of an overall project of liberalization which is hostile to worker interests, the political compromise of the labour side accord creates some opportunities for new forms of transnational interactions and new strategies in domestic politics for trade unions in the three countries. This book will review the cases dealt with to date to assess these competing evaluations, and determine the NAALC's potential to foster positive adjustment in worker rights and labour standards in an integrated North American market. It will assess evidence of the impact on domestic labor practices and the creation of transnational structures and practices among decision-makers and labour rights organizations. A neo-institutionalist approach will help evaluate the prospects for the labour accord's long-term impact. Despite its weaknesses, the NAALC may be the best side agreement which could be negotiated, given differing needs and interests of developed and developing states on the trade-labour link, the asymmetrical regionalism in North America, the weakness of labour and social movements and the intractability of domestic presidential and federal institutions. But these new transnational institutions can themselves become a constitutive force creating new outlets for cross-border collaboration among officials, unions and allied groups, to partially offset the deleterious effects of liberalization.

NAFTA and its labour side accord present an interesting case study of institution building in a transnational region. North America is unique in its pairing of the world's predominant economic, military and political superpower, with a mid-sized developed economy and a newly industrialized country, both largely dependent on the American hegemon as an economic partner. This affects the character of regionalism in this context, and shapes and limits supranational arrangements in trade, labour and other matters, which are distorted to reflect the asymmetrical character of regional economic and political power. NAFTA is, in its genesis, a response to regionalism elsewhere, an instance of defensive regionalism, with North America seeking a counterweight to the growth and deepening of the European Union and emerging competition from Asia. Since competitive pressures are increasing and multilateralism in the WTO is limited by resistance from the developing world, the US pursued bilateral negotiations with its neighbours which then translated into trilateralism in NAFTA.[9] Novel arrangements on the social side were thrown together hastily in the context of threatened US unilateralism and protectionism, producing untried, innovative but limited side agreements for labour and the environment. This contrasts with well-tested, vigorous enforcement provisions on trade and intellectual property, modelled on WTO measures. The side agreements

---

7   Jerome Levinson, *NAFTA's Labor Side Agreement: Lessons from the First Three Years* (Washington: Institute for Policy Studies and International Labor Rights Fund, 1996).

8   Bennett Harrison, 'Averting a race to the bottom' *Technology-Review* 98 (1995), 74.

9   Edward D. Mansfield and Helen V. Milner, 'The New Wave of Regionalism,' in Paul F. Diehl (ed.) *The Politics of Global Governance: International Organizations in an Interdependent World*, 2d ed. (Boulder, Colo.: Lynne Rienner, 2001).

thus fit rather uncomfortably with a largely neo-liberal integration scheme, making their immediate effectiveness limited and their future potential uncertain.

Did the NAFTA labour accord alter the character of regionalism in North America away from neo-liberal integration? Or did the asymmetrical regionalism on this continent prevent adoption of a substantive social dimension to free trade? The effectiveness of the NAALC will be assessed through an examination of the operation of the core institutions, National Administrative Offices and trinational Secretariat, over the past twelve years. The study assesses the main functions of these institutions – hearing public submissions on violations of labour laws, and conducting research and cooperative activities. The analysis is based on interviews at national labour departments and at the Secretariat, interviews with trade union and business actors, and a study of public documents and correspondence. The strengths and weaknesses of NAALC will be reviewed to assess its contribution to a stronger labour relations regime in North America and its influence on transnational actors in government and civil society. It will assess whether the institutions live up to the promises of their founders, and whether they can serve as a model for labour relations institutions in a hemispheric Free Trade Agreement of the Americas (FTAA).

The NAFTA side agreement is an important exemplar of institution building in the new regionalism. Neo-institutionalist approaches suggest that this institutional configuration could have effects on state and social constituencies involved in labour relations. But the side agreement may reveal the limits to broadening and deepening of the social dimension of regional integration, given the intractable North-South divide on labour issues, asymmetrical regionalism in North America, the rigidity of domestic institutions and the weakness of labour and allied social movements domestically and transnationally.

Overview of the Book

This study commences with an overview of the links between labour rights and international trade, highlighting the difficulties in reconciling this connection between developed and developing states. It then provides an examination of the literature on the new regionalism in North American context and will outline a framework for examining the limits to the inclusion of a social dimension in NAFTA, with brief comparative references to the European Union. Then it will discuss the genesis of the NAALC, and describe its institutions and their intent. The bulk of the analysis will involve in depth examination of the activities undertaken using the NAALC, especially the public submissions, made by actors in one nation to highlight labour law violations and lapses in another country. Several chapters will be devoted to a review of these submissions, which are the core opportunity to use the NAALC to expose problems in labour relations and seek potential solutions. Then a more cursory examination will be made of the research, publication and cooperative functions of the NAALC and its institutions, which provide less visible but potentially longer term integrative benefits. These empirical investigations will be used to assess the impact of the NAALC's institutions in generating or strengthening cross-border union and social coalitions, bureaucratic networks and, potentially, trans-national norms, practices and values in labour relations. Does this trans-national institutionalization substantively broaden NAFTA beyond a liberalizing arrangement focussed on trade and investment flows, not human conditions?

Part 1 introduces the intentions of the text. Chapter 1 examines the debate surrounding the relationship between labour rights and trade liberalization, as it has evolved in the past two decades. Chapter 2 situates the NAALC in the comparative context of the new regionalism and neo-institutionalism. Chapter 3 discusses the negotiation of the North American Agreement on Labour Cooperation, as part of the larger negotiation of the NAFTA. It provides an overview of the machinery established under the labour side agreement, which is innovative in the context of trade deals. This section will illustrate why NAFTA's labour accord remains limited in its capabilities and conception, and will evaluate its potential contribution to labour regionalism in North America.

Part II covers the most visible and controversial dimension of the NAALC; the public submissions – complaints about labour law enforcement made by actors in each state against the other nations. It first treats the numerous cases against labour violations (mainly in Mexico) dealt with by the American NAO in three phases; the early testing of the accord; a later group of cases seeking to broaden its application with more enforceability; and recent cases indicating a more sporadic use of the accord and the dwindling enthusiasm by the Republican administration. Then Mexico's cases are reviewed, to illustrate that country's strategic emphasis on protection of its expatriate and migrant workers in the United States. Canada's more limited usage of the agreement, and its difficulties in securing provincial adherence, will next be canvassed. Throughout, the emphasis will be on the emergence of transnational bureaucratic networks, and social coalitions of labour and union activists, to assess whether there has been any significant deepening of the institutional space and reach of the NAALC.

Part III will survey the less visible, but potentially more substantive, cooperative activities under the labour accord. These will be assessed for their impact in forging transnational awareness of labour law traditions and union cultures, and their contribution to a regionalized character to aspects of labour relations (restricted by their advisory, unenforceable nature). Next, transnational effects of NAALC processes and institutions will be reviewed to assess their contributions to regionalization in labour matters. These effects could include new or reinforced transnational bureaucratic and union networks, improvements in enforcement of domestic laws or creation of stronger transnational norms in labour relations. The recent Free Trade Area of the Americas (FTAA) discussions and the prospects for inclusion of a NAALC-style agreement will be briefly referenced, to indicate obstacles to replication of the limited NAALC arrangements, let alone any deepening to European-style labour transnationalism in this hemisphere. The text will conclude by assessing how significant the NAALC is as an exemplar of the new regionalism, and whether this model can be strengthened or extended to the hemisphere, especially in light of global competition from China and the security focus of regionalism after the terror attacks of September 2001. Decisions undertaken so far under the NAALC indicate limited potential to foster upward adjustment in labour standards in an integrated North American market, alter domestic labour practices or create transnational structures and values among decision-makers and unions.

NAALC provides an opportunity to evaluate how new transnational institutions affects social and state actors, and both reflect and mould social forces. For neo-institutionalists, the values and practices of social actors are inextricably intertwined with the institutional matrix. Political behaviours and advocacy are shaped by the institutional framework. Institutions provide opportunities and veto points for social interests, and exert constraints on their behaviours. Therefore, introduction of a new regime like NAFTA and its labour accord could have implications for the behaviour of affected interests, and could transform political and social institutions. Analysis of the labour side agreement must note these institutions' ability to influence labour norms and practices and affect the organization and demands of social interests, notably labour, business and state actors. Transnational social movements and unions helped shape the original NAALC formula and then adjusted to its subsequent implementation, within a context of domestic political constraints, asymmetrical regionalism and globalized commerce.

The analysis will focus on key factors influencing NAALC's genesis, performance and future potential: asymmetrical regionalism in NAFTA, labour power in restrictive domestic institutions, and union and social movement interaction across the North-South divide. Several effects will be assessed in light of the cases arising under the NAALC so far, as practices and norms develop and as societal actors respond to its rulings and precedents. These include incentives for cross-border union and social movement organizing, anticipated reactions by business and state actors, and shared knowledge and perspectives among officials assigned to the new transnational institutions (the NAOs and NAALC Secretariat). The limitations of the side agreement cause some to advocate reconfiguration along European lines, but these factors suggest the EU experience may not be replicable in North America. Major changes in the global environment – post 9/11 security concerns and China's emergence as a dominant trading nation – could limit progress in improving or extending the NAALC, or otherwise linking trade and labour at a regional or a global level.

Throughout, the analysis raises issues of critical import to the welfare of workers in the continental trading system – union rights to association and bargaining, occupational health and safety, gender and workplace equality, child and forced labour, the rights of migrant labour, and the importance of new social movements in alliance with labour. This wide range of issues indicates the broad human impact of the trade-labour nexus, but also the severe difficulties in reconciling such complex issues across diverse societies, cultures, economies and polities. On top of the policy complexities, this analysis will grapple with the analytical and theoretical dimensions of new regionalism, straddling the North-South divide. It will use neo-institutional analyses of domestic and transnational configurations and the constraints and opportunities institutions, formal and informal, create for policy making domestically and transnationally on contentious labour rights matters. Social movement and labour power in North America have been, if marginally, affected by NAALC; throughout, the study will illuminate the potential and limits for unions and allied networks in civil society to secure policy concessions amidst the general neo-liberal directions of economic, trade and investment policy in NAFTA's new regionalism.

Chapter 1

Labour Rights and Trade:
From Global to Regional Approaches

Evolution of the Trade-Labour Linkage

The relationship between trade and labour rights is highly contentious. A variety of philosophical, economic and political motivations are at play resulting in divisive and intractable debates. Of particular import to North America are the debates on what Bhagwati calls 'distributive justice', or concern for a decline in labour standards from competition with low wage employers in developing nations. Critics fear a 'race to the bottom' with concern for worker conditions in countries like Mexico, and posit moral 'obligations beyond borders' the human community[1]. In the NAFTA context, Mexican employers arguably hold an unfair advantage because of lower costs for environmental and labour standards, which could force North American employers to adjust to lower standards to remain competitive.

Since the interwar years and the establishment of the International Labour Organization (ILO), the relationship between labour rights and international trade has spawned controversy which escalated with increased trade liberalization. The ILO was not granted enforcement powers, but defined worker rights and sought voluntary national adoption of its conventions; it provided international 'monitoring and supervision' and 'assistance to nations in implementing measures, particularly through technical cooperation and advisory services'.[2] After World War II, nations rejected a proposed International Trade Organization, which would have explicitly recognized the impact of unfair labour practices on trade. The General Agreement on Tariffs and Trade (GATT) focussed exclusively on commerce and tariff reductions. Except for restrictions on prison labour, incorporation of labour rights in the Bretton Woods institutions remained limited.[3]

The 1950s Ohlin report proposed common labour standards so developed states would not have to compete against countries which ignored worker rights. The 1980 Brandt report argued that fair standards were essential to prevent unfair competition

---

1   Jagdish Bhagwati, 'The Demands to Reduce Domestic Diversity Among Trading Nations' in J. Bhagwati and Robert E. Hudec eds. *Fair Trade and Harmonization: Prerequisites for Free Trade?* (Cambridge: MIT Press, 1996), 10–.

2   Drusilla K. Brown, Alan V. Deardoff and Robert M. Stern, 'International Labor Standards and Trade: A Theoretical Analysis' in. Bhagwati and Hudec, 232.

3   Brown, Deardoff and Stern, 1996, 232.

and maintain support for free trade. No action followed these reports.[4] Efforts to create enforceable labour rights after World War II fell victim to Cold War animosity, which produced interminable wrangles over social and economic versus civil and political rights. Labour rights remained in limbo, with little prospect for enforcement beyond voluntary ILO conventions.[5] Post-war welfare states provided social guarantees and protected collective action by workers. This reflected the Fordist model, with high wages and generous benefits for workers in developed states. The ISI model pursued in larger developing states also permitted welfare provision and union rights. Hence, there was no urgent pressure to link labour standards to trade; liberalization proceeded in isolation from national labour laws.

However, the crises in political economy from the 1970s and 1980s eroded this model, and promoted renewed debate over trade and labour standards. Deficits and debt, coupled with stagflation in global economies, prompted attacks on the welfare state from all sides, and induced support for anti-statist neo-liberalism, which reduced welfare and weakened worker protections. Debt crises impelled welfare state rollbacks, to the detriment of working families. Structural adjustment, including dismantling of trade barriers, accelerated transnationalization of production, as developing economies like Mexico's opened to foreign investment and took on an export orientation. This increased capital mobility from North to South, and firms relocated to places with lower production costs, including lower wages and benefits. Exports from the South competed for developed countries' markets; in North America, this accentuated a trend evident since the Border Industrialization Program, or maquiladora system, from the late 1960s. As Montgomery notes, 'Multinational corporations, able to move operations and processes around the world to the environments they find most attractive, exert a powerful force homogenizing economic, social and environmental standards globally'.[6]

Liberalization and an emphasis on human rights created new circumstances for linking labour rights and trade regimes. Yet the rapid expansion of trade pacts occurred in a context of reduced labour power and technological change which left worker organizations poorly placed to assert influence. The rise of human rights NGOs as a transnational political force, plus the emergence of assertive developing states seeking to influence global trade also transformed the picture.[7] Hence social issues including labour standards assumed greater importance in trade negotiations through GATT and WTO. This accompanied an extension of trade negotiations to investment, intellectual property, procurement, privatization, the environment and other social standards. This trend peaked in WTO negotiations as US and European

---

4   Steve Charnovitz, 'The Influence of International Labour Standards on the World Trading Regime' *International Labour Review* 126, (1987), 567.

5   Christopher McCrudden and Anne Davies,'A perspective on trade and labor rights' *Journal of International Economic Law* 3, (2000), 45.

6   David Montgomery, 'Labor Rights and Human Rights: A Historical Perspective' in Lance A Compa and Stephen F Diamond eds. *Human rights, labor rights, and international trade* (Philadelphia : University of Pennsylvania Press, 1996), 15.

7   McCrudden and Davies, 2000, 46.

negotiators countered domestic criticisms of negative consequences of global commerce by seeking common labour standards. This generated a standoff with developing states, which 'perceived attempts to link further liberalization of free trade to adherence to certain labor standards as protectionist or neo-colonial in their motivation'.[8]

Global Stalemate on Trade and Labour?

Critics of unregulated globalization argue that international competition for investment encourages states to compete by depressing wages and repressing labour rights. Transnational integration has generated new limits on labour protections in northern states, while encouraging developing states to lower their standards. The transnational economy has undermined the Fordist welfare state which supplied high wages, benefits and protections to workers in the North. Productive activity shifted to the South, where states lack the finances, culture or willingness to provide high standards. Debt crisis in many nations eroded labour protections as states restored fiscal balance. Structural adjustment promoted restrictive policies and discouraged strong unions. High unemployment reduced living standards for workers, especially in developing states. With child and prison labour rising, transnational action seemed indispensable. But the GATT and WTO focussed on trade and investment and ignored their social consequences.[9]

Hence, globalization increases the need to link trade and labour rights through effective international standards. Transnational firms have great mobility and nations cannot effectively regulate working conditions; international organizations like the ILO lack power to correct this imbalance. The ILO encourages ratification of core conventions on child and forced labour, rights to worker associations and collective bargaining, and the elimination of discrimination. Its 1998 declaration noted that 'all members, even if they have not ratified the Conventions in question, have an obligation arising from the very fact of membership in the Organization, to respect, to promote and to realize, in good faith and in accordance with the Constitution, the principles concerning the fundamental rights which are the subject of the Conventions'.[10] This declaration remains advisory prompting some in the developed world to advocate alternatives, to balance liberalized trade with improved working conditions and union rights.

---

8   McCrudden and Davies, 2000, 45.

9   Pharis Harvey, 'Trade and Labor' *Foreign Policy In Focus* 2, 15 January 1997 [cited Dec. 16, 2003]. Available at http://www.foreignpolicy-infocus.org/briefs/vol2/v2n15trd.html.

10   International Labour Organization, 'Declaration on Fundamental Principles and Rights at Work' ILO 86th Session, Geneva, June 1998 [cited Dec. 11, 2003]. Available at http://www.ilo.org/dyn/declaris/DECLARATIONWEB.static_jump?var_language=EN&var_page name=DECLARATIONTEXT.

Several approaches have been proposed by developed nations to protect their workers from competitive pressures from low wages and poor working conditions in less developed states. Large states like the US can extend trade access or lower tariffs only to countries which enforce worker rights. This does not require bilateral or multilateral negotiation, but can be imposed unilaterally by the largest economies to ensure that imports from aboard do not undercut domestic production because of abuses of labour rights. Alternately, a multilateral agreement such as the WTO could be the venue, with labour rights conditionalities imposed on all members. Major organizations representing developed states, such as the OECD and the European Union, have advocated a social clause in the WTO, which would require members to respect a basic set of labour standards.[11] This approach requires transnational negotiations, and agreement has been elusive. WTO measures are rejected by southern states as disguised protectionism which neglects differences in development and culture. Finally, bilateral or regional trading agreements can incorporate labour standards, seeking commonality across partners. Regional labour pacts have proven more fruitful, as illustrated by the European Union and NAFTA, though their effectiveness is strained by extra-regional competition in a global economy.

The US General System of Preferences (GSP) system, which grants most favoured nation status to desired trade partners, required developing states to provide basic labour rights, including freedom of association, the right to organize and bargain, a ban on forced labour, a minimum age for child workers, minimum wages, regulated work hours, and occupational health and safety guarantees. Bilateral trade pacts like the Caribbean Basin Economic Recovery Act and federal insurance programs for overseas corporate investments included similar guarantees.[12] 'Section 301 of the 1988 Trade Act authorizes the president to treat as an unfair trade practice the competitive advantage that any foreign country derives from the systematic denial of internationally recognized worker rights.'[13] The Clinton administration required negotiators at GATT and WTO to seek inclusion of labour rights. But, this administration did little to alter a neo-liberal vision of regionalization or globalization.[14] Towards the end of the Clinton years, efforts to spread the labour guarantees in WTO and other trading regimes faced increased opposition from developing states. Clinton pushed for minimal guarantees for child labour and worker rights, but even a modest proposal for a study group was rejected by WTO partners.[15]

---

11   Kevin Watkins *Globalisation and liberalisation: Implications for poverty, distribution and inequality* UNDP, Human Development Reports, Occasional Paper 32, 1997 [Cited Feb. 14, 2004]. Available at http://hdr.undp.org/docs/publications/ocational_papers/oc32c.htm.

12   Brown, Deardoff and Stern, 1996, 236.

13   Harvey, 1997, 2.

14   Doug Henwood, 'Clinton's Trade Policy' in Fred Rosen and Dierdre McFayden eds. *Free Trade and Restructuring in Latin America: A NACLA Reader* (New York: Monthly Review Press, 1995).

15   Steven Greenhouse and Joseph Kahn 'U.S. Effort to Add Labor Standards to Agenda Fails' *New York Times* Dec 3, 1999, A1.

Critics saw these policies as hypocritical unilateral impositions by the US covering even labour rights which it did not enforce domestically.[16] The US has ratified few ILO conventions and critics allege there are 'widespread and growing' violations of rights to organize and bargain in many American states.[17] Developing states see labour protections as a means to remove the comparative advantage of low cost labour and to preserve 'developed countries' global dominance. Neo-liberal economists suggest that violations of labour rights might be necessary to permit catch up development in emerging economies. A 1995 World Bank Study argued that the use of trade sanctions to encourage labour standards on economic or moral grounds would be harmful to the global economy. The 'real danger of using trade sanctions as an instrument for promoting basic rights is that the trade-standards link could become hijacked by protectionist interests attempting to preserve activities rendered uncompetitive by cheaper imports'. Such measures disrupt markets, since 'low-cost unskilled labor is the main comparative advantage of developing countries'.[18]

At the 1996 Singapore WTO ministerial meeting, the developing states blocked any reference to labour rights in the WTO framework, and got developed states to agree to refer such matters to the ILO.

We renew our commitment to the observance of internationally recognized core labour standards. The International Labour Organization (ILO) is the competent body to set and deal with these standards, and we affirm our support for its work in promoting them. We believe that economic growth and development fostered by increased trade and further trade liberalization contribute to the promotion of these standards. We reject the use of labour standards for protectionist purposes, and agree that the comparative advantage of countries, particularly low-wage developing countries, must in no way be put into question. In this regard, we note that the WTO and ILO Secretariats will continue their existing collaboration.[19]

Unions complained that this was a hollow promise as no new cooperation was proposed between the WTO and the ILO, which gained no enforcement powers. However, unified opposition from developing states produced a watered down declaration. By 'passing the protection of labor's interests from an organization

---

16   Henry J. Frundt, *Trade Conditions and Labor Rights : US Initiatives, Dominican and Central American Responses* (Gainesville, FL: University Press of Florida, 1998); Philip Alston, 'Labor Rights Provisions in U.S. Trade Law: Aggressive Unilateralism?' in Compa and Diamond, 1996, 72.

17   Human Rights Watch, *Unfair Advantage Workers' Freedom of Association in the United States under International Human Rights Standards* [cited July 20, 2004]. Available at http://www.hrw.org/reports/2000/uslabor/.

18   World Bank, *World Development Report, 1995: Workers in an Integrating World* Washington World Bank/Oxford University Press, 1995, 79.

19   World Trade Organization 'Singapore Ministerial Declaration' Ministerial Conference, Singapore, December 13, 1996. [Cited Jan. 15, 2004]. Available at http://www. wto.org/english/news_e/pres96_e/wtodec.htm.

expected to be strong to one known to be weak, the ministers took another step to marginalize labor in the planning for a global economic architecture'.[20]

Labour Rights as Human Rights

Advocates claim that the campaign for labour rights is a moral imperative, involving fundamental human rights; a prohibition on child or forced labour, minimum standards and acceptable conditions should be available in all states. As Vam Liemt argues, the 'solidarity or moral argument emphasizes that core workers' rights are human rights. It is morally wrong to exploit workers or repress trade unions.[21] Workers in developed states should assist their brethren in the developing world by promoting equitable global economic arrangements to facilitate development. This should include linking a country's access to transnational trade blocs to its adoption of protective legislation for workers.[22] Observers admit there may be costs for individuals and for the global economy, but suggest that employment relationships are human relations, not economic transactions. If rights like collective bargaining are recognized as human rights, they should be enforced despite such costs, like other basic rights, to protect 'human dignity'.[23]

Some analysts stress altruistic motivations in linking labour rights with trade, since it is immoral to deny workers in developing states fundamental rights which are available in the developed world. Informed consumers are less willing to accept that goods they purchase may have been made in poor conditions by children or workers facing repression, illness or injury because of lax regulations. Human rights advocates suggest that countries should advance their social protections as they move forward economically, as a prerequisite for 'sustainable development'. Another moral concern involves the status of women, often exploited in export economies.[24] Unskilled workers in developed states also lose out if there is no effort to enforce transnational standards. If consumers in the North are willing to pay higher prices rather than buy goods produced in adverse conditions, then pressure to link labour

20   Kathleen Newland 'Workers of the world, now what?' *Foreign Policy* 114, (1999), 58.

21   Gijsbert van Liemt, 'International trade and workers' rights', in Brian Hocking and Steven McGuire eds. *Trade Politics: International, Domestic and Regional Responses* (New York: Routledge, 1999) 113.

22   van Liemt, 1999, 113.

23   Hoyt N. Wheeler, 'Viewpoint' Collective Bargaining is a Fundamental Human Right,' *Industrial Relations* 39, (2000) 535–6.

24   Christine Elwell, *Human Rights, Labour Standards and the New World Trade Organization: Opportunities for a Linkage* (Montreal: International Centre for Human Rights and Democratic Development), 1995, 23–5.

standards and trade pacts will remain, especially in deals which protect investor and intellectual property rights.[25]

Adoption of improved labour standards could also be a prerequisite or a catalyst to development. Distortions in the market occur if firms exploit children or other workers; companies trying to take a moral position find themselves at a competitive disadvantage. The problem in the developing world arises from a lack of enforcement, not a failure to adopt laws or to ratify ILO conventions. Absence of worker organizations able to demand fair wages and benefits depresses labour costs below market levels, creating distortions versus competitor nations. Other studies deny that lax standards have a significant impact on trade, but argue that there are competitive advantages in not facing union demands for enhanced wages and benefits secured through free collective bargaining. Some economists suggest that distorting deficiencies in labor standards can harm emerging economies rather than help them, making transnational standards unnecessary as states recognize that core rights are essential to development; enhanced labour standards may contribute to greater national productivity in a mutually reinforcing fashion.[26] Core rights may contribute to growth by creating 'favourable conditions for developing wages and working conditions in keeping with a country's economic strength'.[27]

Ulterior Motives: Profits versus Protectionism

Some observers suggest that protagonists in the debate have motives other than economic efficiency or worker protection. Some proponents of NAFTA in the business community sought to lock Mexico into liberalizing reforms, and to induce Canada to move to a deregulated, limited state approach. Such actors would welcome 'downward harmonization' of labour standards to serve their economic agendas.[28] Opponents of the social clause in developing states such as Mexico and China also may want economic and political elites to retain profit at the expense of workers in sectors like textiles and manufacturing. Chan and Ross argue that this explains the rising gap between corporate profits based on productivity and competitiveness and poor wages and appalling conditions for workers in these sectors.[29] Some domestic actors who know that transnational competition will not generally be harmful to them as producers nonetheless exploit fears of competitive disadvantage to restrain labour

---

25   Kimberley Elliot and Richard Freeman, 'Globalization versus Labor Standards?' in Elliot and Freeman *Can Labor Standards Improve Under Globalization?* (Washington: Institute for International Economics, 2003), 10–11.

26   Paul Krugman 'What should trade negotiators negotiate about?' *Journal of Economic Literature* 35, (1997), 118.

27   Elwell, 1995, 28.

28   Morley Gunderson, 'Harmonization of Labour Policies Under Trade Liberalization' *Relations Industrielles/Industrial Relations*, 53, (1998), 4.

29   Anita Chan and Robert JS Ross, 'Racing to the bottom: international trade without a social clause' *Third World Quarterly* 24, (2003), 1011–28.

standards.[30] Dorman argues that countries which suppress unions and bargaining gain an unfair competitive edge, since artificially low labour costs disrupts efficient allocation of production across states, and makes global markets 'less responsive' to scarcities, efficiencies or labour quality.[31]

Alternately, proponents of 'fair trade' seek not only to prevent downward harmonization, but to limit reversals of past policy concessions secured by labour and to extend these rights and benefits to non-union workers at home or abroad. They may be seeking to preserve higher wages and benefits at the expense of consumers, non-union workers or surplus labour in the developing world.[32] While unfairness may be the allegation, the actual political motivation is often protection, for firms in threatened sectors and unions concerned lest 'social dumping' undermine benefits and wages. Protectionism can be legitimated if external competitors are portrayed as succeeding via unfair practices.[33] Limits on unions and bargaining may be justified, since unions in developing states may protect a small 'labour aristocracy' at the expense of surplus workers.[34] Brown et. al. argue that import competing and export firms and their unions may cite lower labour standards to further their interests at the expense of the national economy by promoting fair trade requirements 'obstensibly aimed at getting the foreign nation to raise its labor standards'.[35] Proponents of the social clause must concede that some use their views to seek protection from competition from emerging exporters in labour intensive sectors.[36]

Critics suggest that the US is promoting a 'false humanitarianism' designed to cover for hegemonic and protectionist desires.[37] The real effect could be to disadvantage developing states as they move towards market-oriented, export based economic policies which could enhance their economic prospects. Enforceable trade sanctions harm the workers they are trying to help by limiting job growth in developing states and forcing workers into marginal, unregulated informal activities.[38] Economists argue that even international standards for occupational health and safety are trade distorting and should be dealt with by markets, by increasing the choice of workplaces for workers so they can avoid unsafe ones or changing worker attitudes so they avoid risky employment. Finally, treating labour standards as human rights

---

30 Krugman, 1997, 118.

31 Peter Dorman, cited in Elwell, 1995, 33.

32 Gunderson, 1998, 4.

33 Bhagwati, 1996, 32.

34 Golub, 1997, 21.

35 Brown, Deardoff and Stern, 1996, 231.

36 Jagdish Bhagwati, 'After Seattle: Free Trade and the WTO,' *International Affairs* 77, (2001), 24.

37 William E. Scheuerman 'False humanitarianism? US advocacy of transnational labour protections,' *Review of International Political Economy* 8, (2001), 359–88.

38 Keith Maskus *Should Core Labor Standards be Imposed Through International Tade Policy?* World Bank Working Paper 1817, 1997 [cited May 11, 2005]. Available at http://www-wds.worldbank.org/servlet/WDSContentServer/WDSP/IB/2000/02/24/000009265_3971110141359/Rendered/PDF/multi_page.pdf., 1997, 2.

overlooks differences in development, culture and national preferences. Standards designed by developed countries, like prohibitions on child labour and minimum wages, are not feasible or desirable for developing states and may have perverse results, notably poor labour market performance and heightened inequality.[39]

Ultimately, the debate hinges not only on the North-South divide but also on ideological divisions in the North between 'free trade' and 'fair trade'. De Wet notes how free traders dismiss the WTO as the venue for labour standards, based on a neo-liberal vision which suggests that social concerns constitute 'interference in the market process, impeding efficiency, creating suboptimal allocation of labor, stifling competition, deterring investments, and constraining growth'.

> The neoliberal doctrine sees the best protection for workers in a highly competitive, unregulated labor market that almost entirely is unrestrained by artificially imposed minimum standards. The market mechanism is the best way to regulate standards. Those employers who offer low wages, unsatisfactory or unsafe working conditions, or inadequate leave or other benefits will be unable to retain their workers and will, as a result, lose the skills, experience, and other benefits of a stable workforce, unless they offer improved conditions.[40]

Elliot and Freeman note that neo-liberals have corporate and state sponsorship in the billions and authority to impose policy, against dogged, under-funded outsider opposition in NGOs, unions and trans-border social movements.[41]

In contrast, a regulatory model suggests that the mobility of capital in the global economy makes national policy inadequate to address adverse consequences for workers. Fair traders argue that 'optimal social protection requires political negotiation and standard-setting and cannot be left entirely to market forces' given the possibility for 'social dumping' by countries which accept low wages and standards to secure investment and development.[42] Only intervention at the transnational or global level can eliminate this debilitating, socially destructive competition. These contrasting ideological positions and national interests make it difficult to secure a resolution satisfactory to all parties, especially across the North-South divide. While opposition to neo-liberal globalization has started from weakness, it has forced compromises in global trading arrangements.[43]

---

39   Golub, 1997, 22.

40   Erika de Wet, 'Labor Standards in the Globalized Economy: The Inclusion of a Social Clause in the General Agreement On Tariff and Trade/ World Trade Organization,' *Human Rights Quarterly* 17, (1995), 447.

41   Elliot and Freeman, 2003, 8.

42   De Wet, 1995, 447.

43   Elliot and Freeman, 2003, 8.

Can a Consensus Develop on Fundamental Rights?

Some argue that a consensus can be reached on essential labour rights, under ILO or WTO auspices. The ILO Declaration on Fundamental Principles and Rights at Work and the WTO Singapore statement on core labour standards give evidence of some commonality. A short list of fundamental rights, based on ILO conventions, is accepted by most states, though enforced with differing degrees of effectiveness. This list includes essential rights to form unions and bargain collectively, protections against forced and exploitative child labour, and non-discrimination in the workplace. The International Confederation of Trade Unions deems these 'enabling rights'[44], the OECD's Trade Union Advisory Committee calls them 'framework conditions'.[45] The core rights are based ILO Conventions on Freedom of Association (No 87), Right to Organize and to Collective Bargaining (No 98), Forced Labour Convention (No 29), Equal Remuneration Convention (No 100), Minimum Age Convention (No 11), and Non-discrimination in the workplace (111). These rights establish the conditions for collective bargaining which then determines wages, benefits, and working conditions, in accordance with national economic capacity.[46]

Few observers would argue that specific standards for health and safety, wages, protection or benefits could be equally or quickly achievable in developing states, which lack the social, physical and economic capacity to implement them.[47] Freeman distinguishes between core standards and 'cash' standards which must vary depending on the level of development. These include wages and benefits and social security but also health and safety provisions, given the limited ability of less developed states to enforce standards and protections. Freeman notes a category of Arguable Core Standards involving minimum age for workers, prevention of exploitative child labour and minimum standards for health and safety.[48] However, the extent of agreement should not be overestimated, as there remains controversy over which rights to include. US trade laws exclude prevention of discrimination but

---

44   International Confederation of Free Trade Unions. 1999. *Building Workers' Human Rights into the Global Trading System* (Brussels: ICFTU, 1999); James Howard and Winston 'Core Labour Standards and Human Rights in the Workplace' *Opinion 2001* International Institute for Environment and Development, World Summit on Sustainable Development, [cited April 23, 2005]. Available at http://www.iied.org/docs/wssd/bp_corelabor.pdf.

45   OECD, *International Trade and Core Labour Standards* Paris: OECD, 2000 [cited April 12, 2004]. Available at http://www.oecdbookshop.org/oecd/get-it.asp?REF=2200041E. PDF.

46   Kimberly A. Elliott, 'International Labor Standards and Trade: What Should Be Done? In Jeffrey J. Schott ed. *Launching New Global Trade Talks* (Washington DC: Institute for International Economics, 1998), 167.

47   Virginia Leary, 'Worker's Rights and International Trade: The Social Clause, in J. Bhagwati and R. Hudec eds. *Fair Trade and Harmonization, Vol. 2* (Cambridge, MA: MIT Press, 1997), 177–230.

48   Richard B. Freeman, 'International Labor Standards and World Trade: Friends or Foes' in Jeffrey J. Schott ed. *The World Trading System: Challenges Ahead* (Washington, D.C.: Institute for International Economics), 1996, 99, Table 3.

include 'acceptable working conditions' limits on hours of work, minimum wage and health and safety standards; and unions and NGOS insist on inclusion of such 'cash' standards, fuelling developing country suspicions of protectionism.[49]

Some in the developing world oppose recognition of even ILO standards as protectionism adopted under the guise of human rights. They argue that union rights and activities are political, and the growth of unions could undermine efficiency by imposing worker monopolies. Prohibitions against child labour are culturally and economically unsuitable for developing states, where children often provide income for the family. For the most vocal critics of labour rights, only forced or slave labour should be subject to international norms. Bhagwati decries the argument by fair trade advocates that workers in the North and South will fair poorly under free trade, since workers gain opportunities in developing states if capital moves from the North to take advantage of lower costs and wages. The denial of trade access to countries like Mexico based on fairness concerns about the distribution of benefits would prove costly to both North and South.[50]

A World Bank survey suggested that 'linkages between varying international standards for labor protection and international trade policy, both in theoretical and empirical terms, are tenuous' and the benefits from the linkages are small while the costs from may be high.[51] The World Bank rejects trade sanctions, advocating education, information-sharing and poverty reduction through market-driven reforms. There is no clear advantage for developing states based on labour costs; since low wages reflect low productivity, 'international differences in unit labor costs are much smaller than different wage rates suggest', and costs in some developing states exceed those in the North, making any upward pressure on wages damaging to their competitiveness.[52] Ratification of ILO standards may do little to improve labour conditions in developing states, since these are advisory measures and countries ratify only those standards that they have already reached in practice.[53]

Southern scholars suggest that social clauses proposed by Northern states reflect a desire to preserve privileges at the expense of job creation on the periphery:

> Workers in poorer and less-developed nations often view unions based in the advanced industrial countries as defenders of privilege. Their suspicions persist that such unions' insistence on increased wages, conformity with labour standards, and environmental safeguards for Third World workers is simply a disguised form of protectionism, designed

---

49   Stepehn S. Golub, 'Are International Standards Needed to Prevent Social Dumping?' *Finance and Development* December, 1997, 21 [cited Dec. 15, 2002]. Available at http:// www.worldbank.org/fandd/english/1297/articles/041297.htm.

50   Bhagwati, 1996, 16, 18.

51   Maskus, 1997, 1.

52   Golub, 1997, 21.

53   Robert J. Flanagan 'Labor Standards and International Competitive Advantage' in Robert J. Flanagan and William B. Gould IV eds. *International Labor Standards: Globalization, Trade and Public Policy* (Palo Alto CA: Stanford University Press, 2003).

to undercut the developing world's main source of comparative advantage: low labour costs.[54]

Could any core labour standards could be applied to many developing states without restricting their competitive advantage? There is a distinction between basic rights (freedom of organization, collective bargaining), and standards (minimum wages, benefits, etc.) which mirror a country's development level. The former are essential in all states and contribute to competitiveness and growth; the latter are unrealistic in less developed settings, until development proceeds sufficiently to make them more affordable. Trade can contribute to the climate for eventual promotion of labour rights, by increasing middle class demands for rights and spreading liberal values consistent with such rights. Since collective bargaining would occur in local market contexts, cash standards would adjust according to local economic conditions and trends in developing states, hence preserving their competitive position.[55]

There may be positive links between core labour rights and economic development. Elliot suggests that the ILO's core standards can be seen both as important attributes of markets by giving workers a choice of what conditions to accept in the workplace; they are also fundamental rights essential to democratic development. As such they do not differ from other transnational norms of market liberalization or democratization, which are essential for admission to transnational institutions. These norms do not impose commonality on legal frameworks or practices any more than other universal rights, such as those to property or markets, which are implemented in different national contexts. There is no evidence that poor standards assist productivity and attract foreign investment, or that higher standards undermine competitive advantage; rights like health and safety or child restrictions are not costly and may contribute to productivity in the long term.[56] Freeman notes that eliminating human rights violations, such as forced or prison labour and discrimination would not remove China's labour cost advantage, for instance.[57]

An OECD analysis of worker rights and economic performance affirms that a narrow set of core standards would have positive effects on economic competitiveness. OECD data indicates a positive correlation between union rights to organize and strike and levels of industrial growth. This suggests a 'high road' to development via collective bargaining, which encourages worker support and productivity and helps optimize the distribution of income. Collective bargaining and worker rights boost productivity and innovation. Protecting child workers allows for education and skills development, economically beneficial in the long run. Developing states with democratic practices like worker rights withstand global economic disruptions more successfully than less democratic states. OECD analyses indicates that countries without core labour rights did not gain a competitive export advantage, though lower wages and benefits linked to levels of development can help export competitiveness.

---

54   Newland 1999, pp. 56–57.
55   Elliot, 1998, 165.
56   Elliot, 1998, 174.
57   Freeman, 1996, 99.

Excluding China, foreign investors do not prefer countries with poor labour protections, though unregulated export processing zones do pull investment.[58]

But there is no agreement on the nature of core rights or mechanisms for enforcement, beyond a ban on slave or forced labour which is often circumvented. Developing states cannot match the cash standards of the developed world. Any list of core rights must be limited to a essential 'process' rights, which establish labour markets allowing for effective adjustment of wages, rights and standards commensurate with levels of development. It is not feasible to insist on rights to specific outcomes irrespective of national wealth. But even then, as Brown illustrates, it is impossible to generalize about the efficiency, equity and humanitarian results of core standards which vary depending on the conditions in each country's labour market.[59]

Approaches to the Enforcement of Labour Standards

Even if diverse nations, North and South, could agree to common labour standards, there are a variety of ways in which these standards could be enforced transnationally. Block et. al. identify legislative, trade sanctions, multilateral enforcement and voluntary standards models.[60] A *legislative* approach was first demonstrated in ILO conventions and recommendations. The former have treaty status while the latter provide 'guidance' to governments. But countries vary widely in their willingness to adopt core conventions, which are not enforceable. The ILO recognizes that standards are not universal, and must be applied in accord with national circumstances and economic development. Complaints of non-compliance can be investigated by the ILO's governing body, which can only publish a report with recommendations to the offending government. Hence the ILO approach is one of investigation and moral pressure. Countries which ratify conventions might be expected to follow through with implementation. But without any meaningful consequences, 'it is unlikely that the ILO can prevent a country from violating its obligations under a convention or a recommendation if a country is truly inclined to violate them' and those 'countries that ratify conventions retain some 'flexibility' to adapt the standards to their circumstances'.[61]

A second legislative approach is exemplified by the European Union, where transnational directives can be legally enshrined and enforced. But the EU has

---

58   OECD, *International Trade and Core Labour Standards* (Paris: OECD, 2000), 32–3 [cited April 12, 2004]. Available at http://www.oecdbookshop.org/oecd/get-it.asp?REF=2200041E.PDF.

59   Drusilla K. Brown 'Labor Standards: Where Do They Belong on the International Trade Agenda?' *Journal of Economic Perspectives* 15, 3 (2001), 95.

60   Richard N Block, Karen Roberts, Cynthia Ozeki, and Myron J Roomkin 'Models of international labor standards,' *Industrial Relations* 40, 2 (2001), 258–93.

61   Block, et. al., 2001, 271.

introduced few enforceable directives on labour matters to this point, on the mobility of workers (essential to complete market integration), and health and safety (to limit possibilities for social dumping by new members). Other aspects of labour relations, including part-time employment and management-labor relations have been contentious, and EU directives have been opposed successfully by business and some governments. While EU legislation was made easier after 1992 via qualified majority voting on health and safety, non-discrimination and worker consultation, unanimity is required on worker organization, layoffs and migrant labour. The principle of subsidiarity, resistance to regulation by some states and the limited transnational reach of employer and labour groups inhibits EU intervention, though steps have been taken on Works Councils, sex discrimination and part-time workers. Even this limited transnational legislation may be hard to replicate in other regional or global arrangements, since the complex, EU system took 40 years to evolve and is based on a wider integration project. [62]

The US general preferences system is an example of a *trade sanctions* model which uses labour standards as a criterion for trade access. Complaints about non-compliance are investigated by the US International Trade Representative. Several countries have had trade benefits revoked or suspended for failing to comply with labour standards, though improving states have been reinstated. There are similar provisions in the US trade initiatives in the Carribean Basin and the Andean states. The Omnibus Trade and Competitiveness Act requires a report on the implementation of internationally recognized labour standards in any country and sector in which the US has investment. This unilateral approach to trade sanctions has induced positive changes in America's trading partners.[63] However, the complaints-driven system does not provide for comprehensive monitoring of compliance and leaves room for variations in labour standards. It also is uneven in application as it rests on lobbying by particular economic sectors. Its unilateral character makes it an object of resentment by foreign countries.[64]

An *NGO* approach involves actions by human rights and social policy groups to pressure states or corporations to change their labour practices. Approaches include ethical investment guidelines, shareholder activism, codes of practice and labeling systems, under the rubric corporate social responsibility. These tactics may not work unless companies feel sufficient pressure to respond or if public interest is sustained over time. While some firms have realized the advantages, it appears limited to some consumer goods sectors where MNCs want to sustain the reputation of a brand among an increasingly aware transnational public. The approach may be limited for firms with less visible benefits like increased productivity or for firms facing strong competition from those with poor standards. There is no means to compensate workers or families who lose income from consumer boycotts against child labour

---

62 Block, et. al., 2001, 268.

63 Alston, 1996.

64 E. Cappyuns, 'Linking Labor Standards and Trade Sanctions: An Analysis of their Current Relationship' *Columbia Journal of Transactional Law* 36, (1998), 666.

or other abuses.[65] Some prefer market driven approaches. Private firms and NGOs in civil society should inform consumers about the importance of labour rights, and punish violations by rejecting unfairly produced goods or paying a premium for fair trade products. Beyond that, labour rights should be promoted by persuasion and education via NGOs, consumer boycotts, strengthening of civil society in developing states, exposure of non-compliance by the ILO and other voluntary means.[66]

What forms of penalties could be imposed under these various models? Penalties can include withdrawal of trade benefits or fines, proportionate to the damage caused to trade by labour rights violations, but sufficiently sizeable and targeted to discourage such behaviors. Differences in sizes of economies and degrees of trade dependence make it difficult to balance penalties, which usually weigh more heavily on small, dependent economies. Positive incentives could encourage improvements, though this has as rarely been tried. The US-Cambodia agreement increases quotas for Cambodian exports if labour laws and international standards are enforced. This gives incentives for firms to comply to improve their market share in the US. Many trade agreements also provide technical assistance and capacity building to improve the ability of developing states to implement labour laws.[67] International financial institutions, regional development banks and bilateral development agreements can also encourage states to limit labour exploitation. [68]

Some NGOs and activists have pressed for voluntary codes of conduct, backed by consumer awareness. Some private firms, pressed by political and non-governmental advocates, have agreed to respect certain standards in their overseas operations, to avoid negative publicity and potential consumer retribution. Such companies insist that contractors and suppliers avoid the use of sweatshop conditions in manufacturing products for sale in consumer markets. To succeed companies must see that it is in their self-interest to follow voluntary guidelines favourable to workers. Advantages must outweigh the downside of higher labour costs to work in a voluntary way in the long term. Some consumer organizations and ethical investment groups have introduced certification processes to ensure that goods have been produced under desirable conditions, such as fair trade coffee. The criteria include standards for child labour, health and safety, work hours and conditions, representation and collective bargaining, non-discrimination and non-retaliation against activists. To make such codes work, effective pressure is needed to convince managers that socially responsible behavior has a market payoff.[69]

Some free trade supporters recognize the need to 'maintain the legitimacy of the global trading system', but prefer the voluntary compliance and 'peer pressure' of the ILO system to any enforcement regime; product labelling as 'worker friendly' goods

---

65   Block et. al., 2001, 54.

66   Elliot and Freeman, 2003.

67   Sandra Polaski 'Protecting Labor Rights Through Trade Agreements: an Analytical Guide' *Journal of International Law and Policy*, 10, (2004), 9–10.

68   OECD, 2000, 53–60.

69   Block, et. al., 2001, 279–80.

and corporate 'codes of conduct' backed by consumer pressure and corporate self-interest may be a 'less intrusive' and less distorting way of encouraging termination of controversial practices in developing states'; this would alleviate protectionist pressures if combined with appropriate labour market adjustment in the North.[70] Industry-wide efforts to improve standards for workers in the apparel industry indicate the problems of securing agreement from all companies, though high profile successes have been reported (as will be discussed respecting garment producers in Mexico below). This has lead to the search for a nuanced mixture of voluntary and legislated enforcement with penalties, which presaged the multilateral approach of investigation and cooperation of the NAFTA labour accord.

A *multilateral enforcement* model like the NAALC does not try to create common standards across all nations, encourage voluntary adherence to ILO standards or threaten countries with loss of trade privileges to compensate for poor working conditions. Instead, it calls on each nation to enforce its own labour laws. The principle means to encourage enforcement is public consultations and publicity, to put pressure on domestic actors. This model respects sovereignty by making national laws and enforcement paramount. It produces limited, gentle pressure to improve standards through investigation, consultation and publication. Countries are expected to provide impartial, effective law enforcement, and to voluntarily improve standards. In a few areas, tougher measures like trade or financial penalties may be imposed as a 'last resort'.[71] This multilateral model, balancing sovereignty and pressure for improvements in labour standards, with no transnational imposition and limited sanctions, will be evaluated in the NAALC context below.

A Global Approach to Trade and Labour?

Even if consensus existed on core rights and the means of enforcing them, there remains the issue of the level of enforcement. Should this be done by individual nations in bilateral trade relations? Or should a multilateral approach be used? Some promote creation of a system of fair trade via supplemental labour accords in trade deals, or labour rights guarantees in the heart of trade pacts, to bring fairness to transnational integration. If many nations are involved, can this be implemented at a global level or only at a regional one?

A *unilateral* approach, as adopted by the US, extends domestic standards abroad through legislation requiring foreign operations of domestic firms to meet labour standards, allowing domestic legal remedies for overseas labour rights disputes and linking trade access to labour rights, as in the GSP system. Import restrictions penalize countries which failed to protect workers according to standards set by the importing nation. Countries could treat social dumping as unfair competition and impose punitive duties to correct for unfair price advantages gleaned from mistreating workers. A nation could be denied most favoured nation status for mistreatment of

---

70   Golub, 1997, 23.
71   Block et. al, 2001, 275–7.

workers or actions against unions as happened when Poland suppressed the Solidarity trade union in 1980. Countervailing duties could offset a perceived government subsidy for exporters from lax labour laws. Companies could be targeted with import bans for producing goods using undesirable labour conditions or poor renumeration; overseas subsidiaries could be required to implement standards similar to those at home. Other approaches include sanctions, government or consumer boycotts, or selective tariff decreases to reward improvements.[72] Although the easiest approach, unilateralism is selective, protectionist and discriminatory and risks alienating others; only major importers could use this approach, as only such states can withhold access to a significant market.

Others still seek a *global* approach, with the incorporation of worker rights directly in the WTO to give them equal prominence with investor rights, trade disputes, and intellectual property. This could take the form of a social clause, backed by sanctions, which could deprive countries of WTO privileges if they violate core ILO labour rights.[73] The key champion of this approach has been the International Confederation of Free Trade Unions (ICFTU), which has advocated a labour dimension to trade agreements since the 1980s, though usually without significant results.[74] But the proposal is opposed by leading transnational agencies representing developing states, including the UN Conference on Trade and Development, and northern employers groups.[75] A united stance from developing states, lead by ASEAN, has precluded any enforceable labour component in the WTO.[76]

According to opponents, including the UK Conservative government, the 1996 Singapore ministerial rejected a protectionist connection of labour and trade and affirmed that competitive advantage using labour costs was not unfair competition.[77] Proponents held out hope that Singapore marked the recognition of core standards by the WTO. But most observers felt the declaration precluded the addition of labour standards in an enforceable fashion.[78] The issue was again raised at the ill-fated Seattle summit and proposed for inclusion in the Millenium round, where it again faced concerted resistance from developing states. It has remained divisive in

---

72   Charnowitz, 1987, 576–9.

73   David Chin, *A Social Clause for Labour's Cause: Global Trade and Labour Standards – A Challenge for the New Millennium* (London: Institute of Employment Rights, 1998).

74   Laura Sefton-MacDowell, 'The International Confederation of Free Trade Unions,' *Labour/Le Travaileur* 49, (2002), 345.

75   'UN agency opposes WTO 'labor clause'' *Journal of Commerce* Nov 30, 1999, 15; 'UNICE Rejects Wto's Labour Standards Definition' *European Report* Jul 14, 1999, 1.

76   'ASEAN follows its heart' *Business Times* (Kuala Lumpur) Oct 17, 1997, 4.

77   European Trade Commissioner Leon Brittan cited in 'WTO: Ministers Agree to Do Nothing on Labour Standards' *European Report* 14, 2183, Dec. 14, 1996, 1.

78   Virginia A. Leary 'The WTO and the Social Clause: Post-Singapore,' *European Journal of International Law*, 8, (1997), 119.

subsequent WTO negotiations, with countries squabbling over whether to include any social dimension in discussions.[79]

Some observers argue that developing states harm their workers by allowing import firms in the North to play them against one another and press them for cheaper labour costs, irrespective of the social damage. They argue that the developing world would benefit from a global minimum wage and other standards which would end this bidding war.[80] But this has remained a non-starter in the South, where unions joined government and business to opposing any punitive regime, on grounds of 'neo-colonialism' and competitiveness. Only in rare instances should a country face collective or even bilateral suspension of trade rights; selective bilateral action under WTO rules against goods produced under egregious conditions could encourage newly industrialized exporters to switch practices.[81]

Proposals to incorporate a social clause in the WTO or to increase the enforcement capacity of the ILO are unlikely to succeed, since labour issues are subject to different interpretations in different domestic contexts. Even some transnational union movements, such as the ICFTU now advocate WTO referral of complaints to the ILO, which would investigate in its normal fashion backed with assistance and incentives as opposed to trade penalties. Block et al recommend a strengthening of the ILO-WTO nexus, with the former able to submit unresolved labour issues to the latter for trade sanctions. If confined to fundamental process rights this arrangement might not be as offensive to the developing world, as working conditions and compensation would remain sensitive to the level of national development.[82] Ehrenburg also suggests a 'synergistic combination of ILO and GATT/WTO expertise' allowing the ILO to identify inadequacies in standards, and the WTO to assess if these convey unfair trade advantages and invoke its disputes settlement process against 'gross and persistent violations'.[83] McCrudden and Davies likewise argue that a *voluntary multilateralism* with nations agreeing to WTO action against egregious labour violations would be preferable to *involuntary multilateralism* where powerful states and trade blocs punish weaker states not conforming to unilaterally determined standards. A voluntary multilateral approach might be phased in gradually, with the

---

79   'India: 'No one country can decide WTO agenda'' *Businessline* (Chennai) Jan 13, 2000, 1.

80   Robert J.S. Ross and Anita Chan 'From North-South to South-South' *Foreign Affairs* 81, (2002), 8.

81   Jagdis Bhagwati, 'Free Trade, 'Fairness' and the New Protectionism: Reflections on an Agenda for the World Trade Organisation' *24th Wincott Memorial Lecture,* Westminster, Oct. 25, 1994 London: Institute of Economic Affairs/Wincott Foundation, 1995, 22–23, 32–34.

82   Block et. al., 2001, 285–6.

83   Daniel S. Ehrenberg, 'From Intention to Action: an ILO-GATT/WTO Enforcement Regime for International Labor Rights' in Lance Compa and S. Diamond eds. *Human Rights, Labor Rights and International Trade* (Philadelphia: University of Pennsylvania Press, 1996), 165.

WTO resolving labour issues, or restricting full membership to states conforming to core labour standards.[84]

Others prefer to encourage unions in the South to recognize the damage of wage competition among developing states and to respond by promoting enforceable minimum wages and conditions.[85] Northern claims to superiority are questioned by the differences in standards between the US and Europe, poor treatment of migrant workers, declining union density and the absence of meaningful economic democracy or worker participation. And biases in Northern negotiating priorities haven't helped. The Clinton administration, while pressing for inclusion of labour rights based on union lobbying, did little to compromise with the developing world on market access in textiles or steel, migrant worker rights, intellectual rights protection for traditional agriculture and multilateral monitoring of antidumping to limit protectionism. Failure to link these core issues with worker rights is a key obstacle to developing country acceptance of a global labour clause.[86]

Therefore, at the global level, it 'is doubtful whether a consensus can be obtained on anything except well-meaning and broad principles without consequences for trade access.'[87] Despite recognition of core labour rights as fundamental human rights, there remains debate on how to implement them without engaging in disguised protectionism. While a limited core of labour standards can be identified which may not harm the competitiveness of the developing world, this consensus is 'too shallow' to permit adoption of a WTO social clause.[88] Some hold out hope that the ILO could rise to the challenge of Singapore and improve its ability to enhance standards or that the OECD or UNCTAD could fill the void.[89] In the current political climate in the WTO, with the reduction of US pressure under the Bush administration, even a modest increment in enforcement is unlikely to be achieved at a global level.

New Regionalism in Labour Affairs

Given the inadequacies of unilateralism, and in the absence of a global consensus, labour advocates have looked to the new regionalism and the emergence of regional trading regimes as the means to advance labour rights. A regional model involves promotion of the trade labour-linkage among states in a regional economic bloc. The European Union and the NAALC provide examples where states recognize the inability of the global system to address many issues, and have moved on to regional arrangements. Major organizations such as the ICFTU have recognised that regional trading blocks may be the only available venue, especially given the limits to the

---

84   McCrudden and Davies, 58–60.
85   Ross and Chan, 2002, 8.
86   Brewster Grace, 'WTO Trade and Labour Standards' *Foreign Policy in Focus* 5,5 (2000), 3.
87   Bhagwati, 1994, 28.
88   Elliott, 1998, 166.
89   Leary, 1997, 122.

emergence of viable union partners in many areas of the developing world under neo-liberal restructuring. But the effectiveness of the regional model depends very much on its specific design.[90]

Some use the EU experience as an archetype for a trade-labour linkage, though the broader social dimension in European integration does not necessarily incorporate significant harmonization of labour rights and standards on unionization and bargaining. Despite variations in union organization, collective bargaining, and worker rights among member states, EU institutions have sought to introduce some commonality. The complex array of social charters and chapters affecting workers which have been introduced have 'been long on generous intention and short on concrete delivery'.[91] 'Pre-emptive legislation' via EU directives, can impose transnational rules for labour, which acquire 'priority' over national laws, encouraging uniformity on some matters. Few treaty provisions deal with labour and the Council of Ministers has been reluctant to enforce directives. Prevention of gender discrimination, worker mobility, migrant workers rights and occupational health and safety have been dealt transnationally.[92]

The original Social Charter listed fundamental rights to health and safety, association and bargaining, social welfare benefits, worker consultation and participation, protection for children, the aged and the disabled. But even though the Commission could impose common rules, the EU has emphasized voluntary 'harmonization' of laws and regulations by member states. EU directives call on states for ratification of measures in a manner consistent with domestic laws resulting in 'approximation' as opposed to 'uniformity'. Examples of EU directives which have been adopted include prior notification for mass layoffs, protection of contracts and rights after ownership changes, benefits and wages in case of insolvency, safety, gender equality, part-time and contract worker rights, and worker councils. While the social charter required states to accept essential economic and social rights, including worker and union rights, it was not enforceable by the European Court of Human Rights or backed by trade penalties; a Committee of Independent Experts could rule of whether countries are in violation and press for improvements, but only with a 2/3 majority, and only if countries voluntarily report violations of essential rights.[93]

The European Union Charter of Fundamental Social Rights, in the Maastricht Treaty in 1992, advanced worker rights. Its social chapter is enforceable by the European Court of Justice. Maastricht inaugurated a 'social dialogue' between social partners and promoted collective bargaining at a EU wide-level, as a substitute for binding legislation. A change from unanimous voting to qualified majority votes in

---

90   McCrudden and Davies, 56.

91   Denis McShane, 'Human Rights and Labor Rights: A European Perspective' in Compa and Diamond, 1996, 57.

92   Katherine Van Wezel Stone, 'Labor and the Global Economy: Four Approaches to Transnational Labor Regulation,' *Michigan Journal of International Law* 16, (1995), 1000.

93   Elwell, 1995, 13–14.

the European Commission, made it easier to adopt measures on health and safety, working conditions, worker consultation, gender discrimination, and reintegration of the unemployed. [94] Pensions, dismissals, and worker and employer representation remain under the unanimity rule, so EU directives are valid only in instances of distortion of market integration. Bargaining rights, strikes and lock-outs also remain subject to unanimity, restricting harmonization.

The Commission proposed a directive to limit social dumping through firm relocation caused by the UK's opt out of the Social Chapter, by requiring multi-state firms to create works councils to consult on relocation to other EU states. Court rulings allowed workers to sue governments for failing to enforce directives and protect their rights which could encourage greater harmonization, alongside new EU directives on corporate structures or bankruptcies. [95] Finally the EU created a Social Fund to help nations meet targets for workers rights and working conditions. While the general thrust of the European Union integration was meant to focus on markets and to leave social policy to national states, Leibfried and Piersen argue that spillovers from the complex integration process have lead to a 'gradual erosion of national welfare state autonomy and sovereignty, increasingly situating national regimes in a complex, multi-tiered web of social policy'. [96]

Advocates of labour rights recognize that the European situation is atypical, and cannot be replicated elsewhere. This has prompted differences of opinion over what mechanisms and enforcement devices could be employed to implement labour standards regionally. In North America, the labour dimension was handled differently, given the very different character of the NAFTA from the European Union and the distinctive nature of the member states. First, the US implemented its labour laws in extra-territorial fashion backed with the threat of loss of trade access. Courts extended the reach of American labour laws to US companies' operations overseas or to foreign actors with operations in the United States. Age discrimination and civil rights legislation was extended to US workers in US subsidiaries overseas, though a broader extension of the National Labor Relations Act to US subsidiaries failed in Congress. As discussed above, the GSP system and other US trade initiatives explicitly linked trade access to labour rights. So NAALC was brought into an existing system of US unilateral extension of its labour practices to overseas locales. Although easier to implement and potentially potent, this unilateral effort was 'piecemeal', ineffective, and an irritant in trans-border relations[97], especially given the asymmetry between North American trade partners, which meant that extra-territoriality would largely work from the US outwards.

---

94   Gerda Faulkner, 'The EU's social dimension' in Michelle Cini, ed. *European Union Politics* (New York, Oxford, 2003), 268.

95   Van Wezel Stone, 1003–05.

96   Stephan Leibfried and Paul Piersen, 'Social Policy' in Helan Wallace and William Wallace eds. *Policy-Making in the European Union* (New York: Oxford, 2000), 268.

97   Van Wezel Stone, 1026–27.

NAALC as an Example of New Regionalism?

Thus, when NAFTA was debated, new solutions were sought to deepen the integration and coordination of labour rights and standards. Advocates of labour rights sought inclusion of a 'social clause' in NAFTA which would prevent Mexico from taking advantage of its unfairly low labour standards to secure competitive gains in North American trade. But in North America, a liberalizing trade and investment system was modified with a labour side agreement focussed on education and information sharing, not trade sanctions. While no effort has been made to harmonize laws or create transnational standards, the NAALC system as discussed below has created some new mechanisms for addressing worker rights and conditions, focussed on cross border monitoring of domestic law enforcement. The NAALC outlines 'aspirations rather than enforceable obligations'.[98] It is a 'multilateral enforcement model'[99] where states aspire to improve their domestic enforcement regimes to augment standards throughout the region. This text assesses how effectively these 'aspirations' have been realized, in the implementation of NAALC principles and procedures after 12 years.

Did the labour side agreement do anything to broaden NAFTA regionalism beyond a neo-liberal trade and investment agreement by incorporating a counterbalancing social dimension? Some observers see NAFTA and its attendant institutions as a first step towards a process of 'widening and deepening' the integration of regional economies, political and social entities. Charles Doran suggests that the 'interpenetration of cultural attitudes will eventually result in a more regional way of thinking about problems, opportunities and the place of North America in World Affairs'[100] Some observers do not see this trend as alarming or confining for Canadian or Mexican policy choices, and see deeper and broader integration as beneficial since it would maximize economic efficiency and productivity on the continent. Robert Pastor advocates creation of a North American Community directed by stronger central institutions like a North American Commission.[101] But critics argue that this threatens sovereignty and would Americanize policy, including labour relations.

The literature on new regionalism sometimes suggests that regionalization is both inexorable and irreversible. Fuelled by contemporary technology and capitalist ideology, regionalism influences the character of transnational organizations and commitments, and binds nation states to long-term trends of integration. For many, this integration has proceeded more rapidly at the regional than the global level, due to impatience with the complexities and cumbersome qualities of global organizations like the GATT-WTO. As Leibfried and Piersen argue for Europe,

---

98   Van Wezel Stone, 1008.

99   Block et. al, 2001, 275–7.

100   Charles F. Doran, 'Building a North American community' *Current History*; 94, 590 (1995), 98.

101   Robert Pastor, *Towards a North American Community* (Washington: Institute for International Economics, 2001), 100.

economic integration and liberalization may spill over into social realms, broadening the project over time. [102]

This text will suggest that while liberalizing tendencies among the NAFTA partners will persist and grow, the potential for broader transnational social integration and institutionalization may be limited on a continent featuring immense asymmetries in power and dependence. As the case study of the NAALC will show, the institutionalization of a social dimension of trade in North America was limited by by US dominance in the asymmetrical partnership, by the different institutions of the three states, by the lack of strong transnational social forces to counterbalance the immense and by the growing power of transnational capital which seeks deepening of liberalization without countervailing social regulation. But the NAFTA labour accord did generate new institutions which in turn had notable, though limited, effects on social actors and practices in labour relations across national boundaries.

---

102 Leibfried and Piersen, 2000,268.

Chapter 2

NAFTA, Labour and the New Regionalism

The Rise of New Regionalisms

NAFTA provides an example of transnational new regionalism, based around trading blocs, with profound implications for economic and social organization. It is a largely neo-liberal variant of new regionalism, with only modest concessions on labour and the environment. Some proposed that North America emulate Europe in adding a strong social dimension to its trading arrangements. There was talk early on of a 'social charter' to ensure that trade integration did not occur at the expense of labour rights and working conditions.[1] However, this analysis will demonstrate the constraints on regionalization of the social and labour dimension in North America. While some still anticipate a deepening and broadening of North American regionalism, it is unlikely to generate a stronger transnational social dimension on a continent marked by weak social and union movements, rigid domestic institutions, and extreme asymmetry between the economic weight of the three partners. While stronger formal institutions in labour affairs may prove elusive, NAALC provides some impetus to deepening informal institutions, through transborder social movements, bureaucratic networks, policy learning and to a limited degree, a 'cognitive construct' in labour affairs.[2]

Hettne and Soderbaum analyze the emergence of a new regionalism based on the increased transnational and globalized character economic and social life. New regionalism is a global phenomenon reflecting the enhanced interdependence of states in the global economy. Regionalism involves the 'phenomenon' of new forms of regional integration, but also an 'ideology' of regionalism, the search for a 'regionalist order' in a particular geographical region, which 'may lead to formal institution building'.[3] While regional integration takes many forms, trading blocs such as NAFTA and the EU are notable institutional examples. However, social

---

1   See for instance Harley Shaiken, 'The NAFTA, A Social Charter and Economic Growth' in Richard S. Belous and Jonathan Lemco eds. *NAFTA As a Model of Development: The Benefits and Costs of Merging High- And Low-Wage Areas* (Albany: SUNY Press, 1995), 27–36.

2   James Wesley Scott, 'European and North American Contexts for Cross-border Regionalism' *Regional Studies* 33, (1999), 607.

3   Björn Hettne and Frederik Söderbaum, 'Theorising the Rise of Regions,' *New Political Economy* 5, (2000), 457.

movements and networks, transnational companies, and new communities emerging irrespective of old national boundaries constitute other elements of the new regionalism. As proponents of global and regional trade and economic liberalization succeed in generating new regional structures, opposition social movements, labour organizations and their allies are forced into similar organizational changes. Transnational economic regionalism is matched by corresponding social organization across national boundaries.[4] This is evident in an emerging nexus of labour and human rights groups in the NAFTA region.

New forms of regionalism pose an important challenge to national sovereignty and policy. There is a simultaneous development of supranational and subnational regionalism in North America's integrated economic system.[5] States retain significant scope for policy independence in such integrative arrangements.[6] But regional integration inherently challenges national sovereignties and traditional state functions. Regionalization is a facet of globalization as multinational firms create a base in regional markets to withstand global competitive pressures, forcing states to facilitate these alliances through regional trading arrangements. As Grinspun and Cameron note, regionalization has profound impacts for domestic politics and society, by imposing neo-liberal deregulation and forcing 'downward harmonization' in environmental, social and labour standards.[7]

Earlier functionalist interpretations of regionalism predicted that form would follow function, that institutional integration would progress inexorably out of functional needs as non-state economic and social integration proceeded. As Söderbaum asserts, 'Liberal institutionalists argue that supranational institutions are political actors in their own right and represent a new polity beyond or above the nation-state. Institutions and supranational laws 'matter' and they can help states negotiate mutually beneficial outcomes because of their impact on the calculations, expectations, and interests of the actors.'[8] However, these models were drawn from Europe where integration occurred among a number of common powerful core states, with peripheral states balancing the mixture. Even proponents of NAFTA agreed that institutionalization along EU lines might not be attainable in North America, where the focus is on an economic partnership governing the voluminous

---

4   Marianne H. Marchand, Morten Boas, Timothy M Shaw, 'The political economy of new regionalisms,' *Third World Quarterly* 20, (1999), 899.

5   Wilfred J. Ethier , 'The new regionalism in the Americas: A theoretical framework,' *North American Journal of Economics and Finance* 12, (2001), 161–62.

6   George Hoberg, 'Canada and North American Integration,' *Canadian Public Policy* 26, (2000), S45.

7   Cited in Marchand, Boas and Shaw, (1999), 903.

8   F. Söderbaum 2002. "Rethinking the New regionalism", Paper for the XIII Nordic Political Science Association Meeting, Aalborg 15–17 August 2002. [Cited July 9, 2004]. Available at .http://www.socsci.auc.dk/institut2/nopsa/arbejdsgruppe23/soderbaum.pdf.

interactions across the northern and southern American borders.[9] The negotiators' approach focussed on liberalization and removal of barriers to trade and investment. However, political complexities required addition of side agreements on labour and the environment. It remains to assess whether these late additions altered an essentially neoliberal agreement.

Labour, Neoliberalism and NAFTA

Observers are divided over the nature of NAFTA. Some argue that it is a free trade arrangement only, liberalizing commerce with little impact on other government powers and policies. Others argue that it is a deeper integration arrangement, which will bring the junior partners into line with American preferences on tariffs and trade with the rest of the world. The integration and dependence of Mexican and Canadian economies with the U.S. will increase and pressure for overarching institutions and norms will mount. As Wilkinson observes, NAFTA's 'wide ranging provisions ... establish it as an economic community in the making'.[10] Pasquero refers to 'regional market integration' on the NAFTA model as a neo-liberal response to 'efficiency needs'.[10a] Bhagwati implies that the side agreements on labour and the environment mean that NAFTA was broadened into a political as opposed to economic space.[11] But the lesser enforcement capacity afforded to these accords as opposed to trade and investment issues raises doubts that NAFTA deviates significantly from a neo-liberal strategy.

Critics decried NAFTA for facilitating the free movement of capital and production to the detriment of labour and the environment. Wilkinson noted that NAFTA lacked the EU's labour mobility rights and mechanisms to promote upward adjustment of social and labour conditions.[12] Critics in both Canada (such as the, CLC, Action Canada Network and New Democrat Party) and the United States (like the AFL-CIO, Ralph Nader and Ross Perot) argued that NAFTA would result in job loss and wage decreases in these countries. Low Mexican wages, weaker unions and poorer benefits, combined with lax environmental standards would reduce costs of

---

9   Alan Rugman cited in Andrew F. Cooper, 'NAFTA and the politics of regional trade,' in Brian Hocking and Steven McGuire eds. *Trade Politics: International, Domestic and Regional Responses* (New York: Routledge, 1999), 234.

10 Bruce Wilkinson, 'NAFTA in the World Economy: Lessons and Issues for Latin America,' in Richard G. Lipsey and Patricio Meller eds., *Western Hemisphere Trade Integration: A Canadian-Latin American Dialogue* (London: MacMillan, 1997), 31.

10a Jean Pasquero, "Regional Market Integration in North America and Corporate Social Management. Emerging Governance Frameworks for Business and Public Policy". *Business and Society*, 39: 2000. 9.

11 Jagdish Bhagwati, 'The Demands to Reduce Domestic Diversity Among Trading Nations,' in J. Bhagwati and Robert E. Hudec eds. *Fair Trade and Harmonization: Prerequisites for Free Trade?* (Cambridge: MIT Press, 1996), 36.

12 Wilkinson, 1997, 33.

production, and create an incentive for 'social dumping' as companies chose Mexico as a site for low wage commercial and manufacturing activities.

Economists countered that NAFTA should be a win-win scenario as integration reduced inefficiencies and created employment in all three trading partners. Market logic dictates that free exchange of goods and services will increase net prosperity across the entire region, by creating an efficient allocation of investment and activities.[13] Losses in low-wage, labour intensive sectors will be offset by gains in high-wage skilled sectors like computers, communications, and auto-parts, as Mexican restrictions on imports are phased out. Mexico's cost advantage is exaggerated, since industries must absorb statutory benefits and lower productivity per worker, which make wages roughly equal on either side of the Rio Grande. Some low wage companies in textiles and electronic assembly will relocate to Mexico but GNP growth will increase the Mexican market for American goods, fuelling job creation. NAFTA provisions for North American content would make American and Canadian suppliers of parts and raw materials crucial to new Mexican industries. Supporters predicted that 'the opening of the Mexican market to U.S. investment will sustain Mexico's high growth rate. Sustained growth will allow the country to meet its increased appetite for American consumer and industrial goods'.[14]

However, the free market system of NAFTA is incomplete, since labour is denied free movement across borders. Hence some of the gains in efficiency of the full integration of labour markets are lost in North America. Capital retains the 'exit' option as it can move to amenable locations more readily than labour. This creates the possibility for 'regulatory competition' as NAFTA partners attract capital at the expense of labour, whose movement is restricted by immigration regimes.[15] As proposition 187, post 9–11 security concerns and the actions of the California highway patrol and Arizona minutemen demonstrate, there is a strong reaction against immigration and a move to restrict movement, except for limited categories of professionals.

Moreover, in conditions of high unemployment, the link between productivity and wages is lost; Mexican workers have experienced erosion of incomes despite higher productivity since Mexico mostly attracts low wage or part time jobs. While the benefits of trade liberalization may exceed the costs, these are 'net benefits' as losers are evident in particular regions, sectors and industries.[16] Mexico as a whole

---

13 Paul Krugman, 'The uncomfortable truth about NAFTA: it,'s foreign policy, stupid,' *Foreign Affairs* 72, (1993), 13–20.

14 Norman Bailey, 'The Economic Effects of NOT Passing the NAFTA,' in Amber H. Moss, ed. *Assessments of the North American Free Trade Agreement* (New Brunswick, N.J.: Transaction Books, 1993), 7.

15 Brian A. Langille, 'Labour Standards in the Globalized Economy and the FreeTrade/ Fair Trade Debate,' in W. Sengenberger and D. Campbell eds., *International Labour Standards and Economic Interdependence* (Geneva: International Institute for Labour Studies, 1994), 229.

16 Howard Rosen, 'Adjustment and Transition Mechanisms for a U.S.-Mexico Free Trade Agreement,' in M. Delal Baer and Sidney Weintraub eds. *The NAFTA Debate: Grappling With*

may benefit from increased employment, but may do so by maintaining poorer wages and benefits than in the other NAFTA partners. Potential increases in inequality could ultimately undermine democratic responsiveness and stability.[17]

NAFTA advocates believed integration would create 'greater commercial efficiencies', reduced 'transaction costs' and 'economies of scale'. NAFTA reflected the neo-liberal vision, which provided 'ideological/policy coherence'.[18] Those supporting liberalization remained powerful in the governing coalition of the three nations as NAFTA was forged. This contrasted with divisions among foes of NAFTA among unions, human rights groups, environmental activists and opposition parties. In the electoral situation in the US and Canada, these opponents were able to press for negotiation of the side agreements. Some have since hailed the NAFTA as innovative because its extension into investment, labour, and the environment moved beyond most other regional or global agreements at the time. But the thrust of NAFTA remained liberalizing and deregulatory, as demonstrated by the cooperative nature of the accords on labour and the environment, as opposed to the compulsory, sanctions-based regime on trade and investor rights.

The imbalance of forces in this tussle over labour rights and trade is significant. Corporate and state advocates of globalization and regional integration hold the authority to shape transnational institutions and the economic power to force liberalization measures on developing states. Proponents of labour rights must use moral suasion, public opinion and appeals to democratic rights to assert their cause. With the shift to a transnational, post-Fordist paradigm in labour-management relations, the prospects for unions and social movements to force changes to trade regimes are diminishing. Some remain optimistic about the countervailing forces at work as social movements and unions mobilize transnationally and generate pressures on corporations, consumers, governments and supranational agencies.[19] Labour rights activists have forced proponents of transnationalism to acknowledge the impact of integration on workers. They have caused some corporations to become more socially responsible towards workers, and encouraged consumers to demand fair working conditions in selecting products. But the imbalance of forces between advocates of trade liberalization and worker rights remains problematic.

NAFTA and the NAALC present an interesting case study of these debates, as one of the first free trade areas linking developed and developing states. They provide a test of the potential of new regionalism across the North-South divide to incorporate a social and labour rights dimension which is mutually agreeable and beneficial. The inclusion of the labour and environmental side agreements in NAFTA indicates potential for resolution of North-South divisions on a social dimension to

---

Unconventional Trade Issues (Boulder, Col., Lynne Reiner, 1994), 35.

17 Wilkinson, 1997, 52–3.

18 Cooper, 1999, 230.

19 Robert O,'Brien, 'The Agency of Labour in a Changing Global Order,' in Richard Stubbs and Geoffrey R.D. Underhill eds. *Political Economy and the Changing Global Order* (3rd. ed.) Toronto: Oxford, 2005, 230–31.

trade pacts. Yet the characteristics of North American economics, institutions and social movements make NAFTA different from other trading blocs which have incorporated social and labour dimensions. To assess the prospects for transnational labour arrangments in North America, scholars must examine the asymmetrical character of North American regionalism, the strength of unions and their social partners, and the nature of domestic institutions in the NAFTA countries.

Constraints on Social Regionalism in North America

North American integration in labour matters was shaped by the balance of economic power, domestic institutions and social context in which NAFTA and NAALC were negotiated. Three key factors – the form of regionalism, strength of social and labour movements domestically and transnationally, and the character of domestic political institutions – influenced the process of integration. Asymmetrical regionalism between the US and its neighbours did not permit genuine, effective supra-national institutions, as in a more balanced, multi-lateral regionalism like the EU. The weak power of transnational labour and social movements also limited pressure for an effective social dimension. Domestic political institutions also constrained national participation in transnational regional institutions. These factors limited the effectiveness of NAALC's design and may constrain prospects for its enhancement.

Asymmetrical regionalism

NAFTA was built around asymmetrical bilateral relations of the United States with Canada and Mexico with one dominant partner and two trade-dependent countries, which entered free trade for defensive purposes, to limit (albeit only partly) harmful unilateral action by their powerful neighbour. America's preference for unilateralism, and rejection of supranationalism, based on constitutional supremacy and Congressional authority, provides a major barrier to European-style transnational standards as the American hegemon was unwilling to cede sovereignty to transnational institutions. On the other hand, Mexico and Canada feared that enforceable standards backed by trade or financial penalties would work mostly against them. But they recognized the costs of protectionism and accept continental or hemispheric institutions designed around American interests. As Ethier notes of the new regionalism in North America, 'NAFTA liberalization involved more 'concessions' by Mexico and Canada than by the US' as the smaller partners made 'a host of reform commitments'.[20] The smaller partners conceded to their stronger partner for defensive purposes, to prevent negative actions by the hegemon. Ethier suggests, 'the new regionalism typically involves reform-minded small countries

---

20 Wilfred J Ethier 'The new regionalism in the Americas: A theoretical framework,' *North American Journal of Economics and Finance* 12, (2001), 161–62.

'purchasing,' with moderate trade concessions, links with a large, neighbouring country that involve 'deep' integration but confer minor trade advantages.'[21]

These asymmetries are sharpened by the fact that NAFTA spans the boundaries between North and South. It is the first trading bloc to bring together developed and newly industrialized states. Mexico is a prime example of a state forced away from protectionism, to accept liberalization and integration with the American core. Semi-peripheral states like Mexico and Canada find that they must 'participate in new regionalist associations as a way to avoid marginalization' in the interdependent global economy.[22] These semi-peripheries sought market access and influence over the hegemon's policies.[23] Transnationalized production and neo-liberal ideology spawned regional institutions in the highly integrated North American continent as economic and political elites sought a framework to perpetuate liberalized trade and investment. But asymmetry did not give all the advantages to the Americans, who faced internal political and institutional constraints, which forced them away from their initial insistence on enforceable labour standards.

Although there was no mutuality in the bargaining power of the players, Canada and Mexico were able to resist a labour accord with broad enforcement powers. Asymmetries in trade flows between the parties, and the dependence of Canada and Mexico on US markets made them unwilling to accept a strong labour side agreement. Canada and Mexico were reluctant to accept Clinton's proposal for financial and trade penalties for labour law violations, based on sovereignty concerns, and a fear that sanctions would be disproportionately effective for the US which relied less on its neighbours markets. As Grinspun and Cameron note, the smaller partners might 'threaten' retaliation, but would be loath to worsen a trade war which hurt them, as trade dependent peripheries, more than the American hegemon.[24] The smaller states, profoundly affected by regional integration, were cautious and guarded their sovereignty. But despite their reluctance, they eventually acceded to a labour since agreement, though keeping it weaker than the Americans originally intended. Regional asymmetry greatly influenced the NAALC negotiations since Canada and Mexico could not accept a strong trade penalty component. The US was willing to abandon its proposals for sanctions in this area because it was less committed to labour rights than to the core areas of investments, trade flows, and disputes resolutions mechanisms, crafted on its terms.

---

21 Ethier, 2001, 162.

22 Jean Grugel and Wil Hout, 'Regions, regionalism and the South,' in Hout and Grugel eds. *Regionalism Across the North-South Divide: State strategies and Globalization* (London: Routledge, 1999), 6.

23 Wil Hout, 'Theories of International Relations and the New Regionalism,' in W. Hout and J. Grugel eds. *Regionalism Across the North-South Divide: State strategies and Globalization* (London: Routledge, 1999), 15, 17.

24 Ricardo Grinspun and Maxwell Cameron, 'The Political Economy of North American Integration,' in Grinspun and Cameron eds. *The Political Economy of North American Free Trade* (Montreal/Kingston: McGill-Queen's University Press, 1993), 16.

The EU context was more hospitable to agreement on sanctionable clauses and supranational enforcement in social matters. The number of different states and the existence of several large economics able to enforce such actions reduced the fears of asymmetrical benefits from sanctionable measures. In addition, the common level of development of original members meant that a commitment to social integration was established before accession of new members in Southern and Eastern Europe, whose economic differences from the core approximated Mexico's. Van Liemt indicates that the imposition of sanctions remains a 'privilege' for larger states with high bargaining power in a trade relationship.[25] This dynamic made the two smaller NAFTA partners resist American desires for enforceable labour rights, though they made such concessions in trade and investment disputes where US negotiators were adamant and transnational forces were powerful and integrated. Asymmetrical regionalism will limit efforts to strengthen NAALC because Mexico and Canada fear that sanctions favour the US, while the latter doesn't need supranationalism, when well served by unilateralism. Concessions on energy, investor rights, and other issues illustrate that the US could insist on favourable clauses, if it was sufficiently motivated and if it was internally united.[26]

Labour and social movement power

Asymmetry alone cannot explain why labour was marginalized, while enforcement was permitted in trade and intellectual property; the social constituencies promoting the latter were more extensive, powerful, transnational and single-minded than labour. Social and union movements acting domestically and transnationally, created enough pressure to force negotiation of the NAALC. But problems reconciling the interests of civil societies and unions across the North-South divide and the declining power of unions in post-Fordist economies limited this political pressure. Robinson suggests that labour movement power is defined by '(1) structural characteristics of the movement's principal organizations, and (2) the capacity of these organizations to mobilize their members and wider public support for their collective actions.'[27] These factors are affected by the level of union density, strength of social democratic or left parties, the degree of union cohesiveness and the potential for centralized collective bargaining.[28] All three of these states have union movements with limited power relative to European counterparts, with declining density, limited political influence and reduced bargaining power in the economy. In addition, weak transnational

25 Gijsbert van Liemt, 'International trade and workers,' rights,', in Brian Hocking and Steven McGuire eds. *Trade Politics: International, Domestic and Regional Responses* (New York: Routledge, 1999), 121.

26 For a developed overview of the institutional parameters of the side agreement negotiations, see Maxwell A. Cameron and Brian W. Tomlin, *The Making of NAFTA: How the Deal Was Done* (Ithaca: Cornell University Press, 2000), Chapter 9.

27 Ian Robinson, 'NAFTA, social unionism, and labour movement power in Canada and the United States,' *Relations Industrielles/Industrial Relations* 49, (1994), 658.

28 Robinson, 1994, 65.

alliances prior to NAFTA limited the ability of these social constituencies to strengthen the social dimension and protect workers.

The transnational interaction among trade unions in North America is complicated by the very different nature of these nation's economies; one global superpower, one emerging newly industrialized but largely underdeveloped states and the other, developed but export and resource-oriented. These different models prompt very different interactions between the state and unions in each society, generating different laws and regulations governing union rights, workplace conditions and collective bargaining. Vested interests in unions and politics in each state sought to preserve a distinct legal and regulatory climate, prompting resistance from all three union movements to adoption of transnational standards. Above all, the North-South divide split the movement in its approach to the trade labour linkage. Mexico's large official unions resisted this linkage, which they viewed as protectionist. US, Canadian and Mexican independent unions were distrustful of the process but advocated a fair trade model or a social charter in the heart of the NAFTA.

This gulf is extended by the very different evolution of the three union movements and industrial relations systems. America's unions are liberal, non-partisan and economistic, emphasizing gains via collective bargaining. The American system allows for input from interest groups, and is a lobbyist's paradise. Though influential in the past, organized labour has been marginalized by the strong influence of employers and other lobbies in Washington. And the American labour movement has been characterized by elements of voluntarism and economism, preferring to win benefits via a demonstration of strength in the marketplace rather than rely on state assistance or regulation. The labour movement has professed non-partisanship though unions have been allied with the Democratic Party since the New Deal and Great Society coalitions.

But organized labour is a declining force in that system, wielding diminishing power as lobbyist or vote mobilizer.[29] Andrew Martin notes how weak US unions and the ability of governing elites to exclude labour from decision making helped the decline of the Fordist, welfare-state paradigm. Labour, which had previously supported internationalization of the global economy when US MNCs were generating high wage domestic employment from their overseas ventures, now saw itself in opposition to the deepening of this liberalization in NAFTA. But US unions' weak political position ensured that liberalizing elements of NAFTA would be paramount and the social dimension would be limited.[30] The union position on NAALC was one largely of disengagement with attention focused on defeating NAFTA, not improving the side agreement.

---

29 Frederick Englehart, 'Withered Giants: Mexican and US Organized Labor and the North American Agreement on Labor Cooperation' *Case Western Reserve Journal of International Law* 29 (1997), 327–8.

30 Andrew Martin, 'Labour, the Keynesian Welfare State and the Changing Global Economy,' in Richard Stubbs and Geoffrey R.D. Underhill eds. *Political Economy and the Changing Global Order* (Toronto: McClelland and Stewart, 1994), 64.

Mexican unions emerged in a post-revolutionary system of corporatism, where worker organizations were integrated with but dominated by the governing Institutional Revolutionary Party, or PRI. Mexico had a highly centralized trade union movement under the Congresso de Trabajo, led by the Confederación de Trabajadores Mexicanos (CTM), Confederación Revolucionario de Obreros y Campesinos (CROC) and Confederación Regional Obrera Mexicana (CROM). Mexican labour has been dominated by official unions, with a gradual increment in independent unions seeking to challenge the status quo. Mexico's quasi-authoritarian political structures have historically produced a weak civil society. The corporatist organizations surrounding the long-governing PRI provided some input from labour and peasants in this essentially one-party system. However, these organizations served to co-opt these interests into a non-adversarial approach which did not fully represent worker or peasant inerests. This industrial relations system served a labour aristocracy of union leaders and party insiders at the expense of the rank and file. The strength of these official unions had decreased within the governing councils of the dominant PRI by the time NAFTA was negotiated.[31] Vanderbush notes how Mexican unions appeared 'unwilling' or 'incapable' of resisting 'onerous' liberalization and privatization under Presidents de la Madrid and Salinas.[32]

Official unions' proximity to government limited their ability to represent worker interests, which undermined Mexico's labour laws and protections. Though some union leaders played a role in NAALC negotiations, they did so mainly to ensure that existing union privileges were not undermined. In the context of the NAALC negotiations, Mexico's major 'official' unions supported the PRI negotiators and resisted enforceable transnational labour standards, which would work against Mexican workers interests by discouraging investment. They argued that their presence in governing councils provided enough protection for workers, who did not require a regional labour accord.[33] Independent unions and allied social movements were stimulated in part by opposition to NAFTA, and sought to derail NAFTA or alter it to a fair trade model. But marginalized subsistence farmers, migrant workers and informal-sector employees remain vulnerable and hard to mobilize for political action. Hence, Mexican unions opposition helped weaken the NAALC, and the smaller fair trade voices went unheeded.

Canada's union movement and labour laws were influenced by American models, but evolved in different directions, with the greater unionization of public sector workers, and more 'social unionism' around a social democratic party. Canada's industrial relations system, like much of its national legislation, is fragmented by divided jurisdiction between Ottawa and the provinces and by the diverse regional character of the national economy. Federal leadership strengthened Canadian unions before 1970, particularly when collective bargaining rights were granted

---

31 Englehart, 1997, 329.

32 Walt Vanderbush 'Mexican Labor in the Era of Economic Restructuring and NAFTA: Working to create a Favorable Investment Climate,' *Labor Studies Journal* 20, (1996), 58.

33 Englehart, 1997, 329.

to public sector unions. Canada also faces divisions based on linguistic identity (between Quebecois and English Canadian Unions) and between national and so called 'international' (US-affiliated) unions. This leads to fragmented, weak unions compare to the European case, though with greater social activism lead by national, Quebecois and public sector unions. With 4 million union members in 1,000 unions with 25,000 distinct bargaining units, Canadian union density remains near 31.3%, higher than recent US levels.[34] Yet the country faces a post-industrial decline in unionization rates in the private sector, with numbers remaining higher because of public-sector unions.

Neo-liberal restructuring has taken a toll on Canadian unions, with reduced union rights and a decreased ability to resist employer demands for concessions.[35] Labour standards in general remain higher than in the US, but this is not consistent across all elements of core or cash standards, and free trade may induce harmonization for competitive reasons.[36] Robinson in particular argues that NAFTA will reduce the organizational capacity of Canadian unions to remain influential, by eroding union density, limiting the strength of left or social democratic parties, undermining labour unity and diminishing centralized collective bargaining.[37] Hence neo-liberalism, downsizing and transnational integration are weakening the position of Canadian unions, though the union movement remains somewhat more politically influential than in the US.

This weakness was augmented by transnational distance between the union movements in the three nations. American economistic unionism has been influential in all three states. But US union outreach from the Cold war to the 1980s was directed against radicalism, and aligned with US foreign policy. Only from the 1980s did an alternative populist unionism emerge among rank and file US workers, who began to see the importance of mutually beneficial transnanational interaction.[38] This distance between national union movements was bridged to some degree by the emergence of transnational social activism. NAFTA talks stimulated the creation of transnational union networks and allied social movements mobilized against this neo-liberal venture. Thus, organizations in Canada and the US concerned for the protection of social and labour rights linked up with similarly minded unions and social networks

---

34 Akivah Starkman, 'The Structure and Role of Canadian Labour Boards,' presented to the NAALC Trilateral Seminar on Labour Boards in North America, March 2003. [cited August 16, 2004]. Available at http://www.naalc.org/french/pdf/labor_boards_sem_starkmant.pdf.

35 Barry Brennan 'Canadian Labor Today: Partial Successes, Real Challenges,' *Monthly Review* 57, 2 (2005), 46–61.

36 Richard N Block and Karen Roberts 'A comparison of labour standards in the United States and Canada,' *Relations Industrielles/Industrial Relations* 55, (2000), 299–300.

37 Robinson, 1994, 657.

38 Hobart A. Spalding, 'The Two Latin American Foreign Policies of the U.S. Labor Movement: The AFL-CIO Top Brass vs. Rank and File,' *Science and Society* 56, (1992–93), 421–39.

in Mexico.[39] But the gulf of interests between workers in these states is extensive and common trends to weakness and declining density in Canada and the US, with stagnant public sector unionism, decreased labour's ability to influence public policy and transnational agreements in desirable directions. [40]

This compares with the trends in Europe at the time of the Maastricht negotiations, which occurred prior to some of the structural trends to post-Fordism, which have more recently influenced the European economy and union movement. The higher levels of protection provided for labour in Europe reflects the power of union centrals; unions were politically powerful and essential to governing coalitions in many European states. These interlinked, trade-dependent states have a tradition of transnational union solidarity and activism which makes them a force in EU forums. European union densities varied by state, ranges as high as 70% in some Scandinavian states and is well above 30% in most Western European states.[41] This higher density coupled with a structural tradition of strong, unified trade labour centrals, with a social union dimension, explains their political role. The Maastricht social chapter 'suggests that strong national labor movements can influence the shape of international trade agreements', while NAFTA's weak labour clause 'bears witness to the humbling of the labor movement in the United States [and Canada] that preceded the drafting of the treaty'.[42]

Domestic institutions and transnational social policy

Although they differ in configuration, the three North American federations, two with presidential separation of powers, and one with decentralized provincial authorities dominating labour relations, were not well suited to securing national commitment to transnational regimes in labour or social policy. The American political system was designed explicitly to balance and limit powers. The fragmented nature of decision making in the US polity created opportunities for supporters and opponents of NAFTA to mobilize. This was especially so around the so-called 'fast track' authorizations, required by the American president to negotiate trade deals with other states. While insiders in the corporate and trading community held the upper hand, the opposition sought to mobilize a grassroots coalition of those fearful of the impact of free trade. The open system has afforded organized labour opportunities to shape policies and this helps explains why, in the electoral season of 1992 that labour was able to secure the limited concession of the NAALC before NAFTA could be ratified. While unions

---

39 Robinson, 1994, 668.

40 Leo Troy, 'U.S. and Canadian Industrial Relations: Convergent or Divergent?,' *Relations Industrielles/Industrial Relations* 39, (2000), 695–713.

41 ILO, *World Labour Report 1997–98: Industrial relations, democracy and social stability* Table 1.2. [cited Jan. 23, 2004]. Available at http://www.ilo.org/public/english/dialogue/ifpdial/publ/wlr97/annex/tab12.htm.

42 David Montgomery, 'Labor Rights and Human Rights: A Historical Perspective,' in Lance A Compa and Stephen F Diamond eds. *Human rights, labor rights, and international trade* (Philadelphia : University of Pennsylvania Press, 1996), 17.

had a share of this influence in the past, their role has declined as corporate interests hold greater influence over the Washington scene. Labour and its allies had greater difficulty in securing attention to their agenda let alone securing a powerful labour side agreement. Given the time limits imposed in the fast track system, the entire agreement could have been scuttled if Clinton had held out for a stronger labour accord; Republican threats to defeat NAFTA and continued resistance from some anti-free trade Democrats meant a deeper commitment to transnational standards in labour could not emerge from the Congress.[43]

At the time of the adoption of NAFTA, Mexico had a very centralized system of government, with powers concentrated in the national executive and the office of the president. Camp described Mexico as a 'semiauthoritarian political system' with a unique blend of liberal and authoritarian characteristics.[44] The Institutional Revolutionary Party, or PRI, held power both in Los Pinos and in Congress, buttressed by a corporatist system of official interest groups. Official representatives of labour, peasants, business, and other core interests worked through the PRI to shape policy without resort to genuine party competition.[45] Hence the PRI, with its union and business allies, had no difficulties in securing adoption of the neo-liberal NAFTA. And official union opposition to a strong transnational labour accord ensured the government did not face the same pressures as the Clinton administration, and could resist a strong side agreement. Since NAFTA, Mexico has moved towards a more genuine balance of powers among branches and levels of government. With the election in 2000 of Vincente Fox, the PRI lost the presidency, but the presidency also lost its dominance, as Congress, controlled by the opposition, would not accept his legislative direction. As Mexico adopts democratic reforms, the powers of the president is constrained, and gridlock at the national level may prevent meaningful changes to NAALC.

Canada's British derived Westminister system places most decision making power in executive and administrative forums around the Prime Minister and senior cabinet ministers. This creates a very different dynamic from the congressional model, making blocking coalitions more difficult and allowing more comprehensive, coherent policies. Conceivably it could mean that the Canadian government could pursue a more coherent strategy than its NAFTA partners and commit to transnational standards to deepen the social dimension of its international trading agreements. But Canadian labour policy faces obstacles from its federal character. The fragmentation of labour matters in federalism has limited national policies. Federalism also hinders transnational policy; Ottawa cannot readily commit to transnationalism in labour relations, since it has limited ability to impose such accords on the provincial regimes or to require conformity to transnational standards of labor protection. In Canada, with provincial predominance in labour matters, most provinces do not yet

---

43 Cameron and Tomlin, 204–06.

44 Roderic Ai Camp, *Politics in Mexico* (2nd. Ed.) (New York: Oxford, 1996), 11.

45 Yemile Mizrahi, 'Will Vicente Fox be able to breathe new life into Mexican federalism?,' *Federations* 1, 1, (2000).

participate in NAFTA's labour side agreement. More than half of the provinces have still not signed an intergovernmental agreement on the NAALC, meaning many cases cannot even be raised, despite comparable issues to those under review.

Hence, in the case of NAFTA, domestic institutions worked against a strong transnational commitment to labour rights. This contrasted with the European Union, where most states were unitary, parliamentary systems capable of negotiating and committing to broad economic and social integration. Even if domestic and transnational constituencies in favour of a social dimension to NAFTA had been politically stronger the institutional configuration of each state did not facilitate commitment to transnational labour norms. In particular the complexity of the American policy making process makes it exceedingly difficult for even the most well-meaning administration to deliver on its promises as embodied even in detailed treaties; in this case, the Clinton administration had to back away from its earlier insistence on enforceable, transnational labour standards. Canada has historically learned how special interests in the United States attempt to sway the implementation of any accord in their favor, using 'immense size and complexity of the U.S. policymaking agencies and the forces they respond to. It means simply that any agreement is subject to a range of pressures for changes or interpretations which may run against the apparently benign overall plan centering on bilateral cooperation.'[46] Complex institutions, breeding corporate dominance in domestic politics in all three partners, limited prospects for a strong labour dimension in continental trade regimes.

Constraints on a regional labour regime

Many supporters of trade liberalization agree that policies supportive of labour standards are needed to prevent political alienation and opposition which could prove a hindrance to integration. Transnational and domestic policy developments are equally important. Yet the North American context was not hospitable for such policy integration. The complexities of federalism and congressionalism work in favour of blocking coalitions while the neo-liberal agenda has been advanced by well-funded lobbies in all three states. This explains why labour unions and their allies could only secure a limited side agreement in the form of the NAALC, and even then only in the situation of electoral immediacy in both the US and Canada. The constraints of Congressional coalition-building, tensions between the administration and key congressional players, the fast track deadline, and Canadian and Mexican intransigence forced Clinton to concede on this issue to secure the adoption of the trade and investment provisions,; the indifference and weakness of labour outside the electoral context after 1992 made this concession easier for the administration.

The domestic political weakness of unions and their allies and great distance between labour movements in the three countries was also a limitation. These

---

46 Gordon T. Stewart, 'Three Lessons for Mexico from Canadian-American Relations,' *Frontera Norte* 3, (1992), 43.

movements were not politically powerful enough to override the sovereignty concerns and secure equitable treatment of labour issues in NAFTA. The very different labour policy traditions of the various nations are also a barrier. Despite similar origins, Canadian and American labour and social security policy have gone in different directions in the postwar years for instance, and are difficult to harmonize, especially where Canadians have provided higher levels of protection and security. Mexico's corporatist tradition has produced a labour relations system based on constitutionalized arrangements and national codes which has evolved in isolation from American and Canadian practice. These differences inspired distrust of any common labour rights regime in each of the three countries.

Complicating matters was the inevitable difference in bargaining power within NAFTA. America's huge GNP is less dependent on trilateral North American trade, putting it in a strong position to hold out for a suitable accord. But on labour matters, weak domestic unions and adverse partisan alignment made it willing to concede to a non-enforceable accord. Canada's great dependence on trade with the U.S., the greater North-South pull of integration in its economy, and the nature of American trade laws all make it vulnerable to American threats of punitive actions or even withdrawal from the NAFTA; pressure for further concessions could readily be exerted in future if the Americans chose to exercise this leverage.[47] Mexico was in an even more difficult position fearing that any sanctionable agreements could be disastrously imbalanced towards the Americans; this coupled with a desire to preserve its distinct corporatist labour relations made an enforceable labour accord unworkable. This created sovereignty concerns which hindered integration, and caused both Canadian and Mexican resistance to an enforceable labor side agreement. Both countries asserted their right to sovereignty over labour markets and rejected labour standards linked to trade policy, as 'disguised protectionism'. On issues of greater import to the US, supported by more powerful trasnational constituencies, Canada and Mexico agreed to sanctions. Union supporters note with bitterness the hypocrisy of Canadian and Mexican concessions on 'sovereignty' in trade disputes and investor rights, for which the Americans conceded little.

Therefore, unsurprisingly, NAFTA emerged as a largely neo-liberal arrangement, without an enforceable social dimension. Given asymmetry, social movement weakness , and institutional rigidities, it would be unreasonable to expect NAFTA to move readily towards a broader, more equitable or socially sustainable 'plurilateral regionalism'.[48] Yet labour movements remained vociferous in condemning exploitation of child workers, discrimination based on race and gender, low wages, excessive hours and health and safety violations.[49] NAFTA's critics provided revelations about Mexico's competitive advantage from lower labour standards and

---

47 Maxwell A. Cameron, 'North American Free Trade, Public Goods and Asymmetrical Bargaining: The Strategic Choices for Canada,' *Frontera Norte* 3, 6, (1992), 57.

48 Wilkinson, 1997, 32.

49 Lance Compa, 'International Labour Rights and the Sovereignty Question: NAFTA and Guatemala, Two Case Studies,' *Journal of International Law and Policy* 9, (1993), 123–5.

costs, and abuses by American firms operating in that country. This political pressure induced Bill Clinton to promise a labour agreement to secure passage of the NAFTA. That side agreement was limited by the constraints of asymmetry, institutional rigidities and social movement weakness. The result was an accord with limited ability to protect workers from hazards which proliferated in the economic upheaval caused by NAFTA.

Potential Impacts of NAALC's New Institutions

While NAFTA's labour accord was designed in an institutional and transnational social context inhospitable to a more enforcement-driven regime, the creation of these innovative institutions became a factor influencing the character of labour relations transnationally. Given the weak institutions, one might expect these effects to be limited. Nonetheless, neo-institutionalists note the mutually constitutive character of institutions and social organization. A variety of neo-institutionalist approaches have emerged recently, characterized by rationalist, historical and sociological elements.[50] Assessment of NAALC's impact requires a careful reading of its effects on labour relations, the strength of unions and social movements, the character of transnational associations and institutional linkages, and ultimately, the quality and content of norms and practices in labour affairs.

The potential effects of institutional change are nuanced and variegated. Depending on their emphasis, neo-institutionalists target different elements of institutional constraint and causality. Historical institutionalists suggest, akin to constructivists, that institutions shape the character and degree of influence of particular social actors, privileging or strengthening some versus others; creation of new institutions, however weak, may alter the path dependent character of policy development by altering the institutional context for future policy choices.[51] Rational choice institutionalists look to the incentives structures which institutions provide to policy makers, social movements and other actors, which constrain and influence their behaviours and policy calculus. In this fashion, institutions, and the rules and procedures they incorporate, shape and limit the policy options pursued by decisions makers across agencies and nations. Sociological or organizational institutionalism considers the underlying norms and policy maps which permit decision-making in institutions characterized by limited knowledge and bounded rationality. In this variation, institutions incorporate cultural elements which can affect individual 'cognitive scripts' and evaluative frameworks, inducing changes in preferences and behaviour.[52]

---

50 Peter A. Hall, and Rosemary C.R. Taylor. "Political Science and the Three New Institutionalisms." *Political Studies* 44, (December 1996): 936–957.

51 Hall and Taylor, 938–ff.

52 Ellen M. Immergut "The Theoretical Core of the New Institutionalism." *Politics and Society* 26, (1998), 14–16.

While, as March and Olsen concede there is little commonality in methods and frameworks[53], neo-institutionalism analysts focus on how institutional configurations – formal and informal, national and transnational – affect policy constituencies and outcomes. Neo-institutionalism allows us to trace the dynamics effects of the introduction of new regional institutions like the NAFTA labour accord. Dimaggio and Powell posit a gradual institutionalization from increased interactions, to new patterns of relations and domination, increased information exchange and eventual development of common interpretations and ideological orientations as a new organizational field with its own culture emerges.[54] New regionalist analysts suggest that the effects of trans-border integration and new transnational institutions could prove extensive and self-sustaining. If European Union trends are indicative, the constitutive effects of institutions on social and political actors can have profound effects in breaking down previous differences in practices and norms across significantly different economies and cultures.

Such integrative tendencies are complicated by profound differences in labour relations values and practices and economic and developmental prerequisites across the North-South divide. While asymmetry, social movement weakness and domestic institutional constraints limited its reach, the NAFTA labour accord created institutions, transnationally and domestically, which produced new openings, incentives and constraints for state officials and social actors in labour relations in all three nations. The wide range of issues and activities undertaken by NAALC institutions over the past decade must be scrutinized thoroughly to assess their potential for deepening transnational interactions and values. Neo-institutional and new regionalist approaches predict that NAALC could potentially transform the practices, norms, policy networks and expectations surrounding labour relations. In Hurrell's term, a process of 'regionalization' on an informal level involving exchanges of 'ideas', 'attitudes and ways of thinking' or the emergence of a 'transnational regional civil society'[55] could be produced over time by the interactions fostered by NAFTA and NAALC.

Several potential impacts of institutions will be assessed here. NAALC induced stronger transnational union activism and collaboration; tri-national alliances multiplied in part because of the shared costs of liberalization for employees in the three states and the incentives for collaboration provided by NAALC's submission process. NAALC engendered a transnational bureaucracy pursuing common goals in the trinational institutions and national labour departments. Some participants argue that this instills a greater commonality in labour relations law and regulation,

---

53 James G. March and Johan P. Olsen. "The New Institutionalism: Organizational Factors in Political Life." *The American Political Science Review* 78, (1984), 747.

54 Paul J DiMaggio and Walter W. Powell, The *New Institutionalism in Organizational Analysis* Chicago: University of Chicago Press, 1991, 65.

55 Andrew Hurrell, 'Regionalism in Theoretical Perspective' in Andrew Hurrell and Louise Fawcett eds), *Regionalism in World Politics: Regional Order and International Order* (New York: Oxford University Press, 1995), 40.

indicating emergence of a shared labour relations culture. The analysis must assess evidence that national law and enforcement practices have adjusted in anticipation of the norms and constraints imposed by the NAALC. It will also catalogue a degree of policy learning from cross-border sharing of best practices, technology, expertise and legal values. While its weakness may limits such effects, NAALC, and the supranational, state-level and societal interactions it fosters, could generate what a constructivist would label a 'cognitive construct'[56] in labor relations, featuring increased commonality in practices and values. But as a small component in a larger neo-liberal project of integration, NAALC's impact in this regard may be limited. As the analysis will show, if commonality is emerging, it may not be in the direction of a fair trade regulatory model, but rather a free trade neo-liberal approach.

These effects and the limits of NAFTA's labour institutions will be evaluated systematically in light of the variety of public submissions reviewed in its first decade of operation. Did NAALC serve to deepen labour regionalism as societal and state actors seek solutions to 'international policy externalities'[57] generated by NAFTA? Or did the weakness of NAALC's original design limit prospects for deepened regionalism in labour affairs? The opportunities and constraints provided by these new regional institutions, however limited, have implications for labour relations, living standards for millions of workers, working conditions faced by employees, and discrimination based on gender, age, ethnicity or migrant status. The empirical chapters below will illustrate the implications of NAFTA's liberalizing elements and its compensatory new regional labour institutions for the direction of labour policy and the social conditions faced by workers in all three states.

---

56 Scott, 1999, 607.
57 Hurrell, 1995, 63.

Chapter 3
Negotiating the NAALC: Political Compromise

Labour Side Accord: Political Compromise

The 1992 elections in the United States created an opportunity for NAFTA's labour opponents to exert pressure for addition of a labour accord. The Clinton campaign originally promised not to approve of the NAFTA unless it was accompanied by guarantees to ensure that the free movement of goods and investments did not promote the draining of US jobs to lower wage factories in Mexico. However, the Mexicans rejected the strong medicine originally proposed by Washington, including the use of trade sanctions to counter instances of denial of worker rights or the use of low wages to gain competitive advantage. Jean Chretien also pledged substantial revisions to the NAFTA arrangements before he assumed office as Canadian Prime Minister in 1993, but ultimately resisted an enforceable regime for labour rights. These countries claimed the sanctions were unfair; given their greater reliance on the US as an export market, sanctions would bite more heavily if used by rather than against the US.

President Clinton was eventually forced to concede that he could not insist on sanctions for labour issues, which were backed by a weaker domestic and transnational coalition. He also had to steer NAFTA and its side agreements through a complex institutional maze in Congress, which forced him to abandon the goal of common enforceable, labour standards. Administration officials found it hard to defend the lack of teeth in the NAFTA side agreements or the failure to hold out for EEC-style policies for promoting upward levelling of wages and benefits under the NAFTA. But the constraints of asymmetry, institutional rigidity, and social movement weakness limited prospects for a stronger accord. NAALC was an innovative compromise between the sovereignty concerns of Mexico and Canada and the US desire for improved labour standards.

Free Trade and the Labor Movement

Prior to adoption of NAFTA, there was polarization in Canadian and American debates and hyperbole by supporters and opponents. Critics argue that the greater mobility of capital and industries mean that labour would be forced to accept lower wages and benefits and unsafe and unhealthy workplaces to attract firms. Across countries, industries would engage in a bidding war; offers to induce investment could include less protection for unions, weakened health and safety standards, and lower salaries and benefits. The labor movements in Canada and the United States feared that free trade would force them to compete with Mexican workers who received only a fraction of their pay and benefits.[1] Major Mexican unions supported free trade, since it would generate jobs in an economy where gaining employment is often more important to workers than wage levels or benefits. Their leaders believed that free trade would not cause adverse changes in labor laws or practices in Mexico.[2] Other Mexican analysts acknowledged that low wages were likely to persist for some years in Mexico after NAFTA, but welcomed this as a 'comparative advantage' which would help Mexico attract new investment and employment.[3]

Some Canadian and American unions also were willing to work with the NAFTA regime, if it were amended to secure the rights of workers, through a European-style social charter. But major unions like the American Federation of Labor and Congress of Industrial Organizations (AFL-CIO) and the Canadian Labour Congress (CLC) remained opposed to NAFTA.[4] For these unions, the NAFTA was a neo-liberal strategy to undermine the post-war industrial relations system and to implement a low-wage, flexible manufacturing strategy involving concessions from workers.[5] NAFTA allowed countries to protect themselves from import surges after the elimination of tariffs, and permitted slow tariff phase-outs in import-sensitive industries. Most labour commentators expected such provisions to be ineffective.[6]

Supporters hailed NAFTA as a free market model which would improve efficiency, productivity and growth in all three societies. However, NAFTA did not provide for the free movement of peoples, meaning that distortions could occur in labor markets, wages, benefits and working conditions. NAFTA allowed capital and goods to move

---

1   Shellyn G. McCaffrey, 'North American Free Trade and Labor Issues: Accomplishments and Challenges' *Hofstra Labor Law Journal* 10, (1993), 461–65.

2   Pablo Pascual Moncayo and Raul Trejo Delarbe, *Los Sindicatos Mexicanos Ante el TLC* (Mexico: Instituto de Estudios para la Transición Democrática, 1993), 12.

3   Dr. Victor Manuel Godinez Zuniga, Testimony to the *Foro Permanente de Informacion, Opinion y Dialogo Sobre los Negociaciones del Tratado Trliateral de Libre Comercio entre Mexico, los Estados Unidos y Canada*, Senado de la Republica, March 14, 1991, (Mexico: Senado de la Republica, 1991), 35.

4   Richard Martin, 'Canadian Labour and North American Integration' in Stephen J. Randall ed. *North America Without Borders?* (Calgary: University of Calgary Press, 1992), 182; Victor Gotbaum, 'American Labor Looks at the U.S.-Mexico Free Trade Agreement' in Rapheal Fernandez de Castro, Monica Verea Campos and Sidney Weintraub eds. *Sectoral Labor Effects of North American Free Trade* (Austin: University of Texas, 1993), 104–5.

5   Robert Kreklewich, 'North American Integration and Industrial Relations: Neoconservativism and Neo-Fordism?' in Ricardo Grinspun and Maxwell A. Cameron, eds. *The Political Economy of North American Free Trade* (Montreal: McGill-Queen's University Press, 1993).

6   Robert F. Housman and Paul M. Orbuch, 'Integrating Labor and Environmental Concerns into the North American Free Trade Agreement' *American University Journal of International Law and Policy.* 8 (1993), 756.

across borders but did not facilitate worker migration, so supply and demand alone would not determine wages and benefits, which would be distorted. Corporations could move to Mexico, with lower wages and weaker protections against workplace hazards. The Canada-U.S. Free Trade Agreement (CUSFTA) previewed this problem; lower cost, anti-union US states attracted factories from high cost Canadian centres, with union protections and social programs. Canadian workers believed the drop of 22% in manufacturing employment after CUSFTA involved permanent loss of jobs to the US Sunbelt, where states restrict unions and bargaining. NAFTA critics were concerned about the effects on wages and employment, since corporations could establish low wage maquiladora factories in Mexico, which lacked effective unions, or health, safety and environmental standards. NAFTA would exacerbate the CUSFTA model of 'lowest common denominator competition or competitive poverty among workers and communities'.[7]

Worker concern was increased by a continental trend to stagnant or declining wages, increased inequalities, high unemployment, withdrawal of workers from job markets, and increased part-time, low wage, service sector employment. Critics associated these trends with free trade, though CUSFTA coincided with a recession affecting other industrial nations. Some of the decline in incomes and increased unemployment reflected economic integration and technological change, which would exist irrespective of NAFTA. However, Canadian and American policy encouraged competitiveness based on reduced labour costs, rather than increased productivity in a high wage model. Free trade produced downward convergence of wages and standards if there is no intervention to upgrade labour skills, or to encourage business to compete on a high productivity basis. While Mexican wages would not quickly catch up with its northern neighbours, improved policies could encourage upward convergence in incomes and standards, such as transnational programs, to encourage adjustment to high wage, high productivity jobs and to bring poor economies and regions towards a higher performance standard.[8] NAFTA critics worried that the agreement contained no such initiatives, making downward convergence towards Mexican standards likely.

Mexico's Problematic Industrial Relations

On paper, Mexican workers' rights appear enviable. Ann Bartow notes that the 'Mexican people live and work under an astounding collection of protective labor statutes, policies and practices which provide them, as employees with an extensive list of detailed rights and privileges'.[9] The 1917 constitution rewarded labor for its

7   Bruce Campbell, 'A Canadan Labour Perspective on the North American Free Trade Agreement' in Fernandez, Campos and Weintraub, 1993, 65.

8   Ray Marshall, 'The North American Free Trade Agreement: Implications for Workers' in Fernandez, Campos and Weintraub, 1993, 12–13.

9   Ann M. Bartow, 'The Rights of Workers in Mexico' *Comparative Labor Law Journal* 11, (1990), 182.

revolutionary role by providing union rights, an eight hour day, six day work week, mandatory childbirth leave, equal pay for both genders, overtime pay, safe working conditions, compensation for injury or illness, and profit-sharing. It guaranteed wages 'sufficient to satisfy the normal material, social, and cultural needs of the head of a family and to provide for the mandatory education of his children'.[10] Article 123 assures the right of free association. Union organizers and supporters are protected against arbitrary firings. Strikes are legal if designed to balance power between workers and management; conciliation and arbitration is used to settle disputes in public services, or to resolve disagreements about the enforcement of worker rights. The Federal Labor Law of 1970 also balanced the power of the employer in the market, by ceding the benefit of the doubt and procedural bias in disputes to economically weaker workers.[11]

Yet despite this impressive list of protections, observers question if rank and file workers are well protected by Mexico's industrial relations system. While independent unions are legal, most major unions were allied with the Institutional Revolutionary Party (PRI), which governed Mexico for 70 years. While ostensibly speaking for workers, these unions were close to government and business associations, so their independence was doubtful. In prosperous times, this system worked reasonably well, as the government could provide better protection and benefits. However, with the 1980s economic downturn, tensions emerged between unions and the state, which could no longer respond positively to labor entreaties. While government became less enamored of corrupt official unions, which placed costly demands on its diminished resources, workers distrusted union leaders, who were unable to protect their interests or to stem a decline in real wages.[12]

Unions turned to collective bargaining and strikes, as backroom bargaining declined in efficacy; but government power over bargaining limited their success. Federal and state conciliation and arbitration boards, composed of worker, business and government representatives (in practice all affiliated with the governing party) could declare strikes non-existent if they did not secure majority support, if the strike was not for legal purposes under the 1970 labor law, or if the six–day notification period was not observed.[13] Often strikes would be declared illegal on technicalities to limit bargaining. The connection between labour and the PRI undermined the effectiveness of labour legislation. Union leaders were more concerned with protecting privileges, having been co-opted into party and state positions; they were reluctant to challenge the government even if worker interests were better served by opposition.

---

10 Bartow, 1990, 183.

11 Bartow, 1990, 190–1.

12 Ruth Collier, *The Contradictory Alliance* (Cambridge: Cambridge University Press, 1995); Davis, Diane E. "Mexico's New Politics: Changing Perspectives on Free Trade" *World Policy Journal,* 9, (1992), 655–671.

13 Bartow, 1990, 197–98.

While maintaining close relations with official unions like the *Confederación de Trabajadores Mexicanos* (CTM), *Confederación Revolucionario de Obreros y Campesinos* (CROC) and *Confederación Regional Obrera Mexicana* (CROM), governments encouraged rifts or the formation of new unions when these unions became too strong or leaders grew too critical. Independent unions were denied recognition, and prevented from negotiating agreements or representing their members on conciliation and arbitration boards and wage commissions. While the official PRI unions served in these capacities, the co-optation of their leaders made their independence in arbitration or wage negotiations doubtful.[14] This system of co-optation, with occasional repression against dissident unions cemented government control. Even business representatives, who believe labour laws favour workers, admit that the lack of independent union representatives on labour boards means that the arbitration processes does not operate to the benefit of workers.[15]

The tripartite system of bargaining produced disappointing results for workers, and an erosion of real wages after the 1970s. Wage 'negotiations' were illusory; crucial decisions were made in backroom deals and public discussion was a facade to save face for union leaders. Wages fell behind inflation, and subsidized food, health, transport and housing were insufficient to compensate.[16] The 1980s debt crisis brought pressure to freeze wages, reduce spending, and decrease state intervention. Unions did not have the independence necessary to oppose austerity measures. The state divided the official unions, by aiding the smaller CROC and CROM against the CTM. And alliances of the CTM and independent unions were transitory, as the government offered worker access to state subsidized goods to secure electoral allegiance. Although critical of the economic program of President de la Madrid, the CTM joined the 'Pacto', accepting wage freezes in exchange for less effective price controls. Official unions opposed political reform, which would diminish their privileged access to public office and patronage.[17]

Economic restructuring and downsizing of government after 1988 under President Carlos Salinas de Gotari required a new approach to industrial relations, in which centralized corporatist structures played a diminished role. Instead of backroom deals with leaders of labor federations, local union negotiations with firms assumed greater significance. This could produce more independent, participatory unions, greater worker involvement with workplace decisions, and the decline of the old-style, PRI affiliated union bosses. While workers faced pressure to improve productivity and quality, their organizations could assume new importance as more democratic and

---

14 Amy H. Goldin, 'Collective Bargaining in Mexico: Stifled by the Lack of Democracy in Trade Unions' *Comparative Labor Law Journal* 11, 1990, 206–11.

15 Interview with business representative on the district labour board, State of Guanauato, January, 1995.

16 Goldin, 1990, 219–23.

17 Victor Manuel Durand Ponte, 'The Confederation of Mexican Workers, the Labor Congress and the Crisis of Mexico's Social Pact', in Kevin Middlebook, ed. *Unions, Workers and the State in Mexico* (San Diego:Centre for U.S.-Mexican Studies, University of California, 1991), 101.

responsive organizations whose cooperation with management will affect firms' competitiveness. Luis Rubio anticipated a spill-over into greater participation by workers, which could bode well for the future of Mexican democracy.[18]

Yet government interference with union locals was allegedly frequent. Government policies ensured that unions were less effective in the maquiladoras, for fear of alienating foreign investors. Susanna Peters suggests that 'the official unions offer foreign employers 'control' of the workforce and promote themselves as willing to 'take care' of labor problems by denying claims or demands by workers in order not to frighten off foreign investors'.[19] Federal labour laws and constitutional guarantees are difficult to enforce in maquiladoras. Profit sharing is minimal, as foreign companies record little profit in Mexico. High turnover and extended 'probationary' periods deprive employees of statutory severance pay; transnational legal complexities limit enforcement of compensation for plant closures or industrial accidents. While the maquila's reliance on female workers is an important route to gender independence in Mexico, critics note employers' preference for female 'docility' and non-union status, and limited opportunities for training and promotion.[20]

Officials with independent unions criticize both government policy and official union practices, which diminish worker protections in the maquiladora zone. The Authentic Workers Front (Freinte Autentico des Trabajadores or FAT) argues that the neo-liberal strategy of opening Mexican markets to international competition encouraged investors to engage in 'social dumping' by taking advantage of low wage labour in the maquiladoras. NAFTA is part of a neo-liberal strategy which works against worker and small businesses in favour of multi-national firms in search of low cost labor to reduce costs for transnational competition. Official unions have done little to help workers in jobs with maximized productivity, minimized wages, unhealthy and unsafe workplaces and little training in new technologies; defenseless workers are deprived of their legal protections by ineffective, co-opted official unions.[21]

Mexico's independent unions rejected NAFTA, rather than seek transnational more constructive integration with free movement for labour, worker, new technologies, and high quality production like the European Community. Government and official union domination deprived workers of the free association needed to create a progressive labour movement which could facilitating a socially responsible transnational economic integration. Mexico's independent unions' rejection of NAFTA reflected their experience in the maquiladoras, where transnational firms are free from union constraints on productivity, with disastrous consequences for

18 Luis Rubio, 'Economic Reform and Political Change in Mexico'in Riordan Roett ed. *Political and Economic Liberalization in Mexico: At a Critical Juncture?* (Boulder, Col.: Lynne Reinner, 1993), 39–41.

19 Susanna Peters, 'Labor Law for the Maquiladoras: Choosing Between Workers Rights and Foreign Investment', *Comparative Labor Law Journal* 11, 1990, 242.

20 Peters, 1990, 237–9, 244–7.

21 'La otra agenda del Tratado de Libre Comercio' *El Cotidiano* 7, (Sept.-Oct., 1991), 6.

workers. Lack of liberty for unions, police surveillance, firing of organizers, and unequal power between business and workers, mean that, despite increased demand for labor, worker organizations cannot increase salaries or improve conditions. Freedom to organize independent unions is an essential prerequisite for improved working conditions to prevent Mexico from remaining a site for neo-liberal 'social dumping'.[22]

Mexican development has been 'extensive' rather than 'intensive', lagging in productivity despite the influx of technology and production facilities in the maquiladoras. Despite efforts to improve industrial efficiency, most workers still labour in industries with low productivity. Productivity gains are not transferred to workers, so low wages persist despite improved productivity.[23] Free trade critics asserted that NAFTA would generate only more low-wage employment in Mexico. Capital is more mobile than labour in the NAFTA and regions which do not permit downward flexibility in wages, taxes or regulations may face capital flight and loss of jobs to lower wage regions.

NAFTA supporters regarded labour's critique of Mexican practices exaggerated, and noted US and Canadian deficiencies in labour protection which would also require adjustment. The US labour market is 'less regulated than workplaces in most industrialized nations', leaving workers to face the vagaries of collective bargaining to secure rights and benefits.[24] Hence the cost differential is exaggerated and only limited labour protections were required in the side agreement The stereotype of Mexican labour inadequacies carried significant weight with politically important unions in the charged atmosphere surrounding adoption of NAFTA. Well organized labour funded political action committees swayed many in Congress to oppose NAFTA without concessions for labour.[25] Government reports indicated serious problems in US-owned maquiladoras, in areas like health and safety and noted deficiencies in Mexican enforcement systems.[26] During the 1992 presidential election campaign, Bill Clinton pledged to address the concerns of the labor movement, by reopening NAFTA, to provide greater protection for workers.

---

22 Luis Reygades, 'Libertad laboral y Tratado de Libre Comercio' *El Cotidiano* 7, (Sept.-Oct., 1991), 19.

23 Victor Gotbaum, 'American Labor Looks at the U.S.-Mexico Free Trade Agreement' in Fernandez Campos and Weintraub, 1993, 105.

24 Stephen F. Befort and Virginia E. Cornett, 'Beyond the Rhetoric of the NAFTA Treaty Debate: A Comparative Analysis of Labor and Employment Law in Mexico and the United States' *Comparative Labor Law Journal* 17, (1996), 278.

25 Jeffrey W. Steagall and Ken Jennings, 'Unions, PAC Contributions and the NAFTA Vote' *Journal of Labour Research* 17, (1996), 515–21.

26 US General Accounting Office, *U.S.-Mexico Trade: The Work Environment at Eight U.S.-Owned Maquiladora Auto Plants* Report to the Chairman, Committee on Commerce, Science, and Transportation, U.S. Senate, Nivember, 1993, 5–6.

Negotiation of the Labour Side Agreement

The Americans initially proposed a broad accord covering many aspects of labor relations, and subjecting countries falling below common standards to trade penalties. The proposal was based on the US GSP, where countries lost preferential trade access because of violations of labor rights.[27] Canada and Mexico, which rely heavily on US markets for their exports, felt sanctions would be more punitive for them than for the US. They resisted the use of trade penalties over a wide range of issues, since US standards were considered inferior on some labor issues.[28] Mexico's negotiators acknowledged that demands for labour protections were in part inspired by genuine concerns for workers and fear of unfair competitive pressures. But they also noted that these also reflected 'big brother reactions that consider – without obviously admitting it in the open – that some countries because of their higher development status or power have a moral right to impose their notions on other peoples'.[29]

With Democratic ascendance after the 1992 elections, Mexico had to relent and negotiate the side accords. Initial uncertainty over the US position was heightened by statements from the new trade representative, Mickey Kantor, who sought strong labour provisions. Mexican negotiators were relieved to find that President Clinton only sought conditional alterations which did not reopen the heart of NAFTA. Three key principles were defended in these talks; national sovereignty, with no foreign intervention in domestic laws; no disguised protectionism in labor guarantees; and no reopening of the NAFTA itself. The negotiators sought a side agreement which was neither too ineffective nor too 'intrusive'; they eventually had to allow Mexico to take advantage of lower labor costs or risk the complete collapse of the NAFTA.[30]

De Buen notes that as negotiations began, the three countries new little of each other's labour legislation, regulations and traditions and Mexico mostly reacted defensively to prevent foreign impositions on sensitive matters such as the corporatist system. Hence the negotiators had to devise a weak document which did little to enhance the collective rights to organization and bargaining for unions.[31] Though Americans frequently criticized the laxness of Mexican labour standards, Mexican unionists pointed out how inferior American standards were, at least on paper, in some

---

27 Lance Compa, 'The First NAFTA Labor Cases: A New International Labor Rights Regime Takes Shape' *U.S.-Mexico Labor Law Journal* 3, (1995), 161–62.

28 'Comisiones trilaterales, sin caracter supranational: Mexico y Canada' *El Dia* (Apr. 15, 1993), 1.

29 Hermann von Bertrab, *Negotiating NAFTA: A Mexican Envoy's Account* (Washington: Praeger, 1997), 75.

30 Benjamin Rozwood and Andrew R. Walker 'Side Agreements, Sidesteps and Sideshows: Protecting Labor from Free Trade in North America' *Harvard International Law Review* 34, 2 (1993), 355.

31 Néstor de Buen, 'El Acuerdo de Cooperación Laboral de América del Norte.' *El Cotidiano*, 15, (March/April 1999), 5–12.

states, and predicted a deterioration of labour rights under transnational standards.[32] Mexico's resistance to transnationalism and enforceable standards was supported by those who feared NAALC would bring a form of disguised protectionism on labour matters to an already asymmetrical trading relationship.

Negotiations proceeded throughout the fist few months of the Clinton administration in 1993. The Labor Secretary, Robert Reich, proposed stronger enforcement provisions, but Mexico firmly rejected such 'imperialistic' outside interference. Mexican offficals wanted a weaker agreement which would not dissuade firms from relocating to Mexico to secure cheaper labour, which was what proponents of the side accord desired.[33] US NAFTA supporters also insisted on a clear distinction between the intrusive settlement processes expected for trade disputes, and milder binational review and monitoring of labour and the environment. Meanwhile Mexico could not concede to common standards which would threaten its corporatist labour relations model; and Canada had to deal with the impossibility of imposing any deal on provinces that controlled labour relations in most industries. Despite strong pressure from leading Democrats for a tough side agreement as a condition for ratifying NAFTA, increased Republican resistance to the side agreements and the ticking clock on fast-track authorization forced the administration to promote a compromise, which respected national laws and limited the prospects for sanctions to a few core areas. As the US position weakened in the institutional constraints they faced, the negotiations ultimately met most of Canada and Mexico's desire for a weaker agency. One Mexican negotiator stated that the labour accord would produce 'Lots of public discourse, nothing more. This is the result we wanted'.[34]

While Mexico's government and unions were pleased that their system would not be disrupted, and Canada's government was glad sanctions were off the table, US and Canadian labour advocates noted that this reflected a double standard; Mexico and Canada used sovereignty against a strong NAALC, but accepted trade penalties on countervailing, dumping, and investor rights. But Compa noted that the 'NAFTA labor side agreement on labor simultaneously preserves and breaches traditional sovereignty in labor matters' by affirming the paramount character of national laws, while creating 'tripartite oversight' on labour standards.[35] Penalties on labour were milder than those for intellectual property for instance, where seizure of assets or trade penalties could be easily applied. For many labour rights advocates, this imbalance would pave the way for abuse of workers.[36]

---

32 Moisés Cetré Castillo, 'Comercio internacional y normas laborales: el debate actual.' *Comercio Exterior* 48, (October, 1998), 797–803.

33 Maxwell A. Cameron and Brian W. Tomlin *The Making of NAFTA: How the Deal Was Done* (Ithaca: Cornell University Press, 2000), 188.

34 Cameron and Tomlin, 200.

35 Compa, 1995, 161–62.

36 Jerome I. Levinson, *The Labor Side Accord to the North American Free Trade Agreement: An endorsement of the Abuse of Worker Rights in Mexico* (Washington: Economic Policy Institute Briefing Paper, 1993), 13.

The NAALC Agreement's Cooperative Emphasis

The North American Agreement on Labor Cooperation (NAALC) emphasized consultation and cooperation, with limited sanctions. It committed all three nations to improvements in labour rights, working conditions, and living standards commensurate with economic development induced by free trade. NAALC's objectives included:

> To improve working conditions and living standards in each Party's territory.
> To promote, to the maximum extent possible, the labor principles set out in the Agreement.
> To encourage cooperation to promote innovation and rising levels of productivity and quality.
> To encourage publication and exchange of information, data development and coordination, and joint studies to enhance mutually beneficial understanding of the laws and institutions governing labor in each Party's territory.
> To pursue cooperative labor-related activities on the basis of mutual benefit.
> To promote compliance with, and effective enforcement by each Party of, its labor law.
> To foster transparency in the administration of labor law.[37]

NAALC incorporated references to core International Labor Organization (ILO) conventions. These include freedom of association for unions, the right to strike, right to collective bargaining, a ban on forced labor and limits on child labor, enforcement of health and safety and minimum wage laws, parity in men and women's pay, prevention of and compensation for on-the-job accidents, and protection for migrant labor.

The NAALC did not create common standards or establish supranational mechanisms to enforce labour rights or regulations. It did not stress adversarial enforcement; rather the 'preferred approach of the Agreement to reach this objective is through cooperation – exchanges of information, technical assistance, consultations – a concept that is explicitly recognized in the very title of the instrument'[38]. NAALC committed each country to enforce its own laws, but recognized their sovereign right to establish standards. The parties agreed to investigate alleged labor law violations in the other countries submitted by employers, employees or their representatives.[39]

Each party agreed to ensure that its labour laws and regulations provided high standards and safe work sites and to promote compliance with laws via effective law enforcement. The signatories agreed that private parties (unions or citizens) would

---

37 Commission for Labour Cooperation, 'Objectives, Obligations and Principles' [cited July 5, 2004]. Available at http://www.naalc.org/english/objective.shtml.

38 Commission for Labour Cooperation, 'Ministerial Council Meetings' cited July 12, 2005]. Available at http://www.naalc.org/english/meetings.shtml. U.S. National Administrative Office *North American Agreement on Labor Cooperation: A Guide* (Washington: U.S. Dept. of Labor, 1998), 1.

39 Luis Miguel Diaz, 'Private Rights Under the Environmental and Labor Agreements' *U.S. Mexico Law Journal*. 2, 1994, 23.

have access to tribunals and judicial fora to enforce labour laws, and that proceedings would be 'fair, equitable and transparent' and 'impartial' with opportunity for appeals and published reasons for any decisions. Labour laws, regulations, procedures and rulings were to be published and made available through public education, including creation of 'labour defense offices' to educate and advise workers and their representatives.[40]

The NAALC made a 'leap of faith' assumption that the three countries' labor laws were enforced and that they met minimum OECD standards; the three governments pledged not to encourage investment by lax enforcement of labor laws or by reduced protections.[41] Complaints were allowed only when all countries have similar guarantees; Mexico's broader laws could not be challenged by the Americans where they provided no statutory protection, such as severance pay and maternity benefits. And the agreement minimized the use of labour issues as disguised protectionism, by creating a procedure to determine if a complaint was related in a substantial way to trade.[42] While cooperation was stressed over compulsion, supporters believed the procedures for external scrutiny of law enforcement could evolve into an influential mechanism. Public investigation of labor law violations was expected to contribute to stricter law enforcement as the parties tried to avoid negative publicity. It was notable how willing the same governments were to surrender sovereignty and accede to enforceable standards on matters such as trade disputes, investor rights, and intellectual property.

The NAALC explicitly prevented the signatories from creating "a private right of action' for other parties violations; hence the signatory governments had to initiate any action to make the NAALC deterrents effective.[43] Formal and informal trilateral government consultations were the first possibility. NAALC allowed labour organizations and advocates in one country to raise concerns about lapses in law enforcement in the other countries, via a public submissions process. This could result in formal investigation, consultation and cooperation to resolve concerns raised in the submissions, including bilateral consultations at the ministerial level. In a few areas a more substantial investigation by an evaluation committee of experts (ECE) could be invoked. But the NAALC only allowed for sharing of information on most issues. Only on child or forced labour, minimum wages and health and safety could monetary or trade penalties be applied for persistent failure to enforce laws. The main concerns of unions, such as freedom of association, right to bargain and prohibition on firings of organizers, were excluded from sanctions and ECEs.

---

40 Commission for Labour Cooperation, 'Objectives, Obligations and Principles'.

41 Interview with admistrative staff, North American Commission for Labor Cooperation, Dallas, June 19, 1995.

42 Spracker and Brown, 369.

43 Teresa R. Favilla-Solano, 'Legal Mechanisms for Enforceing Labor Rights Under NAFTA' *Uniersity of Hawaii Law Review* 18 (1996), 319.

These contentious areas, where national cultures, ideologies and politics have been decisive, were subject only to cooperation and consultations.[44]

Basic Structures of the NAALC

The NAALC included innovative institutions, some transnational, and some embedded in national administrations. NAALC differed from the trade and environmental disputes mechanisms, which relied on binational or trinational panels. Union leaders were wary of a transnational institution in labour since the laws of each country had developed independently. Mexican unions were especially wary of transnational agencies, even if current laws were problematic for rank and file and non-union workers.[45] The different systems, ranging from Mexico's corporatist closed shop to the 'right-to-work' prohibitions on union contracts in some US states, became an obstacle to the development of transnational standards.[46]

Hence the emphasis was on government to government relations. In each country's Department of Labor, a National Administrative Office (NAO) was created. The NAO is 'a domestic focal point for parties interested in NAALC issues'.[47] It serves as a point of contact in bilateral and trilateral interactions, and coordinates dissemination of information and bilateral and trilateral consultations. Its most prominent function is to hear complaints from its citizens about the failure of another party to enforce its labor laws. Complaints proceed not through a transnational enforcement mechanism, but through the domestic NAO's, to binational NAO consultations under Article 21, then to ministerial consultations under Article 22. If matters cannot be resolved through consultations, evaluation committees of experts (ECEs) can be formed, run bilaterally by the NAOs, to report on practices in the complainant and respondent country and exert pressure for improvements.[48]

The NAO mechanism is unique in international labor matters, and unusual in international law as a domestic agency empowered to rule upon complaints about legal practices in other countries. A complaint can lead to public hearings if the domestic NAO accepts that it is trade-related. The US NAO faced business pressure to limit the process to cooperative activities and not to hold hearings. Employers wanted the NAO to require that all appeals in the offending country be exhausted before a case could be reviewed. Unions sought public hearings on complaints to be held in a city close to the border, with only frivolous complaints excluded. The NAO struck a compromise, by avoiding the term 'complaints' (called submissions)

---

44 Kleinman and Shapiro, 1994, 28–9.

45 'Rechaza la CTM crear una Comisión que supervise cumplir los paralelos' *Economía* June 3, 1993, 30.

46 Interview with business association president, Mexico City, February, 1995.

47 General Accounting Office, *North American Free Trade Agreement: Structure and Status of Implementing Organizations* (Washington: GAO, Oct. 1994), 27.

48 Ronald W. Kleinman and Joel M. Shapiro, 'NAFTA's Proposed Tri-Lateral Commissions on the Environment and Labor' *U.S. Mexico Law Journal* 2 (1994) 28–9.

and requiring that domestic appeals be sought. But the US NAO decided to hold hearings and issue reports even in cases involving only consultations, not only on sanctionable matters.[49] This decision was viewed by Mexican officials as excessive and beyond the spirit of the accord, but was also decried by labour advocates as insufficient to meet the intentions of NAALC.

The NAALCs Transnational Institutions

Transnational institutions were created to support the NAOs' activities. The NAALC established the North American Commission for Labor Cooperation (NACLC), based originally in Dallas, and headed by a Canadian, John McKinnery.[50] It has since moved to Washington DC and has been headed by a Mexican appointee, Alfonso Oñate, and then by an American, Mark S. Knouse. Its main function is to support the NAOs by providing analyses for ministerial consultations and organizing ECEs. The NACLC assembles public data, provides reports on labor relations and conducts special studies on the direction of the Council of Ministers. The NACLC also supports the NAO 'cooperative programs' designed to share information and support adequate law enforcement.[51]

The parties agreed to rotate the post of executive director and ensure a relatively equal balance of nationals on the secretariat's modest staff. The research director guides a team of labour lawyers and economists to conduct research and foster transnational awareness of labour laws, practices and conditions. A director of Cooperative Consultations and Administration was added later on, along with a labour law advisor; the Secretariat also employs labour economists. The Secretariat supports the NAO's cooperative ventures and public submissions. But it also conducts ongoing research and produces publications on issues like labour market conditions, employment trends, labour law, union organization, women in the work force, contract labour, occupational safety and health, child labor, workers benefits, and minimum wages.[52]

The NACLC is directed by the Council of Ministers of Labor, comprised of the three labour ministers. The Council was intended to meet twice a year to evaluate NAALC, and in binational panels for ministerial consultations. As governments have changed in all three states, the regularity of these meetings has varied and ministers have never met more than once a year. No Council meetings were held between 1999 and 2003, as ministers were represented by designees. These meetings occasionally tackled policy matters, but often deal with routine issues of NAALC budgeting and

---

49 Compa, 1995, 164.

50 Allen Myerson, 'Dallas gets three-nation labor office' *New York Times* March 19, 1994, 30.

51 Interview with officials at the North American Commission for Labor Cooperation, Dallas, June 19, 1995.

52 Interviews with officials at the NACLC Secretariat, Washington, July, 2001.

personnel policies, the move to Washington, and conferences. Delegating the activity to bureaucrats limits the potential for high-level policy initiatives at these meetings.

Public Submission Process

Public Submissions are filed by organizations or individuals in one country, alleging failure by another country to enforce its labour laws. For instance, American groups or persons file a submission with the National Administrative Office in the Department of Labor in Washington, about lax law enforcement in Mexico or Canada. The NAO investigates, and consults its counterpart NAO in the country where the alleged violation occurred. The NAO must decide whether to accept a submission for review, based on whether it meets the criteria for acceptance drafted by the NAO itself, in light of the principles and obligations outlined in the NAALC. Criteria for acceptable submissions and investigation requirements are not spelled out in the NAALC but have been devised by each NAO as cases have arisen. These have often involved public hearings to assess the submission, and to determine if national labour laws have been inadequately enforced.

NAOs issue 'public reports of review' providing a determination of the merits of a submission, and outlining potential cooperation to address the matter. If these suggestions cannot be implemented by way of cooperative activities, such as seminars, or information exchanges, the NAO may recommend that the labour secretary or minister seek ministerial consultations with his counterparts to discuss the problems and to consider solutions. All of the labour principles contained in the NAALC may be addressed to the level of NAO reports, cooperative activities and ministerial consultations, which provide mechanisms to expose problems and exert diplomatic pressure, but only result in voluntary compliance by each country's authorities. The NAO investigation and report is meant to be completed in 120 days, though some cases have been drawn out for longer periods. Ministerial consultations are not time-limited and have been subject to frequent, often lengthy, delays.

The NAALC provides three different levels of treatment for public submissions depending on which labour principles are involved. All 11 principles can receive NAO consideration, proceed to ministerial consultations, and be the subject of cooperative activities. However, principles 1–3, on freedom of association and protection of the right to organize, the right to bargain collectively, and the right to strike can not go beyond this level. This has been a major disappointment to unions, which regard these core rights as essential to the promotion of worker organization and protection. Ironically, it is these basic rights which have the most potential for transnational application, since they are not dependent on level of development like cash standards, benefits or working conditions.

Principles 4–11, covering so-called technical labour standards, can proceed to two further levels of treatment. If consultations are not effective in promoting a solution, and if an issue is trade related and deals with a mutual area of recognized law in health and safety, technical labour standards, child labour or minimum wages,

Table 3.1   Levels of Treatment of Labor Principles of the NAALC

Level 1: NAO Hearings, Cooperative Actitivites Ministerial Consultations
Freedom of association and protection of the right to organize.
The right to bargain collectively.
The right to strike.

Level 2: Evaluation Committee of Experts
Elimination of employment discrimination.
Equal pay for women and men.
Prohibition of forced labor.
Compensation in cases of occupational injuries and illnesses.
Protection of migrant workers.

Level 3: Arbitral Panels
Labour protections for children and young persons.
Prevention of occupational injuries and illnesses.
Minimum wage standards.

---

an Evaluation Committee of Experts (ECE) can be created. Each ECE consists of three members, drawn by mutual agreement or lot from a roster of experts in international trade and labour law and administration, set up by the ministerial council. The ECE follows a Council mandate to investigate a particular aspect of health and safety or technical labour standards in all three states, in an objective and 'non-adversarial' manner.[53] The ECE is designed as an autonomous entity but is assisted in research and record keeping by the Secretariat. The ECE can receive submissions from citizens and organizations in all three states, but must examine comparable laws and practices in each country, rather than focus only on the nation whose practices have been challenged by a public submission. The ECE can organize information sessions, with experts and organizations in the affected area of labour law. National governments, NAOs and the NACLC secretariat can be called on for further information. No case has moved to this point after 12 years of the NAALC.

If one of the parties finds that the ECE has not resolved persistent trade-related labour law violations in another party, regarding child labour, health and safety and minimum wages, further consultations can be requested. If these do nothing to resolve the matter, an Arbitral panel can be created. This five person panel would examine the enforcement of laws and regulations to seek a further action plan to resole the situation. If the action plan agreed by the arbitral panel is not carried out, then a nation could face fines or trade sanctions. Again, no case has gone this far in the first 12 years of the NAALC. Critics decry the lengthy process to get to this

---

53 Commmission for Labour Cooperation, 'Rules of Procedure for Evaluation Committees of Experts of the North American Agreement on Labor Cooperation' [cited July 14, 2004]. Available at http://www.naalc.org/english/rules.shtml#ECE%20Mandate.

point, as well as the limited number of issues which could be subject to arbitration. In particular, the failure to include issues relevant to the strengthening of unions and worker rights is seen by many as the Achilles heel of the system, limiting its ability to improve labour rights and standards in North America.

Public Submission: by any domestic individual, group, or union, about practices in other NAALC states

NAO Consideration: accepts or rejects within 60 days; if accepted, reviews within 120 days

Consultations with other NAOs: NAO asks for information on relevent laws, practices; seeks details on case

Public Report of Review: NAO issues report summarizing findings, making recommendations

Ministerial Consultation: official discussion leading to recommendations to address problems

Evaluation Committee of Experts: if unresolved, experts from 3 states may study issues, recommend solutions (health and safety, technical labour standards only)

Ministerial Council: consultations and special meetings to address experts report, recommend actions

Disputes Resolution: arbitration process for health and safety, child labour, minimum wage violations

Sanctions: trade penalties or fines for persistent violations in health, child labour, minimum wages

Figure 3.1   NAALC Submissions Process

Conclusions

NAFTA's labour accord is a limited mechanism for cooperation and scrutiny of the enforcement of domestic labour laws in the three NAFTA partners. It contains no enforceable transnational standards, provides no direct legal rights for workers, and relies on government action to succeed. Given the lack of any action beyond ministerial consultations after ten years, critics question the political will of the parties to enforce their commitments to improve labour laws and conditions. NAALC supporters note the problems in reaching a transnational consensus in favour of more punitive actions, and stress the usefulness of the cooperative and consultative approach to consideration of a full range of labour law issues. Supporters believe the NAALC could promote the creation of stronger, independent unions in Mexico, allowing for greater increases in wages, leading to expansion of working class purchasing power, and to consumer demand for US and Canadian imports.[54]

It remains to examine the public submissions and cooperative activities undertaken to this point, to see if the NAALC has lived up to its intentions or instead has been a toothless creation. The institutional effects of these new mechanisms on societal forces also warrant careful assessment. Even if it has been weak in design and implementation, NAALC has created a new institutional matrix which could gradually generate stronger transnational bureaucracies, social movements and norms in labour relations.

---

54 Marianne Lavelle, 'Labor's charges test NAFTA rules in Mexico' *National Law Journal* 17, Sept 19, 1994, A16.

PART II
Public Submissions:
Promoting Labour Regionalism?

Chapter 4

Testing NAALC's Regional Institutions: Early US Cases

Introduction

Despite their dissatisfaction with the NAALC, US unions and human rights advocates quickly tested the mechanism, to pressure for implementation or to prove its impotence. Expectations were low among labour groups, yet sympathetic observers like Lance Compa, who accepted a post in the NAALC secretariat, urged unions to test the system fully. These initial cases are summarized in Table 4.1. Union advocates focussed initially on core rights to freedom of association, organization, collective bargaining and strikes, which they deemed most crucial to strengthening worker rights, wages and labour standards in Mexico. These were also the issues which NAALC relegated to the lowest levels of scrutiny, because of intractable national differences.

The early cases delimited the US NAO's parameters for accepting submissions. Significantly, these cases resulted in public hearings and ministerial consultations, which went beyond Mexican expectations and created pressure on that regime. Nonetheless, the results disappointed the submitters, as they did not provide direct redress to workers or independent unions who suffered from lax Mexican law enforcement. In addition, the predominance of US unions and rights groups in the preparation of these cases, with select Mexican allies, reinforced the impression of asymmetry in the arrangements, but also beneficially inspired greater cross-border collaboration among labour rights advocates. Such initial transnational interactions, engendered in part by the NAALC's requirements for public submission in the interest of workers in one country by unions or rights advocates in another state, paved the way for more complex coalitions of unions and rights advocates in later cases.

Honeywell and General Electric

In late 1994, the U.S. NAO dealt with the first submissions. In the Honeywell case (US NAO 940001), allegations were made about a plant in Chihuahua, where the company made thermostats, circuit boards, heating and air purification equipment. The International Brotherhood of Teamsters, allied with the Metal Workers union (STIMAHCS) of the Frente Autentico de Trabajo (FAT) to complain about infringements on freedom of association. The submission alleged that workers were fired 'for seeking ... an independent union'.[1] The Teamsters argued that wages were

---

1 International Brotherhood of Teamsters, *Complaint Before the United States National Administrative Office, Bureau of International Labour Affairs, United States Department of Labour,*

Table 4.1   U.S. NAO Submissions, 1994-1996

Submission	Issues	Resolution	Follow-Up
US NAO 940001 HONEYWELL	Freedom of Association, Right to Organize	Reviewed, with no ministerial consultations	Seminar
US NAO 940002 (GENERAL ELECTRIC-1)	Freedom of Association, Right to Organize	Reviewed, with no ministerial consultations	Seminar
US NAO 940003 (SONY)	Freedom of Association, Right to Organize	Consultations and Implementation Agreement	3 seminars on registration; talks with unions, firm; Mexican studies
US NAO 940004 (GENERAL ELECTRIC-2)	Freedom of Association, Right to Organize	Accepted for review but withdrawn	None
US NAO 9601 (SUTSP-SEMARNAP)	Freedom of Association, Right to Organize	Consultations and Implementation Agreement	Seminar
US NAO 9602 (MAXI-SWITCH)	Freedom of Association, Right to Organize	Accepted for review but withdrawn	None

kept low through threats and firings which prevented unionization in contravention of Mexican laws. The leader of the organizing drive was allegedly pressured to expose pro-union employees.[2]

The company stated that 22 workers were fired to cut costs, and received legal severance pay. A worker dismissed for violating plant rules reached an out of court settlement. The state governor allegedly sympathized with the established CROC union against foreign 'agitators' who were fuelling discontent.[3] The Teamsters claimed that workers signed resignations only to receive severance. Some workers insisted managers had told them they were being fired for supporting the independent metalworkers union. There were also claims of electronic surveillance, closed interrogations, and bribes to block the new union. These firings and interrogations violated Article 123 of the Mexican constitution and the labour principles in NAALC

---

in re Honeywell Inc. Feb. 14, 1994.

2   Robin Alexander and Peter Gilmore, 'The emergence of cross-border labor solidarity' *NACLA Report on the Americas* 28, (1994), 42–48.

3   'Denuncian a agitadores en maquilas' *Norte de Ciudad Juarez* July 4, 1996, 28.

Section 1. The Teamsters sought public hearings and wanted the NAO to declare the company in violation of labour rights, to require rehiring of workers with back pay, and to insist on enforcement of Mexican laws; plant managers should be required to post notices on labour norms, and accept good-faith bargaining.[4] The demands should be backed by ministerial consultations.

The United Electrical Workers filed US NAO 940002 about Compania Armadora S.A., a subsidiary of General Electric in Ciudad Juarez. This firm allegedly prevented distribution of union information and fired employees who met with a UEW delegation. It purportedly pressured those fired to accept severance pay instead of challenging their dismissals, which was impossible for these impoverished workers to refuse. The complaint alleged heavy labour for pregnant women, lack of ventilation and protective equipment, failure to test for harmful chemicals, and lack of overtime pay.[5] Submitters claimed the Mexican government failed to enforce both its domestic laws, and its ILO obligations. Mexican officials 'not only failed to safeguard organizational and associational rights, but on numerous occasions has been directly involved in depriving workers of such protections' through interventions, refusal to apply laws, delays, and use of technicalities 'to vitiate the rights of workers and unions'.[6] The US NAO should pressure Mexico to ensure that arbitration boards protected worker rights, recognized independent unions, prevented 'protection contracts' with phantom unions, enforced safety and health standards, and eliminated worker blacklists. Finally, the company should stop interfering with union organizing and allow dissemination of union information in the plant.[7]

The US NAO accepted these cases and public hearings were scheduled, which established a precedent which was not required by NAALC. Witnesses included union representatives, labour lawyers, experts and workers from affected plants. Workers expressed concerns about wages, safety, and union organizing, and the negative repercussions of firings and blacklist of activists. They discussed pressure on union leaders to resign with legal severance, to avoid the appearance of dismissals for union activities. Workers complained about the futility of appeals, given inaction by local arbitration boards and biases towards 'official' unions. Mexican labour lawyers outlined the need for registration for unions to operate effectively, the use of open-ballots and associated intimidation, limits on legal strikes, *sindicatos blancos* (phantom unions) to block genuine representation and systematic firing and blacklist of unionists. US and Canadian labour experts noted that a concerted effort was required to protect core union rights.[8]

---

4   International Brotherhood of Teamsters, *Complaint ... in re Honeywell Inc.* Feb. 1994.

5   Department of Labor, National Administrative Office, *Public Report of Review: NAO Submission #940001 and NAO Submission #9400002* (Washington, October 12, 1994), 2–6.

6   Brief of the United Electrical, Radio and Machine Workers of America (UE) Before the US NAO 'In re: Case No. 940002, General Electric Company' Sept. 16, 1994.

7   Brief of the United Electrical, Radio and Machine Workers of America (UE) Before the US NAO 'In re: Case No. 940002, General Electric Company' Sept. 16, 1994.

8   US Dept. of Labor, Bureau of International Labor Affairs, National Administrative Office, *Transcript of Public Hearing,* Mon. Sept. 12, 1994.

The companies opposed the hearings and did not send witnesses, but responded in writing. US business associations argued that NAALC only allowed consideration of whether Mexico effectively enforced its laws. In these cases, domestic remedies were not exhausted as workers accepted severance and did not contest dismissals. This precedent meant the NAO could accept any case about a company's personnel decisions; complainants could bypass domestic appeals to seek favourable international rulings.[9] NAOs should stress cooperation, not confrontational hearings and should focus on law enforcement, not corporate practices. Mexican officials felt these complaints were devised by 'minority' unions which did not represent most workers. The hearings took the Mexicans by surprise, since they expected more low-key action.[10]

In its public report of review, the US NAO argued that there was a lack of mutual understanding of the other countries' laws governing rights to association and organization. The NAO called for 'cooperative programs' including trinational seminars of officials, business and labour leaders, and training for law enforcement officers. On the dismissals, the NAO decided that because workers,

> for personal financial reasons accepted severance, thereby preempting Mexican authorities from establishing whether the dismissals were for cause or in retribution for union organizing, the NAO is not in a position to make a finding that the Government of Mexico failed to enforce the relevant labour laws.[11]

Therefore, the NAO did not recommend ministerial consultations, and clearly focussed on law enforcement, not the adequacy of laws or corporate practices. Although alarmed that the NAO would consider complaints on non-sanctionable issues, U.S. business leaders 'praised' the NAO 'for focussing the inquiry on Mexican enforcement of its laws rather than on the specific labour practices of the two companies'.[12]

For unions, this ruling revealed the inability of NAALC to redress the workers' weak position in a nation with grinding poverty and high unemployment. The Teamsters suggested that NAALC allowed for a '*broad* scope of NAO Review: 'labor law matters arising in the territory of another party'. Allegations of inadequate enforcement were unnecessary for ministerial consultations, which could touch on any aspect of labour law.[13] The United Electrical Workers called for a broad interpretation, not excluding health, safety or dismissal, with direct NAO inspection of the plants. Unionists protested the ban on cross examination of company and government witnesses and the exclusion of television and radio which limited awareness. The lack of simultaneous

---

9   See correspondence on file at the US NAO to Irasema Garza from US business associations, Aug. 31, 1994, 3.

10   Interview with officials at the National Administrative Office of Mexico, February 13, 1995.

11   *Public Report of Review: NAO Submission #940001 and NAO Submission #9400002*, 30.

12   'First NAFTA Labor Hearing Held', *U.S.-Mexico Free Trade Reporter*, Sept. 30, 1994, 4.

13   IBT, 'Post-Hearing Brief of the International Brotherhood of Teamsters .... In re Cases nos. 940001 and 940002'. Sept. 19, 1994.

translation and the choice of Washington for the hearing limited participation by Mexican workers.[14]

Despite the union reaction, the NAO's report held open the possibility for wider explorations of Mexican law enforcement. And it established the precedent of public hearings which forced Mexican business and government officials to respond publicly.[15] However, while these cases spawned valuable consultations on organization, association and bargaining rights they did not result in workers' reinstatement and the plants were still represented by 'official' CTM unions.

Dissatisfaction with this outcome led to the withdrawal of US NAO 940004 about a General Electric plant where workers were allegedly denied rights to organization through company interference with a union representation election.[16] Company officials suggested that the complaint was invalid, as the independent metal workers union and individual workers did not pursue Mexican appeals, and the NAALC did not require Mexico to adopt stronger protections. This case was an attempt to use the NAO process for anti-NAFTA purposes. Business groups felt NAO acceptance of this submission was premature before domestic remedies were pursued, and would discredit the company, not assess enforcement. Public hearings were 'confrontational' and would provide little understanding of Mexico's laws; cooperative programs would provide a better forum.[17] The US NAO accepted this submission, which was consistent with NAO responsibilities to promote NAALC principles and encourage effective law enforcement.[18] But because the workers had not sought domestic remedies, no finding of non-enforcement was possible.[19] The submitters decided to withdraw, reflecting disappointment with the NAO's decision to consider only law enforcement, not inadequacies in Mexican laws.

Magneticos de Mexico (Sony)

In US NAO 940003 human and worker's rights groups complained about the Sony subsidiary, Magneticos de Mexico, in Nuevo Laredo, whose 5 plants produced computer disks, audio tapes and video cassettes. The complaint alleged violations of freedom of association, right to organize, and minimum standards for hours and holidays. Complainants reported suspensions, demotions, dismissal or blacklisting of union organizers challenging the official CTM union. Open, not secret ballot, union elections were held on short notice and police used force against protestors. Submitters claimed the labour tribunal's rejection of the independent union's registration because

---

14   Asra Nomani, 'Unions angry after administration rejects complaints about Mexico plants' *Wall Street Journal*, Oct. 14, 1994, A2; Jesus Campos Linas, 'la primer audiencia pública en el marco del tlc' *Evidencias*, Fall, 1994, 5–6.

15   Compa, 1995, 177–78.

16   'United Electrical Worker Submission Accepted for Review' US Department of Labor, *News Release* Nov. 10, 1994.

17   See correspondence on file at the US NAO to Irasema Garza from US business associations, Feb. 1, 1995.

18   *Federal Register* 59, 217 Nov. 10, 1994, 58094.

19   Irasema Garza to John Hovis, Feb. 9, 1995.

the application was not supplied in duplicate proved that Mexican authorities hindered an independent union on technical grounds. Submitters called for a hearing in Laredo to facilitate Mexican participation, and sought ministerial consultations.[20] The NAO held hearings in San Antonio, open to television cameras, with simultaneous translation.[21] Jerome Levinson of the International Labor Rights Education and Research Fund, argued 'the Mexican government, instead of affirming the right of free association, is an active collaborator with the company and the official union in effectively preventing the workers from exercising that right'.[22]

The US NAO rejected company denials that workers were fired for union organizing or that dismissals were validated by acceptance of severance. But it resisted union pleas to censure the company, focussing on the actions of officials. The US NAO called for trinational talks on worker rights and a study of Mexican unfair dismissal laws, sought consultations on remedies for electoral unfairness in union democracy, and asked Mexico's NAO for information on police violence to disperse a work stoppage.[23] Finally, the NAO called for ministerial consultations to examine Mexican laws on union registration. Arturo Alcalde of the National Association of Democratic Lawyers observed that this 'decision calls attention to the basic problems faced by Mexican workers, namely that government authorities hold the labour law in contempt and that official unions do not respect the democratic rights of their rank and file members'.[24]

Mexico agreed to a review of its laws on registration by independent experts, and to meetings between labour officials and affected employees, company and local officials respecting remedies. All three countries initiated a joint program of workshops and studies to 'improve implementation and public understanding of procedures regarding union certification'.[25] Ultimately, three seminars were held on union registration, a study of registration procedures was conducted by Mexican experts, and ministry officials met with local officers and CTM leaders.[26] But the submitters criticized the Mexican NAO for limiting participation and advertising for the seminars.[27] Mexican representatives testified in contradictory fashion on whether a new union could challenge an existing one, prompting scepticism. Nonetheless this was 'the first time that … liberty of association has been discussed publicly in Mexico' which could 'help

---

20   Department of Labor, National Administrative Office, *Public Report of Review: NAO Submission #940003* (Washington, April 11, 1995), 2–6.

21   U.S. Department of Labor, National Administrative Office, *Public Hearing* San Antonio, Texas, February 13, 1995, 7.

22   Jerome I. Levinson, 'Opening Statement: In re: Sony Corporation d/b/a/ Magnetico de Mexico', Proceeding before the U.S. National Administrative Office, Feb. 13, 1995.

23   U.S. National Administrative Office, *Executive Summary: Report of the National Administrative Office on Submission #940003* (Washington: Department of Labor, 1995).

24   James Shields, ''Social dumping' in Mexico under NAFTA' *Multinational Monitor* 16, 4 (1995), 20–5.

25   Pamela Prah, 'U.S., Mexico Unveil Plans in Response to Sony Charge Filed Under NAFTA Accord', *Daily Labor Review* 123, June 27, 1995, A–10.

26   US Department of Labor, US NAO, 'Ministerial Consultations – Submission 940003 Agreement on Implementation, Statement on Public Release of Documents Washington, 1996.

27   Dora Delgado and Peter Menyasz, 'Mexico's Union Registration Procedures will be Examined by Panel of Experts' *Daily Labor Report* 175, Sept. 11, 1995, CC1–2.

to prevent abuses and law violations in future'.[28] Submitter's felt the study was an academic exercise, which did not address workers' problems; the NAO process had 'integrity', but consultations were 'fundamentally flawed' and 'severely compromised the credibility of the NAALC.'[29]

No workers regained their jobs despite the NAO finding that they were fired for union organizing. None won their arbitration complaints, and none were offered compensation besides severance pay. And the composition of the arbitration boards was not altered. This lack of sanctions and inability to reinstate or compensate workers meant that, '[n]othing changed as a consequence of the NAALC'.[30] Proposals to remove local officials' discretion in union registration and to transfer authority to the courts remained mired in legislative committees, despite support from union and business. Supreme Court rulings permitting formation of more than one union in a workplace had little effect since lower courts were not bound by this precedent.[31] Submitters petitioned the US Secretary of Labor, Robert Reich, to reopen the case because of alleged biases on the arbitration boards, which included members of 'official' unions who blocked registration of new unions. Reich declined, but asked the NAO to conduct an additional review of the situation of the affected workers and developments in Mexican labour laws.

The Public Workers ('Pesca') Union Case

In US NAO 9601 a coalition of labour and human rights groups, including Human Rights Watch (HRW), the International Labor Rights Fund (ILRF) and the Mexican National Association of Democratic Lawyers (ANAD), launched a complaint when the union representing government employees in the Fisheries Department was dissolved by the Federal Conciliation and Arbitration Tribunal (FCAT or Tribunal) when the department merged into the ministry of Environment, Natural Resources, and Fishing (SEMARNAP). The independent Sindicato Unico de Trabajadores de la Secretaría de Pesca (SUTSP or fisheries department union) was decertified because workers elsewhere in the new department were represented by the Sindicato Nacional de Trabajadores de la Secretario de Medio Ambiente, Recursos Naturales y Pesca (SNTSMARNAP or the environment, ministry union), with ties to PRI-linked official unions. The Tribunal ruled that the fisheries department union ceased to exist when the fishing ministry disappeared.

---

28   Dora Delgado, 'Labor Officials from U.S., Mexico and Canada Discuss Union Registration' Daily *Labor Report* 175, Sept. 18, 1995, A–9.

29   Jerome I. Levinson, 'Response of the International Labor Rights Education and Research Fund to the Ministerial Consultation under the North American Agreement on Labor Cooperation in the Case of the Sony Maquiladora Operation in Nuevo Laredo, Mexico' Washington, June 28, 1995, 5.

30   Jerome Levinson, *NAFTA's Labor Side Agreement: Lessons from the First Three Years* (Washington: International Labor Rights Fund/ Institute for Policy Studies, 1996), 20.

31   US Department of Labor, Bureau of International Labor Affairs, US NAO, *Follow-Up Report: NAO Submission #940003*' Washington, Dec. 4, 1996.

The submission accused Mexico of violating its NAALC obligations to promote freedom of association, and to ensure fair, impartial adjudication of labour laws.[32] Petitioners alleged that laws requiring public workers in any ministry to belong to one union violated Mexico's guarantees for freedom of association and its commitment to ILO conventions on impartial labour tribunals. This practice contradicted freedom of association by recognizing only the Federation of Labour Unions of Workers Representing the State (FTSTE or Federation of State Workers) as a registered union. The petition alleged that the Tribunal was biased because of its appointment procedures, which favoured FTSTE and that it had unlawfully decertified the fisheries department union, despite its proven support.[33] After court rulings ordering the recertification of the fisheries department union and decertification of the environment department union, the Tribunal delayed in letting the ministry know of SUTSP's registration and the ministry continued to work as if SNTSMARNAP was the legitimate union. These actions were violations of Mexico's commitments under Convention 87 of the ILO Covenant on Civil and Political Rights, which submitters claimed, was constitutionally enforceable.[34]

To petitioners, the case illustrated how Mexican legal and political structures hindered independent union registration. They wanted the Federal Tribunal to order a new election, with a secret ballot and a legitimate voters' list: union dues and bargaining rights should be given to the fisheries department union immediately. SUTSP leaders believed NAALC would help them in their battle and hoped that the 'international spotlight could eventually trigger internal political change'.[35] Joel Solomon of Human Rights Watch noted the importance of using 'the NAALC petition process to see just how much use can be made of it to improve the situation'; NAALC could increase 'public awareness', and create 'operating space for independent labor activities' in Mexico.[36]

The Mexican NAO insisted that the submission was inappropriate because laws had been enforced and the ILO was reviewing the matter[37]; the NAO resisted calls for a public forum, as the fisheries department union had been able to petition for redress.[38] But the US NAO accepted the submission because it raised concerns over law enforcement and would further binational dialogue. Submitters hailed this decision since laws which go

---

32   Human Rights Watch/Americas, International Labor Rights Fund and Associacíon Nacional de Abogados Demoncráticos, 'Summary, Petition 9601 Submitted to the US National Administrative Office' , July, 1996.

33   'U.S. NAO Will Review Mexican Labor Practices' *BorderLines* 27 (Vol. 4, No. 8, Sept. 1996) [cited July 12, 1998]. Available at http://www.zianet.com/irc1/bordline/index.html.

34   National Administrative Office, Bureau of International Labor Affairs, US Dept. of Labor, *Public Report of Review: NAO Submission No. 9601* Washington, Jan. 27, 1997.

35   Dora Delgado, 'Side Accord Seen As a Mechanism for Change in Mexico, Groups Say' *Daily Labor Report* 156, August 13, 1996, CC–2.

36   'New NAFTA challenge over labor rights' *Working Together* July-August, 1996.

37   Armando Vivanco, Secretary, Mexican NAO, to Irasema Garza, Secretary US NAO Re: 'Communicacion Publica U.S. NAO 9601' July 11, 1996.

38   'Mexico Had Asked United States to Reject Latest Labor Complaint', *Daily Labor Review* August 16, 1996.

against the spirit of NAALC could now be reviewed as 'violations' of the accord.[39] The Mexican NAO was asked to clarify how conciliation and arbitration tribunal members were selected and the status of international treaties in Mexican law. The Mexican NAO confirmed that the Tribunal included a representative of FSTSE, problematic for its treatment of the fisheries department union. The new department claimed neutrality in its dealings with the unions and its respect for workers' representatives. Mexico's NAO argued that, as the legally recognized union, the fisheries department union could apply to the Tribunal for redress, highly problematic given the Federation of State Worker's role on FCAT.[40]

While US NAO action was pending, the petitioners complained that the Tribunal scheduled a flawed 'recount' vote. The fisheries department union was not allowed to scrutinize voter lists and some polls were held at the headquarters of the official union. The ministry denied the fisheries department union the right to collect union dues or time off for union organizers, while extending these rights to the environment department union, despite its loss of registration. SUTSP was blocked from organizing workers in some sectors of the ministry. Petitioners believed these violations prevented the fisheries department union from contesting the recount, in violation of Mexico's ILO commitments.[41] Despite these concerns, the recount proceeded and the independent fisheries department union lost to the official union amid charges of voting irregularities and intimidation, although loyalty to the official union also played a role.[42] The Tribunal then revoked SUTSP's registration.

At the public hearing, petitioners claimed that, despite denials by the Mexican NAO, the violation of worker rights persisted. The Environment, Resources and Fishing Ministry denied the fisheries department union access to its workers, and treated its rival as the legitimate representative even before it was registered. The Tribunal refused to consider the fisheries department union complaints that the Ministry was ignoring it. SUTSP workers signed affidavits indicating that they had been denied 'licences' to engage in union activity, while such licences were offered to the environment department union, which also gained control over union funds and housing. The Tribunal called the recount election despite the fisheries department union's lack of access to the workplace, distorting the results. Petitioners claimed the FCAT failed to make the Environment, Resources and Fishing Ministry respect the court rulings favouring SUTSP, undermining law enforcement.

Petitioners alleged that the Mexican NAO was misleading in focussing on court victories, and not actual enforcement by the Tribunal. Mexican law allowed unions to exist independently of the Federation of States Workers but did not recognize them for

---

39   'NAFTA Office Okays Review of Mexican Federal Union Practices' *Inside NAFTA* 3, Aug. 7, 1996, 2.

40   US NAO, 'Answers Provided by the Mexican NAO to Questions on U. S. NAO Submission #9601', Oct. 8, 1996 (U. S. NAO staff translation).

41   Pharis Harvey (International Labor Rights Fund) and José Miguel Vivanco (Human Rights Watch/Americas) to Lic. Emilio Chuaffet Chemor, Secretario del SEMARNAP, Oct. 1, 1996.

42   UE-FAT, *Mexican Labor News and Analysis* 1, 19 Oct. 16, 1996 [cited July 25, 1998]. Available at http://www.igc.apc.org/unitedelect/vol1no19.html.

bargaining.[43] The Tribunal only ruled for the fisheries department union when forced by the courts *amparo* decisions, but simply did not inform the ministry, freeing it from obligations to the independent union.[44] While the Tribunal promised it would not intervene, it ordered a recount on short notice. For submitters, this indicated FCAT's biases and led to deregistration of the fisheries department union. The Mexican NAO's endorsement of the Ministry's 'neutrality' between SUTSP and SNTSMARNAP entailed acceptance of the denial of the fisheries department union's legal rights.[45] Neutrality was a 'rhetorical shell game hiding labor rights violations'.[46]

Mark Hager of the International Legal Rights Fund noted that Supreme Court rulings outlawing the single union for university employees should be applied to the public service to implement constitutional rights of free association. Also, 'NAALC does not prohibit the U.S. NAO from criticising fundamental deficiencies in Mexico's law'.[47] Labour lawyers pointed out how laws privileging the official unions violated ILO conventions. The NAO should require the creation of impartial tribunals for Mexican public workers, facilitate independent unions, and organize a new, free and fair election; 'only a rigid and fanatic interpretation would preclude the U. S. NAO from recommending changes in a law that clearly subverts core NAALC objectives'.[48]

The Environmental, Resources and Fisheries Department union indicated surprise at the fisheries department union's claims, since the fisheries ministry and its union ceased to exist after the merger. FSTES used a 'highly democratic and participatory process' to establish a representative union for the new ministry, including workers from fisheries, agriculture and the environment. But when the fisheries group lost the vote even in the fisheries section, they revived SUTSP as a separate entity rather than join the larger union. When a recognition ballot was held for the new ministry, the fisheries department union lost and its registration ended. SUTSP was an undemocratic union which had not improved the contract for fisheries workers, made unproven allegations of government bias and did not respect the majority of workers or the spirit of the laws.[49]

Mexico's NAO commented that NAALC did not allow outside agencies to determine which laws should be in place but only to 'make sure that what is currently in force is

---

43 Testimony of Roberto Tooms, *Public Hearing, U.S. NAO Submission 9601*, Washington, Dec. 3, 1996, 51.

44 Testimony of Eugenio Narcia Teobar, *Public Hearing, U.S. NAO Submission 9601*, Washington, Dec. 3, 1996, 49.

45 HRW/Americas, ILRF, ANAD, 'Brief Filed by Co-petitioners in Case #9601' Dec. 2, 1996.

46 Testimony of Joel Solomon, *Public Hearing, U.S. NAO Submission 9601*, Washington, Dec. 3, 1996, 15.

47 Testimony of Mark Hager , *Public Hearing, U.S. NAO Submission 9601*, Washington, Dec. 3, 1996, 20.

48 Testimony of Mark Hager , *Public Hearing, U.S. NAO Submission 9601*, Washington, Dec. 3, 1996, 21.

49 Testimony of Alfonso Armendariz Duran , *Public Hearing, U.S. NAO Submission 9601*, Washington, Dec. 3, 1996, 87–95.

complied with'.[50] The approach should not be 'adversarial' or suggest that 'everything is rotten' though he acknowledged that 'we do seriously need to improve'.[51] Business wanted the NAO to assess existing Mexican laws, not to seek improvements; US laws only permitted one union in a workplace, so it would be outside the boundaries of NAALC to require Mexico to provide this right. ILO conventions were not part of Mexican laws, and were broad principles which could not be used to invalidate national laws; the submitters' requests would violate Mexican sovereignty and undermine labor relations.[52]

The US NAO recommended ministerial consultations on laws and constitutional provisions affecting freedom of association in Mexico 'with full respect for the national sovereignty of the two countries'.[53] A seminar on 'International Treaties and Constitutional Systems of the United States, Mexico and Canada' assessed the status of international labour law and ILO provisions in Mexico.[54] 'The conference offered no opportunity to resolve the labor rights problems highlighted by the petitioners, and labor rights defenders were not invited to participate.'[55] Submitters requests to the NAO to reopen the case because of new evidence about the application of court rulings were declined because 'Mexican appellate court decisions and secret ballot elections ... had addressed matters that had been raised as concerns in the submission'.[56] Thus, court rulings in favour of the fisheries department union were sufficient even though the Ministry never allowed this union to exercise its rights before the official union won the recount.

Maxi-Switch

The Communication Workers of America initiated US NAO 9602 involving, Maxi-Switch, which made computer keyboards and computer game equipment in Cananea. Two independent Mexican unions, the Union of Telephone Workers of the Republic of Mexico (STRM) and the Federation of Goods and Services Workers of Mexico

---

50   Testimony of Dr. Louis Diaz , *Public Hearing, U.S. NAO Submission 9601*, Washington, Dec. 3, 1996, 71.

51   Testimony of Dr. Louis Diaz , *Public Hearing, U.S. NAO Submission 9601*, Washington, Dec. 3, 1996, 73–4.

52   Correspondence on File at the US NAO to Irasema Garza from US Business association, Sept. 18, 1996.

53   'Agreement on Ministerial Consultations U.S. NAO Submission No. 9601' Sept. 3, 1997.

54   US NAO, 'Communications submitted to the United States National Administrative Office' http://www.naalc.org/english/publications/summaryusa.htm. The conference covered issues of whether treaties are 'self-executing' or require legislation; the difference between treaties and executive agreements; how international treaties fit into 'the legal hierarchy of domestic laws', what is needed 'to make a treaty enforceable domestically' and 'actual experience with the domestic application of treaties'.

55   Human Rights Watch Word Report, *Mexico: The Role of the International Community* [cited July 27, 1998]. Available at http://www.hrw.org/worldreport99/americas/mexico3.html.

56   US NAO, 'Communications submitted to the United States National Administrative Office' [cited July 25, 1998]. Available at http://www.naalc.org/english/publications/summaryusa.htm.

(FESEBES) cooperated with the Communication Workers in the submission which cited the alleged failure of Mexico to faithfully enforce laws respecting union certification and protection of union organizers from retaliation or dismissal. Workers claimed they tried to organize in response to poor wages, health violations, poor ventilation, and abuse by supervisors. The company allegedly resisted unionization using intimidation, firing of organizers and violence.[57] The labour board refused certification for the Telephone Workers' union, claiming a CTM union, Sindicato de Trabajadores en Maquiladoras, Tintorerias, Zapaterias, Tiendas de Ropa e Industrias y Commercios en General del Estado de Sonora (STTZTRRCGMH) represented the plant. Workers were unaware of this union, which allegedly held an illegal 'protection contract' to keep out union organizers.[58] This case was important, for one unionist indicated that 80% of Mexican factories had such 'ghost' unions to conform to mandatory union laws, without providing effective representation.[59]

The Communication Workers complained that the Mexico 'failed to enforce its labor laws in the face of the brutal anti-union activities' and alleged 'government collusion with the CTM ... and its creation of 'phantom unions''.[60] The CWA alleged violations of Part II of the NAALC, as Mexico failed to enforce its laws, constitution, and ILO commitments. The Telephone Workers' union had demonstrated worker support, and should not be denied registration because of the existence of a collective agreement; instead the CTM union should demonstrate that it represented more workers than STRM before receiving bargaining rights. The denial of access to the contract or union bylaws prevented workers from assessing if the CTM union was defending their rights. After its decision was annulled in the courts, the Board simply did not hold another hearing, thereby continuing its ruling in favour of the CTM.[61]

The local board initially refused to hear worker requests for reinstatement after illegal firings for union organizing[62]. When hearings were held, workers were not properly notified, giving management an advantage. The company claimed the workers had resigned, even though one manager was fined in a criminal case for coercing a resignation; other workers had been forced to sign blank pages as a condition of hiring, a tactic allegedly used to prepare false resignation letters.[63] The Communication Workers called for action to make union registration in Mexico open and independent, and free

57   'CWA Files NAFTA Complaint to Aid Mexican Telecom Workers' *CWA News*, 1996, 9.

58   Robert Collier 'NAFTA Labor Problems Haunt New Trade Debate' *San Francisco Chronicle* Sept. 10, 1997; [cited August 11, 1998] Available at http://www.latinolink.com/biz/biz97/0910bnaf.htm.

59   'Ghost Haunts Maxi-Switch' [cited August 13, 1996]. Available at http://www.sweatmag.org/0_industry/no1ghost.htm.

60   'Communication Workers of America Files NAFTA Complaint Charging Failure by Mexico to Enforce Labor Laws' *CWA News*, Oct. 11, 1996.

61   US NAO, 'Submission #9602 – Maxi Switch', Reviewed by US NAO, Oct. 11, 1996.

62   CWA, 'Submission to the United States National Administrative Office Regarding Persistent Pattern of Failure to Enforce and Discrimination in the Administration of Mexican Labor Law: The Case of Maxi-Switch, Inc. in Cananea, Mexico', Oct. 11, 1996.

63   'Observations from the CWA, FESEBES and STRM concerning the responses with regard to the document entitled 'Questions for the Mexican NAO'' translation, April 16, 1997.

of coercion by government officials, employers and rival unions. These actions should go beyond consultation to 'ensure that procedural guarantees are met'.[64]

The AFL-CIO, long averse to the NAALC, associated itself with this complaint. This large union central did not express a preference for a particular union, but was concerned that Mexican 'government agencies and company management are intervening to impose the choice of unions and contracts on workers without their knowledge or consent.'[65] An American delegation reported health and safety violations, including ventilation so poor that it made workers faint and required 3–4 ambulance calls daily. Workers as young as 16 were subjected to harsh conditions for 10 hours a day, for only $3.50. The observers noted the 'catch 22' faced by workers, who were blocked from organizing their own union, but denied access to a contract allegedly signed by the CTM.[66] Despite serious problems, health and safety issues were not emphasized, as the submitters concentrated on freedom of association and fair procedures. This meant that the NAO would be limited to consultations and cooperation, and could not invoke ECEs or sanctions.

In the first intervention by a Canadian union, the Communication, Energy and Paperworkers Union (CEP) joined the complaint, and condemned Mexico's alleged failure to provide impartial tribunals, since the chair and labour representative on the local board were CTM members.[67] The CEP noted that the decision to deny recognition 'raises the very important issue of the right to be heard before a local conciliation and arbitration board' as the process was 'tainted with partiality and lack of transparency'.[68] Withholding of information on the CTM union and delays in proceedings for fired workers were condemned as denials of rights. These deficiencies resulted in a lack of due process for the FESEBES union. Although NAALC did not permit outside parties to force changes in Mexican laws, the CEP wished to use the public hearings to comment on deficiencies in Mexican practices and to create pressure for their rectification.[69]

The US NAO accepted the complaint, planned a hearing for Tucson, and posed questions to the Mexican NAO to clarify the relevant facts and laws. The Mexican NAO reported that the Board had accurately dismissed the claims for reinstatement, since the workers did not show up (though they claimed lack of notification); the NAO acknowledged than one worker had been fined for violence, but denied he was a supervisor, or that this was related to the dismissals. The NAO affirmed the existence of the CTM union and supported the Board's denial of registration to the Telephone workers. The Board was not biased as its government representative was not affiliated with the CTM, though the labour representative was in a CTM local.[70]

---

64 CWA, 'Submission ... The Case of Maxi-Switch, Inc.', Oct. 11, 1996, 14.

65 John Sweeney to Irasema Garza, Oct. 21, 1996.

66 David Jessup, AFL-CIO American Institute for Free Labor Development (AIFLD) 'A Report on Working Conditions at Maxi-Switch, Cananea, Mexico, April 7, 1997.

67 'CEP Supports NAALC Petition', January 24, 1997 [cited July 24, 1998] Available at http://www.cep.ca/en/reg/reg1.htm.

68 Communication, Energy and Paperworkers Union of Canada, 'Submission to be heard Before the United States National Administrative Office ... Regarding Submission #9602...' April 14, 1997, 5.

69 CEP 'Submission', April, 1997.

70 'Public Communication US NAO 9602 (Maxi-Switch) Questions for the NAO of Mexico' March 5, 1997 (responses translated into English).

A public hearing was aborted two days before it was to be held in April, 1997, when the Mexican government agreed to certify the union. The Telephone Workers' union wrote to the Communication Workers to announce that the Board had accepted the certification. While this did not result in reinstatement for those fired, or in an acceptable collective agreement, due process had been restored. Since the 'main objectives' had been reached, STRM requested that the petitioners ask the NAO to terminate the case.[71] The presenters withdrew the NAO submission, expecting that the situation was resolved.[72] The alliance of the Communication Workers and the Telephone workers union was credited with forcing Mexico's hand.[73] The decision was 'a major step forward for Maxi-Switch workers who are determined to build their union, and for other workers throughout Mexico.'[74] US officials hailed the move as evidence that NAALC could make a difference.[75]

But the celebrations were premature. Despite the certification, local authorities refused to enforce union rights, indicating the limits of ministerial consultations in a federal state. Company management did not reinstate the union leaders and changed the legal name of the plant, requiring certification to recommence.[76] Although the Governor of the State ordered reinstatement, he left office immediately afterwards. Communication Workers President Morton Bahr asserted, this 'painfully demonstrates the ineffectiveness of our current trade agreements to protect the right of workers to elect independent unions.'[77] The matter went into Mexican courts where it languished. Workers were not reinstated and the independent union was blocked. Serious health and safety violations, a potential sanctionable issue, were not addressed despite alleged problems with ventilation and safety.

Assessment of Early Cases

Therefore, precedents slowly developed from decisions by the US NAO. Even though the issues raised in these cases were not sanctionable, the NAO put pressure on Mexico to enforce its labor laws. The head of the NAO, Irasema Garza, suggested that the

---

71   Francisco Hernandez Jaurez to Louis Moore, CWA, April 15, 1997.

72   Irasema Garza, US NAO to Jorge Castañon Lara, May Morpaw, and John McKinnery, April 15, 1997.

73   'CWA Filing Brings Victory for Maxi-Switch Workers Mexico Recognizes Independent Union,' *CWA News*, [cited August 2, 1998]. Available at http://www.cwa-union.org/art6.html.

74   'Union wins recognition at Taiwanese computer plant in Mexican maquiladora' *ICFTU OnLine*, 25 April, 1997, [cited July 28 1998]. Available at http://www.icftu.org.

75   Tim Shorrock, 'Mexico approves union at Taiwan-owned firm' *Journal of Commerce* April 18, 1997.

76   'Border Briefs: Maxi-Switch Workers Win Union Recognition' *BorderLines* 37 [cited July 22, 1998]. Available at http://www.zianet.com/irc1/bordline/bl37bb.html; 'Switch at Maxi-Switch', *CLC – What's New: The Morning NAFTA* June 1997 No. 9. [cited August 6, 1998]. Available at http://www.clc-ctc.com/news/m-nafta2.html.

77   'Union Campaign Helps Scuttle Fast Track As CWA Points to NAFTA Failures' *CWA News* [cited July 27, 1998]. Available at http://www.cwa-union.org/action/aboutcwa/cwapubs/9712news/art15.htm.

public review process was designed 'to obtain information to better understand and publicly report on the Government of Mexico's promotion of compliance with and enforcement of its labor laws'.[78] On issues like freedom of association and right to organize, the NAO could do no more than ask for consultations, so it was not insignificant that this step was taken in the Sony case.[79] Employers were critical of the NAO for considering allegations which focused on corporate practices, not Mexico's law enforcement, which they considered an invitation for unions to harass companies.[80] The NAO considered complaints even where enforcement is not at issue to fulfill NAALC's pledge to promote free association, improve labor standards and develop 'transparency' in law enforcement.[81] But the NAO limited requests for ministerial consultations to inadequate enforcement such as delays in union recognition, even though NAALC permits non-enforcement issues to be sent to ministerial talks.[82]

Unions used the agreement to generate adverse publicity for corporations which shift employment to Mexico to take advantage of weak labor protection. Focusing public attention and political pressure on Mexico through public hearings may be a deterrent. The NAALC gave Mexican labor activists new recourse when domestic processes fail. But the US NAO rejected efforts to turn itself into a supranational judicial body giving rulings on coporations' actions. The NAO did not condemn corporate practices as unionists requested, but evaluated Mexican efforts to deal with violations. As the first review report suggested, 'the NAO is not an appellate body, nor is it a substitute for pursuing domestic remedies'.[83] Political pressures induced the NAO to hold public hearings and to promote cooperative activities on worker dismissals, union organization, and health and safety. The NAO interpretation of its role was a far cry from the supranational European agencies on social issues, reflecting continued sovereignty for national actors and supremacy for domestic labor laws.[84]

Thus the NAALC was weaker than unions wanted, since complaints could not lead to sanctions in areas vital to the strength of Mexican unions: right of association, collective bargaining and strikes. These rights could promote stronger independent unions in Mexico, increase wages, and expand working class purchasing power, and consumer demand for imports. Independent Mexican unions suggest the first cases favoured unrepresentative official unions. Critical workers in Mexico argued that official unions maintain their dominance by the denial of rights to free association and union democracy, with the government complicity.[85] These practices continued after

---

78 'Labor Department to Review Allegations of Sony Corporation Violations of Mexican Workers' Rights' *News* (Washington, Department of Labor, Office of Information, Oct. 19, 1994).

79 *Public Report of Review: NAO Submission #940003*, 6.

80 U.S. Council for International Business, 'Statement on Submissions #940001 and #940002', August 31, 1994 and 'Statement on Submission #940003', February 1, 1995.

81 U.S. Department of Labor, National Administrative Office, *Public Hearing* San Antonio, Texas, February 13, 1995, 5.

82 Compa, 1995, 168.

83 *Public Report of Review: NAO Submission #940001 and NAO Submission #940002*, 28.

84 Manfred McDowell, 'NAFTA and the EC `Social Dimension'' *Labor Studies Journal* 20,1 (Spring, 1995), 39–41, 47.

85 Statement of Ezequiel Garcia, (STIMAHCS), 'Organizing Workers in Mexico, A NAFTA Issue', *Hearing Before the Employment, Housing and Aviation Subcommittee of the Committee on*

NAFTA, as Mexico received investments from companies benefiting from lax labor laws. Unions also complained about how long it took to provide staff for the NAOs and the trinational office, which delayed the early cases.[86]

Mexico's 'official' unions and businesses denied that there are problems with freedom of association and suggest that American unions and their 'radical' allies in Mexico wanted to discredit NAFTA. They attacked the alliances of US and Mexican workers as a destabilizing force undermining labour peace in the maquiladoras, to discourage investment in Mexico.[87] They objected to public hearings as meddlesome interference in Mexico's labour affairs, including industrial relations matters not covered by the disputes resolution process.[88] The Mexican NAO regarded public hearings as 'not consistent with the spirit of cooperation of the NAALC.'[89] Even the limited gains made in these cases stirred opposition at the highest levels. President Ernesto Zedillo led other hemispheric leaders in declaring that 'As a matter of principle, labor and environmental worries must not be allowed to be used as instruments to affect free trade in the world.'[90] American business argued that the NAO should evaluate law enforcement, not company practices, and most avoided participation in hearings, preferring written submissions.[91]

US officials defended the accord and pointed to 'successes' such as secret ballot elections in the GE and the fisheries department union cases, and registration of the independent union at Max-Switch[92] (which critics saw as transitory victories). Cooperative activities, research studies and seminars were praised for producing an increased greater public awareness of labour practices across the three countries. This contributed to mutual understanding and facilitated the improvement of relationships among actors across borders. Freedom of association and union registration had been brought to the fore by the submission process, even if Mexican decisions were not reversed and specific workers were not reinstated. The Clinton administration argued that NAALC strengthened awareness of core rights. While the process was considered valuable, there were no plans to extend the protections in NAALC or provide more

Government Operations, U.S. House of Representatives, 103rd. Congress, 1st. Session, July 15, 1993, 8.

86   James Shields, '"Social dumping" in Mexico under NAFTA' *Multinational Monitor* 16, 4 (April, 1995), 20–25; Anthony DePalma, 'Unions complain of delays involving trade pact' *New York Times* (Mon, March 21, 1994), C2.

87   'Denuncian intromisión de sindicalistas de EU' *Norte de Ciudad Juarez* Set. 6, 1994, 4F.

88   Interview with Adolpho Tema, head of the labor commission, COMPARMEX, February, 1995; Interview with Roberto Castellanos Tova, Vice President, Confederacion Regional Obrara y Campesino, February, 1995.

89   Miguel Angel Orozco, Mexican NAO to Irasema Garza, Feb. 7, 1995.

90   'Union Campaign Helps Scuttle Fast Track As CWA Points to NAFTA Failures' *CWA News* [cited July 22, 1998]. Available at http://www.cwa-union.org/action/aboutcwa/cwapubs/9712news/art15.htm.

91   'Mexican NAO Asks Labor Chiefs to Discuss U.S. Laws, Sprint Case' *Inside NAFTA.* 2, (June 14, 1995), 8.

92   Testimony of Ambassador Richard Fisher, Deputy United States Trade Representative Before the Senate Committee on Foreign Relations on the 'Economic Effects of NAFTA' Tuesday, April 13, 1999 [cited Jan. 11, 2001]. Available at http://usembassy-mexico.gov/et990419TLC.html.

enforcement power, which would be resisted by the other parties. The administration claimed success in spreading support for labour-trade linkages in some developing states, and pushed the issue at WTO forums.[93]

From a neo-institutionalist perspective, the early cases showed limited potential for NAALCs institutions and processes to create regionalization in labor affairs. The submissions, which required bilateral cooperation to bring complaints about one country's practices to the NAO of another NAFTA state, contributed to trans-border contacts among affected parties, including officials and unions. Canadian and American unions, along with sympathetic associations for labour and human rights, established stronger ties with their Mexican counterparts.[94] These early cases saw pioneering coalitions between independent Mexican unions in the Frente Autentico de Trabajo, such as its Metal Workers Union, the Union of Telephone Workers of the Republic of Mexico (STRM) and the Federation of Goods and Services Workers of Mexico (FESEBES) with activists US union like the United Electrical Workers, the International Brotherhood of Teamsters and the Communication Workers of America.

It also provided a forum for collaboration with human rights NGOs like the International Labor Rights Education and Research Fund, Human Rights Watch, and the Mexican National Association of Democratic Lawyers, which sought to test NAALC's suitability for advancing labour rights in trade arrangements. Although not creating such alliances, the NAALC did help cement some binational networks of unions and NGOs originally generated by the anti-NAFTA campaign. And these groups began to articulate a view which equated fundamental labour rights with human rights, which should not be dispensed with in the name of liberalized trade. Mexican labour lawyers noted that the process provided 'a mechanism for denouncing... the Mexican government's past unnoticed abuses of workers' rights'.[95]

But major unions like the AFL-CIO and Mexico's official unions remained aloof from such contacts for the most part.[96] The early decline of real wages in service and informal sectors encouraged skepticism and rejection of the agreement as well.[97] One report challenged the claim that 100,000 jobs would be created in the first year of NAFTA; the high number of applications for Transitional Adjustment Assistance (TAA) because of job transfers to NAFTA partners indicated otherwise.[98] And the sunshine capabilities of the NAALC did not produce immediate benefits for workers

---

93   Pamela N. Prah, 'Clinton to Continue to Link Trade/Labor; Renegotiation of NAFTA Seen as Unlikely' *Daily Labor Report* 219, Nov. 13, 1996, A–12.

94   'Mexican unionists find common ground in U.S.' *Working Together* 21 Nov.-Dec., 1996, 3.

95   Dora Delgado, 'Side Accord Seen As a Mechanism for Change in Mexico, Groups Say' *Daily Labor Report* 156, August 13, 1996, CC–1.

96   Russell E. Smith, 'An Early Assessment of the NAFTA Labor Side Accords' in Industrial Relations Research Association, *Proceedings of the Forty-Ninth Annual Meeting* (New Orleans, Jan. 4–6, 1997), 234–35.

97   Tim Shorrock, 'Drop seen in real wages in all three NAFTA countries' *Journal of Commerce,* May 29, 1996, A2.

98   Sarah Andersen, John Cavanagh and Dan Smith, '1st. Anniversary Report: Clinton's NAFTA Promises to Congress and Workers' Alliance for Responsible Trade/Citizen's Trade Campaign, Nov. 17, 1994.

or independent unions in Mexico, or alleviate the concerns of northern unions and workers about 'social dumping'.

The limited results reflected in part the character of the cases selected for the first submissions, which dealt with issues of freedom of association, right to organize and collective bargaining rights. These issues were selected because they are critical to the strength of unions in Mexico, where official unions benefit from lax enforcement of laws. But these matters were exempted from sanctions and expert evaluations, and therefore ministerial consultations were the limited of possible action. Therefore, it was not insignificant that three cases did proceed that far. As Perez-Lopez argued:

> Ministerial consultations have raised to a higher plane the importance of issues such as freedom of association and union registration and have opened a trinational, tripartite dialogue that is bound to have a positive impact on the well being of workers in the three nations.[99]

The Accord avoided adversarial sanctions and allowed 'difference to be addressed through constructive, cooperative means'.[100] For supporters, while the Mexican system often ignored law violations, the NAALC created a forum for unionists to seek redress and to expose corporate practices via the 'intrusive sunshine' of the complaints process.[101]

There is no question that in raising issues which were not included as sanctionable in the side agreement, the American unions were making a political statement, testing Clinton's pledge that worker rights would be protected after NAFTA. In the Sony case the AFL-CIO's Ed Feigen said: 'when this case reaches the NAO, the American people will find out whether the administration is willing to stop corporations that intend to use free trade as a tool for dragging down wages and violating workers rights.'[102] Despite their doubts, the unions' use of the side agreement indicates their willingness to test the potential of the NAALC to transform Mexican labor relations. Indeed, even those associated with the Communication Workers's disappointment after Maxi-Switch still advocated trans-national union collaboration.[103] But US unions were disappointed that these cases resulted only in ministerial consultations and adverse publicity. This inspired a search for cases which would test the next stages in the complaints process; evaluation committees and possible monetary or trade sanctions. In the search for such cases, NAALC inspired broader collaborations among unions, human rights, gender rights and other NGOs, deepening to a limited degree the nature of regional integration in the labour and social spheres.

---

99   Jorge F. Perez-Lopez, 'Conflict and Cooperation in US-Mexican Labor Relations: The North American Agreement on Labor Cooperation' *Journal of Borderlands Studies* XI, (1996), 57.

100 Perez-Lopez, 1996, 56.

101 Reed J. Slogoff, 'Mexico: Living with the NAFTA Labor Laws', *Trade & Culture Magazine* March/April 1995.

102 Talli Nauman, 'Lawmakers Protest Attack on Workers,' *El Financiero International,* May 9–15, 1994.

103 Larry Cohen and Steve Early 'Defending Workers' Rights in the Global Economy: The CWA Experience,' in Nissen, Bruce, ed. *Which Direction for Organized Labor? Essays on Organizing, Outreach, and Internal Transformations* Detroit, MI: Wayne State University Press, 1999.

Chapter 5

Stretching the Institutions: Later US Cases

Introduction

Having pioneered the process, the US NAO faced novel cases, as American unions and their Mexican and Canadian allies tested the boundaries of the NAALC. Submitters pursued cases which could move beyond ministerial consultations to an Evaluation Committee of Experts (ECE) or to arbitration, trade sanctions or fines. The Pregnancy Discrimination case challenged the practice of dismissing pregnant women from employment, which could be the subject of an evaluation committee. The Han Young case involved union organization, but also highlighted health and safety violations, which could lead to sanctions. The Echlin-ITAPSA case raised concerns about the prevention of occupational injuries and illnesses, again a sanctionable issue.

These cases could have tested the stronger enforcement aspects of the NAALC. That they terminated in ministerial consultations and seminars highlighted a lack of political will by the three governments to advance worker concerns. The cases highlighted how gender and class inequality were exacerbated by NAFTA; and they illustrated how these worsened conditions inspired more transnational coalition building to assert a broader interpretation of the NAALC and promote core labour and human rights. But their resolution also illustrated the limited efficacy of NAFTA's labour accord, and increased the scepticism of social actors; this limited NAALC's contribution to regionalization of networks, norms and practices in labour relations.

Pregnancy Discrimination (Gender) Case

The Pregnancy Discrimination case (U.S. NAO 9701) challenged companies which fired or refused to hire pregnant women in violation of Mexican laws. This first complaint on matters other than union rights was launched by Human Rights Watch Women's Project (HRW/WP), the International Labor Rights Fund (ILRF), Human Rights Watch/Americas (HRW/A), and Mexico's National Association of Democratic Lawyers (ANAD). It alleged violations of laws banning discrimination against pregnant women. US-owned maquiladoras were accused of forcing women applicants to take pregnancy tests, to avoid paying compulsory maternity benefits. Women who became pregnant claimed that they were fired or faced intimidation and mistreatment which forced them to quit. These acts violated Part II of NAALC, which required equal rights for men and women and non-discrimination during pregnancy. The case also involved Mexico's alleged failure to provide effective courts or tribunals to enforce non-discrimination laws.[1] The case was significant, since NAALC provided for a step beyond ministerial consultation in discrimination cases – an Evaluation Committee of Experts to investigate practices in the NAFTA states. While Mexican officials insisted no laws were violated, even some US management representatives felt the case had merit.[2]

Table 5.1   U.S. NAO Submissions 1997–1998

Submission	Issues	Resolution	Follow-Up
US NAO 9701 (GENDER)	Employment Discrimination	Consultations and Implementation Agreement	Conference; outreach sessions; NAALC report; officials meetings
US NAO 9702 (HAN YOUNG)	Association, Right to Organize; health and safety in addendum	Consultations and Joint Declaration	Mexico commitment on secret ballot and transparent contracts; Seminars; health and safety cooperation
US NAO 9703 (ITAPSA)	Association, Right to Organize, Bargain; prevention of illness and injuries	Consultations and Joint Declaration	See US 9702
US NAO 9801 (AERO-MEXICO)	Right to Strike	Not Accepted for review	None
US NAO 9803 (FLORIDA TOMATOES)	Child Labour	Not accepted/ insufficient information	None

Source: North American Commission for Labor Cooperation Website

---

1   US NAO Summary, 'U.S. Submission #9701 – Pregnancy-Based Sex Discrimination' Received May 15, 1997.

2   Tim Shorrock, 'Labor panel to hear pregnancy test case' *Journal of Commerce* Nov. 19, 1997, 3A.

The submission followed a fact-finding mission by Human Rights Watch's Women's Project, which investigated allegations of gender discrimination. Maquiladoras, which produced low-cost manufacturing exports to the US, preferred women workers who were considered less likely to be assertive or support unions. Interviews with women in the maquiladora region found evidence of discrimination, including forced pregnancy testing of applicants, and refusal to hire pregnant women. At least 38 companies allegedly engaged in these practices, in five cities. Women had to give urine samples and answer intrusive personal questions to determine if they were (or were likely to become) pregnant. Women who became pregnant purportedly were mistreated, given heavy work, excess overtime and difficult shifts, and denied the right to sit or rest to make them resign. Those denied jobs could not avail themselves of worker rights, and those forced out often lost rights by resigning. Some labour boards defended pregnancy discrimination as a legitimate business practice, despite anti-discrimination laws. The Women's Project report concluded that 'the Mexican government has done little to acknowledge or remedy violations of women's rights to nondiscrimination and to privacy'[3] because of the economic importance of maquila investments. Women were reluctant to challenge these practices for fear being blacklisted, which might force them into domestic service, with less pay and no benefits.

The submission by Human Rights Watch, the International Labor Rights Fund and Mexico's National Association of Democratic Lawyers was based on the Women's Project report, but emphasized Mexican law enforcement deficiencies, in recognition of the NAO's mandate. The petition outlined Mexico's failure to enforce laws against sex discrimination and the lack of judicial review. It noted how the conciliation and arbitration board in Tijuana defended discrimination, since 'employers may rightfully avoid the costs associated with maternity leave mandated by Mexican law'[4]. The submission claimed Mexico's failure to enforce its laws violated its NAALC commitments to promote worker's rights and to provide fair tribunals, with substantial harm to the women, some of whom were single mothers or primary wage earners. The health of unborn children was jeopardized as women concealed pregnancies, avoided medical care, and did not request shifts away from toxic materials for fear of dismissal.[5] Since domestic laws and treaty obligations required anti-discrimination measures this case was subject to the NAALC.[6] The submission sought hearings in border cities with participation by women workers,

---

3   'No Guarantees: Sex Discrimination in Mexico's Maquiladora Sector', *Human Rights Watch Women's Project* 8, Aug., 1996, 2.

4   Human Rights Watch, ... International Labor Rights Fund and Association of Democratic Lawyers *Submission Concerning Pregnancy-Based Sex Discrimination in Mexico's Maquiladora Sector*, submitted o the US NAO, May 15, 1997, 5.

5   *Submission Concerning Pregnancy-Based Sex Discrimination*, 9.

6   The Mexican Constitution, article 4, and federal labour laws, articles 3, 133(I), 164, 170(I) and several international commitments to which Mexico was a signatory required equal treatment of men and women. *Submission Concerning Pregnancy-Based Sex Discrimination* 13–18.

followed by efforts to encourage Mexico to enforce its laws and end violations of women's rights.

This submission was accepted and the US NAO held a public hearing in Brownsville, Texas. Representatives of Human Rights Watch stressed the vulnerability of these women, often with dependents, who migrated to the border in search of work. With few opportunities outside the maquilas, these women 'do and endure whatever it takes to obtain and keep their jobs'.[7] Women reported miscarriages when denied leave. Illegal 'provisional contracts' for permanent jobs made dismissal for pregnancy appear legitimate. Women did not know of their rights to appeal to the conciliation boards or did not have faith that the boards were impartial. Officials as high as the ministry of labour denied that pregnancy testing was gender discrimination.[8] Officials accused the women of seeking jobs merely to collect maternity benefits, or of misrepresenting their abilities by hiding pregnancies. US firms admitted seeking to avoid maternity benefits, as they had to 'adopt Mexican practices to be competitive'.[9]

In its public report of review, the US NAO singled out pregnancy testing and firings. But it stopped short of condemning pregnancy tests in pre-hiring screening. The NAO relied on Mexican analyses of whether this was illegal, and found conflicting evidence. While the Mexican NAO indicated that pre-hire pregnancy testing was legal, the Mexican Human Rights Commission found it violated constitutional prohibitions on gender discrimination.[10] This confusion prevented the US NAO from making a declaration on pre-hire testing. This disappointed the submitters, who considered any forced pregnancy testing a violation of women's rights.[11] Secretary Herman called pregnancy discrimination a 'serious issue' and the US developed an ambitious agenda for consultations[12]. But she praised Mexico's awareness and attention to this issue.[13]

> The HRW/WP was less impressed and argued that the U.S. position going into these consultations should be unambiguous: pregnancy exams as a condition for employment are a form of illegal sex discrimination, whenever they occur. Every minute wasted

---

7   US Department of Labor, *Public Hearing on Submission No. 9701* Brownsville, TX., Nov. 19, 1997, 8.

8   Rachel Watson, 'Maquiladora discrimination: 'A serious issue" *Ms*, May/Jun 1998, 13.

9   Vivienne Walt, 'A test for NAFTA over pregnancy' *U.S. News and World Report*, Jan 26, 1998, 41; US Department of Labor, *Public Hearing on Submission No. 9701* Brownsville, TX., Nov. 19, 1997, 16.

10   US NAO *Public Report of Review of NAO Submission No. 9701*, Jan. 12, 1998, ii.

11   'U.S. Labor Department Review Finds Sex Bias at Border Plants in Mexico' Campaign for Labor Rights, *Labor Alerts* [cited May 12, 2002]. Available at http://www.summersault.com/~agj/clr/alerts/sex_bias_mexico.html.

12   Bureau of International Labor Affairs, 'ILAB Press Release: Labor Secretary Herman Requests Consultation with Mexican Counterpart on NAFTA Pregnancy Discrimination Complaint' Washington, Jan. 12, 1998.

13   Alexis Herman to Javier Bonilla, Jan. 13, 1998.

discussing the possible legality of a patently illegal practice is a minute lost for women in Mexico facing sex discrimination.[14]

Human Rights Watch suggested that NAALC required countries not just to enforce laws, but to raise standards; the NAO should press US firms in Mexico to 'cease these discriminatory practices'.[15]

After consultations, Secretaries Herman and Bonilla planned meetings of officials to discuss pregnancy discrimination, to review legal redress for women, and to evaluate the enforcement of gender discrimination laws in all 3 countries. The NAOs organized a conference on protection of women workers' rights. A joint ministerial implementation agreement made clear that the focus was on 'pregnancy discrimination in the workplace' and 'relief for post-hire pregnancy discrimination'.[16] Since Mexican law did not cover pre-hire discrimination, the NAOs did not consider it, following the narrow focus on enforcement of laws not expansion of rights. However, the NAO noted that a revised Mexican policy on gender equality did suggest that pre-hire pregnancy tests should be eliminated. Several seminars were organized in border and migrant communities to provide information to women workers on their rights and legal options.

Union and human rights activists hoped this case could test the Evaluation Committee process, which they regarded as an untapped potential in the NAALC, even though ECE's could only issue advisory reports which did not lead to enforcement or trade penalties.[17] However, Mexico wanted to resolve this case without an evaluation committee. At the trinational conference, Mexico announced a new women's bureau in the labour ministry and an educational outreach programme for women in maquiladoras. Mexico agreed that pre-hiring or post-employment pregnancy tests were illegal under international commitments.[18] US subsidiaries announced they would end pregnancy testing. But human rights groups claimed that women were still required to reveal pregnancies, allegedly to allow for workplace health protection. A later report by Human Rights Watch revealed continued gender discrimination in the maquiladoras.[19]

---

14 'U.S. Labor Department Review Finds Sex Bias at Border Plants in Mexico'.

15 Watson, 1998, 13.

16 'US NAO Submission No. 9701: Ministerial Consultations Implementation Agreement' October 21, 1998. These cooperative activities are detailed below in Chapter 10.

17 'U.S. NAO to Probe Forced Pregnancy Testing in Mexico' *Borderlines*, 38, (August, 1997) [cited Nov. 15, 1998]. Available at http://www.zianet.com/irc1/bordline/bl38bb.html.

18 'Mexico Signals Stepped Up Efforts to Resolve Labor Dispute on Gender' *Americas Trade* Mar. 11, 1999, 17.

19 Human Rights Watch *A Job or Your Rights: Continued Sex Discrimination in Mexico's Maquiladora Sector* December 1998 [cited June 12, 2002]. Available at http://www. hrw.org/reports98/women2/Maqui98d.htm.

Han Young Case

U.S. NAO 9702 alleged violations of freedom of association, occupational safety and health, and minimum employment standards at the Han Young plant in Tijuana, which made chassis and trailer platforms for a Korean Hyundai subsidiary. The submission alleged corrupt union elections, firings and intimidation of independent unionists, failure of conciliation boards to enforce the law, and health and safety violations. Han Young workers wanted an independent union, the Metal Workers Union of the Frente Autentico de Trabajo, to replace the official Confederation Revolutionario de Obreros y Campesinos (CROC) which held no meetings but had signed a 'protection contract'. The unionization drive was inspired by low wages, disputed job classifications and bonuses, and the lack of on-site medical care. The union wanted to address serious health and safety violations, which were documented by inspectors but not corrected. The CROC union allegedly had not taken action to force regulators to act on these problems. Han Young allegedly did not fulfill its legal obligations on profit sharing, as amounts paid to workers fell short of the mandated 10% of company earnings.[20]

A wildcat walkout in July, 1997 forced a recognition election, which was marred by alleged fraudulent voting. In October, the independent Metal Workers Union won this vote, even though recent hires sympathetic to the official union participated. The election was conducted in an atmosphere of coercion, in the presence of government officials and outside union observers. Because management produced the CROC contract, the conciliation board ruled that the workers were represented and denied registration to the new union, despite its victory. One American observer suggested the government was 'trying to swindle this election'.[21] A deal was almost brokered in December, but the conciliation board balked, and federal officials pressed for a second election and certification. Despite alleged bribes to workers to vote for a CTM union to replace the CROC, the Metal Workers again won a narrow victory.

After the NAO submission, and second election the federal conciliation tribunal agreed to register STIMAHCS. This followed a 26 day hunger strike by workers, a cross-border protest targeting Hyundai, and a meeting between Presidents Clinton and Zedillo.[22] But local officials refused to grant registration. The company hired official union members to manage personnel, and decide which workers should be hired or fired. Federal officials did get the local board to register the Metal Workers union in 1998. But Han Young blocked plant access for Metal Workers representatives and

---

20   ILRF, SCMW, ANAD, STIMAHCS, *Submission to the United States National Administrative Office (Nao) Regarding Impending Irreparable Harm Against the Right to Freedom of Association, Protection of the Rights to Organize and the Right to Bargain Collectively and Persistent Pattern of Failure to Enforce Labor Law:the Case of Han Young De Mexico, S.a. De C.v. in Tijuana, Mexico* October 28, 1997, 2.

21   Sam Dillon, 'Union Vote in Mexico Illustrates Abuses' *New York Times,* Oct. 13, 1997.

22   'US Seeks High-Level Talks on Labor Issues' *El Financiero International* May 4–10, 1998.

refused to negotiate in defiance of board orders. Local employers suggested that US unions sought to 'destabilize' the maquiladoras.[23] But unionists hoped the federal regime would enforce recognition.[24]

The case was submitted by the Support Committee for Maquiladora Workers (SCMW), the National Association of Democratic Lawyers (ANAD), the International Labor Rights Fund (ILRF), and STIMAHCS . Petitioners claimed that the local conciliation board failed to enforce Mexican law respecting a representation challenge by a new union in a factory where an existing union was in place. They argued that Mexico violated its NAALC commitments by denying Han Young's workers an impartial, open and timely review by an independent Board. Submitters put the company's practices in the spotlight and claimed 'a history of attacks against union activists including firings, surveillance, harassment, offers of money or threats'. But they also alleged tainted local labour enforcement noting 'the CAB's apparent collusion with representatives of the CROC and Han Young management to defy workers' right to organize themselves into a union of their own choosing.'[25] The company hired a personnel manager who allegedly led 'a campaign of harassment, intimidation and attack' against STIMHACS supporters, including suspensions and berating of union organizers for trivial violations. The recognition election violated the Federal Labor Law by giving votes to disenfranchised *trabajadores de confianza* (managers) and workers hired after the vote was called. Submitters claimed a violation of federal laws requiring written notice of reasons for termination, which cannot include union activities.

In February 1998, an addendum was filed alleging occupational health and safety violations at Han Young. The submitters were joined by the Maquiladora Health and Safety Network (MHSN), United Steel Workers, Worksafe California, National Automobile, Aerospace, Transportation and General Workers of Canada, (CAW) and the United Automobile, Aerospace, and Agricultural Implement Workers (UAW). The addendum alleged that despite 11 inspections and numerous health and safety violations, the Mexican government never forced the plant to correct problems. Violations included a lack of safety gear, unsafe equipment and inadequate ventilation. Workers complained of burns, broken bones, respiratory illnesses, and vision and hearing loss. The government failed to levy fines or to impose penalties for non-compliance even though some violations were life-threatening, risking crane accidents and electrocution. The plant lacked the mandatory health and safety committee, and allegedly fired workers who complained about safety. The allegations were documented with inspection reports and experts assessments from UCLA. Despite identifying violations inspectors did not sanction the company,

---

23   Dillon, 1997.

24   Han Young Struggle Nears Victory' *Working Together: Labor Report on the Americas* 28, Jan.–Feb., 1998, 2.

25   *Submission ... Regarding... Han Young De Mexico* October 28, 1997, 2.

increase fines, or close the plant.[26] Inspectors did not return after September, 1997 to verify compliance. Critics condemned the inaction; 'only multiple worker deaths in a catastrophic accident will jolt the Mexican Labor Department into Action'.[27]

This case was the first to raise health and safety concerns, which made it eligible for arbitration, trade sanctions or fines. Mexico could face a penalty up to .007% of its trade with the US, totalling over $50 million.[28] Submitters urged the NAO to proceed through consultations, to ECE, to arbitration; if problems remained unsolved, the US should assess fines sufficient to correct problems plus 'punitive damages to be paid to the victims of governmental and industrial neglect at HYM sufficient to serve as disincentive for further negligence and misadministration (sic) of health and safety laws ...'[29] Submitters regarded this as a defining test: if NAALC 'cannot prevent or correct an abuse as flagrant as the Han Young case, its value in defending the rights of workers is nil.'[30]

Hearings were held in February 1998 in San Diego. The Metal Workers union testified of phoney unions linked to businessmen who paid their leaders to keep workers quiet; plants where real unions formed were closed to avoid bargaining and violence was used to dissuade union supporters.[31] A ban on STIMAHCS' presence on company property undermined the union's position, despite its victory in two votes. Failure to grant the contract to the Metal Workers for lack of local (versus national) registration was a violation of Article 388 of the labour law. Workers were unaware of the CROC union, and did not have access to the contract. Lower pay and verbal abuse were allegedly directed at union activists, who were replaced by outside recruits.[32] When voting occurred, there were physical assaults by rival unionists. Strict ID checks were ordered for Metal Worker supporters only in full view of government officials and outside workers were brought in from Veracruz. Workers testified about the lack of safety equipment, poor hygiene, and dangerous conditions including cranes moving heavy objects above workers' heads, flooding in

---

26   *Amendment to Submission No. 9702: STPS pattern of failure to enforce work place health and safety regulations with Han Young de Mexico, S.A. de C.V.* Jan. 26, 1998, 11.

27   'First Workers' Health and Safety Complaint to Be Heard under NAFTA Labor Side Agreement' *Mexican Labor News and Analysis* 3, 4 February 16, [cited June 11, 1999]. Available at http://www.ueinternational.org/vol3no4.html. 'Network Testimony at Han Young NAO Hearing' *Border/Line Health and Safety* 2, 1 March, 1988, 2.

28   Dean Calbreath 'U.S. Officials Look at Baja Labor Strife' *San Diego Union-Tribune* February 19, 1998 [cited May 13, 2002]. Available at at A-Infos (en) Han Young NAO reporthttp://www.ainfos.ca/98/feb/ainfos00348.html.

29   *Amendment to Submission No. 9702* January 26, 1998, 15.

30   'NAO Case Filed To Stop Illegal Firings At Korean Firm In Mexico' October 31, 1997, [cited Nov. 13, 1998] Available at http://www.laborrights.org/press/nao103197.htm.

31   US Dept. of Labor, US NAO, *Public Hearing on Submission No. 9702* San Diego, Feb. 18, 1998, 9–15.

32   Testimony of Jose Fernando Flores Cruz, *Public Hearing on Submission No. 9702*, 75–76.

electrically-sensitive areas and 'metal fume fever' from poor ventilation. Inspections were brief and workers were usually not allowed to speak to inspectors.[33]

Mary Tong of the Support Committee for Maquiladora Workers testified that the labour board, whose members were selected for pro-management positions and were susceptible to inducements, 'played a direct role in undermining and attacking workers' efforts to organize ... independent unions' in collaboration with management and the official unions.[34] The state's governor purportedly intervened to dismiss the labour board president when he ruled for the Metal Workers. Death threats and other intimidation prevented harassment of unions from becoming public.[35] Garrett Brown of the Maquiladora Health and Safety Support Network testified about the Labor ministry's failure to act on health and safety violations. 'Han Young has been allowed to continue operating a work place which is immediately dangerous to the life and health of workers'.[36] This was a symptom of Mexico's need for hard currency from foreign corporations to pay off its debts under IMF austerity measures.

Han Young representatives argued that the Metal Workers lost majority support of the workers, some of whom supported the October 6th CTM union or the CROC. The company paid profit-sharing and wages above minimum wage. Safety equipment was provided and 90% of the hazards identified by inspectors were fixed.[37] Workers were aware of the CROC, which revised the contract yearly, but became discontented and sought outside representation. The 'company played a passive role' in the inter-union conflict; registration was denied to the Metal Workers because it failed to supply documents.[38] Pressure from outside forced another vote, which the Metal Worker's won, but the company did not receive notification of registration, and could not bargain with the union.

In April 1998, the U.S. NAO Public Report of Review about freedom of association found evidence that the company and local officials colluded to keep the Metal Workers union out. But the NAO focussed only on official, not company, conduct. The NAO asked Secretary of Labor Alexis Herman to seek consultations with her Mexican counterpart, Javier Bonilla concerning freedom of association and law enforcement, and on Mexico's reforms to conciliation boards designed to increase their professionalism and their independence. Garza stressed that the attention to labour reforms at the highest levels of Mexican government showed that NAALC was working. STIMACHS was only the second independent union to gain recognition, though it had trouble getting the company to bargain.[39] State labour board representatives rejected the NAO report, claiming that they had followed the

---

33   Testimony of Miguel Angel Meza Arroyo, *Public Hearing on Submission No. 9702*, 88–89.

34   Testimony of Mary Tong, *Public Hearing on Submission No. 9702*, 48.

35   Testimony of Mary Tong, *Public Hearing on Submission No. 9702*, 51.

36   Testimony of Garrett Brown, *Public Hearing on Submission No. 9702,* 139.

37   Testimony of Pablo Kang, *Public Hearing on Submission No. 9702,* 34–37.

38   Testimony of Ricardo Estrada, *Public Hearing on Submission No. 9702,* 41.

39   'NAFTA' Labor Department Seeks Top-Level Talks with Mexico About Organizing at Han Young' *Daily Labor Report*, April 29, 1998, A-1.

law and the US was trying to 'discredit' them; NAALC was being used to require 'certification for our labor practices from a foreign nation'.[40]

In August the U.S. NAO issued a second Public Report of Review on health and safety, which concluded that Mexico had improved its enforcement with new regulations in 1997. At Han Young, despite repeated inspections, some violations were never rectified.[41] The NAO praised Mexico for levying 'substantial' fines but was uncertain if these were ever collected.[42] The report recommended consultations on health and safety as well.

Consultations were accepted by the Mexicans in October, 1998, though follow-up was slow. Following the ministerial agreement, Mexico's Secretariat of Labor and Social Welfare (STSP) organized a seminar on freedom of association and collective bargaining, in Tijuana, in June, 2000. This case also terminated at ministerial consultations and trinational seminars, even though the health and safety violations could have lead to trade sanctions. For its violations the company was fined $9000 only after the NAO agreed to consider the addendum.[43] The company relocated to a safer facility in 1998.

Despite NAO rulings and consultations, workers at Han Young received few benefits. The company refused to negotiate and was not ordered to do so by the board even after the *amparo* trial was won by the Metal Workers.[44] State officials allegedly worked in legal and covert fashion against the union, including efforts to reverse the *amparo* ruling.[45] This forced the union into lengthy strike action, marked by bitter confrontation including periodic violence.[46] Han Young even attempted to operate illegally with replacement workers (a fact cited by US opponents of FTAA fast-track authority).[47] The strike lasted over 2 years, and was complicated by union infighting, as some workers moved from STIMAHCS to the new October 6 Union;

40 Dean Calbreath, 'U.S. accused of meddling in Mexican labor law' *San Diego Union Tribune* April 29, 1998. [cited May 15, 2002]. Available at http://www2.uniontrib.com/news/uniontrib/wed/business/news_1b29hanyoung.html.

41 U.S. National Administrative Office *Public Report of Review of NAO Submission No. 9702 Part II: Safety and Health Addendum* [cited May 11, 2002]. Available at http://www.dol.gov/dol/ilab/public/media/reports/nao/9702partII.htm.

42 ILAB Press Release: 'National Administrative Office Calls for Ministerial Consultations with Mexico on Safety and Health at Tijuana Plant' August 11, 1998.

43 Jacqueline McFadyen *Nafta Supplemental Agreements:Four Year Review* Working Paper 98-4 Washington, Institute for International Economics, 1998 [cited May 11, 2002]. Available at http://www.iie.com/catalog/wp/1998/98-4.htm.

44 Carlos Roberto Gil Villa, 'Fallo a Favor de Trabajadores: Fin al Añejo Conflicto de la Han Young' *La Voz de La Frontera* April 20, 1999, 13–A.

45 Javier Moctezuma Barragan, STPS, to Andrew Samet US Dept. of Labor, July 26, 1999.

46 Sandra Dribble, 'Call for strike brings on brawl over union at Tijuana factory' *San Diego Union-Tribune* May 23, 1998, [cited Nov. 26, 1998]. Available at http://www2.uniontrib.com/news/uniontrib/sat/business/news_1b23hanyoung.html.

47 David Bacon, 'Tense Chapter in Mexico Union Fight' *San Francisco Chronicle* June 2, 1998, A10.

despite its victory in May 1998, the labour board stalled in recognizing the October 6 union. Despite three court orders overturning board findings that the strike was illegal and 'non-existent', workers were subject to police harassment, and the company refused to bargain, hiring non-union replacements workers from away.[48] Hence the appearance of success in organizing an independent union, as at Maxi-Switch, proved illusory.

More ominously, this case demonstrated the dangers of pressing for union democracy in Mexico. During the strike, workers claimed assaults by managers.[49] Subsequent votes were allegedly stacked with replacement employees and union leaders faced arrest in contravention of court orders. At a trinational seminar, Metal Workers unionists who attempted to speak claimed they were roughed up by rival CROC workers in full view of US NAO representatives. This incident prompted one activist to suggest NAALC was moving from 'useless to dangerous' for Mexican workers.[50] While the strike was interminable, headway was made on health and safety in January, 2002, when the company was forced to post a $2 million bond, to be forfeited if improvements in health and safety did not occur.[51] This case was highlighted in Congress by David Bonior as a symbol of the need to resist 'fast-track' authority for FTAA. Bonior exerted pressure on Clinton to raise Han Young with President Zedillo to encourage Mexico to enforce its laws.[52]

Echlin-ITAPSA

The Echlin-ITAPSA case, (U.S. NAO 9703) involved alleged violation of Mexican laws on freedom of association, right to organize and bargain, and prevention of occupational injuries and illnesses. This submission was filed by the International Brotherhood of Teamsters (IBT), United Electrical, Radio and Machine Workers of America (UE), Canadian Auto Workers (CAW), Union of Needletrades, Industrial and Textile Employees (UNITE), United Paperworkers International Union (UPIU), United Steelworkers of America (USWA) and the Steelworkers' Canadian National Office. These unions formed the Echlin Workers Alliance which challenged the multinational firm Echlin through actions in all 3 NAFTA states, over alleged abuses at its autoparts plant outside Mexico City.

---

48   Can NAFTA Protect Han Young Workers? *Solidarity* May, 1998, [cited Nov. 13, 1998]. Available at http://www.uaw.org/solidarity/magazines.html.

49   David Bacon 'Border Bosses Go All Out to Stop Strike at Han Young' May 30, 1998. [cited Nov. 21, 1998]. Available at http://www.igc.org/dbacon/Mexico/04HanYng.htm.

50   'NAFTA Labor Side Deal: From Useless to Dangerous' *Working Together: Labor Report on the Americas* 39 Fall, 2000, 1.

51   Diane Lindquist 'Hyundai plant told to mend its ways' *San Diego Union-Tribune*, Jan.19, 2002, [cited May 11, 2002]. Available at http://www.signonsandiego.com/news/mexico/20020119-9999_1b19hyundai.html.

52   David Bonior et. al. to President William Jefferson Clinton, Jan. 28, 1999.

The company was accused of using thugs (helped by CTM unions) to prevent workers from voting to affiliate with the independent Metal Workers Union of the FAT. The CTM union purportedly signed a 'protection contract' which did not address health, safety and wages. As the union election neared, up to 52 union leaders were dismissed and their families were threatened. A vote was held on September 9th during which employees allegedly were trapped in the plant by armed persons. The CTM union won over the Metal Workers in an open voice-vote with the suspected perpetrators of violence still present.[53] Some fired workers accepted severance; others were reinstated on government order, but later dismissed at the CTM's urging, according to the Metal Workers Union.

Although unions despaired that this case revealed the weakness of the NAALC in preventing company and government coercion, they filed a submission arguing that Mexican authorities had not enforced laws protecting workers from dismissals, harassment or intimidation. The low-paid workers were aware of the CTM local but did not have access to the contract. The Metal Workers Union began to organize in response to complaints about unhealthy, unsafe conditions, notably asbestos contamination which produced illnesses and deaths.[54] Petitioners noted that 'when they would tell the [CTM] union representative at ITAPSA of problems such as abuse by supervisors he would just tell them that they should be thankful that they have jobs at all and that they shouldn't be complaining.' [55] When the Metal Workers petitioned the conciliation board to hold an election, the company and the CTM allegedly responded with intimidation and threats against union leaders and families.

The Board delayed the August union vote at the CTM's request without informing the Metal Workers union. Echlin's regional manager allegedly warned workers of serious consequences if they did not vote for CTM. 170 armed *golpeadores* (thugs) allegedly blocked STIMAHCS supporters from entering the plant to vote. Officials permitted persons to vote who may not have been workers. Despite observing these abuses, Board officers certified the results. In the submitters' view, 'labor authorities are responsible for this unfair election because it was they who conducted the verbal election while doing nothing to shield voters from intimidation. And, the labor authorities certified the vote notwithstanding the fact that they knew it was coerced'.[56] The board did order workers reinstated if they had not accepted severance, but the company stalled, and allegedly responded with a 'reign of terror'.[57] Petitioners

---

53   'Echlin Agrees to Probe Of Mexican Election' *UE News* , January 1998 [cited Nov. 11, 1998]. Available at http://www.ranknfile-ue.org/uenews.html.

54   CAW, IBT, UAW, UNITE, UE, UPIU, USWA et. al,, *U.S. NAO Public Submission 9703, Public Communication on Labor Law Matters Arising in Mexico: Election Contest Between Government and Independent Unions Before the US NAO...* http://www.dol.gov/dol/ilab/public/media/reports/nao/Sub9703.htm.

55   *U.S. NAO Public Submission 9703.*

56   *U.S. NAO Public Submission 9703.*

57   'Workers' Groups in Three NAFTA Countries Bring New Charges Against U.S. Firm for Beatings at Mexican Plant' *Echlin Workers Alliance News*, Feb. 35, 1998.

wanted Mexico to enforce rights to organize, including secret ballot elections and to protect unionists from firings and violence. Bolstered by a study of human rights violations in Mexican labour relations,[58] they proposed a public registry of unions and contracts, and job protection for workers who voted against a majority union.[59]

Health and safety problems, outlined in an amended complaint, made this case eligible for ECEs and sanctions. The petitioners alleged that the government failed to enforce its Reglamento Federal de Seguridad, Higiene y Ambiente del Trabajo (Federal Regulation on Workplace Safety, Health and Environment – RFSHS). These regulations specified limits for exposure to harmful substances standards for safety equipment, workplace health and safety committees, workplace training, and machine maintenance. Worker affidavits indicated numerous violations. Dust in the plant allegedly contained asbestos, and workers were exposed to dangerous solvents and chemicals. Machines lacked safety devices, and some workers lost fingers in the machinery. Loss of hearing and vision were reported.

Petitioners claimed the company did not provide training, warning signs and labels, safety information or protective gear and supplies. Workers who sought safety equipment faced dismissal as troublemakers. Submitters called for consultations, followed by ECE, arbitration and sanctions to compel Mexico to enforce its regulations.[60] The submission was backed by a Mexican workplace safety expert who noted the lack of ventilation near asbestos-handling machines, contaminated non-disposable uniforms, inadequate cotton masks, and insufficient controls for contaminated air.[61]

In response to adverse publicity, Echlin's US parent company promised to consult with workers over the flawed elections and to consider a union-drafted code of conduct. Unions credited this quick response to the trinational alliance, which had staged demonstrations at the company's Connecticut headquarters and at plants in California and Indiana. Unionists made presentations at the company's shareholder meeting, though their resolutions were defeated.[62] Teamsters leaders argued that 'cooperation among workers in the three NAFTA countries is putting a new level of pressure on companies that violate workers' rights in North America... NAFTA's weak labor side agreement has left us no choice but to get in the face of

---

58   Centro de Reflexión y Acción Laboral de Fomento Cultural y Educativo, A.C., *Derechos Humanos Laborales en México: entre la imagen protectora y una política de represión, Informe de violación de los Derechos Humanos Laborales en México, durante 1997*, (Mexico, March, 1998).

59   *U.S. NAO Public Submission 9703*.

60   *U.S. NAO Public Submission 9703*.

61   Affidavit of Rafael Moure-Eraso, Ph.D., CIH, Jan. 13, 1999.

62   'After 4 Years of NAFTA, Labor Is Forging Cross-Border Ties' *New York Times*, Dec. 20, 1997, A1; 'Union Group's Resolutions Lose in Echlin Inc. Voting' *Wall Street Journal*, Feb 4, 1988, 1.

the companies responsible for this kind of abuse.'[63] But the meeting to draft a 'code of conduct' never materialized.[64]

The US NAO accepted the communication in January, 1998. At the hearing, the Echlin Worker's Alliance cited a letter from the company vowing to resist unionization. The Alliance described election intimidation and violence, inaction by the labour authorities, and biases in the registration process. Workers outlined how they were fired for union activities, while labour experts clarified how the government violated domestic laws and international commitments. Another panel outlined health and safety problems, including a failure to convene a health and safety committee. A toxicologist reported careless use of asbestos with no warnings or safety supplies; workers 'often paid with their life and their health for the irresponsibility of the authorities and officers of the Mexican state ... and the transnational company'.[65] The trinational alliance celebrated the first collaboration of union centrals against a MNC with a rally outside the meeting.[66]

In its Public Report of Review, the US NAO concluded that workers had been subjected to retaliation for union activities by the company, including threats and firings. The union election was disrupted by fear and intimidation. The Report rejected the Mexican NAO's argument that secret ballots were required only when both contending unions agreed. The NAO concluded that the Itapsa plant 'may suffer serious health and safety deficiencies that are hazardous to its employees.'[67] It recommended that Secretary Herman seek consultations with Bonilla on associational rights and health and safety. This request was made in August, 1998 but the case took more than 2 years to resolve. Echlin conceded that it allowed 40 CTM 'associates' into the plant, but denied that they had weapons,[68] Echlin insisted that it 'acted responsibly and ethically before, during and after the Sept. 9 election', and followed 'applicable Mexican laws'. But the US NAO declared the workers' accounts were 'well documented' and 'credible'.[69]

Petitioners declared the decision 'an indictment of Echlin, the Mexican government and the largest of the official unions in Mexico,' and as 'a victory for workers in

---

63   'Echlin Agrees to Probe Of Mexican Election' *UE News*, January 1998.

64   'Action Signals New Era of Labor Cooperation Across Borders: AFL-CIO and National Labor Federations in Canada and Mexico Join Alliance NAFTA Complaint Against U.S. Firm' Teamsters' Press Release, March 18, 1998.

65   Public Hearing on NAO Submission 9703, Before the US NAO.... March 23, 1998, 195.

66   'Testimony Targets Echlin's Abuse of Workers Rights' *UE News*, May 21, 1998 [cited March 22, 2002]. Available at http://www.ranknfile-ue.org/uen_intl04.html.

67   US NAO, *Public Report of Review, NAO Submission 9703* [cited November 10, 2003]. Available at http://www.dol.gov/ILAB/media/reports/nao/9703repo.htm.

68   'After 4 Years of NAFTA, Labor Is Forging Cross-Border Ties' *New York Times*, Dec. 20, 1997, A1.

69   'Abuses Reported in Mexico at American-Owned Plant' *New York Times* Aug. 5, 1998.

all three NAFTA countries.'[70] A steel workers' union representative hoped 'the publicity and the peer pressure' would change company practices.[71] Submitters were disappointed that the NAO had not demanded a secret ballot and safe election venue. They rejected the finding that health and safety inspections were 'comprehensive' given the failure to enforce improvements.[72] But the NAO could not ensure that the tainted election was rerun, or that dismissed workers were rehired. The Teamsters argued, 'the fact that the government can't enforce any remedies against Echlin is an example of what's wrong with free trade agreements like NAFTA'.[73]

An action plan for consultations was agreed to in May, 2000. It covered the same issues as Han Young, including studies on freedom of organization and registration, impartial labour boards, and transparent contacts. The countries agreed to 'exchange information on techniques and policies to promote compliance with safety and health laws and regulations'.[74] The plan called for information sharing on health and safety inspections using the Internet. The company was sold to Dana Corporation, but harassment of workers in Mexico allegedly continued. A US plant of Echlin in Irvine, California, was closed in what workers believed was retaliation for cross-border organizing, though the company blamed overcapacity.[75] Although consultations produced an agreement to require secret ballot elections, the new Fox regime backed away from this commitment.[76]

Abortive Cases: AeroMéxico and the Florida Tomato Exchange

A case at AeroMéxico (US NAO 9801) was brought by the Association of Flights Attendants, AFL-CIO (AFA) after the Mexican government invoked *la requisa*, an executive order to return to work. This allowed it to take over the carrier temporarily to continue an essential service and prevent a strike by flight attendants in the Asociacion Sindical de Sobrecargos de Aviacion (Flight Attendants Union or ASSA) a FESEBES affiliate. This action was taken even though the airline had

---

70   UE, Teamsters Press Release, 'U.S. NAFTA Panel Cites U.S. Firm for Violence Against Workers in Mexico' August 3, 1998, [cited Oct. 25, 1998] Available at http://laboris. uqam.ca/anact/Echlinpress.htm.

71   Courtney Tower, 'US labor secretary calls for talks with Mexico over workers rights' *Journal of Commerce* Aug. 6, 1998.

72   Robin Alexander, UE, to Irasema Garza, Aug. 12, 1998.

73   Echlin Worker Alliance Press Release, 'U.S. NAFTA Panel Cites U.S. Firm for Violence Against Workers in Mexico' August 3, 1998.

74   Joint Declaration, Ministerial Consultations Public Submissions US 9702 and US 9703, North American Agreement on Labor Cooperation , May 18, 2000.

75   David Bacon 'A Plant Closes in Revenge for Cross-Border Organizing' Nov. 30, 1998, [Cited on March 15, 2002]. Available at http://www.igc.org/dbacon/Mexico/01PClose. htm.

76   David Bacon 'Border Labor War Defies Mexico's Fox Administration' Oct. 21, 2001. [Cited on May 12, 2002] Available at http://www.maquilasolidarity.org/resources/maquilas/ bacon2001.htm.

been privatized by President Salinas. Forced back to work after two hours, flight attendants protested using black arm bands and draping at check-in counters. The Flight Attendants Union pledged to fight in international forums, since this violated NAALC commitments on freedom of association and right to strike, using laws which were a 'relic from the past'. [77] The case symbolized the rise of new unionists in the UNT, the role of women workers and the costs of privatization. In the 1980s, the government laid off the entire workforce, claiming bankruptcy, to prepare for privatization. The private company had prospered and its employees sought to share in this success.[78]

Negotiations began in March, 1998, over wages, crew size, overtime, night pay and pensions. The pay issue was deadlocked, provoking *la requesa,* an emergency measure for telecommunications, but applicable to airlines since 1995. The National Association of Democratic Lawyers, women's groups and even the PRI-linked Federation of State Workers supported the flight attendants. American and Canadian flight attendants also supported the strike. The strike was settled after five days, but the contract benefited management, with increased flying hours, decreased rest-periods and longer work days; the union secured a modest pay raise, overtime and pensions. Symbolically, a new union had succeeded but with a foreboding of the strength of management after privatization.[79]

The AFA submitted the case to the US NAO in August, 1998 after the strike ended. The submission argued that the use of *la requesa* was an abuse of government power to force the flight attendants back to work. Section XVII of the constitution established a right to strike, and federal labour laws reaffirmed this 'without exception'[80] Although the contract had expired and the Flight Attendants Union gave due notice, the President overrode this right. The government takeover of the airline required a resumption of work, and permitted replacement workers, terminating the strike. Despite its legal basis, this emergency power undermined Mexico's commitment to NAALC, using 'secondary laws' to override basic principles such as the right to strike and the ban on replacement workers. The petitioners sought hearings, consultations, an ECE and a public forum to promote respect for the right to strike.[81]

The Mexican labour department asked the US NAO to reject this case, which involved a sovereign decision to maintain essential services. Flight attendants voluntarily returned to work but were free to continue the strike. NAALC did not

---

77   Diego Cevallos 'Blocking of Strike Violates Rights, Critics Say' *Inter Press Service* June 2, 1998, 1.

78   Dan La Botz 'Flight Attendants Strike at Aeromexico: Symbolic Victory' *Mexican Labor News and Analysis* 3, 12, June 16, 1998, [cited April 20, 2002] Available at http://www. ueinternational.org/vol3no12.html.

79   Dan La Botz 'Flight Attendants Strike at Aeromexico: Symbolic Victory'.

80   AFA, *Public Communication on Labor Law Matters Arising in Mexico: Strike by ASSA – Mexico Vs Aerovias de Mexico, S.A. de C.V.....* Before the US NAO, Aug. 17, 1998, 4.

81   AFA, *Public Communication on Labor Law Matters Arising in Mexico,* 17.

create new standards for labour, and to apply it in this case would raise expectations about the scope of the accord.[82] This case was rejected by the US NAO, which accepted the Mexican government's argument about economic security. Zedillo's requisitioning of the airline was consistent with the Constitution, with Civilian Aviation Law and the Law of General Routes of Communication, which allowed actions to promote the 'economic security of the State.'[83] In addition, the strike was settled in accordance with labour laws. But the NAO 'agreed to undertake a research project to evaluate how the three NAALC countries reconcile the issue of the right to strike with national interests of safety, security, and general welfare'.[84]

The Association of Flight Attendants challenged the decision, which they believed protected an abusive government. The dispute was settled only after the strike threat was eliminated; while the President's action was constitutional, it undermined labour laws, and hampered independent labour organizing. The US NAO replied that despite the seriousness of the complaint, the objectives of the NAALC would not be furthered by reviewing an executive action taken under Mexican laws. The NAO intended to consult an independent expert on how strike rights are reconciled with national interests such as essential services.[85] The petitioners insisted that the NAO review had not been inadequate and pledged to continue their efforts through Congress. This independent union proved its durability, when a 2001 strike produced a new contract in just 2 days.

The Florida Tomato Exchange case (U.S. NAO 9802), involved alleged use of illegal child labour on vegetable farms. It was never pursued by the claimants, despite its novel content which could have led to trade sanctions. This submission involved a claim that Mexico was dumping tomatoes to the detriment of Florida producers.[86] The Florida Tomato Exchange, a non-profit, growers' association, saw its numbers dwindle after NAFTA, as Mexican imports violated agreed market shares for winter vegetables. A 71% increase in imports of Mexican tomatoes cost Florida producers $750 million and led to 10,000 job losses.[87] After seeking legislative protection[88], Florida tomato growers sought a trade ruling certifying Mexican dumping; although

82   Claudia Franco Hijuelos to Andrew James Samet, Sept. 3., 1998.

83   Irasema Garza to Patricia Friend, Oct. 19, 1998.

84   US NAO, 'Status of Submissions: Updated March 8, 2002 [Cited April 23, 2002]. Available at http://www.dol.gov/dol/ilab/public/programs/nao/status.htm#iia9.

85   Irasema Garza to Patricia Friend, Dec. 21, 1998. See also correspondence from the submitters in the US NAO files.

86   Sandra Sanchez, 'U.S. vegetable growers feeling dumped on' *USA Today* Mar 23, 1995, A4.

87   'Deals for NAFTA Votes: Trick, No Treat' Public Citizen, Global Trade Watch, Oct. 1997, [Cited March 28, 2002]. Available at http://www.citizen.org/cmep/foodsafety/food_irradiation/articles.cfm?ID=1802.

88   'Bill seeks to protect U.S. tomato farmers from Mexican imports' *Wall Street Journal* Jan 26, 1996, A4.

they won preliminary rulings, they did not get a dumping determination,[89] though Mexico agreed to a voluntary price floor.[90] Experts argued that improved product, low wages, and peso devaluation, had given Mexican producers the edge, not illegal dumping.[91]

The Exchange obtained video evidence of children working on farms and contacted the Labour and Agriculture Secretaries to request investigations. These requests noted that child labour probes were underway in American states and that Mexico also needed scrutiny, or its producers could secure an unfair trade advantage. Eventually, the Exchange received a response from the Employment Standards Division of the Department of Labour, outlining the ILAB activities on child labour and suggesting the NAALC process.[92] Shortly thereafter, the Exchange made an NAO submission. But almost immediately, the Exchange requested that 'the communication be held in abeyance pending additional information and a decision on how to proceed'[93] The NAO closed its file on 9802 because of the lack of additional information.[94] Thus the innovative and important issue of child labour did not receive a formal NAALC hearing. But the Labor Department had considered this issue and a trinational seminar was held before this case.[95]

Conclusions: Broadening Regional Coalitions

These cases tested the limits of the NAALC by raising issues that could lead to stronger measures than consultations, including ECEs, arbitration and trade penalties. However, the results were similar to earlier cases. Ministerial consultations in the gender case lead to trinational discussions on pregnancy discrimination and seminars to disseminate information on the rights and protections available to female workers. These made some contribution, particularly in educating female workers about their rights, helping to minimize further gender-based discrimination. The other cases prompted research and exchanges of information on health and safety and collective bargaining. But the high profile evaluation committee process was still not invoked.

---

89 'Florida's tomato growers lose case against Mexicans' *Wall Street Journal*, Jul 3, 1996; pg. A2; Florida tomato growers win round in trade case; *Wall Street Journal*, May 17, 1996 A16.

90 Robert S. Greenberger, 'Mexico agrees to temporary floor on price of tomatoes sold in U.S.' *Wall Street Journal*, Oct 14, 1996 B3.

91 David Poppe, 'Tomato pasting: Florida tomato farmers say dumping by Mexico threatens to destroy them' *Florida Trend* 38, 1 Aug 1, 1995, 24.

92 Corlis L. Sellers to Wayne Hawkins, Sept. 22, 1998.

93 Irasema Garza to John Ritchie, Oct. 21, 1998.

94 Irasema Garza to Wayne Hawkins, Oct. 4, 1999.

95 United States-Canada-Mexico Tripartite Conference, U.S. National Administrative Office, U.S. Department of Labor, *Improving Children's Lives: Child and Youth Labor in North America,* 1997.

The roster of submitters in these cases illustrated the effect of the NAALC in generating or cementing cross-border coalitions of unions and sympathetic rights activists. Engagement by Human Rights Watch, Support Committee for Maquiladora Workers, Maquiladora Health and Safety Network, Worksafe California and others illustrated an increase in binational, cross-border activism, encouraged by the collaborations required in NAALC submissions. The proliferation of union participants from all three nations, including the multi-national Echlin Workers Alliance, also illustrated NAALC's potential to stimulate transborder efforts. Meanwhile, the continued activism by of Mexico's National Association of Democratic Lawyers, the Frente Autentico de Trabajo, FESEBES in utilities, and other independent union centrals indicated the deepening of supportive social constituencies in that country, encouraged in part by the institutional openings created by the NAALC. Finally the Echlin case illustrated the emergence of new cross-border activism, with protests targeted at the same firm in two or more NAFTA partners.

NAALC provided the potential to expose problems in Mexican plants and in law enforcement. It created a venue for independent unions to express their concerns and press for change. American worker advocates felt that the use of NAALC processes to draw attention to the conditions in Mexican industries could 'bring tremendous leverage'.[96] Despite the potential for sanctions in the health and safety cases, action was terminated at ministerial consultations. The MHSSN noted that 'no significant changes have occurred in the functioning of health and safety inspectors in the maquiladoras, or in the U.S. workplaces where complaints have been filed, as a result of the NAFTA complaint process'.[97] Hence, the limits of America's political will to seek higher levels of enforcement was evident even before the change to the Bush administration. Government participants defended the process. The US NAO argued that the gender case clarified Mexico's laws, inspired a Mexican office on gender issues and extended education programmes on discrimination and harassment.[98]

But many assessments of the NAALC from non-labour sources became sour. Business leaders argued that NAALC cases had 'unduly emphasized enforcement over cooperative activities' and set 'the wrong tone and focus'. Business preferred 'cross-border technical assistance' suggesting 'acceptance of public submissions ... should be an exceptional act'.[99] Commentaries in the *New York Times* noted the NAALC's lack of teeth. 'the cause of free trade is not helped when NAFTA's labor guarantees are squashed so blatantly'.[100] Such weaknesses induced Democrats and labour lobbyists to oppose fast-track legislation for a hemispheric trade deal; critics believed that labour and the environment should be brought into the core of

---

96   Dillon, 1997.

97   Maquiladora Health & Safety Support Network *Newsletter* V, 3 September 17, 2001 [cited April 11, 2002] Available at http://www.igc.org/mhssn/news16.htm.

98   Victoria Roberts, 'Side Agreement May Target Employers, But International Dialogues Seen as Valuable' *Daily Labor Report* 31, Feb. 15, 2000, B-2.

99   'Labor, Business Say Labor Side Accord Misses the Mark; Suggest Changes' *Daily Labor Report* 27, Feb. 10, 1998, CC-2.

100   'Mexico's Vulnerable Workers' *New York Times* Dec. 6, 1997.

trade agreements, to make them enforceable.[101] Supporters of the accord argued it was the best which could be expected under the circumstances and had produced unprecedented study of Mexican laws by allowing for public review and discussion. But the limited results may have caused a decrease in submissions in later years, despite the increased strength of regional activist networks. The next chapter will examine later cases heard by the US NAO more recently, to discern why use declined and if these cases further extended NAALC's effectiveness.

---

101 'Mexico's Vulnerable Workers' *New York Times* Dec. 6, 1997.

Chapter 6

Institutional Limits? Recent US Cases

Introduction: Diminishing Returns?

The pace of cases slowed after 1997, with only 6 cases submitted to the US NAO by 2003. The first cases involving Canada dealt with the adequacy of laws, not lax enforcement. Another case dealt with a US complaint against a Canadian subsidiary in Mexico. But the core issues at stake remained the same, and the resolution of the cases still peaked at ministerial consultations, with no movement towards an evaluation committee or arbitration and trade penalties. Activity was slowed by transition in the NAALC secretariat and in the NAOs which disrupted continuity of this bureaucratic community. Transborder regional unions and social movements diversified and retained energy; disillusioned with previous decisions, they did not see NAALC as a useful venue for promoting labour rights.

Elections in Mexico and the United States in 2000 brought governments not known for sympathy towards unions. Hence, the prospects for enforcing NAALC principles vigorously possibly decreased, discouraging some unions and rights groups from using the mechanism. But the NAALC has not as yet been abandoned. Activity has resumed with several new cases submitted after 2004, too recently to be thoroughly assessed here, though raising challenging issues. These cases indicate that some groups may still try to use NAALC strategically in future, though the potential for success remains uncertain.

St. Hubert McDonald's

The 1998 St. Hubert McDonald's case involved an attempt by Teamsters Local 973 to organize workers in St-Hubert, Québec, into the first unionized McDonald's restaurant in North America.[1] Union bids failed in Ontario and Quebec in 1993 and 1994, and there were no unionized US outlets at the time. Workers alleged their hours were cut if they supported unions.[2] Despite past problems, the Teamsters were optimistic and planned union drives at a dozen other restaurants around Montreal. 51 of 62 workers signed union cards; these were older, established workers than at other franchises, giving hope for continuity of membership. Issues included low

---

1   Big Mac et Union s'il vous Plait' *AFL-CIO Work in Progress* March 17, 1997 [cited April 11, 2002]. Available at http://www.aflcio.org/publ/wip1997/wip0317.htm.

2   Konrad Yakabuski, 'Teamsters Taking Another Run at a Mcdonald's Outlet' *Globe and Mail Report on Business* March 6, 1997.

wages and lack of overtime pay. The certification request was submitted to the Québec Labour Commissioner who could grant the certification or request a ballot of the workers.[3] Dissident workers met the Labour Commissioner to object to the Teamsters' petition. They filed subpoenas against union officials, and challenges to the Labour Commissioner's authority. The Québec Court of Appeal dismissed these challenges as lacking quality and constituting 'harassment' and 'obstruction'.[4]

As the certification date approached, the owners closed the location, citing losses.[5] Workers were laid off with only 24 hours notice, contrary to laws, but were given severance pay.[6] The owners argued the location was poor, with a low volume and declining traffic. The Labour ministry accepted the owners explanation, but union leaders suggested it was retaliation for organizing. Claude Godbout of the FTTQ asked the labour minister to investigate: 'When they saw that it was a possibility for us to get the certification in March, they decided to close.'[7] The union asked to see the franchise's accounts to verify the financial basis for closure. The union promised money from its solidarity fund to reopen if the restaurant unionized, but threatened to lead a boycott if the union was blocked.[8]

The submission by the International Brotherhood of Teamsters, Teamsters Canada, Teamsters Local 973, Québec Federation of Labour (QFL) and the International Labor Rights Fund (ILRF) dealt with the lack of legal protection against plant closure to avoid unionization, and with 'unwarranted delays in the certification process'. [9] Québec law did not provide recourse for unions facing closures 'motivated by anti-union animus'. 'Procedural laxity' in Quebec's 'requirement that a formal hearing be held by the Labour Commissioner-General (the certification agent for the ministry) whenever the employer disagrees with the proposed bargaining unit' allowed management to stall indefinitely.[10] Les Entreprises JMC, owner of 6 franchises, claimed that its workers were interspersed and transferred among locations, requiring them all to be in the bargaining unit. The certification agent rejected these assertions,

---

3   Yakabuski, March 6, 1997.

4   'Opinion du Juge Vallerand' Sylvain Dery et. al. v. André Bussière , Teamsters Local 973 et. al.' Oct. 28, 1997.

5   'Unionizing the impossible', *Canadian Dimension*, 32, 5 Sept-Oct 1998, 24.

6   Patrick Borden 'McUnion Busting, McClosure in Quebec' Montreal, 14 Feb 1998. [cited April 11, 2002]. Available at http://www.mcspotlight.org/media/press/toronto_13feb98. html.

7   'Union fight continues despite McDonald's closure' *Toronto Sun* February 13 1998.

8   'Union wants to see McDonald's books' *Canadian News Digest* Tuesday, Feb. 17, 1998.

9   The International Brotherhood of Teamsters, Teamsters Canada, Teamsters ... Local 973, Quebec Federation of Labour and International Labor Rights Fund *Public Communication on Labor Law Matters Arising in Canada (Québec)Before the National Administrative Office of the United States Under the North American Agreement on Labor Cooperation (NAALC)Violations of NAALC Labor Principles and Obligations in the Case of The St-Hubert Mcdonald's Restaurant* Oct., 1999, 1.

10   *Public Communication on ... The St-Hubert Mcdonald's Restaurant* Oct., 1999, 2.

but the Labour Commissioner was obliged to hold hearings; nine days of testimony were held over eleven months before certification was granted in February 1998.

The submitters suggested Québec laws allowing plant closures with impunity violated the side agreement's obligation to 'maintain high labor standards' and threatened freedom of association.[11] The lack of recourse for laid-off workers was a violation of NAALC Article 4 (2). Delays in certification violated NAALC obligations to provide appeal procedures which are conducted without 'unreasonable charges and time limits'.[12] Québec's labour code was based on bargaining in a single facility. It had not been modernized to address multiple franchise locations, which were typical of the service sector. 'Atypical' part-time and contract work made the laws inadequate, resulting in declining union membership in services. Difficulties in defining bargaining units could be used by employers to bar unions. The submitters suggested cooperative investigations to find new rules allowing 'multiple-employer bargaining units and establishing a system of certification by sector'.[13]

The Conseil du Patronat de Quebec (a business central) called the submission 'inadmissible' as it did not concern poor enforcement. The owner closed for financial reasons, not to avoid certification and delays were unavoidable. Article 23 of NAALC required a company to export part of its output before NAALC could apply. McDonalds's served a local market and was exempt. If the NAO accepted this case, the Conseil feared more unjustified cases would follow.[14] The Alliance of Manufacturers and Exporters of Québec suggested submitters should have used Québec laws if they believed 'closure of the St-Hubert restaurant constituted intimidation or a threat to employees …'.[15] Submitters wanted to bypass arbitration under the Labour Code and bring an unfair labour complaint to the NAO. Québec law permitting closures was valid and should not be subject to challenge, since NAALC respected sovereignty. 'Submitter's perceived inadequacy of Québec labour law is beyond the jurisdiction of the U. S. NAO'[16]

The Teamsters responded that while the NAO could not seek legal changes, submissions and reviews could promote higher standards. Québec had enforced its laws, but anti-union plant closures and delays in certification undermined the right to organize. The submission envisioned a better certification process, following NAALC exhortations to improve labour principles. There were 'no remedies' for dismissed workers and no possibility for an unfair labour practice charge in light of legal precedent. Previous NAO cases dealt with legal substance, not merely

---

11   *Public Communication on … The St-Hubert Mcdonald's Restaurant* Oct., 1999, 10.

12   *Public Communication on … The St-Hubert Mcdonald's Restaurant* Oct., 1999, 12.

13   *Public Communication on … The St-Hubert Mcdonald's Restaurant* Oct., 1999, 13.

14   Quebec Employers' Council, 'The present is to state some preliminary objections to the petition the Teamsters filed with the American NAO …' January, 1999. Attached to Ghislain Dufour to Irasema Garza, Jan. 15, 1999.

15   Alliance of Manufacturers and Exporters of Québec, 'In the Matter of Public Communication U.S. NAO – 9803' Before the NAO of the US Under the NAALC', Jan. 20, 1999, 5.

16   Alliance of Manufacturers and Exporters of Québec, Jan 20, 1999, 10, 12.

Table 6.1   U.S. NAO Submissions, 1998-

Submission	Issues	Resolution	Follow-Up
US NAO 9803 (ST. HUBERT MCDONALD'S)	Association, Right to Organize, Bargain	Accepted for review; withdrawn	Quebec and US officials met with union, workers
US NAO 9804 (RURAL MAIL CARRIERS)	Right to Organize; OSH; compensation for illness and injury; discrimination	Not accepted for review	None
US NAO 9901 (TAESA)	Right to Organize; prevention of illness and injury; minimum standards	Consultations and Joint Declaration	Bilateral OSH working group, seminar, information exchanges
US NAO 2001-01 (CUSTOM TRIM AUTO TRIM)	Prevention and compensation of illness and injury;	Consultations and Joint Declaration	Bilateral OSH working group
US NAO 2001-02 (DURO BAG)	Association, Right to Organize,	Not Accepted for Review	None
US NAO 2003-01 (PUEBLA)	Right to Organize, prevention of illness and injury; minimum standards	Accepted for review Ministerial Consultations	Consultations Pending
US NAO 2004-01 (YUCATAN)	Minimum standards; OSH	Withdrawn for investigation	
US NAO 2005-01 (ABASCAL)	Reform Law weakens right to Organize, bargain	Not Accepted for review	
US NAO 2005-02 (PILOTS)	Right to Organize,	Pending	
US NAO 2005-03 (HIDALGO)	All NAALC principles	Pending	

Source: North American Commission for Labor Cooperation Website

enforcement and resulted in 'extremely valuable exchanges of information'.[17] The Canadian Association of Labour Lawyers noted that NAALC could apply to any lax standards which involved 'a pattern of misconduct'.[18]

US Labor Department solicitors advised that the case be accepted as the first Canadian case and because of the important issues. But the NAO could not find Québec in violation of NAALC because the submission made no claim of lax enforcement but rather the submitters' desire that 'Quebec law, including case law, should become more friendly to unions regarding representation and plant closing'.[19] The NAO decided to hear the submission because of its claims on certification delays, plant closings and problems of organizing multiple location businesses.[20]

Ottawa and Quebec jointly responded that employers had the right to object to the bargaining unit, and that multiple locations could be covered by one unit. After a mandatory investigation, the Labour Commissioner could amend the unit in response to employer objections. Québec law 'does not expressly prohibit the full or partial closing of a business or of an establishment, including during an organizing campaign'.[21] But the threat of a closure could be illegal if it hindered organizing efforts. The Commissioner could order workers reinstated if the employer did not prove the closure was unrelated to union activities or if a replacement establishment opened. But 'Québec law does not provide for any remedy concerning the potentially chilling effect of a closing that is genuine and lawful'.[22] Workers could appeal the closure as an unfair labour practice but chose not to in this case. Delays in certification reflected attorneys' schedules; the Minister concluded that 'nothing hindered or unduly delayed the union certification process', including the intervention of dissident workers.[23]

The US NAO met with government, labour and business representatives in Québec in April, 1999.[24] Québec officials agreed to study anti-union plant closings, to propose reforms to the labour code and to review delays in certification. With these concessions, the submitters decided not to pursue the NAO route.[25] For the US NAO, discussions were 'useful in clarifying the issues. This is further indication

---

17 Claude Melançon to Irasema Garza, Dec. 10, 1998. (Mr. Melançon, CALL's international affairs committee co-chair was also the Teamsters' solicitor in this submission.)

18 Claude Melançon to Irasema Garza, Dec. 17, 1998.

19 John Depenbrock to Henry Solano, Dec. 14, 1998.

20 U.S. Department of Labor *News Release*, 'U. S. to Review First NAFTA-Related Labor Complaint Against Canada' Washington, Dec. 18, 1998.

21 'Reponses of the Government of Quebec, in co-operation with the Government of Canada tot he questions from the U. S. National Administrative Office concerning the submission on the closing of a McDonald's (Canada) franchise restaurant in Saint-Hubert, Quebec, March 31, 1999, 11.

22 'Reponses of the Government of Quebec ...' 14.

23 'Reponses of the Government of Quebec ...' 18, 20.

24 May Morpaw to Irasema Garza, Jan. 29, 1999, March 25, 1999.

25 Claude Melançon to Irasema Garza, April 14, 1999.

that the process under the NAFTA labor side agreement works.'[26] But workers did not get their jobs back and no franchises were organized; another location in Montreal also closed when a union seemed poised to succeed. The Teamsters abandoned efforts to unionize McDonald's blaming the lengthy certification process. A quicker certification mechanism allowed the Canadian Auto Workers to unionize a franchise in British Columbia in 1998. Québec's delays were surmounted in 2002 by a Confederation of National Trade Unions local, which certified a McDonald's in Rawdon. Because of the lengthy process and high turnover, only four workers who signed union cards were still on staff went the certification was ordered.[27] The franchise later successfully sought decertification, as the transient workers could not sustain support for the union.

Rural Route Mail Carriers

US NAO 9804 challenged legislation denying Canada Post Corporation's rural route mail carriers rights to unionize and protection for occupational health and safety. The case was submitted by the American National Rural Letter Carriers Association (NRLCA or US Rural Carriers) and National Association of Letter Carriers (NALC or US Letter Carriers) on behalf of the Canadian Organization of Rural Route Mail Couriers (ORRMC or Rural Mail Couriers). It was supported by the Canadian Union of Postal Workers (CUPW or Postal Workers), Canadian Association of Labour Lawyers (CALL), and other Canadian unions. The submission argued that Canada Postal Corporation Act Section 13 (5) violated NAALC by excluding rural carriers from rights held by urban carriers. While the Act withstood two legal challenges, Canada's refusal to repeal this provision violated NAALC obligations to promote the right to organize. The submission also complained that rural carriers received no compensation for accidents and illnesses.

These provisions were serious discrimination against rural workers:

> Rural mail couriers are denied the fundamental right to form a union in order to negotiate a collective agreement. Therefore, they are also denied the right to get reasonable and decent working conditions and achieve the same level of protection as their colleagues serving urban dwellings.[28]

---

26 U.S. Department of Labor News Release, 'Labor Department Ends Review of Freedom of Association Complaint Against Canada' Washington, Apr.21, 1999.

27 'Mcunion Ordered; Burger Workers Sign First Contract' *Toronto Sun* April 18, 2002, 53.

28 Organization of Rural Route Mail Couriers et. al., *Public Communication on Labor Law Matters Arising in Canada Before the National Administrative Office of the United States under the North American Agreement on Labor Cooperation (NAALC) Violations of NAALC Labor Principles and Obligations in the Case of Canadian Rural Route Mail Couriers,* Dec. 1, 1998.

Submitters requested an NAO review, testimony from rural carriers, ministerial consultations and a NAALC report on 'the reasonable limitations that can be placed on freedom of association and the right to collective bargaining'.[29] The US Letter carriers commented: 'It is shocking to us that the government of Canada has singled out a group of Canadian workers for discriminatory and unjust treatment.'[30]

Rural carriers had long complained that Canada Post unfairly blocked unionization by hiring rural workers on individual contracts. They were denied union rights on a 'temporary basis', when the post office was losing millions. Rural carriers never had job security, but their five-year contracts were automatically renewed until the corporation decided on competitive tenders.[31] Up to one third of the rural carriers then formed the Canadian Rural Route Carriers Association, and sought certification from the Canada Labour Relations Board, which ruled rural carriers were employees because their functions were similar to urban workers. This decision was reversed in Federal Court which held that rural carriers were contractors not employees; the Supreme Court refused to review the decision, and rural carriers were prohibited from unionizing. Canada Post amalgamated rural routes and many carriers were forced to take pay cuts to retain contracts.[32] Rural carriers also lacked employment insurance, disability benefits, workman's compensation, paid vacations and other rights of full-time employees.

The US NAO requested information on the reasons for the exclusion of these workers from the Canada Labour Code, which governed federally-regulated employees. The Canadian NAO provided background information on Canada Post's status as a crown corporation. Canada Post officials insisted that rural carriers were contractors and urged the US NAO to decline the case.[33] Canada was in compliance with the NAALC since its laws were enforced. Rural couriers had no bargaining rights and the Act preserved the status quo. The submitters wanted the NAO to 'review Canadian legislation that has already passed through the scrutiny of the Canadian judicial review process'. The NAO did not have jurisdiction 'to conduct an examination of validly enacted and properly enforced legislation'.[34] NAALC's call for 'high standards' was an 'objective ... without specific binding obligations'.[35]

---

29   *Public Communication on ... Canadian Rural Route Mail Couriers*, Dec. 1, 1998.

30   'US Mailmen Lodge Complaint Against Canada' *El Universal* Dec. 3, 1998, [cited April 11, 2002]. Available at http://www.unam.edu.mx/universal/net1/1998/dic98/03dic98/english/03-un-a.html.

31   Marcella Campbell 'Rural carriers join union in fight to save their jobs' *Toronto Star* Nov. 20, 1986 A 17.

32   John Flanders 'Last-ditch fight: Time running out for rural mail carriers' *Hamilton Spectator* Nov. 26, 1991 C5.

33   'NAFTA: NAO Rejects Complaint That Canadian Labor Laws Violate Mail Couriers' Rights' *Daily Labor Report* Feb. 3, 1999; Doug Meacham to Irasema Garza, Dec. 23, 1998.

34   'Response of Canada Post Corporation to Public Communication U.S. NAO 9804 (Rural Mail Couriers) Before the NAO of the United States, under the NAALC', Jan., 1999, 9.

35   'Response of Canada Post Corporation' Jan., 1999, 13.

Solicitors advised that the NAALC requirements respecting submissions 'on labor law matters arising in the territory of another Party' was sufficiently broad to include this issue. But the NAALC makes clear the need to respect other countries' laws, and discourages submissions focussed on legal substance. US NAO 9804, which stressed the unfairness of Section 13 (5) was 'singularly focussed regarding a desire for change in the statutory law of a Party to the agreement'.[36] The NAO declined the submission, even though it raised important issues on the exclusion of rural workers. The submission did not demonstrate enforcement problems since 'the Canada Post Corporation Act does not contradict the Canadian Labor Code or the Canadian Charter of Rights and Freedoms'.[37]

Unions were alarmed that the Canadian government and Canada Post provided information to the US NAO without their knowledge. The Postal Workers considered the lack of opportunity to respond a denial of 'natural justice' and asked in 'fairness' to make a 'full and nuanced reply'.[38] Submitters declared that Section 13(5)'s sole goal was to strip rural carriers of rights they would otherwise have enjoyed. The unions suggested that the 'NAO's position narrows the commitment of the parties to the NAALC to strive to improve labour standards to a point where, in fact, no such commitment really exists'.[39] Claude Melançon of the Canadian Association of Labour Lawyers (CALL) suggested the rural couriers should be considered similar to other excluded workers in agriculture, domestic service, and lower management.[40] After delays, the NAO organized a 2001 seminar on bargaining rights for contractors like the rural carriers.

Rural carriers pressed for legislative change to share in the profitability of Canada Post Corporation, which posted six profitable years and paid $300 million in dividends by 2001. CUPW argued that the government should force Canada Post to use dividends to provide rural and suburban carriers with salaries and benefits comparable to its members.[41] As the Rural Mail Couriers argued, 'It's clear to rural Canadians that Canada Post rakes in big profits because postal services and working conditions are better for people who live and work in cities. It's time that rural Canada got a fair share of the wealth.'[42] But rural carriers failed to secure changes to the

---

36   John F. Depenbrock to Irasema Garza, Jan. 21, 1999.

37   Irasema Garza to Stephen R. Smith, Feb. 1, 1999.

38   'NAFTA Side Dealing: Through rain and wind ... but no union' *The Morning NAFTA* 14, May 1999, 9; Robert White, President CLC, to Irasema Garza, March 8, 1999.

39   Deborah Bourque, 'Denial of Basic Rights – The Situation of Rural and Suburban Mail Couriers' Presented to the Workshop on the Right to Organize and Bargain Collectively in Canada and the United States Toronto, February 1–2, 2001

40   Claude G. Melançon to Irasema Garza, July 2, 1999.

41   Deborah Bourque, 'Denial of Basic Rights'.

42   'Rural Canadians Deserve an Equal Share of the Wealth', *CUPW Communique*, June 21, 2001, [Cited April 4, 2002]. www.cupw-sttp.org/pages/document_eng.php?Doc_ID=144.

Canada Post Act and private members bills failed.[43] US rural carriers were unionized and received 3.5 times minimum wage with benefits, versus minimum wages with no benefits for their Canadian counterparts. This mocked Canada's alleged superiority on ILO and NAALC principles.[44] Rural and suburban mail carriers eventually did secure some improvements when CUPW successfully negotiated a new contract for them in 2003.[45]

Executive Air Transport, Inc. (TAESA)

The TAESA case (U.S. NAO 9901) involved union rights for flight attendants at Transportes Areos Ejecutivos, Mexico's third largest airline. Workers claimed they were prevented from organizing an independent Flight attendants union by Mexico's federal labour board and TAESA managers who preferred a CTM union. 100 workers were allegedly fired for voting for the new union. The submission alleged that Mexico ignored its guarantees on freedom of association, collective bargaining, minimum standards, and prevention of workplace injuries and illnesses.[46] The airline was grounded following a fatal crash in November 1999, which killed 18 people. Fired attendants claimed they had pointed out alleged deficiencies in aircraft maintenance and mechanical problems, including on the doomed airliner.[47] TAESA responded that the plane was in 'perfect shape' and met international safety norms and sued the union president for libel.[48]

43   Campbell Morrison 'Rural mail carriers want act changed' *The Fredericton Daily Gleaner* Oct. 17, 2001, A4.

44   James Sauber, 'Continental Divide: Collective Bargaining Rights and Rural Letter Carrier Compensation in the United States and Canada' Prepared by Union Network International for the NAALC Workshop on the Right to Organize and Bargain Collectively in Canada and the United States Toronto, Feb. 1–2, 2001.

45   Canada Post Corporation, 'Ratification Update September 26, 2003 – Canada Post Union Ratifies Two New Contracts' [cited June 26, 2006]. Available at http:www.canadapost.ca/textonly/personal/corporate/about/newsroom/negotiations/ratification-e.asp.

46   Association of Flight Attendants (AFA) *Public Communication to the US NAO, Executive Air Transport, Inc. (Taesa)Violations of Workers' Right to Freedom of Association and Protection of the Right to Organize; Workers' Right to Bargain Collectively; Minimum Employment Standards; and Prevention of Occupational Injuries and Illnesses and Persistent Pattern of Failure by the Government of Mexico to Fulfill Obligations under Part 2 of the NAALC to Effectively Enforce Levels of Protection, Government Enforcement Action, Private Action, and Procedural Guarantees with Respect to TAESA Violations*, Nov. 10, 1999, 10.

47   'Cae avión de Taesa; meuron al menos 18' *Reforma*, Nov. 10, 1999; 'Mexico suspends Taesa airline following crash that killed 18' *Amarillo Globe-News* Nov. 25, 1999 http://amarillonet.com/stories/112599/usn_LA0410.001.shtml, April 9, 2002; Felipe Cobián and Salvador Corro, 'Desde 1998, las autoridades conocían la inseguridad en TAESA' *Proceso* Nov, 1999.

48   'Crash May Ground Mexican Airline' *Washington Post*, Nov. 11, 1999, A35.

The US Association of Flight Attendants' and Mexico's independent Asociación Sindical de Sobrecargos de Aviación (ASSA or Flight Attendants' Union) submitted the case to the US NAO a day after the crash.[49] The communication alleged that Mexican authorities did not enforce freedom of association for independent unions, and aided the certification of the CTM's National Union of Air Transport Workers, which was recognized without a vote. TAESA supposedly reneged on promises to pay for health insurance, housing, pensions, and overtime and did not send payroll deductions to government. Officials failed to enforce laws on hours, overtime and premium pay, occupational injuries and illnesses, safety training and working conditions; emergency training purportedly decreased after TAESA fell on hard times in 1994.[50]

When workers sought representation by the Flight Attendants'Union

TAESA management, with the complicity of government labor authorities, struck back with a vengeance against the efforts of flight attendants to obtain ASSA representation. They blocked an election for two years, then held an election rife with fear, fraud and intimidation. Finally, TAESA fired the flight attendants who voted by an overwhelming majority for ASSA.[51]

CTM's union triumphed in elections in March, 1999 but the independent union claimed intimidation and threats clouded the vote.[52] The federal labour tribunal, with a CTM representative, ruled against the Flight Attendants' and it took two years to get courts to force a vote. The tribunal then ordered a vote of *all* TAESA workers, not just flight attendants, ensuring a negative outcome. The public vote was made difficult for the flight attendants' supporters whose shifts were changed unfavourably, while non ASSA workers were given transport to voting sites.[53] Such biased and open elections violated laws on the right to form craft-based unions and the constitution's guarantees for fair process and freedom of association. Reprisals allegedly followed, as 100 flight attendants, 40 ground crew and two pilots who supported the new union were discharged.[54] Their only recourse was to the same Tribunal. The flight attendants lamented: 'although our laws confirm the 'Principle of Union Plurality', the illegal action taken by the referenced Federal Board attacks the 'Principle of Free Association' to which our country is committed'.[55]

Submitters attached documents from the union which demonstrated its warnings about alleged unsafe practices. The submission maintained that TAESA

49   'Presentan quja contra la aerolínia en EU' *EL Universal*, Nov. 13, 1999.

50   *Public Communication ..., Executive Air Transport, Inc. (Taesa)* Nov. 10, 1999.

51   *Public Communication ..., Executive Air Transport, Inc. (Taesa)* Nov. 10, 1999, 6.

52   'Empleados de Taesa se quedan con la CTM; intimidacíon: ASSA' *El Financiero* March 23, 1999.

53   *Public Communication ..., Executive Air Transport, Inc. (Taesa)* Nov. 10, 1999, 8–10.

54   'Acusan a Taesa de repesalia' *Reforma* April 22, 1999.

55   'Mexican Flight Attendants Union [ASSA] v. Executive Air Transport [TAESA] and the National Union of Air Transport Workers and Employees [SNTETA]', Special Board Number Two of the Federal Board of Conciliation and Arbitration, April 23, 1999, 1.

did not 'provide sufficient emergency training and retraining for flight attendants' and 'failed to maintain its aircraft cabin areas in safe operational conditions'.[56] Supposed deficiencies included faulty smoke detectors, overhead luggage locks, fire extinguishers and emergency lights, broken seats, blocked emergency exits, leaking bathrooms, inadequate first aid kits and oxygen masks and air contamination from lubricants. Excess hours made flight attendants less alert, allegedly contributing to an earlier crash. Since authorities did not correct these violations, the submitters sought NAO action. The AFA and the Flight Attendants' Union requested consultations leading to union recognition, rehiring of fired workers with of back wages, benefits, and deductions, and better training, maintenance and safety. The NAO should seek ministerial consultations, an ECE, disputes resolution, arbitration and sanctions. The US Association of Flight Attendant's noted that Mexico's violations were serious but similar to US practices. Despite TAESA's bankruptcy, the AFA urged 'concrete remedies' for workers and guarantees for representation at any replacement airline.[57]

The U.S. NAO accepted the submission and held a hearing in Washington. The Flight Attendants' Union claimed that, although flight attendants voted 99 to 42 for ASSA, the CAB accepted the votes of other workers to declare a CTM victory; 'labor terrorism' was used to 'manipulate the vote towards CTM'.[58] Workers had to declare their vote in front of management, CTM representatives, armed security and police with attack dogs. Outside observers were denied entry and the independent union's supporters were photographed and videotaped while waiting for hours outside the hanger to vote. Complaints were made to the labour ministry but the union was told the company was allowed to have police and CTM present.[59] Purportedly, CTM supporters received bonuses and holidays, while members of the Flight Attendants' Union were fired. Workers had to sign agreements supporting the CTM to receive identification cards and pay.

Efforts to alert civil aviation authorities to safety and health hazards allegedly brought little action; the required health and safety committee was dormant. Workers testified about long hours without overtime pay; those who refused overtime faced intimidation. Profit sharing and bonuses were supposedly cut or eliminated. Flight crews were forced to work connecting flights making them too tired to work safely; complaints lead to a worse assignment next time. The company ordered flights with crews too small for the number of passengers. According to workers, maintenance deteriorated as the company approached bankruptcy.[60]

---

56   *Public Communication to the US NAO, Executive Air Transport, Inc. (Taesa)*.

57   U.S. NAO *Public Hearing In The Matter of Submission 9901* Washington D.C. March 23, 2000, 13.

58   U.S. NAO *Public Hearing on Submission 9901* Washington D.C. March 23, 2000, 60.

59   U.S. NAO *Public Hearing on Submission 9901* Washington D.C. March 23, 2000, 93–94.

60   U.S. NAO *Public Hearing on Submission 9901* Washington D.C. March 23, 2000, 80–82.

The US NAO sought an opinion from the National Law Centre for Inter-American Free Trade (NLCIFT). The report focussed on CAB rulings 'to ascertain the extent to which they are consistent or vary from existing Mexican law and precedents'.[61] The Centre's report indicated that the Flight Attendants'Union lacked standing under Mexican law to represent all TAESA employees and was too small relative to the TAESA union. The recount was conducted in accordance with Mexican legal precedent which required that all employees, not a particular trade, be polled. ASSA should have followed procedures to create a union representing flight attendants, and should not have tried to take over the current bargaining unit since flight attendants were a minority. Thus, Mexican laws had been followed and the union's rights had been respected.[62]

The NAO's Public Report of Review noted that Tribunal rulings preventing fragmentation of the existing collective agreement conformed to Mexican norms. It sought clarification on the effects on craft unions organizing on professional lines where a company-wide contract was in place. And the NAO decided there was evidence that flight attendants faced threats and intimidation from management and the CTM union; 'a representation election where workers must declare their choice in the open and in front of hostile management and opposing union personnel, where workers are subject to intimidation and threats prior to and during the election, and where eligible voters are denied access to the voting area, is not likely to have an outcome of free choice'.[63] CTM's representative on the Tribunal gave an appearance of conflict of interest, though this person ruled for the Flight Attendants' Union once.[64] Firing of workers appeared to be retaliation for union activity, though Mexico's 'exclusion' clause allowed dismissals of those outside the recognized union. The US NAO believed the Flight Attendants' Union presented credible testimony on non-payment of overtime and social security taxes, inadequate safety training and non-enforcement of health and safety rules, including aircraft maintenance. Requests to Mexico's NAO for information on safety received no response prior to the report.

Despite the potential for an evaluation committee and sanctions on health and safety, the NAO confined its request to consultations, focussed on the 'integrity' of union elections and secret ballots, tribunal impartiality, the exclusion clause, overtime, payroll deduction and occupational safety and health.[65] Consultations took a long time to complete, due to turnover in the Mexican and US NAOs. When they were held in 2002, TAESA was out of business. A follow-up seminar addressed freedom of association, minimum employment standards, occupational health

---

61   National Law Centre for Inter-American Free Trade, *Legal Memorandum, U.S. National Administrative Office Submission 9901 (TAESA)*, June 2000, 1.

62   NLCIFT, *Legal Memorandum ... (TAESA)*, June 2000, 20.

63   US NAO, *Public Report of Review of NAO Submission No. 9901*, July 7, 2000, 75.

64   *Public Report of Review of NAO Submission No. 9901*, July 7, 2000, 42.

65   *Public Report of Review of NAO Submission No. 9901*, July 7, 2000, 75–76.

standards, and different types of unions representing workers by craft, company, industry or sector.[66]

Auto Trim/Custom Trim/Breed Mexicana

US NAO 2000–01 was the first submission exclusively on safety, health and compensation for work-related injuries. It involved two plants in Tamaulipas, originally owned by a Canadian firm, Custom Trim, but bought in 1997 by Florida-based Breed Technologies. The plants made leather and vinyl seats, head rests, covers for steering wheels and knobs for gear shifts for automobiles. Employees complained of exposure to adhesives, solvents, and chemicals, poor ventilation, repetitive stress and ergonomic injuries, carpal tunnel syndrome and back problems. Workers sought better pay, pensions, safety equipment, profit-sharing and Christmas bonuses.[67] After CTM representatives declined to assist, workers turned to an independent union and pursued an illegal strike despite fears of police violence.[68] 28 workers were allegedly fired for organizing. One worker received death threats for travelling to Ontario to seek support from Custom Trim workers. Death threats reinforced the workers concern that NAALC was dangerous and worker rights were not secure.[69]

The submission was filed by the Coalition for Justice in the Maquiladoras (CJM), the Pastoral Juvenil Obrera (PJO), the Maquila Solidarity Network (MSN), United Auto Workers, United Electrical Workers, Maquiladora Health and Safety Support Network and other labour, human rights and religious groups. The complaint alleged that Mexico failed to enforce health and safety regulations causing workplace illness and injuries. Fast-paced production plus inadequate work stations caused ergonomic problems. Poor ventilation and improper safety equipment lead to illnesses. Symptoms included dizziness, miscarriages, headaches and deaths. The plants had inadequate first aid supplies and accidents or illnesses went unreported, so no treatment or compensation was provided. There was no worker-management health and safety committee; workers lacked information and training on how to prevent injuries. Submitters asked the US NAO to investigate a 'persistent pattern' of inadequate enforcement. After consultations an 'inspection commission' should

---

66 U.S. Department of Labor, *Press Release*, 'U.S.-Mexico Joint Statement on Ministerial Consultations Under the North American Agreement on Labor Cooperation' Washington, June 12, 2002, 2; 'U.S., Mexico Ministers Resolve Three Cases, Creating Working Group on Workplace Safety' *Daily Labor Report* 113, June 12, 2002, A-11.

67 Coalition for Justice in the Maquiladoras, *Press Release*,'Mexican Customtrim Workers Demand Higher Wages' May 15, 1997.

68 James Shea to Irasema Garza, May 22, 1997.

69 Coalition for Justice in the Maquiladoras, *Press Release*,'Custom Trim Worker's Family Receives Death Threat' Sept. 12, 1997; USWA, *News Release*, 'Death Threats Shadow Mexican Workers After Canada Tour', Sept. 15, 1997.

determine if the plants complied with regulations; continued violations should lead to an evaluation committee, arbitration and penalties.[70]

The submission was supported with petitions filed with ministries of labor and health, affidavits from workers, material safety data sheets and studies of health and safety in chemical and production processes. Workers anonymously reported hazards and injuries and stressed the lack of safety equipment and training. Some claimed they endured harmful medical treatment to qualify for disability pay, to force them to quit. Others were sent to counsellors who suggested injuries had outside causes such as spousal abuse. Lack of proper seating caused muscular and skeletal injuries; employees punctured their faces with needles and scalpels because they worked close to these tools. Despite chemical exposure, air extractors were sometimes turned off or poorly maintained. Female workers reported birth defects. Even during a fire caused by sparks igniting solvents, workers allegedly were told to continue working. Yet the health and labour ministries did not respond to petitions and workers could not find out if inspections were conducted.

The US NAO accepted this complaint since it related to fair, transparent, expeditious law enforcement and appeals, protection of worker rights and health and safety.[71] The NAO received petitions from the American Public Health Association and health and safety professionals and activists. As the first case focussed solely on health and safety, these groups hoped the NAO would use arbitration and sanctions 'to send a strong message to governments and employers in all three countries that they have a legal responsibility to ensure that workers' health and safety is not compromised by their employment'.[72] At a hearing in San Antonio, law students who worked on the case argued that inadequate oversight 'resulted in the workers suffering illnesses and injuries, sometimes so severe that their ability to support themselves and their families is compromised and their capacity to perform basic tasks becomes impaired'.[73] Workers who became ill or unproductive were purportedly pressured to quit, by being transferred to an onerous area called 'the junkyard'. Legal experts testified that Mexico was in violation of constitutional, treaty and statutory obligations by not enforcing exposure limits for chemicals.[74] Accident cases were sent to private doctors, not the health ministry (IMSS), so the company could claim accident-free status. One witness blamed the changing work culture, emphasizing

---

70   The Coalition for Justice in the Maquiladoras et. al. Submission to the U.S. National Administrative Office (NAO) … The Case of Autotrim and Customtrim. June 30, 2000. Numerous affidavits were attached to the submission with names redacted.

71   *Federal Register* 65, 174, September 7, 2000, 54301.

72   Among the many identical items on file at the US NAO, see National COSH Network to Members of the US National Administrative Office, 'Re: December 12, 2000 NAO Hearing' Nov. 11, 2000.

73   Testimony of Monica Schurtman, University of Idaho Legal Aid Clinic, to the *US NAO Public Hearing on US NAO Submission 2000–01*, San Antonio, Dec. 12, 2000.

74   Testimony of Alfonso Otero to the *US NAO Public Hearing on US NAO Submission 2000–01*, San Antonio, Dec. 12, 2000.

productivity and internal resolution of problems without recourse to tribunals, strikes or public reports.[75]

Managers insisted that some health problems were psychological or not work related and that health and safety standards exceeded requirements. The firm improved hazard prevention, ergonomic safety, plant ventilation, and protective equipment and workers got thorough medical treatment under IMSS. Workers received training on health, fire safety, first aid, and chemical storage and handling. Safety and hygiene committees composed of workers and managers, conducted frequent inspections, and reported on problems and solutions. Work stations were adjusted for comfort, and repetitive operations were restricted in duration. Ergonomics courses, physical therapy and exercises were provided to reduce muscle strain. Chemicals and solvents had Spanish labels for contents, precautions and emergency remedies. Mexican officials never cited the plants, which received certifications for excellence in safety. Workers were dismissed under legal procedures, and many made voluntary severance settlements.[76]

The Mexican NAO outlined regulations on ergonomics, chemicals and other hazards. The labour ministry conducted timely inspections if requested by employees to enforce health and safety standards and worker rights, backed by fines and remedial orders. The health department provided information, education, training and technical assistance. Routine inspections sometimes cleared the plants of any problems, but all violations were sanctioned. An ergonomic inspection was undertaken in 1995 with a follow-up in 1996. Special inspections were conducted in 1998, and inspectors returned to confirm compliance. A 1997 inspection resulted in a citation, but the firm relocated and fixed all problems. Breed's plants in Valle Hermosa were fined in 1999 but problems found later that year were rectified. Mexico's NAO emphasized that Breed was on a committee of 'responsible employers with regard to health and safety'[77]

National Institute for Occupational Health and Safety (NIOSH) officers accompanied NAO officials on a site visit and submitted recommendations for health and safety programmes at Breed's invitation. They found ergonomic problems which could cause musculoskeletal injuries, tendonitis and carpal tunnel.[78] Workers often did not wear protective masks or gloves; ventilation and extraction devices were converted from other purposes and were not optimal for glues and solvent vapours. Workers suffered respiratory, neurological, and skin problems consistent with prolonged chemical exposure. In confidential interviews, workers noted problems in getting on health and safety committees or being asked to sign statements affirming

75   Testimony of Isabel Morales to the *US NAO Public Hearing on US NAO Submission 2000–01*, San Antonio, Dec. 12, 2000.

76   Auto Trim de Mexico, S.A. de C.V., Matamoros, Tamaulipas, Mexico, and Custom Trim/Breed Mexicana, S.A. de C.V., 'Submission to the U.S. National Administrative' Office (NAO) , no date.

77   'Public Communication U.S. 2000–01 (Auto Trim and Custom Trim)'(Mexican NAO Responses to Questions), 6–8.

78   Aaron L, Sussell and Sherry Baron to Lewis Karesh, March 7, 2001, 3.

they were trained when they had received no training. Inspections were done on 1–2 days notice, and were routine verifications, not focussed on complaints. Worker interviews were non-confidential and available to management, limiting frankness. Inspectors were concerned with company paperwork, not measuring hazards or suggesting corrective measures.[79]

The US government investigated alleged intimidation of workers after the submission. Workers were allegedly questioned about their participation in the submission, and received implied threats of retaliation, according to State Department inquiries. Threats against union leaders may have emanated from official union locals; the media labelled independent unionists as 'terrorists, as destabilizers of the maquiladora industry, as agitators'.[80] Letters from unions, churches, and peace activists noted that a failure 'to protect complainants under the NAFTA Labor Side Accords ... will have an extremely chilling effect on workers who wish to exercise their rights'.[81] The US Labor Department wrote to Mexico's labor ministry to express concerns about intimidation, and threats against those planning to testify at the hearing which 'raise concerns about the efficacy and transparency of our public submission process'.[82]

The US NAO public report of review acknowledged that, after worker complaints and inspections, 'Breed management has taken initiatives in the areas of training and hazard prevention plans to reduce work-related injuries and illnesses, improved ergonomic practices, installation and operation of improved exhaust systems, ventilation and temperature controls, use of personal protective equipment, and provision of medical treatment in cooperation with IMSS'.[83] The NAO criticized the lack of confidential worker interviews or independent tests to verify compliance. Mexico did not provide enough information to evaluate testing, so the effectiveness of enforcement remained uncertain. Health and safety committees focussed on hygiene. Injured workers were not always sent to IMSS; some were seen by company doctors creating conflicts of interest.

The US NAO informed Breed of its right to keep documents on inspections confidential, based on exemption 4 of the Freedom of Information Act, on 'trade secrets' and 'commercial and financial information'.[84] Submitters criticized the US NAO for allowing Breed to veto disclosure, which they felt violated its neutrality. Secrecy left inspections unverified and unquestioned, which was unfair, given open testimony by workers despite threats. The NAO noted that NAALC was a 'government-to-government agreement' focussed on law enforcement, not company practices. Breed released some documents but was not required to answer questions, and did not appear at the hearing. Submitters noted that Mexico refused to provide full information about

---

79   Aaron L, Sussell and Sherry Baron to Lewis Karesh, March 7, 2001, 8–12.

80   Dominican Sisters (Houston) to NAO Office, Oct. 5, 2000.

81   Among numerous almost identical letters in the US NAO's files, see Jane Howald, President CWA Local 14177 to Lewis Karesh, Dec. 4, 2000.

82   Andrew Samet to Carlos Tirado Zavala, Sept. 29, 2000.

83   US NAO, Public Report of Review: US NAO 2000–01, Washington, April 6, 2001.

84   Lewis Karesh to Stuart Boyd, Breed Technologies, Jan. 18, 2001.

inspections; unless all signatories cooperated, NAALC could not promote transparent laws enforcement.

Despite potential sanctions, the case again terminated at ministerial consultations, which dragged on for months, as workers claimed conditions worsened at the plants. Submitters proposed transborder and interagency cooperation to improve inspections, enforcement and prevention. After a year had passed from the public hearings, with no consultations or corrective action, submitting groups called for an evaluation committee.[85] 35 members of Congress wrote the Republican Secretary of Labour, Elaine Chao, to ask why consultations were so slow and to support an ECE.[86] Chao rejected this request.[87] In June 2002, a joint declaration created a bilateral working group on health and safety to make 'technical recommendations' and design 'cooperation projects'. The Labour ministry agreed on 'outreach' to workers about their rights in health and safety cases, 'best practices'on ergonomics, prevention of injuries and handling of hazardous materials.[88] This agreement was bitterly protested by the submitters who condemned it as 'all talk, no action', with no deadline or role for workers or independent experts, and no bilateral examination of deficient practices.[89] The "Joint Declaration' is a charade and a disgrace – and it demonstrates the complete failure of the NAFTA side agreements to protect workers. If NAFTA is the "success story" and model for the proposed Free Trade Area of the Americas trade agreement, working people in the Americas are in serious danger.'[90]

Duro Bag Manufacturing

US NAO 2001–01 involved Duro Bag Manufacturing, which made premium shopping bags for retailers. It featured another open election allowing intimidation by management and rival unions. Workers first sought improved conditions through the Paper, Cardboard and Wood Industry Union of the CTM by trying to elect officers who would represent them effectively. Concerns included exposure to improperly labelled solvents, inadequate gas masks, and accidents resulting in lost fingers. 'Safety guards ... were removed from the rollers that imprint designs on

---

85   Custom Trim Update: CustomTrim/AutoTrim Workers Demand Action by NAFTA Offices, Maquiladora Health & Safety Support Network, January 2002, [cited June 14 2003]. Available at http://www.maquilasolidarity.org/resources/maquilas/customtrim.htm.

86   George Miller et. al. to Elaine Chao, May 7, 2002.

87   'Maquiladora Group Unhappy With Handling of Complaint Filed Under NAFTA Accord' *Labor Relations Weekly* 16, (March 28, 2002), 404.

88   U.S.-Mexico *Joint Declaration on Ministerial Consultations*, June 11, 2002, [cited Oct. 24, 2002]. Available at http://www.dol.gov/ilab/media/reports/nao/jointdeclar061102.htm.

89   'Letter from CJM to Labor Secretaries Chao and Abascal September 6, 2002, [cited Oct. 13, 2003]. Available at http://mhssn.igc.org/nafta13.htm.

90   Statement of the Coalition for Justice in the Maquiladoras Regarding the June 11, 2002, 'Joint Declaration' of the US and Mexican Governments on the Autotrim/Customtrim case' June 19, 2002 [cited October 13, 2003]. Available at http://mhssn.igc.org/nafta10.htm.

the paper lining – the extra time required to clean them was treated as needless lost production.'[91] The workers presented their concerns to managers and asked for a raise from 320 to 420 pesos a week. But the CTM union signed a contract addressing none of the workers' concerns, and expelled activists, who were fired and faced intimidation (one house was burned down in suspicious circumstances). The workers then turned to the new National Union of Workers (UNT). A ballot was held between the UNT and a' CROC affiliate in 2001, but only one-third of workers voted with 498 supporting CROC and 4 supporting the UNT.[92] Witnesses alleged that the election was conducted under threat from 'thugs' who oversaw 'the virtual imprisonment and drugging' of workers.[93] Protesters pressured state officials to allow a fair choice, and shadowed the governor, demanding '*libertad sindical*' (union freedom).[94]

This case was the first covering violations after the inauguration of the PAN President, Vincente Fox. Since similar complaints had been heard by the US NAO, frustrated unions made one last effort to use the NAALC, to give the new President a chance to improve the labour climate. The submitters, including the AFL-CIO and the Paper, Allied-Industrial, Chemical & Energy Workers International Union (PACE) alleged that officials violated the NAALC by blocking a secret ballot in a neutral location.[95] This was a breach of the Mexican constitution, the federal labour law (FLL) and ILO Convention 87. Submitters conceded that Mexican law did not require secret ballots or neutral sites, but it did not prohibit these practices, which were needed to meet treaty and legal obligations.

While this case was similar to Han Young and Itapsa, the submitters argued the violation was more egregious. In the May 2000 agreement on US 9702 and 9703, Mexico agreed to 'promote secret ballots and neutral voting places within the framework of labor-management dialogue for the New Labor Culture'.[96] Yet in the Duro Bag election, supervised by the Federal Conciliation and Arbitration Board, workers had to declare their support for an independent union in front of managers and rival unionists.

91   David Bacon 'Unions Without Borders' *The Nation* Jan. 22, 2001 [cited October 12 2003]. Available at http://www.thenation.com/docPrint.mhtml?i=20010122&s=bacon.

92   David Bacon 'Secret Ballot Denied in Vote at Duro Maquiladora' *Mexican Labor News and Analysis* 6, March 2001[cited October 12 2003]. Available at http://www.ueinternational.org/Vol6no3.html.

93   Gene McGuckin 'Rio Bravo union loses to guns, drugs, intimidation' *CEP Journal* 9, 2 Spring, 2001, 2.

94   David Bacon 'Just south of Texas, democracy faces its hardest test' *Canadian Dimension* 34 (2000), 25.

95   American Federation of Labor and Congress of Industrial Organizations (AFL-CIO) and Paper, Allied-Industrial, Chemical & Energy Workers International Union (PACE International Union) *Public Communication to the U.S. National Administrative Office (NAO) ... on... Violations of NAALC Labor Principles and Obligations regarding the Union Representation Election at Duro Bag Manufacturing Corp., Rio Bravo, Tamaulipas.*, June 2001, 2.

96   Agreement on Ministerial Consultations U.S. NAO Submissions 9702 and 9703, May 18, 2000.

The government of Mexico abandoned this secret ballot agreement, making no effort in the Duro case to fulfill its promise. On the contrary, the government allowed Duro management and the FCAB to force workers into public declarations of their union sentiments in a non-neutral location under conditions totally destructive of free choice of union representation.[97]

Management testified that the ministerial agreement had 'no legal or probitive value' and the Labour Board rejected it as a 'plan of action'.[98] For the submitters, this was a violation of NAALC commitments to protect worker rights and promote 'high labor standards'. [99] The submitters wanted the NAO to review the case and consult with Mexico on ways to implement its secret ballot pledge. The case was supported by a cross-border coalition of unions and human rights NGOs. Martha Ojeda warned 'The Duro election strips away any idea that the NAFTA process can protect workers rights. The side agreement is bankrupt.'[100] Transnational efforts included protests at US Duro plants and pressure on its customers to buy elsewhere, with cards declaring 'Sweatshop abuses are no way to say, 'I love you.''[101]

Secretary of Labour Carlos Abascal noted that some foreign organizations were creating a 'false climate of labor violence'.[102] Abascal suggested that US union activity was designed to 'discourage private investment in Mexico'; 'while they entered the country on the pretext of denouncing violations of workers' rights, their real goal is to seek parity with the wages and conditions of U.S. workers.'[103] Local employers and official unions accused the workers of being pawns in a Texas-led 'dirty war' to 'destabilize' the region and encourage investors to move back to the US.[104] In October, 2001, in another contested vote, CROC supporters allegedly took over the executive of the UNT local without the knowledge or participation of its members.[105]

---

97 *Public Communication ... regarding the Union Representation Election at Duro Bag.*, 2.

98 *Public Communication ... regarding the Union Representation Election at Duro Bag.*, 4.

99 *Public Communication ... regarding the Union Representation Election at Duro Bag.*, 2, 7.

100 David Bacon 'Border Labor War Defies Mexico's Fox Administration' Oct. 21, 2001. Available at http://www.maquilasolidarity.org/resources/maquilas/bacon2001.htm.

101 Maquiladora Solidarity Network, 'Send Hallmark a Valentine's message and support Duro workers' http://www.maquilasolidarity.org/alerts/duro3.htm.

102 Bacon, 'Secret Ballot Denied At Duro'.

103 'Abascal Attacks U.S. Labor Unions' *Mexican Labor News and Analysis* 6, (2001) [cited Feb. 13, 2004]. Available at http://www.ueinternational.org/Vol6no3.html.

104 Bacon, 200, 26–7.

105 Garrett Brown 'Letter from the Coordinator' *Maquiladora Health & Safety Support Network Newsletter* (2001) [cited Oct 24, 2002]. Available at http://mhssn.igc.org/news17.htm.

The U.S. NAO declined the submission, explaining that NAALC only 'obligates each party to effectively enforce its labor law through appropriate government action'. Since 'there is no provision in the [Mexican] law governing the use of secret ballots in trade union representation elections', there was no failure of enforcement.[106] This ruling occurred despite previous condemnation of such practices, including at Custom Trim. An NAO official queried by this author stated 'I am not able to offer any further elaboration on the reason for not accepting the submission'.[107] Since similar cases had been accepted previously, Duro Bag was a sign that the standard for cases might be more stringent in the Republican era of George W. Bush, creating disillusionment and discouraging submissions.

Puebla Garment Factories

It was two years before a new case emerged at garment factories in Puebla. This submission, filed by the United Students Against Sweatshops (USAS) and the Centro de Apoyo al Trabajador (Worker Rights Center), showed the importance of human rights groups in the process. This complaint was directed at Matamoros Garment; an amendment raised concerns about Tarrant Mexico. The case involved maquilas making low cost garments for global brands. Workers at the Izúcar de Matamoros facility tried to organize a union, because of alleged non-payment of wages, violations of minimum wages, forced overtime, verbal abuse by managers and the dangerous practice of locking workers in the factory during shifts. Workers alleged that the existing the Sindicato Francisco Villa de la Industria Textil y Conexos, was a company union which made covert deals with managers.

Workers tried to form the Sindicato Independiente de Trabajadores de la Empresa Matamoros Garment (Matamoros Workers or SITEMAG), and staged a one-day walkout. About 162 of 250 employees signed papers supporting SITEMAG. The employer allegedly threatened to close the plant, and buyers like Puma of Germany withdrew orders after the union filed for recognition.[108] The factory closed after orders were cancelled, citing legal and financial problems. The labour board refused to recognise the Matamoros Workers, citing technical faults, including an unclear name for the local, misspelled name of a leader, and inclusion of management employees on the certification petition.[109]

A similar process unfolded at Tarrant in Ajalpan, whose clients included Levis and Tommy Hilfiger. Workers staged a one-day work stoppage and got 700 of 800 workers to sign in favour of the Sindicato Unico y Independiente de Trabajadores

---

106 Lewis Karesh to Deborah Greenfield, Associate General Counsel, AFL-CIO, Feb. 22, 2002.

107 Lewis Karesh Email to R. Finbow, April 22, 2002.

108 'Puma dumps workers' *The Guardian* April 30, 2003 [cited Feb. 23, 2004]. Available at http://www.cpa.org.au/garchve03/1135puma.html.

109 Matamoros Garment Campaign Update, April 2003 [cited Feb 23, 2004]. Available at http://www.cleanclothes.org/companies/puma-03-04-01.htm.

de Tarrant (Tarrant workers or SUITTAR). Once again, the petition for recognition was rejected by the labour board because of a misspelled name of a union official. Efforts by Levis to get the plant to cooperate with its code of conduct were rejected, a rare occurrence in Levis' experience. Levis suspended orders and wrote Puebla's governor urging that labour laws be respected. Meanwhile, the factory began to dismiss workers, with 300 fired, starting with union leaders. Limited Brands, Tarrant's remaining large customer, joined efforts to get the firm to respect worker rights. Some employees accepted severance pay, but union organizers held out for reinstatement. In December, 2003, the plant shut; submitters were concerned because the factory was planning to reopen as part of AZT International, requiring certification to recommence. The factory claimed a 'technical work stoppage' as opposed to a closure, and did not pay severance benefits.

The submission to the US alleged that Mexican authorities did not enforce laws respecting freedom of association, and the right to organize and bargain. The Puebla Conciliation and Arbitration Board allegedly failed to provide a fair, transparent registration process to independent unions.[110] The urgency of the organizing efforts was heightened by failure to enforce laws and regulations governing minimum standards, minimum wages, back wages or severance pay, forced overtime, illegal suspensions and layoffs. Charges were also made about unsanitary bathroom conditions and occupational health and safety. The submitters referred to previous submissions to show that these practices reflected a systematic disregard for labour rights in Mexico.

At the NAO hearing, workers complained of unsafe, unsanitary workplaces, poor pay, forced overtime, verbal abuse, unpaid benefits, and interference with union organizers. They told of lack of adequate bathroom and lunch breaks, lack of overtime pay, underage workers, and sexual harassment. A female employee told of 26 straight hours of work, mostly standing, causing fatigue and leg problems. Pregnant workers were not exempted and one suffered a miscarriage. Workers lacked protective masks or ear plugs, and were not given legal holidays. A Tarrant worker noted that talk of unionizing brought threats of firing. Workers went on strike over the denial of profit-sharing, but found the local board unsympathetic, since workers were 'represented' by a union that none of them had heard of before. After proposing the independent union, leaders were fired. Workers could not get new jobs because of a blacklist allegedly distributed by the company.[111]

United Students Against Sweatshops representatives detailed their pressure on brand name companies to demand adherence to labour rights by their contractors.

---

110 'Department of Labor, Bureau of International Labor Affairs, U.S. National Administrative Office; North American Agreement on Labor Cooperation; Notice of Determination Regarding Review of U.S. Submission 2003–01' Federal Register 69, February 11, 2004, 6691.

111 ILAB *Public Hearing on US National Administrative Office Submission 2003–01 (Puebla)*, Thursday, April 1, 2004, [cited May 7, 2004]. Available at http://www.dol.gov/ilab/media/reports/nao/submissions/2003-01Transcript.htm.

But Mexico's failure to enforce laws on organizing, bargaining, minimum standards and health and safety required a NAO submission as a 'last resort' to compliment the student groups' work on codes. The Puebla plants resisted pressure from major brands to improve conditions, and Mexican legal remedies were exhausted. The Worker Rights Consortium, used to ensure garments with university and college logos were made in factories with worker protections, testified about Tarrant's alleged denial of union rights. Worker Rights Center's investigations supported claims that workers were fired for union activity. Local labour boards failed to protect workers, through 'filibuster' or inaction, using the excuse that some had accepted severance, virtually impossible for impoverished workers to refuse. The Centre affirmed the workers complaints at Matamoros; according to the Centre, the firm locked workers in the plant to complete work and hid underage workers from inspectors.

Submitters asked the NAO to pressure Mexico to ensure that collective agreements and union registrations were made public, to prevent continuance of phantom unions. A trinational committee should be set up to study violations of rights of association, collective bargaining and strikes, including blacklists and open ballots. Outreach activities should be held in Puebla, with government, labour boards and workers on union organizing and registration. Health and safety, forced labour, child labour and minimum standards for wages and overtime should be addressed by an ECE. [112]

The US NAO public report of review agreed with the petitioners that the board had rejected union registration on 'technical grounds' and had not given the organizers an opportunity to correct problems to permit registration. Unions at Matamoros and Tarrant did not exhaust domestic appeals which may have produced court orders requiring registration. But the NAO acknowledged the similarity of this and other cases, where harassment, intimidation and pre-signed letters of resignation undermined union appeals; 'what is supposed to be a mere administrative formality should not be implemented in a way that effectively obstructs the basic worker right of freedom of association'.[113] The NAO cited conflicting information on whether workers appealed violations of minimum standards or health and safety rules. Despite evidence of informal complaints and prior knowledge by authorities through inspections, the US NAO could not find that Mexican authorities had not enforced the laws. However, the NAO recommended consultations on a 'lack of knowledge and transparency' about complaints procedures, inspections, reports and government assistance.[114] And the NAO was concerned that their Mexican counterparts did not follow up on consultations or permit wider contacts, restricting their feedback to written responses. Two years on, there was little evidence these consultations had produced results.

This submission was linked to a broader campaign against garment sweatshops including pressure on major brands to remedy poor conditions in their contractors

112 *Public Hearing on U.S. National Administrative Office Submission 2003–01 (Puebla).*

113 US NAO, *Report of Review of US NAO Submission No. 2003–01* Washington, August 3, 2004, iii.

114 *Report of Review of US NAO Submission No. 2003–01*, iii.

in developing states. This case tested whether NAALC can help secure voluntary compliance by corporations to improve working conditions and labour standards. It had international impact because of connections between workers and global anti-sweatshop campaigners, who applied pressure on major fashion and garment brands. Anti-sweatshop campaigners in the US and Europe pressured Puma and others to resume orders and to insist that the factory and local authorities recognise unions. Transnational interest was demonstrated by the participation of British anti-sweatshop organizations, among others.[115] This approach worked in Puebla previously in the Kudong (Mexmode) dispute, when sweatshop campaigners persuaded Nike to help secure union recognition; but this occurred outside the NAALC process. USAS was confident that Tarrant suffered a loss of business from the boycott.[116] The Worker Rights Center noted that without 'extraordinary circumstances' like pressure from brand name firms, 'there seems to be at least near universal disregard for the law with respect to the obligation of the local labor boards to grant a registros to a duly constitute independent labor union.'[117] How helpful the NAALC is to this cause remains uncertain.

Conclusions

Recent submissions to the US NAO further diversified the regional linkages in labour affairs. Cases about Canada were brought soon after it became eligible in 1997. These cases dealt not with failures to enforce labour laws, but with the adequacy of laws. As the US NAO indicated in the rural route carriers' case, it would not consider the substance of laws, as opposed to the adequacy of enforcement. Both cases were resolved outside of the submissions process, through cooperative activities or informal, direct engagement at the provincial level. These cases witnessed the extension of transnational networks across America's northern border. New alliances emerged linking international, local and francophone unions. For instance, the International Brotherhood of Teamsters, Teamsters Canada, Teamsters Local 973, and the Québec Federation of Labour (QFL) joined on the McDonalds' case. Public sector unions in both countries joined forces on the rural postal workers complaint, engaging the politically active Canadian public sectors unions for the first time.

Mexico's independent union movement persisted in its efforts to use NAALC to secure relief for workers; the campaign waged by the flight attendants with the emerging public sector and utilities union FESEBES reflected this commitment, despite frustration in national and NAALC forums. Unions were joined by more

---

115 *Pile The Pressure on PUMA* [cited May 7, 2004]. Available at http://www.nosweat. org.uk/files/leaflets/puma.pdf.

116 USAS, 'Maquila Cases Bring Violations, Legal Enforcement' [cited May 7, 2004]. Available at http://www.onekoreaforum.org/kiwa/cgi/read.cgi?board=ala_board_2&y_ number=58.

117 *'Public Hearing on U.S. National Administrative Office Submission 2003–01 (Puebla)'.*

human rights activists organized trinationally, such as the Coalition for Justice in the Maquiladoras (CJM), the Pastoral Juvenil Obrera (PJO) and the Maquila Solidarity Network (MSN) which brought the complex Custom Trim/Auto Trim case. The intervention by the United Students Against Sweatshops (USAS) and the Centro de Apoyo al Trabajador (Worker Rights Center) showed binational collaboration in using NAALC alongside a pressure campaign directed at global firms to dissuade them from accepting contract work produced under repressive conditions.

Finally, despite a decline in submissions, the politically motivated challenge to Mexico's labour law reforms, US NAO 2005–01, discussed fully in Chapter 10, led by the Washington Office on Latin American illustrated the development of transnational activist and think tank networks that had mobilized around labour rights issues in NAFTA. While some of this activism was emerging irrespective of the NAALC, the labour accord did provide a framework allowing encouraging further transnational networking. The NAALC contributed a forum and motivation (in the requisite binational action on public submissions) for social movement players in the three countries to work together to seek redress and social change for beleagured workers facing worsening prospects in the neo-liberal NAFTA region.

Despite these incremental institutional effects, scepticism remained about the effectiveness of the accord. There were several high profile reversals of seemingly positive decisions; and increased threats and intimidation produced a dampening effect, discouraging some from participating. After the rejection of US 9804, Canada's postal workers union declared: 'The NAFTA side accord has not proven to be an effective way of protecting workers' basic rights. And there is no reason to assume that a WTO side accord or working group would do a better job.'[118] CUPW Vice President Bourque opined,

> the Canadian government is either a signatory to an agreement that means something in terms of labour standards and is in breach of that agreement in the case of rural and suburban mail couriers .... . Or the Canadian government has deliberately entered into an agreement that is meaningless and provides no measures of protection for workers rights.[119]

The electrical workers president noted that the agreement on the seminar involving the Itapsa case fell apart when the NAO's changed their mind on worker participation; 'the NAO process has deteriorated into a farce, and under these circumstances we see no value in participating further'.[120]

---

118 Canadian Union of Postal Workers *Your Public Post Service: More than Just the Mail More than Just the Quebec-Windsor Corridor (Submission to the Canadian Government on Public Postal Services and the World Trade Organization's General Agreement on Trade in Services)* Ottawa, June 2000, 57.

119 Bourque, 'Denial of Basic Rights', 11.

120 John Hovis to Elaine Chao, July 24, 2002. [cited Oct. 24, 2002]. Available at http://mhssn.igc.org/nafta11.htm.

Other unions lamented the impact of NAFTA as business laid off Canadian and US workers to employ less protected Mexican labour; North American employers were now 'producing for a high wage consumer economy from a low wage platform'.[121] Despite NAO acceptance of worker concerns in the Custom Trim Case, unions were sceptical that the US would move towards disputes resolution: 'under a new, Republican president, it also seems unlikely that the U.S. Department of Labor will be more enthusiastic about imposing sanctions on Mexico over labor and safety problems in those same plants'.[122] The new Secretary of Labor rejected requests to initiate an ECE for this case. The rejection of the Duro Bag submission seems to indicate that even where secret elections are not permitted, the NAOs will not step in. The argument could be made that successes perceived earlier (after Han Young validated an independent union and Mexico pledged to hold secret ballot elections) were eroded as the pace of cases slowed and intervention appeared less vigorous.

Transnational political collaboration using the NAALC does continue, despite the frustrations. UNITE-HERE and Centro de Apoyo a los Trabajadores de Yucatán brought a case involving violations of minimum employment standards and safety and health standards in the apparel sector in Merida, Yucatan. The submission, US NAO 2004–01, was withdrawn pending further investigation. US NAO 2005–1 on Mexican Labour law reform (to be discussed in Chapter 10) showed a continuing willingness of transnational activists to employ NAALC to press for politically desirable changes.[123] Its rejection by the US NAO in February, 2006, may have a dampening effect on NGO and union use of the NAALC. US NAO 2005–02, respecting Mexican Airline Pilots was submitted in May 2005, but had not yet been accepted by the NAO at time of writing; it returned to familiar themes of denial of rights to free association, and an independent union, blocked by a phantom union with state acquiescence.[124] US NAO 2005–03 dealt with alleged violations of labour rights in the garment sector in Hidalgo; this submission covered almost all of NAALC's principles, including several which were sanctionable like health and

---

121 'Workers Fired by Canadian Company: NAFTA to Blame' (Joint Press Conference of NDP MP Bev Desjarlais, and union and worker representatives), Ottawa, August 20, 1997.

122 David Bacon 'Junked Workers Test NAFTA', [cited Nov. 25, 2001]. Available at http://www.zmag.org/ZMag/articles/feb01bacon.htm.

123 Washington Office on Latin America (WOLA), et. al., *Public Communication to the U.S. National Administrative Office under the North American Agreement on Labor Cooperation (NAALC) Concerning the Introduction of Reforms to the Federal Labor Code of Mexico (Abascal Project), Which Would Seriously Diminish Current Labor Standards, including the Right to Freely Associate, to Organize and to Bargain Collectively, in Violation of the Mexican Constitution, ILO Conventions Adopted By Mexico, and the NAALC*. February 17, 2005.

124 Asociacion Sindical de Pilotos Aviadores de Mexico *Re: Mexico's failure regarding its commitments and obligations arising under labor law matters as defined in the North American Agreement on Labor Cooperation Article 49 and Part Two of the NAALC, in relation to the labor conflict between Consorcio Aviaxsa. S.A. de C.V., dba Aviacsa Airlines and the Mexican Airline Pilots Union, ASPA de Mexico* May 15, 2005.

safety and child labour. This important case was accepted by the US NAO in January, 2006. These submissions came too close to this publication to be considered here. But they demonstrate that, despite frustrations, NAALC has not yet been entirely abandoned by unions and their supporters.

Supporters point to the nature of the NAALC to defend its accomplishments. One official noted, 'None of the three signatories (Canada, the United States and Mexico) gave up sovereignty in this'; the 'whole point of the agreement is that the three signatories have a better understanding of each others' labor laws'.[125] Some progressive voices were more hopeful noting that 'worker issues are being brought to light in a formal setting and are being formally considered by people with power to do something about them. Remedies, while perhaps not the ones we would like best, are being worked out.'[126] The recent cases indicate that optimism persists, though the Abascal reforms could reduce its potential. And cynics warned that NAALC provided no real protection; workers must oppose a hemispheric trade agreement with the same or weaker guarantees for labour.[127]

---

125 Megan Kamerick 'Maquiladoras face NAFTA challenge Local nonprofit group alleges serious health, safety woes' *San Antonio Business Journal* August 11, 2000. [cited May 11, 2002]. Available at http://www.bizjournals.com/sanantonio/stories/2000/08/14/story1.html.

126 'The NAO Hearing' *Newsletter*, Winter 2000 [cited June 26, 2002]. Available at http://www.flash.net/~sric/winter-2001/winter-01-3.htm.

127 'Custom Trim Workers Vindicated But will they be compensated?' Maquila Solidarity Network June 2001, [cited March 23, 2002]. Available at http://www.maquilasolidarity.org/resources/maquilas/customtrim3.htm.

Chapter 7

Protecting Migrant Workers: Mexican Cases

Introduction

The Mexican NAO has pursued cases involving migrant, Hispanic workers in the US, indicating a desire to protect its citizens abroad rather than improve American labour practices. By pursuing a focussed set of cases designed to protect the rights of its nationals, the Mexican NAO has achieved perhaps the most effective results from the NAALC. This does leave doubts about NAALC's ability to protect American workers in general from uneven, inadequate treatment in different states and sectors. And it is not clear that migrant rights have improved sufficiently to offset the costs of liberalization or to mitigate the anti-migrant backlash in recent US policy.

As a result, Mexican observers are also divided on NAALC's usefulness for labour. But there is evidence in these cases of considerable cross-border collaboration and networking. On the one hand, social actors from the US have augmented the submissions and assisted their Mexican partners in these complex cases, which have covered the full range of NAALC principles. On the other hand, new liaisons between local and federal agencies, Mexican consulates and social networks demonstrate some potential for the NAALC to generate transborder regionalization of benefit to migrant workers.

La Conexion Familiar (Sprint): The First Mexican Complaint

MEX 9501 was filed by the Sindicato de Telefonistas de la Republica Mexicana (STRM), with the Communication Workers of America (CWA), against the Sprint long distance company. Sprint disbanded a Latino subsidiary, La Conexion Familiar (LCF), 9 days before a representation election under the National Labor Relations Act.[1] The submission alleged that Sprint's closing of the subsidiary was designed to prevent the Communication Workers from gaining certification. 235 mainly Hispanic workers, employed in 'telemarketing' of long-distance service to Spanish-speakers in the Bay area lost their jobs. Sprint was targeting the lucrative Hispanic market, as many immigrants spent significantly on long distance calls back home.

---

1   Sindicato de Telefonistas de la Republica Mexicana Advertisement *El Universal* March 31, 1995, 10; Francisco Hernandez Juarez, Secretario General de STRM to Oficina Administrativa Nacional de los Estados Unidos Mexicanos, February 9, 1995.

Table 7.1   MEXICO NAO Submissions

Submission	Issues	Resolution	Follow-Up
Mexico NAO 9501 (SPRINT)	Association, Right to Organize	Reviewed, with no consultations	Public Forum; Secretariat study;
Mexico NAO 9801 (SOLEC)	Protection of Migrants;Right to Organize, Bargain; discrimination; minimum standards; prevention and compensation for illness or injury	Consultations and Joint Declaration	Outreach sessions and public forum; Secretariat guide; officials meetings
Mexico NAO 9802 (WASHINGTON APPLES)	See Mexico 9801	Consultations and Joint Declaration	See Mexico 9801
Mexico NAO 9803 (DECOSTER EGG)	See Mexico 9801	Consultations and Joint Declaration	See Mexico 9801
Mexico NAO 9804 (YALE-INS)	Minimum standards; protection of migrant workers	Consultations and Joint Declaration	Spanish materials for migrants; measures to protect migrants
Mexico NAO 2001-1 (NEW YORK WORKER COMPENSATION)	Protection of migrant workers; prevention and compensation for illness, injury	Accepted; no onsultations recommended	US procedural reform, information on migrants rights
Mexico NAO 2003-1 (NORTH CAROLINA VISA WORKERS)	See Mexico 9801	Accepted for review; pending	
Mexico NAO 2005-1 (IDAHO VISA WORKERS)	Protection of migrants; forced labour; discrimination; pay equity; prevention and compensation for illness, injury	Pending	

Source: North American Commission for Labor Cooperation Website

The complaint alleged that Sprint violated US law which guaranteed the right to freedom of organization for unions.

By April, 1994 many workers had signed union authorization cards. The petition for certification was accepted by the National Labour Relations Board and an election was scheduled for July 22. The complaint alleged that Sprint made 'an immediate and direct attack against the workers who were exercising their right to unionization' culminating with their firing on July 14.[2] An court injunction reinstating the workers was denied. Sprint's 'unethical' actions were permitted by the 'slow process of seeking remedies to violations of labor law in the United States'.[3] This was a serious violation of US NAALC commitments. Submitters asked the NAO to hold a hearing to pressure Sprint to comply with laws on freedom of organization and to reinstate fired workers. The plaintiffs sought measures to require Sprint to recognize the Communication Workers local and to encourage dialogue on worker protection and job creation. Finally the Mexican NAO should develop standards to address law violations affecting Mexican workers in the US, like those at La Conexion Familiar. Mexico's Telephonistas union deplored the violations of basic labour rights, declaring 'We do not want this to happen with Sprint in Mexico'.[4]

The Communication Workers union and individual workers filed with the National Labor Relations Board charging that the closure followed 58 alleged illegal actions to prevent unionization. Workers told a labour committee of the San Francisco Board of Supervisors about alleged interference, intimidation and abuses of union supporters, including the firing of protest leaders, managers' warnings that unionization might undermine La Conexion Familiar, and threats that the unilingual workers wouldn't get other jobs. Workers suggested the closing defied senior managers' rosy depictions of the subsidiary's prospects in this rich market.[5] The Labor Board ruled the company had violated 50 labour laws, with evidence that managers had admitted La Conexion Familiar's closure was meant to avoid unionization.[6]

Sprint appealed, arguing that La Conexion Familiar was disbanded because of a yearly loss of $4 million and a drop from 200,000 to 75,000 customers.[7] An administrative law judge acknowledged that workers were 'bombarded with statements by local La Conexion Familiar managers and supervisors that LCF ...

---

2   'Complaint Against Sprint Filed by Mexican Telephone Workers Union' Daily *Labor Report*, Feb. 10, 1995, E-6.

3   'Complaint Against Sprint ... ' E-7.

4   'Mexican Union Jabs Sprint' *Labor Activist* 1995, 2(3) [Cited Sept. 25, 1998]. Available at http://dsausa.org/archive/LA/LabAct23.html#E.

5   Communication Workers of America, 'Illegal Sprint/La Conexion Familiar Shutdown: 'All we Wanted Was a Union'' CWA, Public Affairs Department, Sept. 1994.

6   'Sprint's labor practices turn into cross-border controversy' *San Francisco Examiner* June 29, 1995, B-2.

7   'Sprint Hangs Up on Workers' *Multinational Monitor*, 17, March 1996 [Cited Oct. 13, 1998]. Available at http://multinationalmonitor.org/hyper/mm0396.03.html.

would be closed if the union got in'.[8] But he ruled that closure was economically justified, even if it was related to union organizing. The judge ordered Sprint not to 'threaten to close a facility they've already closed'; the union appealed to the Labor Board to seek reinstatement with back pay.[9]

Mexico's NAO predicted that this case would be resolved through cooperation.[10] However, after the US Sony decision, the Mexicans decided to accept this complaint. The NAO did not hold hearings, but collected information on US laws, and consulted the US NAO and lawyers for Sprint. The NAO report raised concerns about the 'effectiveness' of legal 'measures intended to guarantee ... fundamental ... labour principles' like free association and organization.[11] US laws held these rights in high regard, but new economic realities of free trade required a review of their implementation. The Mexican NAO was concerned with the impact of sudden closures on fundamental rights, and asked US Labor Secretary Robert Reich for ministerial consultations.[12] The CWA expressed 'pleasant surprise'. Although workers would not be compensated, consultations could dissuade companies from violating labour standards.[13] The report did not condemn Sprint, but sought a review of U.S. laws, which the company complied with 'fully'.[14] The US agreed to consultations, though sought to avoid conflict with court review of the Labor Board case.[15] The parties agreed to an exchange of information, a trinational study of plant closings, and a public forum for workers.[16]

At the forum in San Francisco, Mexico's telephone workers testified about the path-breaking effort by Mexican unions to assist US workers who faced 'racist

---

8   LCF and Sprint vs. Communication Workers of America, AFL-CIO, District 9, Before the NLRB Division of Judges, JD (SF) – 96–95, San Francisco, Aug. 30, 1995.

9   'Judge Affirms Charges of Illegal Worker Abuse By Sprint Corp. During Union Drive at Sprint/La Conexion Familiar in San Francisco: Union Will Urge Labor Board to Strengthen Remedy and Cite Sprint for Firing of 235' *CWA News*, Aug. 31, 1995, 2.

10   Interview with Mexican NAO officials, Feb. 13, 1995.

11   Oficina Administrative Nacional de México, *Informe sobre la Revisión de la Communicación Pública 9501OAN Mex* México, DF, May 31, 1995, 17.

12   *Informe sobre la Revisión de la Communicación Pública 9501/OAN Mex'*, 18.; 'Mexican NAO Asks Labor Chiefs to Discuss U.S. Laws, Sprint Case' *Inside NAFTA* 2, (1995), 8.

13   'U.S. Reviews Mexican NAO Charge on Sprint; CWA `Pleasantly Surprised' *Labor Relations Week* 9, (1995), 553–4; Marianne Lavelle, 'NAFTA jars labor laws; U.S., Mexico to discuss criticisms of Sprint's firing of employees' *National Law Journal* 17, 45 (1995), A9.

14   'Mexican NAO Asks Labor Chiefs to Discuss U.S. Laws', 8.

15   'Secretary of Labor Accepts Ministerial Consultations' U.S. Dept. of Labour News Release, June 26, 1995; Pamela Prah, 'Talks on Sprint NAFTA Charge, Chile Accession on Tap in Mexico', *Daily Labor Report* July 27, 1995, C-1.

16   'Ministerial Consultations – Submission 9501 (Sprint Case): Agreements on Implementation' Washington, Feb. 13, 1995; 'Agreement Reached Between Mexico and U.S. on Labor Issue' *U.S. Dept. of Labour News Release*, Dec. 17, 1995; 'Labor Department to Hold a Public Forum as Part of NAFTA Consultations with Mexico' *U.S. Dept. of Labour News Release*, Feb. 22, 1996.

aggression'.[17] The Communication Workers called the hearing a breakthrough, which could focus attention on anti-union policies like sudden closings. The union sought to bolster NAALC with company codes of conduct to recognize unions and to prevent cross-border relocation. The Hispanic workers detailed lack of water or bathroom breaks, unpaid commissions, exorbitant quotas, arbitrary schedule changes and pressure to spy on colleagues to thwart organizers. The Telephonistas wanted Sprint to alter its practices in case its strategic alliance with Telephonos de Mexico gave it a share of the Mexican market. American labour relations practices were depicted 'as the most acrimonious and open to abuse' in NAFTA [18]. The hearing helped correct perceptions that the NAALC was simply about Mexico's inadequate labour laws.

Sprint noted the administrative law ruling that La Conexion Familiar had closed for business reasons. Previous owners misrepresented LCF's profitability and employed illegal immigrants forcing Sprint to hire new workers and take a loss. Sprint noted improved working conditions at La Conexion Familiar, including wage increases, 401k contributions, legal hours of work, and comfortable facilities. After the money losing operation closed Sprint provided severance, career placement and counselling. Sprint recognized workers' rights to unionize, but stipulated to 245 violations of the National Labor Relations Act by local managers.[19] Sprint's lawyer examined Labor Board and court decisions, and determined that the law had been followed and the closure was for legitimate purposes, despite anti-union intimidation at La Conexion Familiar.[20]

The case dealt with freedom of association and sanctions did not apply, despite the costs to workers. The hearing showed the 'extraordinary' visibility of labour issues raised by complainants, even with weak enforcement mechanisms.[21] Despite the lack of recourse for fired workers, the CWA welcomed the opportunities for public review of plant closings, and hoped this would induce changes. 'It is cost-effective for Sprint to wage a legal battle because of the lengthiness of the process and the weakness of U.S. labor laws. Only by putting Sprint in the public spotlight will they be forced to address the violations.'[22] The Labor Board ruled in 1996 that Sprint's plan closure violated the rights to organize, and ordered workers reinstated. This was overturned in federal court in 1997, since Sprint acted for economic reasons. Despite

---

17   Testimony of Francisco Hernandez Juarez, ILAB Public Forum, San Francisco, Feb. 27, 1996, 27.

18   Peter M. Tirschwell, 'NAFTA Case Highlights Charges of US Workers' Rights Abuses' *Journal of Commerce* Feb. 29, 1996.

19   Written Statement of Sprint Corporation, Public Forum on Submission 9501 Filed under the North American Agreement on Labor Cooperation, Feb. 27, 1996.

20   Testimony of Roberto Corrada, ILAB Public Forum, San Francisco, Feb. 27, 1996, 47–8.

21   Diane Lindquist, 'NAFTA Fallout: Related Accord Subjects Sprint to a First-Ever 3-Nation Probe' *San DiegoTelegraph* March 10, 1996.

22   'Labor Secretaries Agree on Action Plan in Sprint Case' *BorderLines* 20 Jan. 1996, [cited March 22 1997]. Available at http://www.us-mex.org/borderlines/1996/bl20/bl20brf.html.

a 'fabricated a paper trail to obfuscate the closure date' evidence of La Conexion Familiar's financial decline was persuasive.[23]

This case demonstrated a new attitude of some US unions, who hoped cooperation with Mexican and Canadian workers could forge transnational 'codes of conduct'.[24] Communications workers forged transnational union links, in response to liberalization in this sector, including US deregulation and Mexican privatization. Structural shifts from this altered climate and from technological change made this sector a test for union responses to globalization. Cooperation between the US Commmunication Workers and Mexico's Telephonistas contributed to common strategies in future NAALC cases. The latter worried that Sprint could acquire some of Mexico's privatized communication market. Globalization and regionalization caused 'interdependency and alliance among companies of different countries'. This caused a 'tendency on the part of multinational companies to implement policies which go beyond mere technological change and new forms of administrative and financial management. The hegemony of multinationals has political and social consequences which impact workers worldwide ...'.[25] This inspired unions to cooperate across borders to seek codes of conduct to avoid low wage competition and poor working conditions. But this transnational alliance was dealt a blow by court rulings which ruled that layoffs were justified by economic decline. The process provided little help for La Conexion Familiar workers, who had 'no enforceable rights' under NAALC.[26]

Protecting Migrant Mexican Workers: Solec

The Solec International case (MEX 9801) involved delays in the National Labor Relations Board process and alleged violations of occupational health and safety and overtime pay laws for Latino workers. Solec, a subsidiary of the Japanese Sanyo and Sumitomo Bank, employed 130 persons in California, making solar panels for Sanyo's Japanese facilities. Workers sought representation with the Oil, Chemical, and Atomic Workers International Union, because of exposure to toxic chemicals like hydrofluoric acid, titanium, nickel and chromium. Despite reports of skin, eye, ear and throat problems, workers alleged the Occupational Safety and Health Administration carried out cursory inspections and workers were not given medical examinations. Aged safety equipment caused burns and respiratory problems. Vague job classifications and pay scales ignored seniority; raises and promotions allegedly reflected connections, not merit. Those challenging low pay faced firing. Workers

---

23   La Conexion Familiar and Sprint Corporation vs. NLRB 96–1500, Nov. 27, 1997.

24   Carey Goldberg, 'U.S. Labor Making Use of Trade Accord it Fiercely Opposed' *New York Times* Feb. 28, 1996, A11.

25   'Complaint Against Sprint Filed by Mexican Telephone Workers Union' *Daily Labor Report*, Feb. 10, 1995, E-6.

26   Robert Collier, 'Sprint Exonerated in Mass Layoff of S.F. Workers: Case tested unions' ability to adapt to NAFTA policies' *San Francisco Chronicle* Nov. 28, 1997, A3.

charged discrimination, as there were no African-American workers and Latinos complained of bias.[27]

The case was submitted to the Mexican NAO by Local 1–675 of the Oil, Chemical and Atomic Workers International Union (OCAW), Sindicato de Trabajadores de Industria y Comercio '6 de octubre' (the 'October 6' Industrial and Commercial Workers Union), Unión de Defensa Laboral Comunitaria (Labor Community Defense Union or UDLC); and the Support Committee for Maquiladora Workers (SCMW). The submission alleged that Solec 'acted in complicity with the U. S. Government … to suppress the labor rights and safety and health rights of Solec workers engaged in lawful efforts to organize'.[28] The Labor Board allegedly allowed a union buster to conduct meetings and threaten workers in violation of the NLRA. When the election was held, a Labor Board agent allowed the company to exclude 'group leaders' as supervisors, despite a prior Board dismissal of this claim. Votes were not counted for 4 months while a company allegation of unfair labour practices was heard. The Board did not act promptly on Solec's appeal, allowing managers to continue alleged demoralization of unionists.[29] The slow process violated NAALC's exhortation to enforce labour rights without undue delays. The US disregarded NAALC requirements to minimize accidents and illnesses, enforce standards for hours and overtime, and eliminate discrimination. The NLRA and ILO conventions were also ignored.[30]

The petitioners wanted Mexico's NAO to address the Labor Board's 'failure to observe the right of freedom of association, inasmuch as this is not a matter of isolated incident'.[31] They sought a hearing in Tijuana, measures to ensure that Solec conformed to U.S. laws and NAALC principles, and investigation of Labor Board and Occupational Health and Safety Administration deficiencies. Submitters requested ministerial consultations if these agencies were biased towards Solec or racist towards Hispanics. Mexico's NAO did not follow the U.S. lead and hold public hearings, but asked the American NAO about US laws. The US NAO confirmed that Solec was cited for health and safety violations, lack of injury and illness prevention, inadequate protection against falls, corroded pipes and blocked access to a fire extinguisher. The company paid a fine and moved to a new location. Workers were interviewed and OSHA found that workers were not exposed to illegal levels of chemicals like hydrochloric acid, nickel or chromium. After the submission, state and federal officials found 11 violations such as lack of protective eyewear, inappropriate gloves, missing equipment guards, improperly stored chemicals and gas cylinders, and hazards like tripping and electrical maintenance. The NAO noted

---

27   OCAW Local I-675 et. al., *Public Communication to the National Administrative Office (NAO) Regarding Irreparable Harm to the Right of Freedom of Association and the Right to Organize and Regarding the U. S. Government's Failure to Enforce the Law: The Case of Solec, Inc. in Carson city, California, United States of America* April 9, 1998, 9–15.

28   OCAW Local I-675 et. al., *Public Communication The Case of Solec*, Inc., 4.

29   OCAW Local I-675 et. al., *Public Communication The Case of Solec*, Inc., 15–22.

30   OCAW Local I-675 et. al., *Public Communication The Case of Solec,* Inc., 22–28.

31   OCAW Local I-675 et. al., *Public Communication … The Case of Solec* , 5.

that the Labor Board imposed no penalties and had unclear time lines for appeals. It acknowledged that US laws did not protect union organizers from reprisals.[32]

The Mexican NAO report on Solec summarized the submission and did not take a position on the claims, leaving this to ministerial consultations. The Mexican authorities emphasized sovereignty and the limits of NAALC, which was 'not intended to create supra-national mechanisms, since it is not its function to judge or attempt to amend laws, but rather promote strict compliance with U.S. law and to protect worker rights'[33]. But Mexican Secretary of Labour Mariano Palacios Alcocer requested consultations on freedom of association, collective bargaining, safety and health, minimum standards, and racial discrimination. By the time consultations were held, the focus was on the problems of migrant agricultural labour raised in the Apple and Egg cases below. The industrial health and safety and organizational issues raised by Solec received limited consideration.

Human Rights Watch summarized this problem:

> The ministerial agreement between the Mexican and U.S. governments did not address the problems in the Solec case. The failure of the Mexican NAO to explain its reasoning, or to include findings and conclusions, made it impossible to know whether the ministerial agreement's weakness stemmed from a belief that the allegations were without merit, or if it indicated that the state parties simply did not wish to address the problems highlighted by the petitioners.[34]

Thus, 'this complaint led to no substantive programming on the issue of collective bargaining'[35], a disappointing result after Sprint. The outcome was a bilateral exchange of information, with no consideration of the effectiveness of federal agencies The Labor Board belatedly recognized the October 1997 representation election; workers in OCAW Local 1-675 negotiated a contract by mid-1998.[36] aided in part by the NAALC.[37]

Protecting Mexican Agrarian Workers: Washington Apples

Mexican and American activists sought cases on the plight of migrant agricultural workers, who were essential to the competitiveness of American farms and orchards.

---

32   U.S. NAO. 'U.S. Responses to Mexican NAO Questions; Additional Occupational Safety and Health Matters Mexican Submission 9801 Solec', Nov. 24, 1998, 1–3.

33   Mexico, Secretariat of Labor and Social Security, NAO, Review Report: Public Notice MEX 9801 Mexico DF, August, 1999.

34   Human Rights Watch, Trading *Away Rights: The Unfulfilled Promise of NAFTA's Labor Side Agreement* April 2001, 40.

35   Human Rights Watch, 2001, 43.

36   Gary Holloway 'Solec Workers Win First Contract!' *The Organizer* (OCAW Local 1–675), 3, 1 September , 1998, [cited May 28, 1999]. Available at http://www.pace8-675.org/articles/organizer0998.html.

37   Kelly Quinn 'Stand And Deliver: The Solec Unit Organizing Campaign' *The Organizer* (OCAW Local 1–675) 3 July 1998 [cited May 28, 1999]. Available at http://www.pace8-675.org/articles/organizer0798.html.

This industry suffered low wages and health and safety problems. Although problems were well documented, little had changed since a 1970s congressional report noted:

> Migrant and seasonal farmworkers have long been among the most exploited groups in the American labor force. Despite their hard toil and valuable contribution to our nation's economy, their lot has historically been characterized by low wages, protracted hours, and horrid working conditions. These families, and particularly the children of these workers, have also suffered from the typical symptoms of chronic poverty – being under-educated, ill-fed, poorly housed, and lacking even the most rudimentary sanitary facilities. The tragedy is further compounded when it is realized that the victims of poverty are in fact the working poor, those who offer an honest day's labor but are denied the full benefits such work should provide, which are so desperately needed to provide the most basic necessities of life.[38]

80% of migrant farm workers are Mexican; many are illiterate and exploitable, speak little English, and do jobs Americans reject for less than minimum wage.[39]

The Apple Pickers case (MEX 9802) considered the failure to protect migrants in Washington State's apple industry. The case covered several NAALC principles and exposed inadequacies in US laws. Problems included exclusion of agricultural workers from labour laws, violations of the right to organize, delays in enforcing rights, falling value of wages, poverty among migrants, poor enforcement of health and safety and minimum wages, and denial of equal legal protection. Apple pickers complained about efforts to prevent them from unionizing with the Teamsters. Workers alleged wage cuts for activists, forced attendance at anti-union meetings, health and safety violations, heavy work for injured workers, and discrimination against Mexicans.[40] After losing two votes, the Teamsters alleged intimidation and threats of INS raids and deportation, and asked the National Labor Relations Board to grant certification.[41]

Unions and their supporters hoped this case would set a precedent for these vulnerable workers, who were denied their rights because of lack of knowledge of language or law and fear of deportation. Covering seven of NAALC's 11 labour principles,[42] it marked 'an important step for scrutinising labor law enforcement in the United States, where there are severe problems of discrimination against workers who try to form unions and where migrant workers face widespread labor

---

38   Quoted in Statement of Columbia Legal Services, NAALC Seminar, Yakima Washington, August, 2001, 2–3.

39   Carole Pearson 'A case of apples: Mexican farm workers in Washington' *Our Times,* 20, 6 Dec. 2001/Jan. 2002, 21–28.

40   National Radio Project 'Empty Promises: NAFTA and the Workforce' [cited June 12, 2002]. Available at http://www.radioproject.org/transcripts/9840.html, June 12, 2002.

41   Jim Lobe, 'Mexicans File Complaint Against U.S. Applegrowers' *Inter Press Service,* May 27, 1998, 1.

42   'Faulting U.S. Labor Laws, Mexican Unions File 'Broadest' NAFTA Labor Complaint on Washington State Apple Industry', *International Labor Rights Fund Press Release* May 27, 1998 [cited June 7, 2002]. Available at http://laboris.uqam.ca/anact/Applepress.htm.

and human rights violations.'[43] This case continued Mexico's concern for the well-being of its citizens; many of the 45,000 migrant workers in Washington's orchards migrated from Michoacan and Oaxaca. Mexico was a large market for US apples; for submitters, 'what's going on is a veritable 'social dumping' of apples exported to Mexico, with companies tripling their profits by violating workers' rights.'[44]

The submission was made by the Unión Nacional de Trabajadores (UNT), Frente Democrático Campesino (FDC), Frente Auténtico del Trabajo (FAT), and its metalworkers affiliate, the Sindicato de Trabajadores de la Industria Metálica, Acero, Hierro, Conexos y Similares (STIMACHS). This alliance of dissident Mexican unions was aided by the International Brotherhood of Teamsters (IBT), the International Labor Rights Fund (ILRF), and the National Employment Law Project (NELP). It targeted Stemlit Growers and Washington Fruit, which were accused of violating NLRA, ILO and NAALC on association and organization, bargaining, minimum standards, non-discrimination, compensation for injuries and illnesses, and protection of migrants. The submitters stated that 'Violations of Mexican and U.S. workers' rights in the Washington State apple industry continue because the United States has failed to develop laws, regulations, procedures and practices that protect the rights and interests of the workers, contrary to its commitment under the Labor Principles of the NAALC.'[45]

Mexican migrants had unequal protection in the right to organize, because illegally obtained evidence could be used against them. Compensation for injuries and fatalities was lower than for US nationals or Canadian immigrants. Immigrants under the H-2-A program did not enjoy guarantees of transportation or workplace safety, salary levels or housing conditions. They were not protected from reprisals for union activities or compensation claims and could be black-listed. They lacked health insurance because they worked too few hours and immigration rules limited emergency care even for legal migrants. Finally, migrants fared poorly in family reunification because they fell below new income minima.

The companies allegedly used threats and discrimination to persuade pickers to vote against the Teamsters even though most had signed union cards. Teamsters' appealed to the National Labor Relations Board for certification because of illegal interference, but faced delays, so the NAO appeal was launched. The Labor Board's process 'has ceased to be a test of free choice for union representation by the workers, and has become, rather, a vehicle for campaigns of intimidation and coercion by the employers'.[46] The Teamsters sought 'voluntary recognition' via a tally of signed membership cards, instead of a certification vote.[47] The NLRA excluded farm

---

43 Lobe, May 27, 1998, 1.

44 ILRF Press release, May 27, 1998.

45 STIMHACS, FAT, UNT, FDC, *Violations of NALCA Labor Principles and Obligations in the Washington State Apple Industry (Public Submission to the Mexican NAO)*, Mexico, DF., May 27, 1998, 3.

46 *Violations of NALCA Labor Principles in the Washington State Apple Industry*, 9.

47 *Violations of NALCA Labor Principles in the Washington State Apple Industry*, 7.

workers and state guarantees were not enforceable. Thus apple workers lacked protection from anti-union discrimination, highlighting inadequacies in US laws. But the submission also claimed deficient enforcement, including complex procedures, delays, and lack of penalties.

The submission alleged violations of NAALC principle 6, on minimum wages, overtime and working conditions. Wages had not kept pace with the cost of living, and agricultural work was seasonal, lasting only seven months. Despite industry profitability, pickers and warehouse workers fell into poverty, and lacked medical insurance. Wages did not reflect productivity.[48] Using contractors as middlemen removed workers from the Fair Labour Standards Act, denying them overtime pay. Despite exposure to pesticides and ergonomic stress, protective gear was minimal. Environmental Protection Agency rule changes allowed workers to return to contaminated areas in 4, not 12 hours. Allegedly, workers who sought investigations of illnesses were fired. Pesticide limits were enforced by the state, which lacked the capacity or, allegedly, the will to act.[49] Budget cuts at the National Labor Relations Board and Occupational Safety and Health Administration 'severely hampered effective enforcement of labor laws'.[50] Submitters asked the Mexican NAO to assess the situation in Washington first hand and to hold information sessions. Ministerial consultations should develop a plan to end violations and produce a code of conduct for employers. If necessary, Mexico should initiate an evaluation committee on technical labour standards, followed by arbitration and sanctions.[51] Arbitrators could 'cancel tariff benefits under the NAFTA for apple exports from Washington' unless workers rights were restored.[52] Teamsters concurred that NAALC 'is a tremendous forum for exposing the reality that workers face'.[53]

The apple industry accused unions of 'abusing' the NAALC to increase their power; the case could 'open doors to a host of frivolous and costly complaints against U.S. employers'.[54] Without low wages, the industry would have to replace workers with machines. 'We are blessed with a bountiful labor supply. If there is something we want done, we throw bodies at it and they cost $7.50 an hour.... If we have to pay

---

48   *Violations of NALCA Labor Principles in the Washington State Apple Industry*, 13.

49   *Violations of NALCA Labor Principles in the Washington State Apple Industry* 14–21.

50   John Nagel,'NAFTA: Mexico Seeks Ministerial-Level Talks on Washington Apples' *Daily Labor Report* Sept. 8, 1999, A-6.

51   *Violations of NALCA Labor Principles in the Washington State Apple Industry* 26–28.

52   Nagel, 1999, A-6.

53   Evelyn Iritani, 'Mexico Charges Upset Apple Chart in U.S.'. *Los Angeles Times*, 20, August 1999, D2. [Cited June 6, 2001]. Available at http://www.american.edu/projects/mandala/TED/picker.htm.

54   'Apple Picker Rights: An Apple a Day, Keeps the Unions Away' [cited June 7, 2001]. Available at http://www.american.edu/projects/mandala/TED/picker.htm.

$12 an hour, those people are gone'.[55] This was an acute issue in an industry facing stiff competition from trade liberalization.

The Mexican NAO accepted the submission and held an informal public meeting to gather evidence from workers and to develop an understanding of conditions in Washington.[56] The US NAO reported that Washington state operated an occupational safety and health program that exceeded OSHA's requirements. State penalties were lower, but there was no direct link to higher levels of illnesses and injuries, which had declined in Washington faster than the national average. Budget cuts and fewer inspectors were offset by state spending and cooperation with employers to improve conditions, which reduced injury and illness. Federal law excluded farm workers from bargaining, but the Labour Department actively helped workers find employment and increase earnings, while the Immigration and Naturalization Service helped 'reduce the oversupply of undocumented workers'.[57] The NLRA, OSHA and the Fair Labor Standards Act (FLSA) applied equally to migrants, who are entitled to compensation for injuries or illnesses. No workers may be dismissed for filing health and safety complaints, but employers could dismiss workers based on 'the frequency or nature of the worker's job-related accidents'.[58]

The Mexican NAO report was again a recitation of petitioners' claims followed by a review of NAALC and American laws. The report noted that the US had not ratified ILO Agreement No. 87 on freedom of association and right to organize. US law did not prevent employers from conducting anti-union campaigns since 'the expression of any point of view, argument, or dissemination of opinions ... does not constitute job discrimination'.[59] But dominating worker organizations, firing or blacklisting a worker because of union activities or refusing to bargain were unfair practices. The Mexican NAO found no legal basis for paying migrant workers below minimum wage or for non-enforcement of health, safety and non-discrimination laws. Mexico requested consultations on freedom of association and right to organize, minimum conditions, discrimination, and prevention of and compensation for safety and health problems. The report noted that under NAALC, migrants' 'legal protection ... must be the same, in labor-related matters, as those enjoyed by ... domestic workers'.[60]

The National Labor Relations Board ruled for workers respecting violations of the right to organize, though it dismissed a worker's claim of dismissal for union activity. Stemlit and Teamsters agreed that authorization cards could determine

55   Philip Martin 'Immigration and Farm Labor: An Overview' University of California, Davis August 31, 1999, 9 [cited June 11, 2002]. Available at www.farmfoundation.org/1999NPPEC/martin.pdf.

56   STPS, OAN de México, *Se celebro en México Reunion Sobre Presunta Violacion de derechos de Trabajadores Migrantes en Washington,* México, DF, Dec. 2, 1998.

57   U.S. NAO, 'U.S. Responses to Mexican NAO Questions Mexican Submission 9802 Washington State Apple Industry', Nov. 30, 1998, 7.

58   U.S. Responses to Mexican NAO Questions Mexican Submission 9802, 11.

59   Mexico, Secretariat of Labor and Social Security, *NAO, Review Reports, Public Notice MEX 9802* Mexico, DF, August, 1999, 9.

60   *Review Reports, Public Notice MEX 9802,* 19.

Worker's desire for certification.[61] But conditions for migrant workers, who lived in squalor, without necessities, would not quickly improve.[62]

Because growers are not required to provide accommodation for their employees, it's not uncommon to see workers camped along the river banks or in the orchards, living in shelters of discarded cardboard and plastic tarps. Others live out of their cars, or crowd into vans to sleep. Some are housed in dreary trailer parks of vermin-infested, rotting, mobile homes.[63]

Teamsters criticized immigration authorities for having illegal workers fired. Such workers remained vital to the industry and an INS crackdown could create increased hardships for the largely female Mexican migrants.[64]

At the public forum in Yakima, migrant farm workers testified about the 'disrespect for persons, inadequate pay, exploitation and discrimination'.[65] They complained of unpaid wages, dismissals for unionism, inadequate rest breaks, and denial of workers' compensation. Some inspectors accepted company claims not to have used pesticides even when doctors demonstrated worker exposure. Workers who reported violations and chemical exposure were denied treatment and faced harassment. Workers allegedly paid high rent to live in housing without adequate kitchens, toilets or basic appliances.[66] Workers depicted the apple industry as suspicious of unions, which were needed to improve standards. Since domestic remedies had not succeeded, the workers had turned to NAALC.

Growers responded that Washington's laws were stronger and wages were higher and rising faster than in other states. Piece-rate pay was less than minimum wage, but growers provided subsidies. The Equal Employment Opportunities Commission provided information on services for migrants and enforced standards irrespective of immigration status. The growers association provided education in pesticide safety. Orchards were regulated by two government agencies, and if 'current laws do not seem effective it is due to inconsistent enforcement'.[67] NAALC was not a proper forum for such issues, which the Labor Board or state agencies should address as unfair labour practices. The Growers asserted that unions like the United Farm Workers (UFW) opposed 'the creation of an agricultural labor relations board in

---

61   'Taste of Victory' *AFL-CIO Work in Progress* September 20, 1999 [cited June 10, 2002]. Available at http://www.aflcio.org/publ/wip1999/wip0920.htm.

62   Lynda V. Mapes 'Fruit Pickers' Summer of Squalor' *Seattle Times* August 2, 1998, [cited June 12, 2002]. Available at http://www.jsri.msu.edu/commconn/latnews/aug98b.html.

63   Pearson, 2002.

64   Philip Martin 'Immigration and Farm Labor: An Overview', 8.

65   NAALC *Public Forum: Promoting Dialogue among Migrant Agricultural Workers, Growers and Government Officials*, Yakima, Washington, August 8, 2001, 1.

66   'Statement of Columbia Legal Services', NAALC Seminar, Yakima Washington, August, 2001, 1–2.

67   *'Public Forum: Promoting Dialogue ...'*, 2.

Washington state because this would outlaw secondary boycotts and mandate secret ballot elections'.[68]

Submitters and their US allies like the National Employment Law Project pressed Washington State to hire more inspectors, and improve policies on health and safety, enforcement and compensation. But the Department of Labor and Industries did not propose timetables for increased penalties for wage and hour violations. Nor did it act swiftly on improved health and safety rules or bilingual access to workers' compensation.[69] Pesticide regulations and safety enforcement remained deficient, though a supreme court ruling on the states' failure to ensure medical monitoring of exposure created pressure for stronger enforcement and better compensation.[70] A United Farm Workers' representative declared, 'We hope to work cooperatively with the state and federal governments to reach a model of labor relations in which fair returns to growers are coupled with fair protection of workers' collective bargaining rights, rights with respect to labor standards, and their health and safety'.[71] Submitters hoped the case could proceed toward an ECE or disputes resolution.[72] But the Fox administration did not appear eager to enforce these elements of the NAALC, despite the President's pledge to defend the interests of migrant workers.

Protecting Mexican Agrarian Workers: Decoster Eggs

The DeCoster Egg Farm case (MEX 9803) involved alleged mistreatment of migrant Mexican workers in Maine. Allegations included violations of laws governing health and safety, living conditions, worker compensation and discrimination based on national origin. The DeCoster Egg facility had been fined $3.6 million in 1996, (eventually settling for $2 million) after being cited for poor work and housing conditions, delays in pay and illegal deductions for rent.[73] Other allegations included unpaid overtime, sexual discrimination, unsanitary housing (with up to 17 persons per trailer), unsafe machines, no assistance for the sick, and retaliation against those seeking improvements.[74] The Mexican government joined a class action suit which alleged that the US had done little to protect workers' rights. The suit, which represented 1500 Mexicans employed at the facility after 1992 claimed

---

68   'Public Forum: Promoting Dialogue ...', 5.

69   Rebecca Smith, NELP, to Lewis Karesh et. al., April 17, 2002.

70   NELP, 'Status of Issues Raised in NAALC Submission No. 9802 and at Public Forum on August 8, 2001', Attached to Smith to Karesh, April 17, 2002.

71   'U.S., Mexican Officials to Hear Workers' Claims in Trade, Labor Rights Dispute under NAFTA; Sanctions Could Result' *National Employment Law Project Press Release* August 06, 2001, [cited June 12, 2002]. Available at http://nelp.org/press/pr080601naalcfull.pdf.

72   Email from Rebecca Smith, NELP to the Author June 12, 2002.

73   Steven G. Vegh, 'Farm's infamy drew unusual suit' *Portland Press Herald* May 25, 1998.

74   Irasema Garza to Lewis Karesh, email, May 18, 1998 (forwarding email from Michael Fluharty of OSHA). US NAO Public Files on MEX 9803.

racial bias, since Hispanics received worse treatment than whites: 'The efforts by DeCoster to stigmatize the class plaintiffs as inferior carries a universal sting against which Mexico seeks to protect Mexican nationals'.[75] Mexico claimed the principle of *parens patrie*, a right to defend its nationals, and paid the costs of the suit (with the settlement payable to workers).[76] Mexico's consul in Boston argued that workers had been 'lured' from jobs in Texas by false claims about conditions in Maine and had to work amidst chicken waste.[77]

The company, which had been divided into smaller firms, responded that most managers were Hispanic and that workers had rejected union representation. It was 'ironic' that Mexico 'which is banning trade unions, jailing political dissidents, having really terrible working conditions, would somehow now complain about working conditions 3,000 miles from its border'.[78] A company lawyer argued that if Mexico wanted to protect its nationals it should sue in states with larger Mexican populations, like Texas or California, and improve protections in Mexico.[79] Managers argued that conditions had improved and were better than those in Mexico. Workers could use state and federal equal opportunities commissions to seek improvements; the suit was 'nothing more than a money grab'.[80] OSHA reduced its penalties when De Coster agreed to hire safety managers, allow independent audits, deliver training in Spanish and provide clean water, basic hygeine and medical care.[81] An independent audit confirmed improvements on many deficincies.

The NAO submission by the Confederación de Trabajadores de México (CTM) marked the first time any PRI-linked 'official' union had submitted a case. This submission alleged a failure by the U.S. government to ensure equal protection of migrant workers. Federal and state officials allegedly did not enforce laws protecting against breaches of contract. Workers had to pay for housing and transport after being promised these were covered. De Coster allegedly violated minimum standards for living quarters for migrants and state authorities did not inspect or certify the housing as acceptable. Submitters noted that Mexican workers did not receive written

---

75   'Mexico vs. DeCoster: Grandstanding or concern for its citizens?' *Associated Press*, May 26, 1998.

76   Embassy of Mexico, 'Mexican Workers File Class Action Suit Against De Coster Egg Farm' *News Release* Washington, May 18, 1998.

77   David L. Marcus, 'Mexico joins workers' suit against egg farm in Maine' *Boston Globe* May 19, 1998, A1.

78   Steven G. Vegh, 'Farm's infamy drew unusual suit' *Portland Press Herald* May 25, 1998.

79   'Mexico vs. DeCoster: Grandstanding or concern for its citizens?'

80   Marcus, 1998.

81   Lisa Finnegan, 'DeCoster scrambles, corrects violations' *Occupational Hazards*, 60 (Sept. 1998), 11; Lisa Finnegan 'OSHA mandates safety program at DeCoster' *Occupational Hazards* 59, (July, 1997), 16.

terms of employment.[82] The submission claimed inadequate enforcement of anti-discrimination laws with workplace harassment, threats and intimidation directed at Mexicans. Non-Mexicans were allegedly treated favourably on performance criteria and unsafe tasks, had better quality, housing, medical coverage, and longer medical leave.[83] Both housing and workplace exposed workers to health and safety risks and Mexicans who suffered injuries or illness were denied legal compensation.[84]

The Mexican NAO accepted the submission and requested clarification on US and Maine laws covering migrant workers. The US NAO affirmed that migrants were entitled to equal protection for minimum wages under the Fair Labour Standards Act. But the FLSA excluded agricultural workers (American and foreign born) from overtime pay. The Migrant and Seasonal Agricultural Worker Protection Act (MWPA) protected migrants dealing with contractors and employers, on hiring, transporting, and housing. Both domestic and foreign born H-2A workers were exempt from MSPA. Federal and state anti-discrimination laws prohibited discrimination against Mexicans. While the NLRA excluded farm workers in the poultry industry, Maine state laws protected the right to organize and bargain for larger operations. Workers were entitled to written guarantees, in their language, of job conditions, and employers must meet minimum standards for housing and sanitation. Foreign workers had the right to make health and safety complaints to OSHA. The Labor Board could investigate violations of standards, discrimination and illegal restrictions on rights to organize. The Equal Employment Opportunities Commission (EEOC) protected Mexican workers against discrimination. The US NAO described specific measures in the DeCoster case, including fines and a new health and safety regime, housing, medical and sanitary improvements, and a bilingual ombudsperson.[85]

The Mexican NAO report documented petitioners' claims and applicable US laws. But no hearings were held, and no independent fact-finding was conducted. The Mexicans requested ministerial consultations

> to obtain further information about the steps that the [US] government is taking to guarantee that Mexican migrant agricultural workers enjoy the same labor protection as nationals with respect to labor rights and minimum employment standards, elimination of discrimination in the workplace, prevention and compensation in cases of occupational injuries and illnesses, and protection of migrant workers.[86]

---

82   Confederación de Trabajadores de México, *Public Communication on Possible Violations of Employment Rights in U.S. Territory; The Case of DeCoster Egg*, Aug. 4, 1998, 6.

83   *Public Communication on ... DeCoster Egg*, Aug. 4, 1998, 7–8.

84   *Public Communication on ... DeCoster Egg,* Aug. 4, 1998, 9–10.

85   U.S. NAO, 'Mexico NAO Submission 9803 (DeCoster) Questions: U. S. NAO Responses' Washington, Dec. 22, 1998.

86   Department of Labor and Social Welfare, Mexican NAO, *Report of Review: MEX Public Communication 9803* (Mexico DF: Dec., 1999), 4.

The lawsuit filed by Mexico was dismissed, as courts ruled that the doctrine of *parens patrie*, normally applied between US states, had no standing in international law and the Circuit court deferred to the executive and Congress. In dismissing Mexico's role as co-plaintiff, the judge noted that Mexico could finance lawsuits by workers and use the NAALC to protect its nationals. Mexico continued to support the plaintiffs via its consulate and covered over $100,000 in costs. This Mexican role as defender of migrants introduced a new line of defence for these marginal workers. Jorge Dominguez noted, 'Mexico is going to great lengths to protect its people like never before.... . The case in Maine shows a commitment and an attitude that's new and refreshing.'[87] A mediator proposed a $6 million settlement , but after two years of negotiations, the sum was reduced to $3.2 million to be split 1500 workers. The migrants' representatives acknowledged improvements in housing and conditions at former De Coster operations, which could now serve as a 'model'.[88]

The Apple and DeCoster cases were addressed together (with Solec), in ministerial consultations after a long delay. The ministers promised to promote the protection of migrants, and agreed to a conference on the legal, social and economic situation of agricultural migrants. The US Department of Labor hosted meetings to discuss the concerns of Mexican workers, 'including inspection programs and systems for determining violations of employment conditions for migrant workers' in health and safety, housing conditions, and workplace conditions.[89] The NAO held information sessions in Washington and Maine to inform migrant workers about their legal rights. The NAO also held a seminar on 'Promoting Dialogue Among Migrant Agricultural Workers, Growers and Government Officials' in Yakima, Washington. Finally, a public meeting on migrant worker rights was held in Augusta, Maine with farm owners, workers, NGOs, federal and state officials, and Mexican labour and consular officials on wages, lodging, visas, and discrimination.[90] Delegates also discussed the US Supreme Court ruling in the Hoffman case which suggested illegal immigrants did not have the same protection as Americans if wrongly fired. The NAALC Secretariat drafted a trinational guide for migrant labourers. However, Mexico did not initiate an ECE, arbitration or trade penalties on these cases.

---

87 Alfredo Corchado 'Case of workers alleging mistreatment in Maine illustrates attitude shift' *The Dallas Morning News,* December 13, 2001.

88 'DeCoster reaches migrant settlement' *Bangor Daily News* June 21, 2002.

89 'Agreement on Ministerial Consultations: Mexican NAO Submissions 9801, 9802, and 9803' May 18, 2000, 2.

90 STPS, OAN de México, Boletin 077, 'Reunión sobre Derechos Laborales de los Trabajadores Migratorios en Estados Unidos' Mexico DF, June 9, 2002.

Expanding the Protective Net: The Yale INS Case

The Yale/INS case (MEX NAO 9804) alleged a failure to provide minimum wages and overtime pay to foreign nationals because of a memorandum of understanding between the Immigration and Naturalization Service (INS) and the Department of Labor.[91] The Clinton policy, called 'interior enforcement', sought to reduce the flow of illegal migrants by targeting them at work, which was the major magnet drawing them to the US. Workers faced dismissal if they could not prove legal residency. The INS used visa status, collected by employers on the I-9 form, to make the determination, and cooperated with Labor inspectors and the Social Security administration, to uncover illegal workers.

Employers allegedly volunteered visa information on union activists to dissuade labour organizing. This discouraged valid complaints and allowed violations of standards by firms hiring illegal migrants. The chilling effect was discriminatory and led to suboptimal enforcement of standards, as many cases never came forward. INS' reporting 'policy amounts to a gag order on immigrant workers ... If no one can complain about slave wages, sweatshop owners have a green light to ignore minimum wage and overtime laws.'[92] INS raids and deportations ensured that the chilling effect was widely known among migrants, who remained silent about violations. INS actions against apple pickers in Washington, janitors in San Francisco, furniture workers in Los Angeles, meat packers in Nebraska and asbestos removers in New York and New Jersey confirmed employer predictions of deportations if workers backed unions. [93]

A coalition of US and Mexican groups, led by the Yale Law School Workers' Rights Project and the American Civil Liberties Union (ACLU) Foundation Immigrants' Rights Project submitted the case to the Canadian and Mexican NAOs. Supporting groups included the Asian American Legal Defense and Education Fund (AALDEF), Asian Pacific American Legal Centre of Southern California (APALC), Korean Immigrant Workers Advocates (KIWA) and Asian Law Cuacus (ALC), indicating the broader constituency. They were joined by the Latino Workers Centre (LWC) and the Mexican-American Legal Defense and Educational Fund (MALDEF). Several organizations with a general interest in immigration joined the case, including the Florida Immigrant Advocacy Centre, NELP, Legal Aid Society of San Francisco and National Immigration Law Centre.

The submitters noted that the memorandum undermined the Labor Department's obligation to protect workers by 'requiring the Department to play the role of agents'

---

91   'Memo of Understanding Between INS and Labor Department on Shared Enforcement Responsibilities' *Daily Labor Report* (June 11, 1992), D-1.

92   David Bacon 'Immigration Law – Bringing Back Sweatshop Conditions' Nov. 10, 1998 [cited June 18, 2002]. Available at http://apctax.igc.apc.org/dbacon/Imgrants/11sanctn. html.

93   David Bacon, 'The Law that Keeps Workers Chained' Labor News, Oct. 2, 1999 [cited June 19, 2002]. Available at http://www.sfsu.edu/~labor/Labor_News.html.

for INS. Inspectors were given no discretion to keep immigration status confidential, even if this aided investigation of labour violations.

This policy sends a clear signal to exploitative employers that they need not pay their immigrant workers a legal wage, because such workers are aware that filing a wage and hour complaint can easily lead to deportation for themselves or their co-workers, friends and family. The inevitable result is to depress the terms and conditions of employment for all workers in the United States.[94]

The memorandum suggested that workers seek DOL 'assistance at your peril' and caused 'systematic under enforcement of U.S. minimum wage and maximum hour laws'.[95]

There was resurgence in sweatshops, as violations of standards became the norm in sectors with many migrants, like garments. Victims included legitimate employers, faced with 'unfair competition', who lost market share by complying with minimum wage laws.[96] Submitters requested that the Mexican NAO ensure that the memorandum was rescinded and that labor inspectors not inquire into the immigration status of workers or report to the INS. As overtime and minimum wages were 'technical labour standards' the case was suitable for an evaluation committee, arbitration and disputes resolution.[97]

INS and Employment Standards Administration (ESA) of the DOL signed a revised memorandum in November 1998 'to achieve compliance with our immigration law and basic employment standards' for 'legal workers'. Both agencies noted their desire to allay workers' fears but also to increase prosecutions for those who hire illegal workers, since 'worksite enforcement is the primary means of reducing the job magnet to draw illegal aliens.'[98] Under the new rules, the DOL would not examine I-9 forms when investigating labour standards complaints, reducing the link between complaints and exposure of illegal migrants. The new memorandum 'is intended and will be implemented so as to avoid discouraging complaints from unauthorized workers who may be victims of labor standards violations.'[99] In response to problems in the Washington Apple case, the new memorandum also discouraged INS field

---

94   Petition ... *Regarding the Failure to Enforce Existing Minimum Wage and Ovetime Protections in Workplaces Employing Foreign Nationals Due to the memorandum of Understanding Between the U.S. Department of Labor and the U.S. Immigration and Naturalization Service on Shared Enforcement Responsibilities' Submitted to the Mexican NAO*, September 16, 1998, 1.

95   *Petition Regarding... Yale*, 2.

96   *Petition Regarding... Yale*, 35.

97   *Petition Regarding... Yale*, 44–45.

98   U.S. Department of Labour, 'Labor Department and INS Sign Memorandum of Understanding to Enhance Labor Standards Enforcement to Aid U. S. Workers' *Press Release*, Washington, Nov. 23, 1998, 1.

99   U.S. Department of Labor and U.S. Department of Justice 'Memorandum of Understanding Between the Immigration and Naturalization Service and the Employment Standards Administration Department of Labor', Washington, Nov. 23, 1998, 10.

agents from conducting raids at plants where union organizing campaigns were ongoing, limiting intimidation.[100]

But immigrant advocates doubted the benefits. Under the new rules,

> the DOL will not inquire into the immigration status of workers who file individual complaints. However, it will forward information to the INS on immigration status in 'directed' cases where employers are monitored as part of an ongoing DOL program of targeting non-compliant industries. Since many of these industries are populated by workers with precarious immigration status, the new memorandum can still have a chilling effect.[101]

The petitioners noted that 'directed' investigations might be 'indirectly prompted by complaints' about standards, so the disincentive to complain could continue.[102]

The US NAO noted that the Immigration and Naturalisation Act did not require labour officials to identify illegal migrants, and INS did not have access to labour department data on complaints. The NAO denied that the 1992 memorandum violated labour laws and the DOL's supervision of labour standards was not hampered.[103] The new memorandum of understanding clarified roles, and helped to 'overcome perceptions or fears that the Department of Labor's role – as it was perceived, often incorrectly – was an obstacle to workers coming forward with complaints alleging labor standards violations, or cooperating in investigations of labor standards compliance'. The new memorandum should prevent 'the victimization of unauthorized workers' by employers who 'may seek to use the enforcement powers of INS and DOL to intimidate or punish these workers'.[104] While seeking to reduce the employment of illegal aliens, labour inspectors would not examine immigration documents unless cases arose outside of employee complaints. This should encourage migrants to make complaints and help the Labor Department focus on law enforcement, improving salaries, benefits and working conditions.

The Mexican NAOs report of review again summarized petitioners' arguments and relevant laws. Despite the new memorandum, Mexico requested consultations on the protection of migrants. Consultations did not occur until 2002, because of changes in government in both countries. The agreement did not address the

---

100 'INS and Department of Labor Sign New Memorandum of Understanding on Workplace Inspections' *Immigrants' Rights Update*, 12, (December 21, 1998) [cited June 19, 2002]. Available at http://www.nilc.org/immsemplymnt/inswkplce/wkplcenfrc006.htm.

101 Campaign for Labor Rights, *Workers in the Global Economy Report on a Labor Rights-Immigrant Worker Advocacy Dialogue: Labor Rights, Migrant Workers' Rights and Immigration Policy in an International Economy*, June 1999 [cited June 18, 2002]. Available at http://www.laborrights.org/projects/globalecon/immigrant/index.html.

102 STPS, *Informe de Revisíon Communicación Pública MEX 9804* (Report on the Review of Public Communication MEX 9804), Mexico, November, 2000, 11.

103 US NAO to Mexican NAO, Nov. 25, 1998; cited in *Informe de Revisíon Communicación Pública* MEX 9804, 15.

104 'U. S. Responses to Mexico NAO Questions Relating to INS-DOL MOU' March 31, 1999, 2–3.

immigration reporting requirement. Rather the two parties agreed that the U.S. government would produce educational pamphlets, videos and flyers in Spanish, detailing migrants' rights. These would be available at Mexican consulates, whose staff would receive training to ensure effective referrals for Mexican workers. The Equal Employment Opportunities Agency and Labor Department developed 'non-traditional partnerships' with worker support groups and the Mexican government to 'educate workers about their rights and remedies for abuse' via 'a toll-free number', 'seminars, radio programs, and other outreach efforts'.[105]

Bureaucratic Nightmares: New York State Worker Compensation Case

MEX NAO 2001–01 involved allegations that New York State did not enforce workers' compensation and occupational safety and health laws. The submission claimed that workers' compensation judges ignored procedures, producing arbitrary decisions and inordinate delays stretching up to two decades. Some workers lost benefits when insurance company doctors avoided meetings. This case was novel in targeting only a state agency's violations of NAALC. The submission was novel Chinese Staff and Workers' Association (CSWA), which represented workers in garment, restaurant, domestic and construction sectors. The National Mobilization Against SweatShops (NMASS) joined to advocate improvements in compensation, including interim benefits during lengthy proceedings. Workers' Awaaz represented South Asian domestic workers, and Asociacion Tepeyac represented undocumented Mexicans. Individuals associated with the complaint included Mexicans and Latinos but also Chinese, Polish, Eritrean, and Middle Eastern workers. The delays were onerous; workers faced 20 hearings over 7–10 years without benefits and injured women were forced to beg for a living. Submitters claimed that death benefits and funeral expenses also were not paid for years.[106]

The submission alleged violations of international law and NAALC. The delays denied essential support to workers and their families. Workers who could not afford medical care were forced back to work to support families. The delays served the interest of negligent employers, who were not required to prevent injuries or illnesses or pay for workplace hazards. Submitters claimed judges postponed proceedings so insurance companies or self-insured employers could earn interest on investments

---

105 U.S. Department of Labor, 'U.S.-Mexico Joint Statement on Ministerial Consultations Under the North American Agreement on Labor Cooperation' *Press Release*, Washington, June 12, 2002, 2; 'U.S., Mexico Ministers Resolve Three Cases, Creating Working Group on Workplace Safety' *Daily Labor Report* 113, June 12, 2002, A-11.

106 Thomas Maier ' Immigrants at Risk: Paying Injury's Price' *Newsday* July 24, 2001, [cited June 20, 2002]. Available at http://www.newsday.com/news/ny-work-comp724.story Thomas Maier 'Mexico To Probe Immigrant Claims' *Newsday* Dec. 4, 2001 [cited June 20, 2002]. Available at http://www.newsday.com/news/printedition/ny-epnaft042496769dec04.story.

or force workers into 'low monetary settlements'.[107] Procedural errors by judges, not subject to any appeal, added to delays. Inadequate or absent translations made proceedings inaccessible and slow.. A New York Bar Association report argued that the procedural delays were used by employers and insurers to pressure workers to settle at low rates or face lengthy proceedings. The delays and the uncertainty of benefits discouraged workers from filing claims, depressing the level of benefits and forcing injured workers to stay on the job.

The state's failure to end delays was a violation of NAALC Article 5 which committed the three countries to fair, transparent proceedings without delays and was a 'persistent failure' to enforce US labour standards. As the issues included violations of 'technical labour standards' on benefits and health and safety issues, the case was eligible for an evaluation committee or even an arbitral panel. NAALC commitments to fair and expeditious procedures were at stake; guarantees like due process 'are a central element of each signatory nation's constitutional and statutory laws and warrant the greatest possible NAO oversight'.[108]

The New York State Workers' Compensation Board (WCB) claimed it did not know how long it took for benefits to be paid, since issues in specific immigrant cases were complex. The Board provided 'the best possible services' for injured workers and had reduced the number of unresolved cases.[109] It offered to meet the submitters but their lawyer suggested previous meetings had been pointless and NAALC processes were speedier. Reforms adopted by New York under pressure from employers and insurance firms decreased benefits and premiums. Governor George Pataki focussed on cost cutting by limiting the amount and duration of benefits, especially for the permanently disabled, rather than raise premiums as insurers' demanded.[110] The National Mobilization Against Sweatshops argued that insurers profited by taking in $2 billion in annual premiums, while paying out only $1 billion in benefits, one of the highest differentials in the country.[111] The anti-sweatshop group sought legislative changes; a Democratic bill would 'provide immediate interim benefits to injured workers within one week of filing a claim, pay injured workers at a liveable weekly

---

107 *Petition ... Regarding the Failure by Governor George Pataki, the United States of America, the State of New York, the New York Workers' Compensation Board (the "Board"), and Board Chairman Robert Snashall to Provide Timely and Adequate Compensation for Occupational Injuries and Illnesses and to Implement Standards to Minimize the Causes of Occupational Injuries and Illnesses in the State of New York Submitted to Mexican NAO*, October 24, 2001, 3.

108 *Petition ... Regarding... the State of New York*, 30.

109 Daniel Hayes, 'Mexico to probe N.Y. workers' comp board' *National Underwriter* 105, 51, Dec. 17, 2001, 20.

110 Daniel Hayes 'N.Y. governor pushes WC reform proposal' *National Underwriter* 103, 21, May 24, 1999, 1.

111 National Mobilization Against SweatShops (NMASS) 'New York State's Workers' Compensation: A Dehumanizing 'Nightmare''. [Cited July 3, 2002]. Available at http://www.nmass.org/nmass/wcomp/workerscomp.html.

benefit level [and] resolve injured workers' cases within three months.'[112] The group hoped the NAALC petition and international coverage, would pressure New York to reform workers' compensation.[113]

Asociación Tepeyac, representing Mexican workers, alleged that long hours increased injuries, stress and health problems. Workers 'languished' in a 'heartless' process; others avoided the system and kept working, worsening injuries, to avoid poverty.[114] Workers' Awaaz noted that delays forced domestics, who had to continue living in their workplace, to continue working despite injuries or illnesses, relying on painkillers to get by.[115] The Chinese Staff Workers association noted that sweat shops in textile, garment and restaurant industries produced health problems from chemicals, poor lighting, repetitive actions, poor ventilation, and hours of heavy lifting. Yet the compensation system allowed employers and insurers to delay interminably, prolonging or worsening suffering. Low benefits were impossible to live on, and insurers delayed to force workers to settle for even less. 'Instead of relief for workplace injuries, workers gain nothing but the misery and humiliation of navigating a deceptive system'.[116]

The Mexican NAO accepted this communication and sent questions through the US NAO to federal and state officials to see if immigrant workers were treated differently from Americans. New York took a long time to respond that NAALC does not empower outside agencies to enforce laws or hear appeals from disgruntled claimants. The Compensation Board called the submssion a 'series of unfounded and unwarranted allegations' and denied 'the Petition's allegations in their entirety'.[117] New York, not a party to NAALC, could not be forced to change the content of laws through the petition process. New York laws did not discriminate against immigrants, even illegal aliens. Conjointly with the Occupational Safety and Health Administration, the State Department of Safety and Health protected workers. Since 1997, the state reduced delays and punished employers or insurers who stalled proceedings.[118] Workers, foreign and domestic, received legal counsel and interpreters. Computerization allowed the Board to track employers' insurance and sanction those failing to properly cover compensation claims.[119]

---

112 National Mobilization Against SweatShops (NMASS), 'NAFTA lawsuit and New York State Workers' Compensation' [cited July 3, 2002.]. Available at http://www.nmass.org/nmass/wcomp/nafta.html, July 3, 2002.

113 National Mobilization Against SweatShops (NMASS)'What is the NAFTA petition?' [cited July 3, 2002]. Available at http://www.nmass.org/nmass/wcomp/nafta-whatis.htm.

114 Affadavit of Asociación Tepeyac, October, 23, 2001.

115 Workers' Awaaz (WA) Affidavit, October 20, 2001.

116 Chinese Staff and Workers' Association (CSWA) Affidavit, October 22, 2001, 4.

117 New York State Workers' Compensation Board, 'Responses to Questions Posed by the Government of Mexico', 1.

118 'Responses to Questions Posed by the Government of Mexico', 16.

119 'Computer Program helps track employer insurance coverage' *Hudson Valley Business Journal* Dec. 17, 2001; '6,200 uninsured employers fined' *Press and Sun Bulletin*, Mar. 3, 2002.

In its report of review, Mexico's NAO declined comment on specific health, safety or injury cases since these were ongoing and not subject to NAALC, which applied only after a final domestic disposition. The NAO also refused to evaluate recent reforms of the compensation board, since domestic law making was not covered by NAALC. The Mexican report urged US authorities to address workers concerns, provide information for migrants, and improve redress, in keeping with an earlier joint declaration. The NAO did not ask for ministerial consultations, but called for dialogue to follow up on progress. The US NAO provided lengthy legal briefings after the Mexican report was issued. Further exchange of information did not resolve all of Mexico's concerns resulting in a second 'Report of Review' which noted continued weaknesses in state statistics on workplace accidents and illnesses, and applicable penalties. Mexico's NAO was concerned that state compensation hearings violated US commitments on 'fair, equitable and transparent' proceedings under the NAALC. The Report cited NGO, union, and medical studies that questioned wait times for claims and criticized state responses to insurance company appeals for denial of compensation. The Mexican NAO acknowledged that cutbacks in the amount and length of compensation could not be challenged, as these were internal matters but pursued further consultations to see if the state had addressed these concerns.[120]

Protecting Visa Workers: North Carolina and Idaho

Mexico continued this pressure with the acceptance of a case involving H-2A farm guest workers visa holders in North Carolina. The case was brought by the Central Independiente de Obreros Agrícolas y Campesinos (CIOAC), an independent Mexican group that represents farmworkers, and the US based Farmworker Justice Fund. The submission alleged the violation of basic rights for vulnerable temporary workers recruited for dozens of agricultural employers by the North Carolina Growers Association (NCGA). The submission alleged unequal treatment of visa workers, who were denied protections under the Migrant and Seasonal Agricultural Worker Protection Act (MWPA), lacked rights to unionization and bargaining, and faced blacklisting of activists. Migrants received little protection or compensation for occupational injuries or illnesses, and faced arbitrary restrictions to length of employment season to preclude required repayment for travel; they even reported limits on visitors in employer-provided housing. The Mexican government accepted this case in September 2003 and almost immediately requested consultations.

---

120 Secretariat of Labor and Social Welfare International Affairs Unit Mexican National Administrative Office for the North American Agreement on Labor Cooperation *Second Report of Review from the Mexican NAO Regarding Public Communication MEX 2001-1'* Mexico City, November 19, 2004 [cited April 5, 2005]. Available at http://www.dol.gov/ ILAB/media/reports/nao/ny_mexico_sror.htm.

The case was politically strategic, since Congress was considering employer requests which might actually further weaken the rights of H2-A employees[121]. This case was innovative, since it involved a collaborative approach to protection of Mexican workers by US and Mexican unions. The petitioners referred explicitly to common areas of labour laws governing recruitment, transport and migrants' housing. The petition also referenced economic pressures in the two countries, since the industries involved exported products to Mexico and H2A visas could be used to undermine US minimum wages with implications for US workers. Watts notes that by 'linking the effects of migration to the U.S. and Mexican economies, the petitioners make a much stronger case to the NAALC than any previous public submission'.[122] This case again illustrates the Mexican proclivity to select cases protective of their nationals in the US, a successful, if limited, strategy. But slow progress in this case also demonstrates a lack of urgency by the affected governments, despite the important implications for migrants.

In 2005, Mexico received a case involving H-2B via workers in Idaho, filed by three US-based advocacy groups: the Northwest Workers' Justice Project, the Brennan Center for Justice at New York University School of Law, and Andrade Law Office. Once again, a wide range of NAALC principles were invoked including some which could be eligible for sanctions, including prohibition of forced labour, minimum employment standards, elimination of discrimination, equal pay for women, and prevention of and compensation for occupational injuries. At issue was the US practice of denying legal aid to visa workers, making it impossible for them to enforce their rights on these and other matters. Visa workers went years without a legal hearing or without medical treatment or compensation for injuries. This violated the NAALC commitment to grant workers legal recourse for infringements of their rights, and to provide access to tribunals which adjudicate such rights, without undue complexity or expense. Fundamentally, the treatment of visa workers violated the principle of equality with US nationals.[123] No decision on acceptance was reported at time of writing.

---

121 Mexico to Investigate Guestworker Abuse in North Carolina *Triangle Free Press* Oct. 2030 [cited May 4, 2005]. Available at http//www.trianglefreepress.org/oct03/local. html.

122 Julie Watts *Mexico-U.S. Migration and Labor Unions: Obstacles to Building Cross-Border Solidarity* University of Califorina at San Diego, Center for Comparative Immigration Studies Working Paper #79 June, 2003 [cited April 23, 2005]. Available at http://www.ccis-ucsd.org/PUBLICATIONS/wrkg79.pdf, 27.

123 Northwest Workers' Justice Project, the Brennan Center for Justice at New York University School of Law, and Andrade Law Office *Petition on Labor Law Matters Arising in the United States submitted to the National Administrative Office of Mexico under the North American Agreement on Labor Cooperation Regarding the Failure of the United States to Effectively Enforce Laws Protecting the Rights of Immigrant Workers* April 13, 2005 [cited March 10, 2006]. Available at http://www.dol.gov/ilab/media/reports/nao/submissions/2005-01petition.htm#i.

Broadening Migrant Workers' Rights?

After frequent US allegations about its labour violations, Mexico responded in kind to demonstrate that NAALC was balanced. In Compa's words 'Mexico appreciates the opportunity to undertake a review of U.S. labor law and practice so that the countries are treating each other as equals under this agreement, and not so much one country taking an arrogant attitude toward another country's system.'[124] The Mexican NAO declared that it was not in a position to tell Americans how to enforce laws, but wanted to bring attention to problems and encourage better collaboration to improve labour rights. The Mexicans criticized early US communications which questioned decisions by Mexican agencies and tribunals. Mexico's NAO initially proceeded differently in submissions it received, focussing on respect for sovereignty, collaboration, and cooperative activities. After many US cases questioned its domestic practices, Mexico accepted cases challenging the substance and enforcement of American laws.

This challenge increased after the US Supreme Court narrowly ruled in Hoffman Plastic Compounds vs. NLRB that undocumented aliens were not entitled to back pay and benefits if fired for union activity, since they had illegally obtained employment.[125] The Mexican embassy decried the ruling, which could 'foment a situation of abuse, exploitation, and marginalization of a great number of undocumented Mexicans.'[126] Mexico appealed the ruling to the Inter-American Court on Human Rights; this contributed to an accord with Republican Labor Secretary Elaine Chao on expanded rights and information for migrants, but did not reverse the court decision. In a 2002 joint declaration the two countries affirmed their dedication to protections for minimum wages, and health and safety for workers irrespective of their immigration status, despite the Hoffman rulings. What this means in practice remains to be seen, though Secretary Chao pledged Hoffman would not diminish DOL's enforcement of standards for immigrants.[127]

Mexico also secured concessions after ministerial consultations. The US allowed Mexican consulates to make anonymous complaints on behalf of illegal migrants (or insecure legal migrants) who suffered abuses in employment or violations of labour laws. The consulates also developed outreach programmes to inform migrants about labour rights, working with state and federal agencies on coordinated information for

---

124 National Radio Project 'Empty Promises: NAFTA and the Workforce' [cited June 12, 2002]. Available at http://www.radioproject.org/transcripts/9840.html.

125 Stanley Mailman and Stephen Yale-Loehr, 'Supreme Court Denies Back Pay to Fired Undocumented Immigrants' [cited Sept, 20, 2003]. Available at http://www.twmlaw.com/site/resources/backpay.html.

126 'Mexican Legislators to Discuss Supreme Court Decision on Undocumented Workers' Yale Law School Web Site April 29, 2002, [cited Sept 20, 2003]. Available at http://www.law.yale.edu/outside/html/Public_Affairs/242/yls_article.htm.

127 U.S Department of Labor, , 'U.S.-Mexico Joint Ministerial Statement Regarding Labor Rights of Immigrant Workers' *News Release* Washington, DC, April 15, 2002.

workers and unions.[128] This system was tested in Dallas, but could extend elsewhere, using materials prepared by both governments informing workers of their labour and immigration rights and providing access to electronic job banks.[129] It is too early to tell if these arrangements will improve access to rights for immigrants.

More evidence of the fruits of this strategy came in a May 2004 joint declaration between Secretary Chao and Mexican Foreign Affairs Secretary Luis Ernesto Derbez, aimed at improving the working conditions of Mexican migrant workers in the United States. The declaration pledged that the US government would increase migrant's awareness of labour rights, and improve employer compliance with standards. The declaration noted that Hispanics, 'are an integral part of the American workforce' and the administration 'is committed to ensuring that they are safe on the job and fully and fairly compensated for their work'.[130] Derbez noted that President Fox had made living conditions for Mexican migrants a key priority for foreign and social policy; this agreement furthered past collaboration with consular officials to protect migrant workers.[131]

The declaration was accompanied by cooperation on wages and hours and on health and safety matters, with liaison between the Labor Department and the Occupational Safety and Health Administration and Mexican consulates. Labor's Wage and Hour Division collected $18 million in back wages for migrants in six months. It collaborated with non-governmental organizations like Justice and Equality in the Workplace in Houston.[132] OSHA increased its outreach by hiring more Spanish speakers. The Equal Employment Opportunities Agency connected officials in justice, employment and health and safety with NGOs and consulates to create support networks for migrants.[133] This may have slowed the high rate of injuries and fatalities in some US industries. So Mexican initiatives, aided by NAALC and NGOs began to address problems for migrants. Given the volume of migration, political hostility to it, and retrenchment in social policy, these steps could be offset by unreported abuses and by cutbacks in health, welfare or education for migrants. As the Idaho submission illustrates, denial of access to legal representation could still undermine enforcement of rights for visa workers.

---

128 Secretaria de Trabajo y Prevision Sociale, Dirreción General de Communicación Social, 'EUA pone en operación un programa para proteger los derechos laborales de los trbajadores migratorios' *Boletines* Mexico, DF, June 17, 2003.

129 Interview with officials at Mexico's National Administrative Office, August, 2003.

130 OSHA 'U.S. Labor Secretary Elaine L. Chao and Mexican Foreign Secretary Luis Ernesto Derbez Sign Joint Declaration to Improve Working Conditions for Mexican Workers', *News Release* Washington, July 21, 2004 [cited April 16, 2005]. Available at http://www.dol.gov/opa/media/press/osha/OSHA20041371.htm.

131 'Elaine L. Chao and Luis Ernesto Derbez Sign Joint Declaration…'.

132 Tom Karson, 'Confronting Houston's Demographic Shift: the Harris County AFL-CIO' *WorkingUSA* 8, (2004) 213–14.

133 US Equal Employment Opportunities Agency 'EEOC Expands Immigrant Rights Partnership to Include OSHA, DOJ and Latin American Consulates' *Press Release* Washington Sept. 27, 2002, [cited May 5, 2005]. Available at http://www.eeoc.gov/press/9-27-02.html.

Conclusions: Migrants and Regionalization

Overall, Mexican analysts have mixed of interpretations of NAALC's efficacy. Ministerial meetings were valuable contacts, and studies and reports from the Secretariat were informative.[134] Mexicans stressed the country's distinct traditions, notably its binding labour code versus North America's case-based common law. NAALC did not compel signatories to adopt common principles. Adversarial complaints should be de-emphasized; submissions should not invoke 'prosecution' or 'controversy'.[135] NAALC exposed the weak protection for collective bargaining in North America, and provided opportunities for transnational collaboration on freedom of association, long in the shadows in Mexico. But NAALC did not promote independent unions or close gaps in wages and benefits between the NAFTA signatories. Nor did it allow quick resolution of grievances for workers facing sanctions or dismissal for union activities or abuses of migrant's rights. Only stronger national laws and international standards would strengthen rights of association and bargaining and prevent the NAFTA partners from following a path towards diminishing standards.[136]

The cases brought by Mexico illustrated the potential for transnational collaboration among societal and state actors. A diverse range of trade unions and social movements were involved in these submissions. Contacts began slowly, with the cooperation between the activist Mexican Telephonistas and the Communication Workers in the Sprint case. Solec broadened the coalitions to include the Oil, Chemical and Atomic Workers International Union, Sindicato de Trabajadores de Industria y Comercio '6 de octubre' Unión de Defensa Laboral Comunitaria and the Support Committee for Maquiladora Workers. In the Washington Apples case, several independent Mexican unions and activist groups joined in, including the Unión Nacional de Trabajadores (UNT), Frente Democrático Campesino, Frente Auténtico del Trabajo, and its metalworkers affiliate, the Sindicato de Trabajadores de la Industria Metálica, Acero, Hierro, Conexos y Similares. US support was provided by the Teamsters the International Labor Rights Fund and the National Employment Law Project, demonstrating the growing US social movement commitment to transborder issues. De Coster Egg witnessed the first use of NAALC by the Confederación de Trabajadores de México, the largest official unions indicating that on the migrant issue, this conservative organization could see the benefits of transnationalism.

The Yale case produced an even wider coalition, demonstrating the leadership role of the US non-governmental rights groups in bringing together transnational support. The submission was led by the Yale Law School Workers' Rights Project

---

134 Interview with officials at Mexico's National Administrative Office, August, 2003.

135 Mexico, Oficina del Secretario, Coordinacion Gral de Asuntos Internacionales, 'Informe del Comité Gubernamental sobre el ALCAN a los cuatro anos de su entrada en vigor confrome al articulo 10.1(a)', 2.

136 Graciela Bensusán, 'Integración regional y cambio institucional: la reforma laboral en el norte del continente.' in Graciela Bensusán (ed.), *Estándares laborales después del TLCAN* (México: FLACSO/Fundación, 1999), 177–209.

and the American Civil Liberties Union Foundation Immigrants' Rights Project. They were joined by the Latino Workers Centre and the Mexican-American Legal Defense and Educational Fund, the Florida Immigrant Advocacy Centre, National Employment Law Project, Legal Aid Society of San Francisco and National Immigration Law Centre. These lead groups secured input and support from the Asian American Legal Defense and Education Fund, Asian Pacific American Legal Centre of Southern California, Korean Immigrant Workers Advocates and Asian Law Caucus, showing that the wider immigrant community could be mobilized. The New York State case, lead by the Chinese Staff and Workers' Association and The National Mobilization Against SweatShops, backed by Workers' Awaaz, and Asociacion Tepeyac, was also a rainbow coalition of Mexicans and Latinos but also South Asian, Chinese, Polish, Eritrean, and Middle Eastern workers. The joint role played by the Central Independiente de Obreros Agrícolas y Campesinos and the Farmworker Justice Fund in the North Carolina case revealed the increased potential for social movement mobilization across rural constituencies as NAFTA affected the lives of thousands of migrants in agrarian work in both nations.

This nexus of legal, rights, immigrant and workers groups demonstrated how the NAALC could facilitate coalition-building of the kind required to counter the complex effects of trade liberalization on the diverse communities of migrant workers. While Mexico has asserted equality in application of NAALC, the effects of regional asymmetry are clear. The disproportionate resources available to US NGOs versus Mexican groups means that, in many cases, American groups have taken the lead, and Mexican partners have played a supporting role in submissions. The Washington and Maine cases were lead by US immigrant advocacy groups, including US-based Mexican-American or Latino groups. The final Mexican case, brought by three US groups, the Northwest Workers' Justice Project, the Brennan Center for Justice at New York University School of Law, and Andrade Law Office, showed the effects of asymmetry in resources and associational cultures; despite promising overtures from Mexican civil society, the task of protecting migrants was often left to US groups. Néstor de Buen suggests that NAALC has not provided Mexican workers and NGOs with effective mechanisms to address their concerns. Transnational organization can contribute, so long as unions are not in competition to attract employment. But the biggest beneficiaries have been US businesses taking advantage of the weaker labour regime in Mexico to increase profits.[137]

---

137 Néstor de Buen,. 'A cinco años del Acuerdo de Cooperación Laboral anexo al Tratado de Libre Comercio.' *Memorias del Encuentro Trinacional de Laboralistas Democráticos.* (México: Universidad Nacional Autónoma de México, 1999), 81–93.

Chapter 8

Canada's Slow Accession
to the NAALC

Introduction

Canadian participation was hampered, typically, by federal-provincial squabbles. Federal accession to NAFTA did not compel provincial acceptance of NAALC, which involved labour matters under provincial control. Except for limited categories of workers in federal employment or federally-regulated, interprovincial industries, most Canadian workers fall under provincial jurisdiction. The Canadian NAO drafted a model intergovernmental agreement for provinces to sign. Four have now signed, including Quebec, Alberta, PEI and Manitoba and cases have been submitted through the Canadian NAO, some of which overlapped with US or Mexican cases. These cases illustrate the potential for transnational collaboration among unions and human rights groups in the three countries. Several important new players entered the process, including public and private sector unions, maquiladora support groups and labour lawyers.

The ITAPSA case took on the Echlin plant in Mexico, after a change of ownership. The Yale/INS case involved the same issues as the Mexican submission, but Canada accepted the adequacy of the new memorandum of understanding and closed the file. The Labor Policy Association case was brought by an employer group and EFCO, a maker of commercial windows, doors and walls. It alleged that the U.S. National Labor Relations Board enforced laws prohibiting employer interference with unions so as to prevent employee-management committees in non-union companies. The Canadian NAO accepted the Puebla garment case in 2003, and has conducted public hearings. More recently, Canada rejected the Abascal law reform case. The Canadian NAO has made clear its emphasis on consultations and information sharing, and not enforcement or adversarial proceedings, and has secured more business input than in some US NAO cases. Despite the emergence of groups supportive of using NAALC to promote labour rights, the bilateral effects have so far been limited; full participation is impeded by intergovernmental divisions.

Federal-Provincial Complications

Canada's labour relations system differs from US and Mexican models because federal regulations and laws cannot override provincial ones. Federal authority extends only over federal public servants and crown corporations, and to a few federally regulated industries, such as broadcasting, interprovincial transportation (railways and airlines), banks, shipping, ports and cargo handling, telecommunications, grain handling, and uranium mining. Federal laws also cover three sparsely populated northern territories (Yukon, Nunavut and North West Territories). Only about 10% of workers are covered by federal laws. The remaining 90% fall into provincial jurisdiction under Section 92 of the constitution, which refers to property and civil rights and local works and undertakings. A landmark 1925 court case recognized provincial labour authority outside wartime, although major federal statutes respecting rights to collective bargaining and arbitration influenced provincial practice. Moreover, constitutional jurisprudence prevents national policies from overriding provincial ones, even if Ottawa uses treaty-making powers to sign international accords. Hence, fragmented Canadian law is less easily subjected to international scrutiny.

Thus, the NAALC was slow to apply to Canada, and implementation was complicated by the need for provincial cooperation.[1] The Canadian NAO could not adopt standards for consultations because these needed joint development with the provinces. Canadian officials did adopt procedures for submissions, and pledged to provide a prompt, 'accessible, open and transparent examination of the issues' through meetings with submitters, independent reviews, and possibly, but not necessarily, public meetings.[2] But submissions could not proceed beyond a very preliminary stage unless complaints dealt with matters under exclusive federal jurisdiction. Threshold levels of provincial acceptance were specified in the NAALC to trigger its application to Canada. Canada had to meet these thresholds before it could submit complaints about the other parties, or before they could submit complaints about Canadian practices.[3] So at first only federal labour matters could be subject to NAALC procedures, and the provinces were slow to sign on; a majority remain outside the NAALC.

The Canadian NAO draft labor agreement with provinces emphasized that 'partnership and cooperation between the federal, provincial and territorial governments are essential in order to achieve the goals of the NAALC'. The preamble noted the need for cooperation since 'labour laws in Canada apply to workplaces and workforces that for the most part fall within provincial or territorial responsibility.'[4] The agreement bound the provinces to accept the obligations of the NAALC, and its disputes resolution procedures. Federal provincial cooperation

---

1   'NAFTA labor talks on with provinces' *Financial Post Daily* March 22, 1994, 8.

2   Canada, Department of Labour, *Guidelines for Public Communications under Articles 16.3 and 21 of the North American Agreement on Labour Cooperation (NAALC)* [cited April 16, 2001]. Available at http://www.hrsdc.gc.ca/en/lp/spila/ialc/pcnaalc/02Guidlines_for_filing.shtml.

3   May Morpaw, 'The North American Agreement on Labour Cooperation: Highlights, Implementation and Significance' Closing Address at the 1995 Conference of the Canadian Industrial Relations Association, Montreal, May 29, 1995, 12.

4   Canada, Department of Labour, *Canadian Intergovernmental Agreement Regarding the North American Agreement on Labour Cooperation*, Ottawa, May, 1995.

included a joint committee of senior officials from each level of government, with a secretariat provided by Ottawa. This committee managed Canadian participation in submissions, trinational consultations and in evaluation committees, and prepared Canada's positions for the Council and the Secretariat. The Federal Minister of Labour represented Canada on the Council, but delegations to trinational meetings would include a representative of a signatory province. Provinces which did not sign could participate in cooperative activities, but not in the submissions process.

The Canadian government hoped the intergovernmental committee would reach consensus on responses to submissions, but could act on its own in accordance with the NAFTA labour accord if agreement was lacking among provinces. When Canadian practices in provincial jurisdiction were subject to complaints, the signatory province was required to provide all information needed by the NAO for consultations with other nations. Affected provinces would have an opportunity to participate in consultations where their labour practices had been challenged, and would lead any arbitral panel for Canada if their laws were the subject of arbitration. Signatory provinces agreed to undertake prompt implementation of an action plan or to pay monetary fines where their laws were involved. Provinces could withdraw from the agreement with six months advance notice.[5]

The first signatory was the Conservative government of Alberta. This province was a strong supporter of NAFTA, though not considered progressive respecting labor. Manitoba's conservative regime, also pro-NAFTA, was next to sign. The Quebec Liberal government of Robert Bourassa also strongly supported NAFTA and agreed in principle to the intergovernmental agreement. However, the election of the sovereigntist Parti Québécois under Jacques Parizeau delayed agreement;[6] this delay continued after the 1995 referendum, given the hostile relations between Ottawa and the new PQ Premier, Lucien Bouchard. However, the sovereigntists' desire to retain a credible claim to participation in NAFTA after separation induced the PQ government to sign the deal to establish a Quebec presence in NAFTA institutions. Prince Edward Island also signed on, when federal Labour Minister Laurence MacCauley, an Island MP, placed pressure on his provincial colleagues. The largest, most industrialized province, Ontario, remains outside NAALC; it was governed by the anti-free trade New Democrats when the NAALC was signed and later by the anti-labour Harris Conservatives. It remains to be seen if the Liberal Regime of Dalton McGuinty will alter Ontario's position. So far, no other province seems prepared to sign on to NAALC.

Union Hostility and Disinterest

Canadian unionists remained hostile to NAFTA, and advocated alternative models of transnational social unionism. Canadian labour was reluctant to use the process.

---

5   *Canadian Intergovernmental Agreement* Ottawa, May, 1995.

6   Telephone interview with officials at the Office of the North American Agreement on Labour Cooperation, Department of Labour, Ottawa, October 26, 1995.

The Canadian Labour Congress (CLC) boycotted the side agreement because of its lack of enforceable standards.[7] But Canadian unions slowly saw some potential in NAALC. The success of American unions in securing attention to violations of workers rights prompted Canadian unionists to rethink this position. Unions like the CLC and Canadian Auto Workers have sent fact-finding missions to Mexico. Canadian concerns about organizational rights involve both Mexican and American practices, as 'right to work' laws have led to the movement of companies from highly unionized Canada to low-wage non-union southern states. But few cases as yet have involved Canada and the resolution of these cases has involved consultations only, which did little to satisfy union concerns.

The NAALC falls short of the demands of Canadian labour for a transnational regulatory regime. But its provisions for consultation and cooperation and its fledgling complaints process do provide the opportunity for generation of new transnational ties in labour relations and new networks of unions, business and government officials. Canadian unions expected challenges to cross-border hiring of strikebreakers in some border states, such as the use of Canadian nurses in strikes in Minnesota.[8] And in the case of proposed privatization of labour standards inspections matters in Alberta, Canadian unionists did coordinate with American and Mexican counterparts to secure pressure on the provincial government to withdraw the measure.[9] Critics could target provincial laws which discourage unions to attract industries; six provinces have laws which deviate from ILO standards, on association and organization, so there could be future complaints[10], though these remain blocked if the affected provinces remain outside NAALC. So skepticism of NAFTA and its labour side accord contributed to limited union usage. However, union leaders have tried to ensure that NAALC is not weakened as free trade expands to Chile and others in the hemisphere.

Dana-Itapsa

Canada was slow to proceed with cases given the need for sufficient provincial ratification, which did not occur until 1998. In June, the Canadian NAO accepted NAO 98-1, a submission on Itapsa, which alleged that Mexico did not protect freedom of association and the right to organize, and did not enforce laws on safety and health. The submission claimed Mexican authorities showed bias towards 'official' unions during legal proceedings. The lack of secret-ballots in union representation

---

7   'Why NAFTA's no love of labour' *Globe and Mail* February 8, 1995, A13.

8   Interview with officials at the NAALC Secretariat, Dallas, June 19–21, 1995.

9   'Border Briefs: NAFTA Labor Challenge Likely in Canada' *BorderLines* 30 4, 1996 [cited Jan. 18, 2000]. Available at http://www.zianet.com/irc1/bordline/bl30bb.html.

10   Leo Panitch, 'Changing Gears: Democratizing the Welfare State' in Andrew Johnson, Stephen McBride and Patrick Smith (eds.) *Continuities and Discontinuities: The Political Economy of Social Welfare and Labour Market Policy in Canada* (Toronto, University of Toronto Press, 1994). 37.

Table 8.1   Canadian NAO Submissions

Submission	Issues	Resolution	Follow-Up
CANADA 9801 (ECHLIN/ITAPSA)	Freedom of Association, Right to Organize; prevention of illness, injury	Reviewed, with ministerial consultations	Canada joined in Occupational health and safety working group
CANADA 9802 (YALE)	Minimum standards; protection of migrants	File closed by NAO	New INS-Labor memorandum accepted by Canada as resolution
CANADA 9901 (LPA)	Freedom of Association, Right to Organize	Not accepted for review	None
CANADA 2003-01 (PUEBLA)	Freedom of Association, Right to Organize, bargain; prevention of illness, injury; minimum standards	Ministerial Consultations pending	pending
CANADA 2005-01 (ABASCAL)	Reform Law weakens right to Organize, bargain	Not accepted for review	

Source: North American Commission for Labor Cooperation Website

elections violated Mexico's commitment to provide high labour standards as required by Article 2 of NAALC. This case dealt with plant conditions and a representation campaign at the ITAPSA plant in Reyes La Paz which was owned by Echlin, a subsidiary of Dana Corporation.

The submission covered labour board and other proceedings which followed from the union organizing campaign. It was submitted by United Steelworkers of America (Canadian National Office), the CLC and AFL-CIO, the Frente Auténtico del Trabajo (FAT), supported by other unions and NGOs. The submission was brought despite scepticism about NAALC; the Steelworker's McBrearty argued that NAALC's "protections' have done nothing to remedy the circumstances of workers in real situations of abuse'.[11] The timing of the case, prior to the talks on expanding hemispheric free trade, suggested a political motive by submitters who opposed a Free Trade Area of the Americas. They hoped to illustrate the weaknesses of NAFTA's side agreement before Canada entered into similar arrangements in any hemispheric trade agreement.[12]

The submission was similar to U.S. NAO 9703. However, there were variations in Canada's approach and in the participation by the new managers, which produced different outcomes. The communication dealt with infringements on freedom of association of workers and the right to organize. The Steelworkers noted 'collaboration' by employer, official union and government to suppress worker rights to select representatives. The submitters summarized the problems which prompted workers to seek unionization, including sexual harassment, supervisor's abuse, and poor wages. The unsafe workplaces had unsuitable and non-working safety equipment causing exposure to hazardous substances like asbestos. Submitters claimed that 'Inspections were perfunctory, and no air samples were taken, with the inspectors relying on company reports' and levying minimal fines.[13] Workers were allegedly subjected to loud noise and received inadequate medical check-ups. A weak health and safety committee, and the lack of Spanish labelling compounded the risks for workers.

The submission claimed company and official union efforts to disrupt the unionization campaign including threats, surveillance, firings, election fraud, and open voting in front of armed supporters of the official CTM union. Mexican officials apparently did nothing to prevent it even though 'Mexican laws prohibit coercion and guarantee fair election procedures. Federal Conciliation and Arbitration Board representatives witnessed numerous incidents of physical violence, intimidation and election fraud, but failed to investigate, initiate proceedings, or provide sanctions for the illegal conduct.'[14] The Board delayed the proceedings, allegedly because of official union and company motions, and cancelled a vote without informing the Metal Workers union, allowing its members to be identified and dismissed. Board officials permitted the tainted election to occur in a climate of coercion, refused to hear evidence from the Metal Workers and did not allow a new vote. The Federal Board did not notify the independent union of a critical meeting, so it could not present evidence. The Board held a second hearing under court order, but dismissed

---

11   United Steelworkers of America, 'Vote Fraud, Abuse Lead to First-Ever Complaint Made under NAFTA 'Side Deal' ' *News Release*, Ottawa, April 6, 1998, 2.

12   Heather Scoffield, 'Mexican case puts spotlight on NAFTA: Canadian labour hopes factory worker's plight will expose weakness of side agreement' *Globe and Mail* August, 21, 1998.

13   United SteelWorkers of America, 'The Dana/Echlin Case – Background Notes' Sept., 1988, 2.

14   *Public Communication to the National Administrative Office of Canada Regarding the Denial of Workers' Rights by Echlin, Inc., Itapsa, American Brakeblock, the Confederation of Mexican Workers (Ctm), and the Federal Conciliation and Arbitration Board of Mexico*, April, 1998.

the union's appeal despite evidence of electoral irregularities, which neither Itapsa managers nor the CTM refuted. The Board did order workers reinstated, but they were expelled by CTM and dismissed by Itapsa citing the union exclusion clause. Submitters challenged the impartiality of the Board, since one of its members was in the CTM, and it took no measures to enforce reinstatement. Mexico was accused of neglecting NAALC commitments to impartial procedures by allowing a bias towards official unions in the Federal Board.[15]

Submitters sought improved Mexican procedures including proper notice for proceedings, accurate voter lists, expeditious proceedings and 'measures to remedy the bias and conflict of interest which is systemic in the composition of the FCAB panels which administer and supervise representation elections.'[16] But petitioners also questioned the adequacy of Mexican laws on secret ballots, or suspension of results pending investigation of alleged voting illegalities. Submitters asked for hearings, consultations, and expert evaluation. Canada should press for 'development by Mexico of enforceable guidelines to prevent future violations' and 'specific measures to remedy the violation of the workers' freedom of association and the right to organize which occurred at the Echlin/ITAPSA plant'.[17] But they sought to go beyond an evaluation of Mexican law enforcement, to induce improvements in the substance of laws. Canada should 'issue a declaration that Mexico and the FCAB have violated Article 2 of the NAALC by failing to ensure that Mexican labour laws provide for high labour standards with respect to protections of freedom of association and the right to organize'.[18] Submitters requested a public registry of union contracts, and an end to firings of workers whose unions lost representation elections. Canadian Steelworkers national director, Lawrence McBrearty, lead the campaign. He declared: 'Things have to change in Mexico. ... Any company that walks out here, sure they're going to make money. There's exploitation, there's child labour, there's harassment, there's no freedom of association.'[19]

The company deemed the allegations 'exaggerated' or 'fabricated': 'The unions are not happy with NAFTA and they are using this as a subterfuge to put pressure on the Mexican government to change their labour laws to, in effect, make Mexican jobs less attractive for companies'. [20] The company alleged that an internecine struggle between unions lead to the complaint, which was designed to discredit NAFTA.[21] One company official admitted that CTM members were allowed in and may have

---

15   Canadian NAO, 'Summary of Submission CAN 98-1', April, 1998.

16   *Public Communication ... the Denial of Workers' Rights by Echlin, Inc.* April, 1998.

17   Jeffrey Sack to May Morpaw, April 2, 1998.

18   *Public Communication ... the Denial of Workers' Rights by Echlin, Inc.* April, 1998.

19   Leah Rumack 'Union complaint says votes rigged' *Now* (Toronto), [cited Jan. 23, 2000]. Available at http://www.nowtoronto.com/issues/17/48/News/front.html.

20   Rumack 'Union complaint says votes rigged'.

21   Gord McIntosh 'Steelworkers file complaint under NAFTA' *Canadian-Press-Newswire* April 6, 1998.

armed themselves with factory debris; but the company did not sanction intimidation and the complaint was a 'publicity stunt'.[22]

The Canadian NAO accepted this submission, citing the NAALC's goal of 'cooperative consultations'.[23] The Dana Workers Alliance noted that this 'unprecedented investigation by the Canadian government shows just how severe Echlin's abuses in Mexico have been'.[24] The NAO held hearings to gather information. Workers testified of sexual harassment; women who would not go out with supervisors were allegedly forced to do heavier work, denied leave or given undesirable shifts. Official union representatives were equally abusive and workers who tried to unionize independently were fired for their actions.[25] The CLC supported Mexican workers despite its scepticism; the CLC's Dick Martin wondered if the NAALC could 'provide even an iota of justice to violated workers', and noted that the 'people of all three countries deserve proof that NAFTA can change the behavior of a multinational corporation'.[26]

By the time Canada held its hearings, the Itapsa plant had be bought by Dana corporation, which participated in the NAALC process. This lead to different issues being aired at the hearings and a different tenor to Canada's report, as the company defended its practices. Dana indicated its commitment to workers' health and safety; its practices had been recognized with awards. The company encouraged a culture of respect for employees' well-being and compliance with laws. After it acquired the Itapsa plant, Dana reviewed the alleged violations, and refuted many claims, especially on health and safety.[27] On asbestos, the Itapsa plant complied with Mexican regulations and excess levels were rectified. Faulty equipment was replaced and training provided. While there was always room for improvement, measurements of asbestos and noise, using exposure tests showed that new quality control systems had protected employees, complied with regulations and met health and safety standards.[28] Dana presented alternative accounts of the elections, which indicated there was no 'chaos and coercion'.[29] Dana answered the Canadian NAOs questions noting that CTM observers had no connection to the company,

22   Laura Eggertson 'Canadian labour backing Mexican workers' *Toronto Star* April 7, 1998.

23   Human Resources Development Canada, 'Canada to Review Public Communication Received under NAALC' *News Release*, June 4, 1998.

24   Dana Workers Alliance *Press Release*, 'Canadian Government Launches Firts-Ever NAFTA Investigation Against U.S. Firm' Sept. 15, 1998.

25   Laura Eggertson, 'Canada Urged to Stop Worker Abuse in Mexico' *Toronto Star* Sept. 15, 1998, A3.

26   'CLC – Media Releases' – September 14, 1998| [cited July 15, 2002]. Available at http://www.clc-ctc.ca/media-releases/archive/pr-98sep14.html.

27   'Opening Remarks to the Canadian NAO by Dana Corporation, Sept. 14, 1998, 3.

28   Randall J. Foster to Marc Rioux (RE: Itapsa Health and Safety Documentation) , Feb. 8, 1999.

29   'Opening Remarks to the Canadian NAO by Dana Corporation', Sept. 14, 1998, 5–6.

and that the CAB was responsible for the election. Workers were dismissed after STIMHACS lost the election because of 'exclusionary clauses' in Mexican labour agreements. Reassignments were based on production needs, not retaliation for union activities.[30]

The submitters were angered that the Canadian NAO travelled to Mexico, toured the plant, and met officials without unions representatives. 'The rights of workers and petitioners in this process are in doubt when closed meetings are held'.[31] In notes from one of meeting between Canadian and Mexican officials, the latter conceded that closed elections were not required and open union votes were considered 'free votes'. The officials noted that coercion could not be precluded but did not fear retaliation by employers. McBrearty wrote of these 'startling revelations' with Mexican officials apparently admitting that workers were routinely fired if they had supported a losing union.[32] In January, 1999, Canadian NAO officials again travelled to Itapsa, carried out an inspection, and interviewed government and company officials.[33] This visit again occurred without notice to the submitters until after the final report was released. The petitioners suggested this threatened 'transparency' and 'fairness' and might discourage future submissions, as plaintiffs could not respond to all information received by the NAO.[34]

In written responses to Canadian NAO questions, the Mexicans acknowledged that there were no legal mechanisms to investigate intimidation in union organizing and elections. Federal labour law did not authorize the Board to investigate claims of violence, which were dealt with in the criminal justice system.[35] Employer rights to respond to evidence, challenge complaints and question the legality of the union lead to delays which were unavoidable. The responses confirmed a lack of health and safety training, high asbestos levels, failure to provide asbestos and noise reports to the government, and non-reinstatement of workers.[36]

The Canadian NAO released a report on freedom of association and right to organize at Dana-Itapsa and recommended that Minister of Labour Claudette Bradshaw seek consultations with Mexican Secretary of Labour José Antonio González. A second report noted that the Mexican government failed to enforce legislation requiring that chemical safety data sheets be provided, that hazardous substances have Spanish

---

30   'Re: Questions Related to Public Communication CAN 98-1', attached to Gary Golden to May Morpaw, Dec. 7, 1998.

31   'Canadian NAO Sends Dana H&S Complaint to Next Step' *Working Together* March-April 1999, [cited July 15, 2002]. Available at http://www.americas.org/News/Working_Together/WT_35/Canadian_NAO_Sends_Dana.htm.

32   Lawrence McBrearty 'NAFTA hearings reveal abuses' *Toronto Star* December 7, 1998.

33   Marc Rioux, 'Rapport de Visite a l'Usine Itapsa S.A. de C.V., Los Reyes, Mexico', January 18, 1999, Ottawa, January 21, 1999.

34   Lawrence McBrearty to Claudette Bradshaw, June 2, 1999.

35   Mexican NAO Responses, First Questionnaire on Public Communication CAN 98-1, (Canadian government translation) Nov. 6, 1998.

36   'The Dana/Echlin Case – Background Notes' Sept., 1988, 5.

labels, and that equipment be supplied to protect workers against asbestos dust. The Canadian NAO sought ministerial consultations on health and safety and inspections, the use of private laboratories to monitor hazardous substances, best practices in protecting workers in plants using asbestos and compensation to those with long-term illnesses like asbestosis. Although enforcement was improving, the NAO felt these issues required consultations.[37]

The submitters welcomed the report as a preliminary victory in a lengthy process, but were disappointed with the weaker condemnation in the Canadian report. Absence of concrete remedies for workers, including reinstatement, demonstrated NAALC's ineffectiveness.[38] Submitters called on the NAO to alter its procedures, to improve the fairness and effectiveness. The USW wanted the NAO to make 'findings of fact' including appointment of an independent investigator who could compel production of documents, and give unions proper notice to respond to claims made by other parties.[39]

Dana was pleased that the report showed the Itapsa plant complied with Mexican health and safety regulations; the company could not be blamed if Mexican regulations were weak.[40] Dana was concerned that 'misstatements' in the NAO findings might suggest it had not complied with Mexican laws respecting Spanish language information about hazards, protective devices and respirators for asbestos. Dana insisted it had complied, and complained that the NAO's failed to acknowledge the company's cooperation.[41]

Canadian officials interviewed by this author did not regard their report as softer. They believed Dana's participation had balanced the findings, especially on health and safety issues. Canada had a different philosophy, seeking gradual influence on Mexican labour laws, rather than immediate action for particular workers. Mexico's labour relations culture had to be respected, and immediate changes could not be expected.[42] Canada's NAO asked for consultations to consider the problems raised by this submission.[43] However, there was no Mexican labour minister at the time, which caused delays; Mexico also asserted a right to refuse consultations, according to some Canadian officials. But some reforms were envisioned with support for secret recognition votes in future.

---

37   Ian Jack, 'Mexican Workers Seek Help Through NAFTA Pact' *National Post* March 16, 1999, C8.

38   United Steelworkers of America, Press Release, 'Steelworkers Say NAFTA report not enough relief for Mexican Workers' *Canadian Press NewWire* March 12, 1999; Heather Scoffield, 'Ottawa upholds labour complaint against Mexico', *Globe and Mail* March 16, 1999, B8.

39   Lawrence McBrearty to Claudette Bradshaw, June 2, 1999.

40   Ian Jack, 'Mexican Workers Seek Help through NAFTA Pact' *National Post* March 16, 1999, C8.

41   'Dana Corporation and the Canadian NAO Reports', May 5, 1999.

42   Interviews with officials at the Canadian NAO.

43   'Canadian Government Launches First-ever Nafta Investigation Against U.S. Firm' *Teamsters News Release* September 15, 1998.

The workers were rebuffed in October, 1999, when their court appeal of Board decisions was dismissed. The court's reasoning mirrored the Board's arguments, which, the petitioners claimed, revealed 'the inadequacy of Mexican legal processes in enforcing the guarantee in Mexican law of worker's rights to be represented through a union of their choice'.[44] The outcome demonstrated that ministerial consultations were needed to encourage Mexico to abide by its NAALC commitments. But the process of consultations was slow. Canadian and Mexican ministers met after the change in government to Fox and the PAN, in 2001 and 2002, but did not conclude consultations until January, 2003. Canada joined the Working Group of Government Experts on Occupational Safety and Health set up by Mexico and the US, to address safety in dealing with hazardous substances, health and safety management and protection, information sharing and inspector training.

Labour Minister Bradshaw lauded the consultations as 'frank, constructive and mutually useful'. She also 'praised the efforts of the Mexican business and labour representatives who participated in reaching a consensus on an initiative to reform the federal labour code'.[45] The labour reforms, though not yet enacted, were viewed as responding to the Canadian concerns on union rights, fair adjudication and effective enforcement. Unions feared the reforms would augment rather than alleviate problems in certification and registration. Submitters warned that the low profile working group of experts on health and safety would not rectify particular hazards and would have 'no meaningful impact on the working conditions of Mexican workers.'[46]

Canadian Yale Submission

Canadian NAO 98-2, dealing with the Yale case, covered the same issues raised in MEX NAO 9804. It addressed the Memorandum of Understanding between the INS and the Department of Labor (DOL) which allegedly deterred immigrant workers from reporting violations of U.S. minimum employment standards laws. The Memorandum required DOL inspectors investigating wage and hours complaints to inspect employer records concerning the immigration status of employees and to report unauthorized workers to INS. This practice deterred immigrants from reporting violations in wage and hour laws, including unpaid overtime and back wages. The submission stated that, if worker complaints were so discouraged, U.S. labour officials were deprived of information required to enforce.

---

44 Jeffrey Sack to May Morpaw, Oct. 19, 1999.

45 Department of Labour, Office of the Minister, *News Release* 'Canada and Mexico Conclude Ministerial Consultations Under the North American Agreement on Labour Cooperation', Jan. 29, 2003, [cited July 16, 2004]. Available at http://www.naalc.org/english/announce7.shtml.

46 United Steelworkers of America 'In the Matter Of: Public Communication 2003–01 Before the Canadian National Administrative Office Pursuant to the North American Agreement on Labour Cooperation' May 28, 2004, 8.

No Canadian groups were involved in this submission, which was again made by the Yale Law School Workers' Rights Project, the American Civil Liberties Union Foundation Immigrants' Rights Project and other civil rights organizations, immigrant groups and unions. Again the submitters sought the elimination of the memorandum, so that labour inspectors would not investigate the immigration status of workers or report illegal immigrants to INS. Canada's labour minister was urged to seek consultation and independent expert investigation, hold hearings and seek disputes resolution and arbitral panels.[47] Although the Canadian NAO was uncertain about accepting a submission from non-nationals[48] it eventually did accept this complaint.

The Canadian NAO posed questions to the US NAO about the memorandum and relevant laws and regulations. Canada sought information on whether the memorandum had been evaluated for its impact on labour law enforcement, what efforts had been made to inform immigrant workers of their rights, and whether the memorandum was consistent with US obligations under NAALC. The US NAO informed the Canadian NAO of the revised memorandum, and assured their Canadian and Mexican counterparts that the Department of Labor 'is committed to ensuring that workers can and are encouraged to file complaints regarding abusive workplace conditions without fear of reprisal'.[49] She emphasized that while the Employment Standards administration may help INS identify employers who hire illegal migrants, its primary responsibility remained enforcement of labour standards for all workers irrespective of immigration status.

The US NAO sent a copy of the new memorandum, dated November 23, 1998, modifying and superseding the earlier one. This document clarified that the ESA would not automatically report on the immigration status of those involved in complaints, except in a few 'directed cases'. 'This means that a labor investigation initiated on the basis of a worker complaint cannot lead to an INS investigation through any communication between the agencies regarding employee sanctions compliance'.[50] Where directed cases occurred, the US NAO was confident that INS and DOL would cooperate to ensure that those raising complaints could stay in the country until the complaint was resolved and receive any back pay owed to them. 'Outreach' sessions would be held to ensure that the workers were informed of their rights and encouraged to make complaints when justified.[51]

The Canadian NAO extended consideration of the communication by 30 days to evaluate the implications of the new memorandum. In April, 1999 the Canadian NAO wrote to the submitters that, since the original MOU had been replaced, 'it is

---

47   Canadian NAO 'Summary: Submission CAN 98-2 Memorandum of Understanding Between the U. S. Department of Labor and the U. S. Immigration and Naturalization Service on Shared Enforcement Responsibilities', Ottawa, October, 19998.

48   May Morpaw to Graham Boyd, Director, Yale Law School Worker's Rights Project Oct. 16, 1998.

49   Irasema Garza to May Morpaw and Rafael Aranda, November 25, 1998.

50   Irasema Garza to May Morpaw and Rafael Aranda, November 25, 1998.

51   Irasema Garza to May Morpaw and Rafael Aranda, November 25, 1998.

our opinion that a review of the original submission is no longer appropriate' and absent new information the file would be closed.[52] There was no response from the submitters, many of whom were law students who may have graduated or moved on to other projects, and the case remained in abeyance. Meanwhile the INS continued efforts to track illegal workers and clarify its relationship with the Labor department by delegating more responsibility to the Labor Department for visa applications for temporary agricultural workers.[53] From Canada's standpoint, the NAALC process was terminated but it is unclear if the new memorandum still stifled worker complaints about labour violations.

Labor Policy Association/EFCO Corporation

Public communication CANA 99-1 set a precedent as the first submitted by an employer and a business association, again both based outside of Canada. The American Labor Policy Association (LPA Inc.), and EFCO Corporation, a Missouri manufacturer of windows, doors, and curtain wall systems for institutional buildings, filed the communication. They alleged that the National Labor Relations Board (NLRB) interpreted American laws prohibiting employer interference with unions too broadly and prevented 'employee involvement' programmes which could represent worker interests in non-union facilities. The submitters argued that these actions by the Board lead to a failure to provide for high labour standards as required by the NAFTA labour accord, and made it difficult to enforce laws on freedom of association and the right to organize. The communication also alleged delays in Board hearings on the legality of 'employee involvement' programmes.

The submission reflected an ongoing effort by employers to legalize employer-created labour-management committees at companies without unions. This practice had a long history prior to the 1930s, as companies countered unionization by creating employee representation at the firm level. These had been outlawed by the National Labor Relations Board, because of concerns about management domination. Section 8(a) (2) of the National Labour Relations Act of 1935 made employer domination of unions illegal, to eliminate 'yellow-dog' company unions. Rulings in the 1990s confirmed that the NLRA outlawed joint programmes in non-union facilities if they were dominated by management.[54] Even informal associations, with little structure, were prohibited, if the purpose was to 'deal with' employees on working conditions, though discussion of product quality and productivity were permitted.[55]

---

52   May Morpaw to Graham Boyd,, April 27, 1999.

53   Fawn H. Johnson, 'Employment Verification Tops INS agenda; Various Nonimmigrant Worker Rules Pending', *Daily Labor Report* Nov. 30, 2000, C-3.

54   Aaron Bernstein, 'Making teamwork work – And appeasing Uncle Sam' *Business Week* Jan 25, 1993, 101.

55   Kenneth A. Janero and Phillip M. Schreiber, 'Revisiting the Legality of Employee Participation Programs under the NLRA' *Employee Relations Law Journal* 25, 1 (Summer, 1999), 121–23.

Management suggested the provision was antiquated, as 'sham unions' had been eliminated by the 1950s.[56] But the Board's positions dissuaded management from introducing joint arrangements, which was an effective means of dealing with safety, productivity and other workplace concerns.[57] EFCO introduced joint committees on safety, benefits, employee suggestions, and workplace rules on 'no-smoking policy, leave policies, dress codes, four-day workweeks, overtime, holidays, vacations and time clocks'.[58] The Board ruled EFCO's initiatives illegal despite benefits to job satisfaction, productivity and efficiency.[59] EFCO lamented the decision, which ended popular committees which empowered workers, and suggested the Board targeted it because of a failed union organizing campaign.[60]

The Clinton administration formed a task force on worker-management relations and was sympathetic to management concerns about teamwork systems.[61] The Republican Congress sought to revive this practice, in the Teamwork for Employers and Managers (TEAM) Act of 1995. President Clinton supported employee-management cooperation to improve competitiveness, but Republicans rejected a narrower effort to clarify the NLRA. This measure was vetoed by Clinton, who was persuaded by labour criticism. The bill 'would undermine the system of collective bargaining that has served this country so well for many decades... by allowing employers to establish company unions where no unions exist and permitting company-dominated unions where employees are in the process of determining whether to be represented by a union'. [62] Clinton opposed efforts to exempt health and safety from the NLRA. An 'employer would be free to create, dominate and unilaterally terminate employee participation mechanisms' and could 'impose on its employees representatives they have not chosen and would not choose for themselves', undermining the NLRA.[63]

The Labor Policy Association argued that NLRA clauses which prohibit joint mechanisms violate NAALC, which calls for employee involvement in workplace management. The LPA stated 'it has been the consistent policy of the United States

---

56   Steve Bartlett, 'Teamwork: The illegal management tool' *Management Review* 85, 4 Apr 1996, 7.

57   William C. Byham, 'Manager's journal: Congress should strengthen the corporate team' *Wall Street Journal* Feb 5, 1996, A14.

58   'EFCO's Illegal Four: Committees that went astray' *Personnel Journal* Feb., 1996, 87.

59   Jenero and Schreiber, 119–130.

60   'Management Teams at Risk' *Chief Executive*, May, 1996 [cited July 26, 2002]. Available at http://www.snc.edu/socsci/chair/336/ebsco2.htm.

61   'Study commends worker participation, but says labor laws may be limiting' *Wall Street Journal* Jun 3, 1994, A2.

62   'Teamwork for Employees and Managers Act of 1995 – Veto Message form the President of the United States (H.DOC. No 104-251), Jul 30, 1996.

63   'Statement of Henry L. Solano, Solicitor of Labor, Dept. of Labor, Before the Subcommittee on Workforce Protections, Committee on Education and the Workforce, House of Representatives', May 13, 1999.

Government, through the U.S. National Labor Relations Board, to prohibit effective employee involvement and participation in non-union workplaces, including labor-management teams and committees that address occupational safety and health issues.'[64] Politically, labour opposed these changes, which they feared would allow management-dominated organizations and undermine efforts to organize genuine unions.[65] They believed 'workplace cooperation' was a Republican effort to undermine unions when they were already waning. The TEAM Act was unnecessary given the range of cooperation currently allowed by law.[66] Republicans reintroduced the measure, to promote 'cooperation in the workplace, not confrontation'. One sponsor contended: 'We need to promote flexibility and give employees a greater voice on the job while protecting their right to choose union representation'.[67]

The Labor Policy Association and EFCO submitted a lengthy document to the Canadian NAO. LPA had intervened to assist companies contesting NLRB rulings on Section 8(a) (2). EFCO had been prosecuted by the Labor Board for five years, before a final ruling outlawed its employee committees. NAALC obligations committed the US to pursuit of 'high-skill, high productivity global economies through the promotion of labor-management relations and employee involvement and participation in the workplace'[68]. NAALC had many references to the need for 'labor-management cooperation', 'greater dialogue between worker organizations and employers to foster creativity and productivity', and 'consultation and dialogue between labor, business and government'.[69] But Board rulings made it illegal 'for employees to be involved and participate effectively in critical decision-making processes within non-union workplaces'.[70] This meant the US failed to uphold NAALC goals on cooperation and participation, or to effectively enforce its labour laws. NLRB delays in adjudicating such matters were also criticized.

The submitters suggested that Board rulings were an 'improper' application of the NLRA which prohibited effective employee participation in non-union settings,

---

64   Labor Policy Association *Press Release*, 'LPA Files Complaint Under NAFTA Citing Failure of U.S. Government To Meet Its Employee Involvement Obligations' April 14, 1999, [cited July 12, 2002] Available at http://www.lpa.org/lpapublic/policy/press/releases/1999/LPA_NAFTA_Complaint.htm.

65   Glenn Burkins, 'Anti-union group files NAFTA suit', *Globe and Mail* April 14, 1999, B8.

66   Jonathan P. Hiatt and Laurence E. Gold, 'Employer-Employee Committees: A Union Perspective', submitted to the Canadian NAO, 1999, 1.

67   Press Release, 'Hon. Harris Fawell Introduces Teamwork for Employees and Managers Act' , Feb. 6, 1997 [cited July 15, 2002]. Available at http://legacy.csom.umn.edu/wwwpages/faculty/jbudd/teamact/intro26.htm.

68   LPA, Inc., and EFCO Corporation, *Public Communication on Employee Involvement in the United States in Non-Union Workplaces as the United States National Labor Relations Board Applies, Interprets and Enforces Section 8(a)(2) of the United States National Labor Relations Act* April 14, 1999, 1.

69   *Public Communication on Employee Involvement in ... Non-Union Workplaces*, 13.

70   *Public Communication on Employee Involvement in ... Non-Union Workplaces*, 1.

allowing only minimal suggestions to which management does not respond. Submitters looked at the legislative history of the Act to suggested Section 8(a) (2) was not meant to prevent worker participation, if properly interpreted by the Board in light of altered industrial conditions and processes. Employee participation is now crucial to competitive firms, and the initial problem – the predominance of company unions – was no longer prevalent. The submission noted the replacement of the Taylorist mode of production by a flexible system, in response to global competition, workplace demographics and technological change. US companies 'have had to adopt more efficient production processes that break down the barriers between employers and employees'.[71] But the Board had not adjusted despite Congressional and Presidential encouragement of employee involvement.[72]

A variety of joint initiatives were in place at US firms, from quality circles, employee support organizations, autonomous work teams, and networks of employees sharing characteristics of race, gender or ethnicity. Involvement helped improve morale, safety, health, job security, skills, and management understanding of workers' needs. Labor Board rulings limited these initiatives, even though programs like OSHA encouraged or required employee involvement. Submitters wanted the Canadian NAO to require the US NLRB 'to apply, interpret and enforce Section 8(a) (2) to allow for effective employee involvement in non-union workplaces'.[73] The submitters considered their case suitable for consultations and an evaluation committee on health and safety, because some joint committees declared illegal by the Board dealt with these subjects. Since prevention of worker participation on health and safety matters constituted a 'persistent pattern' of non-enforcement, the case could be subject to arbitration and financial penalties as well.

The AFL-CIO noted the importance of Section 8(a) (2) to the promotion of a free trade union movement in the US. The submission did not indicate a failure of the National Labor Relations Board to properly enforce the National Labor Relations Act. Instead 'it is LPA's latest attempt to change U.S. law by eliminating the NLRA's prohibition against company-dominated unions'.[74] The Board frequently ruled on these issues, and developed a detailed understanding of the limits of permissible cooperation; the LPA rejected these limits, and sought greater flexibility. The NLRA governed collective bargaining and Section 8(a) (2) was designed to ensure independence for worker organizations by prohibiting coercion or co-optation by employers. Hence, joint organizations or associations sponsored by employers were prohibited. The Board had acted properly in enforcing the prohibition on employee dominated groups.

To demonstrate the US was not in violation of NAALC, AFL counsel cited Board rulings which permitted forms of participation, such as committees with delegated powers on scheduling, open employee meetings, work teams, communication

71 *Public Communication on Employee Involvement in ... Non-Union Workplaces*, 14.
72 *Public Communication on Employee Involvement in ... Non-Union Workplaces*, 6.
73 *Public Communication on Employee Involvement in ... Non-Union Workplaces*, 6.
74 Jonathan Hiatt to May Morpaw, June 2, 1999, 1.

committees and other non-representative forums. Health and safety could be addressed by 'brainstorming' or suggestion boxes, or committees designed to share information with employers, gather complaints from employees, or design training. The Board ruled that employers may not impose a committee on their workers or dominate or interfere with an employee group.[75] Thus, the Board has not failed to enforce laws, or to abide by the spirit of NAALC. The LPA was trying to use the labour side agreement to amend US laws to allow more employer involvement with worker organization. But 'NAALC cannot become the vehicle to achieve changes in American law that *diminish* freedom of association, protection of the right to organize and the right to bargain collectively' and the case should be rejected.[76]

Workers also sought collaboration with employers, in place of hierarchical management which dominates American industries. Traditional structures were 'demeaning' and demoralizing, and limited the skills acquired by individual workers. Unions agreed that this Taylorist system was ill-equipped to meet competition in the new economy, since it created excess management and responded slowly to markets. US unions sought an end to this 'degrading and authoritarian structure' to secure collaborative management. But these improvements were best accomplished 'through collective bargaining, where workers speak with an independent voice secure in the law's protection of their rights'.[77] For unions, this was not the intention of the TEAM Act, which would undermine the labour movement. Its wide provisions allowed employers to 'establish, assist, maintain or participate in' workers' organizations, which could give management control over their creation and termination, influence how they operate, who served in official positions, and even their goals. This could allow 'employer-dominated systems of employee representation' to 'discourage or defeat the formation of truly independent workplace representatives: unions'.[78]

The Canadian NAO posed questions to the US NAO to clarify legal issues.[79] The US NAO outlined the character of the National Labor Relations Board as an independent executive agency, whose decisions are subject to appeal to the US Court of Appeals, which had generally upheld its protection of 'labour organizations'. The NAO described the differences the Clinton administration had with Congress on the TEAM act, which it viewed as undermining longstanding essential protections for labour unions. The NAO agreed that the TEAM act would allow company-dominated unions and could hinder employee acceptance of independent unions; employer-worker committees could also undermine existing unions as bargaining representatives.[80] Laws allowed a wide range of employer-employee consultations, as required by modern industry. In the area of health and safety, worker involvement

---

75   Jonathan Hiatt to May Morpaw, June 2, 1999, 5.

76   Jonathan Hiatt to May Morpaw, June 2, 1999, 5.

77   Hiatt and Gold, 4–5.

78   Hiatt and Gold, 9–10.

79   Thomas Cunningham to May Morpaw, May 9, 1999.

80   'U. S. NAO Responses to Questions Raised Regarding Canada NAO Submission 99-01 (LPA, Inc.), June 1, 1999, 2.

in improving workplace conditions was mandated by the Occupational Health and Safety Administration. But this requirement must be exercised in a manner consistent with labour laws by acting through unions where certified or through autonomous worker committees in non-union workplaces. Employee participation is subject to the requirement that there be no employer domination in matters affecting employment, which would in union work sites be subjects of collective bargaining.

As the EFCO decision revealed, only employer domination of bargaining invalidated joint committees. Board rulings made clear the numerous legal forms of bilateral committee, on 'brainstorming', information-gathering, delegation of management authority, safety conferences, improving efficiency, and all-employee committees where all express individual viewpoints. The Board had effectively enforced US laws, which did not violate NAALC prescriptions on participation and high standards. Up to 30,000 companies had created joint committees without domination, and without impinging on issues of working conditions, wages or benefits. Only 3% of NLRB cases dealt with employer domination and only 25 companies had been ordered to disband joint committees.[81]

On June 15, 1999 the Canadian NAO wrote to LPA and EFCO to inform them that it had rejected CAN 99-01. The NAO noted that information provided by the US NAO, the AFL-CIO and the submission did not indicate non-compliance with US NAALC obligations, or non-enforcement of labor law.[82] The submitters immediately sought a reassessment, including an explanation of the Canadian NAO's reasons, given the apparent contradiction between OSHA requirements for employee participation and NLRB prohibitions.[83] But on May 15, 2000, the file was closed, as the Canadian NAO received no further information from the submitters.[84] An administrative court ruling in 2001 suggested that if employee committees could implement decisions about productivity, safety, quality and other issues, the Board may deem them legal.[85]

Puebla Garment Factories

There were no further submissions to the Canadian NAO until 2003, when it received NAO 2003-1, on the Puebla garment maquiladoras. The communication was submitted by the United Students Against Sweatshops (USAS) and the Centro de Apoyo al Trabajador (CAT) and was twice amended by the petitioners. A Canadian petitioner, the Maquiladora Solidarity Network, joined the submission in January 2004, and the NAO accepted it in March. The original petition involved workers at

---

81   'U.S. NAO Responses', June 1, 1999, 12.

82   May Morpaw to Daniel Yager, June 15, 1999.

83   Daniel Yager to May Morpaw, June 15, 1999.

84   May Morpaw, 'Note to File, Public Communication Can 99-01', May, 2000.

85   Susan Heathfield, 'New NLRB Decision Supports Employee Involvement and Empowerment' [cited June 18, 2004]. Available at http://humanresources.about.com/library/weekly/aa072901a.htm.

Matamoros Garment S.A de C.V. in Izúcar de Matamoros who sought an independent union. The amended submission included similar, ongoing complaints by workers at Tarrant Mexico. This duplicate of the US submission alleged that Mexico neglected its commitments in national and international law to promote rights to organization, bargaining, health and safety, minimum wages and overtime pay. Submitters noted that Mexico did not ensure impartial and independent labour tribunals in violation of Section 5 of NAALC. Their evidence suggested government tolerance of protection contracts involving phantom unions, unbeknownst to workers, designed to preclude genuine worker representation. Given the similarities to other communications, petitioners argued that Puebla demonstrated a persistent failure by Mexico to enforce labour laws.

Workers at both plants claimed to have contacted management frequently about problems in working conditions, to no avail. Existing unions did little to assist, so workers sought to create new unions to represent them (SITEMAG at Matamoros Garment, and SUITTAR at Tarrant México). But organizing at both plants prompted intimidation and illegal firings of activists aided by the established union. The local CAB, which included representatives of the established unions, refused to register the new unions despite their demonstrated support. The Matamoros union admitted that it did not file the legal *amparo* needed to challenge the Board ruling, claiming lack of time to respond. The Tarrant union did file such a challenge, but later withdrew. The workers claimed that not only was the union registration process biased against the independent unions, but the local officials had failed to protect workers rights to minimum wages, timely pay, hours of work and overtime pay, severance pay, and prevention of workplace accidents and illnesses.

At a public hearing in May 2004, Linda Yanz, coordinator of the Canada-based Maquiladora Solidarity Network testified about 'the systematic violations of workers' rights in garment maquila factories in the state of Puebla, and the failure to date of the NAALC process to hold the Mexican government accountable for not enforcing its own labour laws'.[86] Detailed research by the Maquiladora Solidarity network had uncovered systematic abuses of workers rights in garment factories in Puebla. These practices were not challenged by the ghost unions and 'protection contracts' which were the 'norm' in such maquiladora operations; workers were usually unaware of either the union or the contract, which was negotiated in secret to meet legal requirements for representation without giving genuine influence to the workers. Authorities intervened to bloc representative unions and allowed protection contracts to dominate. In Yanz's words, the 'role of the official unions in local and state Conciliation and Arbitration Boards is an institutionalized barrier to fair, equitable and transparent labour boards and processes'.[87]

---

86 'NAFTA ten years later: Why the labour side agreement doesn't work for workers' *Maquila Network Update*, June 2004 [cited July 12, 2004, at http://www.maquilasolidarity. org/campaigns/tarrant/update_jun2004.htm.

87 Lynda Yanz, Coordinator, Maquila Solidarity Network, Canada 'Testimony to the Canadian National Administrative Office (NAO)' Toronto, Ontario, May 28, 2004, 2.

A student with the United Students Against Sweatshops, who observed the situation at Tarrant, testified that she heard allegations of non payment of wages, denial of overtime pay and harassment of workers who sought redress. Management claimed collective action was illegal and destructive to the firm and isolated union supporters from fellow workers. Despite gaining support from 75% of workers, union leaders faced stalling from the Board, which was closed for most of the summer, and some of them were forced to resign by the company.[88] A Centro de Apoyo al Trabajador representative testified that labour authorities were ineffective in defending worker rights in Puebla's new maquilas, which allowed poor treatment of uneducated workers, including children as young as ten. He detailed problems at Kukdong (Mexmode), Matamoros Garment and Tarrant, as workers faced intimidation from employers and rival unions and indifference or bias from authorities, who did not prevent mass dismissals. The result was a 'grave injustice' as the power of government helped sustain abusive practices and meaningless 'protection' unions.[89]

Personal testimonials underscored how, in this ineffective system, workers received inadequate wages which lagged behind subsistence, suffered sexual and racial harassment and pregnancy discrimination, were forced into compulsory, unpaid overtime, and were exposed to harmful chemicals. Unclean washrooms and lack of ventilation added to workers discomfort. Workers were not registered for the social security system, denying them crucial benefits, but saving employer premiums.[90] There was not enough legal recourse for workers, who resorted to 'wildcat' walkouts. The Board received many complaints of illegal firings and unpaid severance, serious injuries and deaths from fumes. But workers trying to change things faced intimidation, threats and violence, including a serious assault on a human and labour rights advisor to the Tarrant workers.[91] An activist from Puebla's Worker Assistance Centre noted that workers exhausted all legal avenues in Mexico, and needed NAO pressure on Mexico to give workers and unions fair treatment.

The Steelworkers noted that ineffective earlier NAALC cases failed to stem problems in independent organizing and worker protections; a failure in this case would further drain the 'credibility' of NAALC.[92] The Steelworkers submission reflected on the Itapsa case, which covered similar issues, but left most of these

---

88   Testimony of Julia Plascencia 'Public Meeting on Public Communication CANA 2003-1 Under the NAALC' Toronto, May 28, 2004, p. 25.

89   Testimony of Blanc Velazquez Diaz, 'Public Meeting on Public Communication CANA 2003-1 Under the NAALC' Toronto, May 28, 2004, p. 31–6.

90   Marisol Enyart, United Students Against Sweatshops 'Testimony to the Canadian National Administrative Office (NAO) – Public Communication CAN 2003-1 (Puebla)' Toronto, May 28, 2004. [cited Jan, 13, 2005]. Available at http://www.maquilasolidarity.org/campaigns/NAO/Toronto%20English/Testimonio_Marisol_Enyart.pdf.

91   Yanz 'Testimony..' 3.

92   'Mexican workers testify to NAFTA panel in Toronto. Ten years of NAFTA and rights still trampled' Maquila Solidarity Network *News Release* May 27, 2004 [cited July 20 2004]. Available at http://www.maquilasolidarity.org/campaigns/tarrant/media_may2004.htm.

concerns unrectified despite NAALC promises. Protection contracts, intimidation, unfair Board rulings and lax health and safety standards were familiar holdovers. Despite the Canadian NAO's request in Itapsa that Mexico ensure publication of contracts and union registrations, workers in Puebla again were confronted with representatives they had never heard of when they tried to form an independent union. The existence of a protection contract posed legal obstacles to independent organizing despite earlier commitments to end such practices. Firings or unpaid 'breaks' for unionists persisted after ministerial consultation on 98-1, indicating how little had been accomplished. Thus 'the facts set forth in the Puebla case constitute not only an indictment of the respect for workers' rights in Mexico, but also a clear indictment of the NAALC as a vehicle for the enforcement and improvement of workers lives in Mexico'.[93] Canada should seek an evaluation committee of experts to avoid the same limited results.

Canada's NAO concluded that the Board's delays were inconsistent with Mexico's federal labour law, which treated registration as a technical issue not subject to arbitrary delay. The Board's failure to point out technical problems in union applications precluded a 'timely and predictable' registration process. The delays required a remedy from Mexico to ensure an effective and expedient process. The Canadian NAO felt that the Tarrant union was denied a timely hearing of its *amparo* action by the Board, but did express concern that the union did not pursue all possible appeals, because of financial pressures on members to settle outside the formal process. The Canadian NAO concluded that these events raised questions about Mexico's fulfilment of its NAALC commitment to ensure timely and impartial law enforcement. As in CANA 98-1, the Mexican legal system did not ensure that the Boards were free of bias, because of the presence of representatives of the official unions. But the Canadian NAO declined to comment on claims of interference via intimidation and coercion, since the fledgling unions had not made formal complaints and could not claim that Mexican authorities had failed to act.[94]

On health and safety, the Canadian NAO noted that workers had again not made formal complaints; but inspectors should have uncovered issues requiring rectification at the plants. The Canadian NAO sought information from Mexico on inspections and enforcement in these plants. On minimum employment standards, including wages, and overtime, workers again made few complaints, aside from one at Matamoros garment which was resolved in favour of the worker. This meant that the appeal procedures were not fairly tested. But the Canadian NAO noted evidence that the Board discouraged workers from making complaints about employment standards. By remaining passive in the face of claims of unfair dismissal, the Board

---

93   United Steelworkers of America 'In the Matter Of: Public Communication 2003-01 Before the Canadian National Administrative Office Pursuant to the North American Agreement on Labour Cooperation' May 28, 2004, 4.

94   Canada, Dept of Human Resources, National Administrative Office, *Review of Public Communication CAN 2003-1* Ottawa, May 2005, [cited May 23, 2005]. Available at http://www.hrsdc.gc.ca/en/lp/spila/ialc/pcnaalc/pdf/report.pdf.

increased pressure on workers to move on rather than pursue appeals so some chose to 'abandon or unduly compromise' their rights.[95]

The Mexican NAO was slow in clarifying whether regular inspections were undertaken to ensure compliance, or whether the Board reported non-compliance to authorities. The Canadian NAO suggested that the reluctance of workers to follow through on complaints processes revealed scepticism with the neutrality and effectiveness of the Board which was unhealthy for complaints-driven law enforcement. The NAO recommended ministerial consultations on effective and expeditious registration, registration, impartial labour boards, protection for workers seeking to organize unions, prohibitions on retaliatory dismissals and transparency on collective agreements to prevent phantom unions from operating without worker scrutiny. On health and safety, minimum standards, suspension of pay or dismissal, the NAO awaited additional information from Mexico, particularly reports on health and safety and minimum standards inspections, and any responses to violations.[96] Labour Minister Joe Fontana accepted the review report and sought consultations to encourage 'a more positive approach on the part of the labour authorities'.[97]

The MSN representative welcomed the growth of transnational collaboration in this case. In the Kuk Dong or Mexmode case, international pressure on the brand name companies who contracted for garments secured company recognition of a union, after adoption of company code of conduct for contractors. Puebla's Conciliation and Arbitration Board still refused to grant registration until the company and union had reached a recognition agreement. Unfortunately, the Board did not follow even this weak precedent at Matamoros Garment and Tarrant. Yanz suggested that transnational connections to companies in Canada and other developed nations could be mechanisms for pressuring Mexican firms and sub-contractors to respect labour rights. But the NAO should join in these efforts by pressuring Mexico to require conciliation boards to operate transparently and by making union registrations and collective agreements available to workers. These efforts could be advanced by creation of a trinational body to investigate enforcement of NAALC principles on association, bargaining and the right to strike, cooperative activities on union registration, and ECE's on child and forced labour, minimum wages and health and safety.[98] Canada did not act on such recommendations, and did not seek trinational enforcement via the first evaluation committee of experts.

---

95   *Review of Public Communication CAN 2003-1*, vii.

96   *Review of Public Communication CAN 2003-1*, vii.

97   Minister of Labour and Housing, *News Release* 'Canada to pursue labour complaint with Mexico under the North American Agreement on Labour Cooperation' May 11, 2005 [cited May 23, 2005]. Available at http://www.hrsdc.gc.ca/en/cs/comm/hrsd/news/2005/050511.shtml.

98   Yanz 'Testimony...' 4–5.

Evaluations of Canada's NAALC Activities

Canada's use of the NAALC submissions process has been limited so far. This reflects in part the attitude of Canadian officials who preferred to emphasize cooperative activities and communication under NAALC, not confrontational submissions. It is also a symptom of federal-provincial complexity on labour issues, as several provinces remain outside the intergovernmental agreement and are exempt from NAALC proceedings directed at local industries. There was also limited motivation from civil society actors for engagement. Union and human rights NGOs in this country always rejected the NAALC as an inadequate compromise. The Canadian Labour Congress (CLC) referred to the 'marginal impacts' of NAALC which 'has primarily been a failure due to its non-binding nature and lack of enforcement mechanisms. It has brought no relief to the affected workers'. The CLC acknowledged that submissions could 'be utilized for fact-finding purposes and to expose problems in order to generate a broader public awareness' of the need for further reform.[99]

Submitting groups quickly became disillusioned as the limited results confirmed NAALC's weakness. The coalition behind the Dana/Itapsa case noted their scepticism:

> Thus far, while a great deal of paper has been generated, and numerous reports have been written making many findings with respect to violations of the NAALC, there have been few, if any, concrete results that improve the lives of workers in any of the three countries ....[100]

The USW's Canadian counsel, Mark Rowlinson, argued that the Puebla submission showed that, 5 years after Itapsa,

> representation votes are still not held by secret ballot in Mexico. The system of administrative justice is no better. Workers still do not have the right to freely choose their union and they still suffer terribly unsafe working conditions. In short, in our view, there has been no progress on the issues identified in our Complaint.[101]

Many Canadian labour advocates agree with Rowlinson's assessment of NAALC: 'It makes many lofty promises, but the enforcement mechanism lacks teeth'.[102]

There is no shortage of pressing deficiencies in Canadian practices which should draw the attention of NAALC institutions and processes. Despite Canada's

---

99   CLC, 'Chapter 5 The Social Dimension of NAFTA: A Work in Progress' *NAFTA: The Social Dimensions of North American Economic Integration* [cited April 4, 2002]. Available at http://www.clc-ctc.ca/policy/trade/nafta5.html.

100   Lawrence McBrearty to Claudette Bradshaw, June 2, 1999.

101   'Mexican workers testify to NAFTA panel in Toronto. Ten years of NAFTA and rights still trampled' Maquila Solidarity Network *News Release* May 27, 2004[cited July 20 2004]. Available at http://www.maquilasolidarity.org/campaigns/tarrant/media_may2004.htm.

102   USWA, '10 Years After NAFTA, Mexicans Still Work in Unsafe Conditions' [cited August 23, 2004]. Available at http://www.uswa.org/uswa/program/content/1235.php.

professed superiority in labour standards and law enforcement, Suen raises concerns respecting the same transborder issues evident in Mexican complaints about the United States. She criticizes Canada's treatment of migrant Mexican and other immigrant farm labourers under its Canadian Seasonal Agricultural Worker (SAW) Program. Workers in this seemingly well-regulated system have been denied access to their rights in practice, however extensive these are on paper. Problems include denial of unionization and bargaining rights, unfair application of overtime rules, prohibitions on moving to other jobs, and threats of termination and repatriation for these vulnerable immigrants. Mexico could take a similar interest in its nationals in Canada and employ NAALC to publicize these deficiencies, notable in a country nominally committed to the UN Migrant Workers Convention. Suen doubts that NAALC can provide protection, and suggests a greater NGO role in advising migrant workers of their rights, including possible use of the Charter and Rights and Freedoms against discrimination on the basis of nationality.[103] Mexico's experiences in pressing such issues in the US could set a precedent, allowing NAALC to assist in allowing migrant workers access to the knowledge needed to safeguard their rights, in collaboration with concerned NGOs.

However, the principle constraint on Canadian participation in the NAALC remains the lack of provincial accession. There has been no movement on this front for some time, and there appear few prospects for this to change. Hence, numerous potential NAALC submissions cannot be raised by complainants, however compelling. Provinces like Nova Scotia have received ILO censure for their labour practices, but cannot be brought to account under NAALC. Not only does this limit NAALC's applicability in Canada; it also undermines Canada's credibility in NAALC forums, and in FTAA negotiations. How can Canada regard its practices as a model when most provinces, covering a majority of workers, are unwilling to sign on to NAALC? But provinces seek to avoid a new form of pressure for improvement of labour laws and standards, in a global context where intra-provincial as well as international competition for investments and jobs has escalated.

NAALC did provide a new venue for union activism on a trilateral basis. Canadian unions affiliated with American unions, like the United Steelworkers of America (Canadian National Office), joined with the major union centrals, the Canadian Labour Congress and AFL-CIO, and Mexico's emerging independent unions like the Frente Auténtico del Trabajo (FAT) on the Itapsa case. Their motives were overtly political, in seeking to demonstrate NAALC's weaknesses before the FTAA negotiations proceeded. There was a notable overlap between cases reviewed in Canada and the other two countries, as non-Canadian NGOs took the lead role in some cases; for instance, the Yale-INS case was submitted by the same groups which had raised the issues in Mexico, the US-based Yale Law School Workers' Rights Project and the American Civil Liberties Union Foundation Immigrants' Rights Project.

---

103 Rachel Li Wai Suen, 'You sure know how to pick 'em: human rights and migrant farm workers in Canada.' *Georgetown Immigration Law Journal*, 15 (2000), 199–227.

The EFCO case was also raised exclusively by American submitters, the American Labor Policy Association and EFCO Corporation, who did not seek any Canadian partners. On the Puebla case, the lead was again taken by the original US and Mexican submitters, the United Students Against Sweatshops and the Centro de Apoyo al Trabajador, though they did find a Canadian partner, the Maquiladora Solidarity Network. Finally, CANA 2005-01, on Mexico's Labour Law Reform, also copied the US submission, led by the Washington Office on Latin America, but involving a coalition of unions, including the Canadian Auto Workers Union, Canadian Energy and Paper Workers' Union, Canadian Labour Congress, Centrale des Syndicats du Québec, Confédération des syndicates nationaux, Federation des travailleurs et travailleuses du Québec, and the Syndicat de la fonction publique du Québec.

The small number of cases and the limited role for Canadian organizations in bringing forth new ones indicates that Canada's engagement in NAALC will remain marginal. This reflects the disillusionment with NAFTA and it side agreements among Canadian unions and human rights groups, which have distrusted the framework from the outset. This disinterest and limited usage is heightened because many provinces, including populous, industrial Ontario, remain outside the agreement. This reflects the impact of domestic institutions of federalism which fragment labour laws and regionalize unions. The ultimate effect will be that NAALC will not serve as a significant stimulant to cross border activism in Canada's case, though transborder engagement by Canada's vibrant civil society organizations will proceed independently of NAALC. As the Abascal labour law reform case (discussed in Chapter 10) shows, Canada's NAALC activities have not ceased. However, the incentive to bring new submissions may be diminished after the rejection of this politically important case in January, 2006.

PART III
NAALC and the Prospects for Regionalism in North America

Chapter 9

Cooperative Activities: Cultivating Commonality?

Introduction

Although submissions have the highest profile, the NAALC secretariat and NAOs also engage in cooperative and research activities mandated by NAALC Article 11. Some are linked to submissions and consultations which provide direction to trinational cooperation and research, with numerous seminars, conferences and research projects undertaken in fulfilment of ministerial agreements. But the Secretariat has advanced a wide-ranging research agenda and engaged in transnational activities and information sharing, directed by the ministerial council, and influenced by national advisory committees and activist groups. This activity has pressed the cause of labour relations perhaps as significantly as the submissions.

Given the range of such activities, and the complexity of their subject matter, these cannot be fully investigated here. Nonetheless, they will be surveyed to provide insight into the possible building of transnational bureaucratic expertise and international understanding of labour norms, principles and best practices, though not as yet a common North American culture of labour relations. Notably, the range of subject matters involved has been quite broad, with a few key emphases. These diverse activities have drawn in different state and federal agencies from all three countries, and provided numerous opportunities for official contacts and interactions. In addition, the conferences, seminar and outreach sessions have involved numerous non-governmental, union, corporate and academic participants, generating greater familiarity with each country's labour problems and traditions, encouraging commonality in some measurements and practices, and inducing more transnational social networking which could contribute to a deepened regionalism in labour affairs.

NAALC enjoined the parties to 'encourage publication and exchange of information, data development and coordination, and joint studies to enhance mutually beneficial understanding of the laws and institutions governing labor in each Party's territory' and to 'pursue cooperative labor-related activities on the basis of mutual benefit'.[1] This prompted the NAALC secretariat, in conjunction with

---

1 Commission for Labor Cooperation, 'Section IV: Cooperative Activities, Research, and Public Information and Education' [cited Sept. 24, 2003]. Available at http://www.naalc.org/english/review_annex3_4.shtml.

national departments of Labour and NAOs, to initiate an active agenda of research and cooperative interchanges. This chapter cannot comprehensively assess these activities, but will survey years of cooperation in major issue areas. Given the wealth of data and analysis, this will not provide a definitive catalogue or evaluation but will highlight prominent themes and provide an overview of perceived effectiveness from stakeholders close to the process. This chapter concludes by evaluating the range of social and state actors who have been involved, and assessing the potential for regionalization of the labour policy community.

NAALC's Cooperative Element

The NAALC website defines cooperative activities as 'the gathering and exchanging of information about labor law, industrial relations, labor markets, and human resources practices in each Party country considered on its own and/or comparatively to the other two'. Activities 'can involve mutual examination of each country's typical practices, best practices, or both, across any portion of the spectrum of work-related matters'. [2] The ILAB website noted that the goal was to focus attention on 'issues that were viewed as meriting particular concern by all three countries and on those issues raised in the submissions filed with the NAOs' to 'facilitate better understanding of each country's labor laws, policies and practices, and to promote awareness of current labor issues'.[3]

The NAALC suggested themes for cooperative activities:

> occupational safety and health; child labor; migrant workers of the Parties; human resources development; labor statistics; work benefits; social programs for workers and their families; programs, methodologies and experiences regarding productivity improvements; labor-management relations and collective bargaining procedures; employment standards and their implementation; compensation for work-related injury or illness; legislation relating to the formation and operation of unions, collective bargaining and the resolution of labor disputes, and its implementation; the equality of women and men in the workplace; forms of cooperation among workers, management and government; [and] the provision of technical assistance, at the request of a Party, for the development of its labor standards...

This hefty agenda inspired early activities, but priorities were later steered by public submissions and ministerial consultations.

This cooperation has taken different forms. Training and technical support involved training in best practices in enforcement, inspections, and operation of technical equipment, often to implement the findings of ministerial consultations.

---

2   'Section IV: Cooperative Activities, Research, and Public Information...'.

3   U.S. Department of Labor, National Administrative Office, Bureau of International Labor Affairs *North American Agreement on Labor Cooperation: A Guide* Washington, D.C., April 1998 [cited September 30, 2003]. Available at http://www.dol.gov/ilab/media/reports/nao/naalcgd.htm#CooperativeActivities.

This approach was invoked on gender discrimination and migrant workers. More conventional information sessions include workshops, seminars and conferences. These allowed stakeholders and analysts to share national or comparative research, and to reconcile disparate records, statistics and measurements, which hampered comparison. NAALC promoted common definitions, data sets and research frameworks, to improve understanding of labour laws and processes.

Cooperative activities evolved around an ongoing Labour Cooperation Program, which reflected priorities shared by all NAALC states, but the agenda was affected by submissions from early 1995. The Mexican NAO indicated that 26 of the 34 activities it has lead were part of the ongoing labour cooperation program, 7 came from ministerial consultations after submissions and one was suggested by the Secretariat.[4] The agenda developed despite a lack of clarity respecting the relation between the secretariat and the NAO's. The NAO role became more prominent as activity focussed on issues raised in submissions. Most activities have been organized by NAOs, sometimes collaboratively, but at times with one country taking the lead. While some activities have been trinational, others have been binational, with more marginal participation by the third partner. Notably, more than half of the cooperative activities were held or organized in Mexico.[5]

The NAALC secretariat planned fewer of these activities and concentrated on an ongoing research agenda, linked to the cooperative programs but responsive to the submissions. Under Article 14, the Secretariat provided reports on labour legislation and regulations in the three countries, law enforcement, labour market trends, human resource policies and other matters requested by the Council of Ministers. Examples included studies on labour markets, labour laws and plant closings.[6] Trinational coordination sometimes involved creation of working groups to assist with data standardization and collection. For instance, in 1998 a working group on Transborder Workers Compensation designed questionnaires for national and state authorities, while another convened on the compatibility of labour market data. Examples of secretariat research and publications are outlined below. Several key themes emerged, which became the central focus of cooperation and research. Table 9.1 outlines some of the major activities on each theme. In these core areas, the NAALC engaged in repeated activities which generated transnational expertise and fostered regional, transborder networks.

---

4 Mexico, STPS, General Coordination for International Affairs 'The North American Agreement on Labor Cooperation (NAALC): Labor Cooperation Program' [cited April 13 2005]. Available at http://www.stps.gob.mx/01_oficina/03_cgai/ingles/seccion_tres. htm#Program.

5 Mexico, STPS, NAALC: Labor Cooperation Program.

6 Commission for Labor Cooperation, 'Section IV: Cooperative Activities, Research, and Public Information and Education' [cited Sept. 24, 2003]. Available at http://www.naalc. org/english/review_annex3_4.shtml.

Table 9.1　　Cooperative Activities, 1994–2005, By Subject Area

---

INDUSTRIAL RELATIONS AND WORKERS' RIGHTS

2005 Trinational Conference on the Labor Dimensions of Corporate Social
　Responsibility March 30–31, Ottawa.

2003 The Labor Boards in North America Trilateral Seminar – March 20,
　Monterrey, Mexico.

2001 The Right to Organize and Bargain Collectively in Canada and the United
　States – February 1–2, Toronto.

2000 Seminar on Freedom of Association in Mexico – June 23, Tijuana, Mexico.

1998 Conference on Contracting Out – December 7–8, Ottawa, Canada.

1998 Fourth Major Conference on Labor Relations – October 29, Washington, DC.

1997 International Treaties and Constitutional Provisions Protecting Freedom of
　Association – Dec. 4, Baltimore.

1996 Industrial Relations for the 21st Century – March 18–20, Montreal, Canada.

1995 Labor Law and Freedom of Association – September 20–21, Washington,
　D.C.

1995 Labor Law and Freedom of Association Workshop – March 27–28,
　Washington, D.C.

1994 Conference on Labor Law and Industrial Relations – September 19–20,
　Washington, D.C.

1994 Workshops on Labor Law and Practice – June 26–30, La Jolla, California.

OCCUPATIONAL SAFETY AND HEALTH

2003 Second Chair's Meeting of the Trinational OSH Working Group – August 25,
　Mexico City.

2003 Technical Seminar on Manufacturing of the Trinational OSH Working Group
　– Subgroup on Training and Technical Assistance – June 16–17, Mexico City.

2003 Technical Workshop on Management Systems and Voluntary Protection
　Programs of the Trinational OSH Working Group – Subgroup on Training and
　Technical Assistance – March 10–12, El Paso, and Ciudad Juarez.

2002 Trilateral Working Group on Occupational Safety and Health, inaugural
　meeting July 8– 9, 2002 Mexico City.

2000 Conference on Safety and Health in the Workplace in North America – May
　17–19, Mexico City, Mexico.

2000. North American Occupational Safety and Health Week (NAOSH) – May
　15–19,

1999 Occupational Safety and Health Laws in the United States, Mexico, and
　Canada

1999 Occupational Safety and Health Laws in the United States, Mexico, and
　Canada – October.

1999 The Future Culture of Safety and Health in the Mining Industry in North
　America – Sept. 22–24, Winnipeg.

1999 Conference on Safety and Health in the Bottling Industry – June 21–23, Mexico City.
1999 Conference on Safety and Health on the Job – May 27–28, Monterrey, Mexico.
1999 North American Occupational Safety and Health Week (NAOSH) – May 17–21
1998 North American Occupational Safety and Health Week (NAOSH) – May 18–22
1997 North American OSH Week – June 2–6
1996 NAALC Petrochemical Study Tour "Preventing Catastrophic Explosions in the Petrochemical Industry in North America" – Oct. 27–31, Orlando.
1996 Occupational Safety and Health Planning Session – March 25–26, Mexico City, Mexico.
1995 Construction Study Tour – November 5–10, Dallas, Texas.
1995 Canadian OSH Centre Seminar – July 13, Mexico City, Mexico.
1995 Annual Meeting of Senior Occupational Safety and Health Officials – June 5–8, Vancouver, B.C.
1994 Technical Seminar on Safety and Health in the Petrochemical Industry – November 14–17, Edmonton, Alberta.
1994 Technical Seminar on Safety and Health in the Construction Industry – September 27–30, Mexico City.
1994 Hazard Recognition training for Industrial Hygienists – September 20–22, Guadalajara, Jal., Mexico.
1994 Accident Inspections training – September 13–15, Monterrey, N.L., Mexico.
1994 Seminar on Occupational Safety and Health Statistics – September 12–13, Mexico City, Mexico.
1994 Industrial Hygiene training session – August 30–September 1, Guadalajara, Jal., Mexico.
1994 Safety and Health in the Construction Industry training – August 23–25, Monterrey, N.L., Mexico.
1994 Biohazards Course – June 28–30, Mexico City, Mexico.
1994 Technical Seminar on Safety and Health in the Electronics Industry – June 13–16, Albuquerque, New Mexico.
1994 Sampling of Environmental Contaminants training – April 26–29, Mexico City, Mexico.
1994 Principles of Ergonomics training – February 22–24, Mexicali, Mexico.
1994 Sampling and Laboratory Analysis of Airborne Contaminants training – February 21–25, Mexico City, Mexico.

MIGRANT WORKERS
2003 Workshop on U.S.–Mexico Labor Rights of Migrant Workers – August 26, Mexico City.
2002 Migrant & Immigrant Worker Forum – June 5, Augusta, Maine.

2001 Public Forum: Promoting Dialogue among Migrant Agricultural Workers, Growers and Government Officials, Aug. 8, Yakima, Washington.

2001 The Application of U.S. Labor Law to Migrant Agricultural Worker Issues – May 23–24, Washington, DC.

2000 Conference on Agricultural Migrant Labor in North America – February 7–9, Los Angeles, California.

GENDER DISCRIMINATION

2004 Workplace Discrimination and the Law (with George Washington University Law School, Nov. 18–19, Washington, DC.

2001 Women Farmworkers, Know Your Rights, July 1 2000, Yakima, Washington

2000, The Protection of the Labor Rights of Women in North America – May 30, Puebla, Mexico.

1999, Women in the Workplace: Know Your Rights! – August 17–18, in McAllen, Texas and Reynosa, Tamaulipas.

1999, Protecting the Labor Rights of Working Women – March 1–2, Mérida, Yucatan, Mexico.

1997, Women and Work in the 21st Century – April 23–25, Queretaro, Mexico.

1995 Equality in the Workplace – June 21–22, Mexico City, Mexico.

CHILDREN, VIOLENCE AND LABOUR TRAFFICKING ISSUES

2004, Conference on Trafficking in Persons in North America – December 6–7, Washington, D.C.

2001, Violence as a Workplace Risk – November 29–30, Montreal, Canada.

1997, Protecting Working Children in North America: A Shared Responsibility – October 15–16, Ottawa, Canada.

1997, Child and Youth Labor in North America: Improving the Lives of Working Children Feb. 25–26, San Diego. California.

LABOUR MARKET DEVELOPMENT

2004, Workshop on Supporting Economic Growth Through Effective Employment Services – Sept. 29–30, Cancun.

2004, Conference on Labor Market Information Statistics – July 12–15, Mexico City, Mexico.

2003, Meetings between BLS and STPS on employment projections and productivity measurement, December 11–12, in Washington, D.C.

2003, Seminar on Linking Job Skills and Education in North America – August 21–22, Mexico City.

2003, Workshop on Standard Occupational Classification (SOC) – June 23–26, Mexico City.

1999, U.S.–Mexico Cooperation on Workforce Development – Mexico June 4–20

1998 Seminar on Labor Market Trends & the Role of Governments – April 1–2, Guadalajara, Mexico.

1996, Tripartite Seminar on Responding to the Growth of Non–Standard Work and

Changing Work Time Patterns and Practices – Nov. 25–26, Ottawa, Canada.
1996, Workshop on Income Security Programs – October 3–4, Ottawa, Canada.
1996, Workshop on Continuous Learning and Development in the Workplace –
April 23–24, Dallas, Texas.
1994, Workshop on Productivity Trends and Indicators – October 24–25, Mexico.
1994, Technical Seminar on Microenterprises and the Informal Sector – June 2–3,
Mexico City.

Worker Rights and Industrial Relations

From the advent of NAALC, union organizing rights took centre stage. Workshops
and a conference in 1994 focussed on implementation of laws governing bargaining,
best practices in labour-management relations, and worker-employer cooperation.
In 1995 the submissions on General Electric, Honeywell and Sony, which stressed
freedom of association and the right to organize, prompted a workshop on 'Labor
Law and Freedom of Association'. A conference on Industrial Relations for the
21st century heard academic presentations on how labour law has been affected by
neo-liberalism, technological change, capital mobility and continental integration.
Stakeholder workshops considered the competitive pressures of globalization, which
affected freedom of association and gender equality and proposed policies to adjust
to competition and family demands in the workplace.[7]

In 1997, the Fishing Ministry case prompted a seminar on 'International Treaties
and Constitutional Provisions Protecting Freedom of Association'. Panellists
presented information on the constitutional status of treaty commitments, especially
ILO conventions.[8] A NAALC publication called *Plant Closings and Labor Rights*,
summarized research, following the Sprint case, on how closings in plants with
pending union certification affected the right to organize. The study recommended
improved data collection, transnational collaboration and 'codes of conduct' or
ethical guidelines on closures under ILO or OECD auspices.[9]

A 1998 conference on 'Labor–Management Relations in North American
Multinationals: Legal, Cultural and Economic Environments' considered 'the
utilization of new, innovative procedures for the purpose of creating a dialogue
between management and labor, and examining labor management processes.'[10]
The conference examined how MNCs adjusted to differing legal, institutional

---

7   Commission for Labor Cooperation, *Industrial Relations for the 21st. Century.*

8   US Department of Labor, National Admininstrative Office, *Seminar on International
Treaties and Constitutional Systems of the United States, Mexico and Canada* University of
Maryland School of Law, Baltimore, Dec. 4, 1997.

9   Commission for Labor Cooperation, *Plant Closings and Labor Rights* Washington:
NAALC Secretariat, 1997 [cited March 26, 2001]. Available at http://www.naalc.org/english/
nalmcp_3.shtml.

10 US department of Labor, ILAB, NAO Cooperative Activities, 1994–2005, [cited April
30, 2005]. Available at http://www.dol.gov/ilab/programs/coopact/sectcoopact.htm#ii.

and cultural environments. MNCs took advantage of different labour relations by delegating these issues to plant managers. These variations affected firms' location decisions along with access to markets and transborder integration of production. This promoted efficiencies and innovation, weakened the potential for transnational, company-wide labour challenges and made workers in the three countries compete for investment and employment.[11]

A conference on 'Contracting Out' assessed changes in a post-Fordist flexible production paradigm. Employers sought flexibility in number of workers, hours and shifts, length of contracts, salary rates, and work specialization. So they avoided traditional contracts and preferred individual deals with workers, who could be shifted or recalled as conditions demanded. The conference examined employers' freedom to 'contract out' to avoid benefits, workman's compensation and other liabilities. Contract work raised 'fundamental questions' about workplace organization, and 'the balance between individual and collective approaches to employment'.[12]

In 2000, the secretariat published a survey of legislation and regulations on union organizing, collective bargaining, and the right to strike. The guide outlined laws, constitutions, statutes and regulations, and evaluated jurisdictional conflicts in these federations. It surveyed the legal status of unions, organization rights, decertification, internal governance, dues and membership, and political roles. This document examined the legal basis of the right to strike, legal actions to show support (picketing, secondary boycotts) illegal work stoppages, legal means to end strikes, use of replacement workers, labour boards and ministries, court redress, publications and information and procedural guarantees. It is a comprehensive guide to labour laws, with insights on national practices and differences, which can help promote transnational learning.[13]

A Tijuana 'Seminar on Freedom of Association in Mexico,' which resulted from the ministerial agreement on Han Young and Echlin-ITAPSA, dealt with freedom of association, access to contracts and protection of union organizers against retribution. This session was controversial because no time was provided for worker testimony and Han Young employees claimed they were kept out by force, allegedly by members of the 'official' union.[14] Canada and the US organized a workshop on 'The Right to Organize and Bargain Collectively in Canada and the United States',

11 *Labor–management Relations in North American Multinationals: Legal, Cultural and Economic Environments* Washington College of Law, October 29, 1998; [cited June 123, 2004,]. Available at http://www.dol.gov/ilab/media/reports/nao/labor_management_relations. htm#iiib.

12 May Morpaw, Opening Remarks to the Conference on *Contract Labor, Contracting Out: The Implications of New Forms of Work For Industrial Relations* Toronto, Dec. 7, 1998; [cited June 13, 2004]. Available at http://www.dol.gov/ilab/media/reports/nao/contractingout. htm.

13 NAALC Secretariat, *Labor Relations Law in North America* Washingon: NAALC, 2000; PDF format available at http://www.naalc.org/english/study2_pdfs.shtml.

14 UE Workers Internationa 'NAFTA Side Agreement Sidelined Labor Rights' [cited April 2004]. Available at http://www.ueinternational.org/WorldTrade/nafta.html.

in 2001. The workshop considered how global trends and transnational agreements like NAALC affected managers, temporary and contract workers.[15] It was notable for the allegations of violence against Mexican workers who attempted to participate on behalf of independent unions. In 2003 a Trilateral Seminar on 'The Labor Boards in North America' focussed on bias in local CABs discovered in the Han Young, ITAPSA and TAESA cases. Participants considered ways to increase the impartiality, transparency, independence and honesty of labour boards, to ensure workers had full access to their legal rights on union recognition and bargaining.[16] The Mexicans presented information on changes in arbitration, and hailed the workshop as evidence of increased openness.[17]

A 2005 Trinational Conference on the Labor Dimensions of Corporate Social Responsibility discussed best practices, and the role of government and transnational agencies like the ILO, OECD and UN. Organizers noted the emergence of multilateral norms encouraging voluntary measures such as the ILO 'Tripartite Declaration on Principles Concerning Multinational Enterprises and Social Policy' and the OECD 'Guidelines for Multinational Enterprises and the United Nations Global Compact'. These promoted corporate 'codes of conduct' on labour, encouraged by NGO activism, as in the Puebla case, which can 'serve to enhance the respect and the promotion of human rights and labour standards'.[18]

Occupational Health and Safety

Supporters and opponents of NAFTA agreed that there were deficiencies in Mexico's capabilities to enforce occupational health and safety standards. Even before the first submissions, the secretariat and NAOs held seminars, technical consultations, training sessions and meetings of experts on health and safety. The Occupational Safety and Health Administration (OSHA) sent experts to train Mexican inspectors in the measurement of airborne contaminants and ergonomics. Canadian officials provided sampling equipment for the STPS laboratory, and trained STPS employees. Technical seminars and training seminars were held for the electronics, petro-chemical, mining, bottling and construction industries, and on biohazards management, industrial hygiene, hazard recognition, and accident inspections. In 1995, an annual

---

15 The workshop themes are outlined on the Laboris website page [cited August 12, 2003]. Available at http://laboris.uqam.ca/toronto.htm.

16 US department of Labor, ILAB, NAO Cooperative Activities, 1994–2005 [cited April 30, 2005]. Available at http://www.dol.gov/ilab/programs/coopact/sectcoopact.htm#ii April 30, 2005.

17 STPS, Dirección General de Comunicación Social Boletín 037 'Seminario laboral de México, Estados Unidos y Canadá', March 20, 2003 [cited May 11, 2005]. Available at http://www.stps.gob.mx/06_com_social/boletines/marzo_03/037_20_mar.htm.

18 Canadian NAO, 'Why a Conference on the Labour Dimensions of Corporate Social Responsibility in North America?' [cited May 12 2005]. Available at http://www.naalccsrconference.ca/en/about_en.shtml.

meeting for top officials in industrial health and safety was inaugurated. The 3 countries began an Occupational Health and Safety week to promote awareness and improvements.[19]

A 3 day mining seminar, with on-site visits to a Manitoba mine and laboratory, emphasized strategies and technologies to reduce fatalities, injuries and health hazards. Sessions addressed protective devices, remote mining to limit human exposure to hazards, disaster avoidance and rescue, ergonomics, respiratory disease, worker-management partnership, measurement of hazards, and prevention. [20] A trinational report was published 'Occupational Safety and Health Program: the legal framework, the development of standards, ensuring compliance, information systems, training, and workers' compensation'. Another trilateral conference on safety and health was held in 2000 on 'globalization of safety and health in the workplace, methodologies for the analysis of dangers in the workplace' and 'the importance of safety and health inspections, and preventive medical services in the workplace.'[21]

With the changes in Mexican and American administration in 2000, there was a lull. After Han Young, Itapsa, Taesa, Custom Trim/Auto Trim, and Yale, a ministerial declaration established the Trilateral Working Group on Occupational Safety and Health with sub-groups on 'handling of hazardous substances; safety and health management systems and voluntary protection programs; training of inspectors and technical assistance staff.' The working group went beyond the submissions, to consider 'technical recommendations' for the governments, develop 'technical cooperation projects' to improve safety and health, and identify additional issues for transnational 'collaboration.'[22] The Subgroup on Training and Technical Assistance hosted activities on health and safety management, voluntary programs, corporate-worker cooperation, hazard and risk prevention and best practices, with visits to construction enterprises in Mexico and Texas. Other projects included a website for information sharing, information visits on hazards and compliance in the automotive sector, a seminar on a Globally Harmonized System of Classification and Labelling of Chemicals, and training for Mexican inspectors on fire safety, life saving, and electrical equipment.[23]

19 US department of Labor, ILAB, NAO Cooperative Activities, 1994–2005.

20 'Trinational Seminar on The Future Culture of Mining Safety and Health In North America' Winnipeg MN: Sept. 22–24, 1999 [cited April 30, 2004]. Available at http://www.dol.gov/ilab/media/reports/nao/mining1.htm.

21 US department of Labor, ILAB, NAO Cooperative Activities, 1994–2005.

22 US department of Labor, ILAB, NAO Cooperative Activities, 1994–2005.

23 'Working Group established to promote NAALC objectives' *Lab Safety Supply – Techlines*, April 2004, [cited April 11, 2005]. Available at http://www.labsafety.com/refinfo/techlines/tchln0404.htm#Article4.

Migrant Workers

While protection of migrants was a core principle of NAALC there was little attention until Mexico's submissions, when the 3 ministers pledged 'to work together to eliminate employment discrimination and assure that migrant workers are accorded full protection under the laws'.[24] The first collaborative activity was the February, 2000 'Conference on Agricultural Migrant Labor in North America' which considered omissions and problems with enforcement among transient agricultural workers, including poor workplaces and housing, problems for women and families, lack of legal representation and deficient social services. Presenters considered how law enforcement could address these problems, and what role NAALC could play.[25] A conference on the 'Application of US Labor Law to Migrant Agricultural Worker Issues' considered the federal and state roles in enforcing migrant worker rights. The meeting promoted cooperation between authorities including collaborations with Mexican consular officials on outreach to migrant communities. [26] A 'Public Forum: Promoting Dialogue among Migrant Agricultural Workers, Growers and Government Officials' discussed health and safety, compensation, housing, pesticide exposure and other issues raised in the Washington Apples case. A similar Migrant and Immigrant Worker Forum in Maine addressed issues from DeCoster Egg.

A Joint Statement in May 2002, called for a deepening of the interaction between consular officials, state and federal authorities, and human rights and labour NGOs, to coordinate enforcement and education. The two labour ministries committed to local experiments which could be transferred to other locales where migrants were concentrated, such as the Justice and Equality in the Workplace experiment in Houston. The joint statement lauded a California initiative 'whereby Mexican Consular staff receive training on the various laws enforced by Federal and State agencies that have application to workers in the U.S. to enable Consular staff to refer workplace issues to the proper authority for review and resolution' [27] A binational 'Workshop on U.S.-Mexico Cooperation on Labor Rights of Migrant Workers in North America' in, 2003 assessed past collaboration and considered new ways to inform migrants of their rights.[28] OSHA officials introduced a Spanish-language web

---

24 Ministerial Consultations – Mexico Submissions 9801, 9802 and 9803 Joint Declaration, May 18, 2000, [cited June 23, 2001]. Available at http://www.dol.gov/ilab/media/reports/nao/minagreemt9801_9802_9803.htm.

25 'NAFTA and Migrants' *Rural Laws* 18, April, 2000 [cited June 23, 2001]. Available at http://www.migrationint.com.au/ruralnews/slovenia/apr_2000_18rmn.asp.

26 US Department of Labor, International Labour Affairs Bureau, *Foreign Labor Trends: Mexico* , Washington: ILAB, 2002, 18.

27 'U.S.–Mexico Joint Ministerial Statement Regarding Labor Rights of Immigrant Workers' April 15, 2002. [cited June 11, 2004]. Available at http://www.dol.gov/ilab/media/reports/nao/jointstate061102.htm.

28 US Department of State, Bureau of Western Hemisphere Affairs *U.S-Mexico Binational Commission Labor Working Group, Report* Washington, Nov. 12, 2003 [cited May 12, 2005]. Available at http://www.state.gov/p/wha/rls/rpt/26212.htm.

site, toll free number and Hispanic Task force to assist migrant labourers. STPS Secretary Abascal indicated the high priority Mexico gave to migrants, who should be recognized as a vital economic force.[29]

The secretariat produced a report on migrant workers, which summarized laws and documented the challenges migrants faced in all three countries in enforcing their rights. The report contrasted the protection available to nationals and foreign-born workers, to illuminate gaps and explore measures to reduce abuse against migrants. Laws covered housing, transportation, legal services, sanitation, water and hygeine, pay rates and due process. Though many similar topics were covered there were significant variances between national practices in the treatment of migrants which made common standards elusive. Some provinces and states exempted farming from labour protection and compensation, and Mexico had difficulty registering farm employees in its social security system. Temporary agricultural workers did not qualifying for health, pension and unemployment coverage because of residency requirements or deficient employment hours.[30] The Secretariat also compiled a 'Guide to Labor and Employment Laws for Migrant Workers in North America', which detailed the rights of foreign workers, with fact sheets on particular subjects for each country, tailored to the needs of a particular migrant.[31] NAALC activities have provided resources to address the impact of trade integration, especially the Mexicanization of US agriculture. It is debatable whether NAALC has sufficiently addressed the problems migrant workers face. But a comprehensive agreement on migrant issues was put on hold after the attacks of September 11, and modest advances may be all that can be expected.

Gender in the Workplace

Gender discrimination assumed a key place in cooperative activities from the start. The 1995 'Training Equality in the Workplace' workshop considered employment discrimination, the glass ceiling on promotions, unequal pay and sexual harassment. It assessed economic restructuring and female workers, the balance between work and family, and gender-specific health and safety issues.[32] A 1997 conference on 'Women and Work in the 21st Century' 1997 covered 'differences and complementary trends

---

29 STPS, Dirección General de Comunicación Social, Boletín 116 'México y EUA acuerdan acciones en beneficio de trabajadores Migratorios' August 27, 2003 [cited May 12 2005]. Available at http://www.stps.gob.mx/06_com_social/boletines/agosto_03/116_27_ago.htm.

30 Commission for Labor Cooperation *Protection of Migrant Agricultural Workers in Canada, Mexico and the United States* Washington: NAALC Secretariat, 2002, 9–10.

31 See for instance, *Guide to Labor and Employment Laws for Migrant Workers in Canada* [cited June 22, 2004]. Available at http://www.naalc.org/migrant/english/mgtabcan_en.shtml.

32 North American Free Trade Agreement (NAFTA) Policy Documents National Administrative Offices 'Training Equality in the Workplace', June 21–22, 1995, Mexico

of economic and labour structures, the levels of female participation in the labour force, part-time labour, flexible working hours, the transformation of female education levels'.[33] The Secretariat published statistics and analysis in *The Employment of Women in North America*; this report revealed similarities in earnings, occupational specialization, and part-time status of women in the 3 countries, but differences in education, participation rates, hours of work and unemployment. This work remained specialized in clerical, educational and health and social services, and was often part-time and low wage, though with growing participation in management and professions. Women faced common challenges of employment discontinuity from child-bearing and domestic roles.[34]

A trinational conference on 'Protecting the Labor Rights of Working Women' in 1999 addressed protections from employment discrimination, including pregnancy testing. The conference increased the profile of womens' rights, by publicizing programs to protect women from discrimination and considering improved enforcement of laws and regulations. Mexican officials outlined their country's laws which prohibited pregnancy or gender discrimination, and provided recourse for those affected before and after hiring. The conference received a report on state and federal jurisdictional complications.[35] The US Women's Bureau outlined how collaboration among agencies, unions and NGOs helped it spread bilingual information to women on pregnancy, wages, disabilities, sexual harassment and the Family and Medical Leave Act. The Bureau shared expertise with Mexico's new Bureau on Gender Equity.[36] This conference spawned outreach sessions, called 'Women in the Workplace: Know Your Rights' in Texas and Tamaulipas, at which government officials, unions, employers and NGOs informed Mexican women and migrants on their rights and protections. American officials introduced core legal protections for women including the Pregnancy Discrimination Act and Family and Medical Leave Act. Employers were informed of their obligations and responsibilities. Women were put in touch with local agencies and NGOS which could provide information and legal advice. Information was also supplied on federal and state collaboration

---

City, Mexico [cited December 11, 2002]. Available at http://www.ilo.org/public/english/employment/gems/eeo/nafta/nao.htm.

33 North American Free Trade Agreement (NAFTA) – Policy Documents – National Administrative Offices 'Trinational Conference on Women and Work in the 21st Century', April 23–25 1997, Queretaro, Mexico [cited December 11, 2002]. Available at http://www.ilo.org/public/english/employment/gems/eeo/nafta/nao.htm.

34 North American Commission for Labour Cooperation, *The Employment of Women in North America* [cited April 11, 2003]. Available at http://www.naalc.org/english/study5.shtml.

35 North American Comission for Labor Cooperation, *Biennial Report, 1999–2000* Washington, D.C,, NACLC, 2000, 15.

36 'Remarks of Delores Crockett at Protecting the Labor Rights of Working Women A Trinational Conference under the North American Agreement on Labor Cooperation' Merida, Yucatan, Mexico March 2, 1999. [cited April 11, 2003]. Available at http://www.dol.gov/wb/speeches/mexico.htm.

in enforcing anti-discrimination laws. The sessions aimed to transfer some of these methods to Mexico to improve women's understanding and enforcement of their rights.[37]

An outreach session for workers, employers and NGOs was held in Puebla in 2000. The brief sessions provided useful information to workers and gender rights advocates, and potentially contributed to the enforcement of women's workplace rights. The sessions illustrated the extensive legal and constitutional protections which existed. Mexican laws established rights to equal pay and treatment, hours and conditions. But studies indicated the gap between men's and women's earnings, as women tended to be in low-paying jobs. Problems of implementing anti-discrimination protections were reviewed, given rapid economic transformation and the preponderance of jobs in informal, agrarian or family enterprises.[38] Despite the intentions of Mexican officials to end gender discrimination, the lack of resources for enforcement meant that these problems persisted, though cooperation and transnational exchanges could increase awareness among workers and officials.

A 2001 session in Yakima Washington, 'Women Farmworkers, Know Your Rights', was designed to help migrant agricultural workers in Washington orchards. A broader training session in Puebla, featured outreach to NGOS, workers, unions, officials and employers on the rights of women workers. Topics included 'legal action against dismissal due to pregnancy' and social security programs to aide women at various stages of working and family life.[39] In 2002, President Fox signed an agreement with the National Council of the Maquiladora Export Industry pledging full enforcement of laws prohibiting gender discrimination.[40] A 2004 seminar on Workplace Discrimination also incorporated concerns of native peoples and persons with disabilities.[41] Despite these interchanges, pregnancy discrimination persists in some industries. But the pressure brought by NAALC cooperative activities may bear fruit over time.

---

37 *Women in the Workplace: Know Your Rights!* McAllen, Texas August 17 1999 [cited March 26, 2003]. Available at http://www.dol.gov/ilab/media/reports/nao/genderoutreach1. htm. Similar presentations were made by Mexican officials and NGOS on August 18, 1999 in Reynosa, Tamaulipas.

38 US Department of Labor, *Foreign Labor Trends: Mexico*, 2002, 12.

39 North American Comission for Labor Cooperation, Biennial Report, 1999–2000 Washington, D.C, NACLC, 2000, 17–18.

40 Alison Gregor 'Fox champions women in maquiladoras' *San Antonio Express News* April 9, 2002.

41 'Seminar on Workplace Discrimination and the Law in North America' November 18–19, 2004 George Washington University Law School, Washington DC. [cited June 12 2005]. Available at http://www.naalc.org/english/pdf/Brochure_SeminarDiscrim1.Nov2004ENG. pdf.

Child Labour

Protection for child labour was one of NAALC's 11 labour principles. Mexico prohibits work by children under age 14, and limits hours, night work and non-industrial employment for those under 16. But because of economic necessity and lack of enforcement, child labour in the informal sector remains widespread. ILO reports estimate that 6% of children aged 10 to 14 might be employed in services, primary resources, agrarian and industrial activities. UNICEF estimates of workers under age 18 ranged up to 3.5 million in 2000. A U.S report noted that the 'protections afforded under Mexican law are difficult to apply in the large and growing informal sector ... in family workshops, and in agriculture, because federal and state labor inspectorates are too small to effectively monitor practices' at these myriad locations.[42]

A 1997 conference on 'Child and Youth Labor in North America: Improving the Lives of Working Children in the NAFTA Countries' considered ways to prevent exploitation of children by enforcing age restrictions, ensuring health and safety, guaranteeing an education for legally employed children.[43] The conference revealed concerns about child labour in all NAFTA partners, including how to ensure that work environments were safe and provided education. Participants discussed lack of data, lack of coordination among government, NGOs and international agencies, failure to evaluate policies, and the lack of public awareness or responsiveness.[44]

A conference on 'Protecting Working Children in North America: A Shared Responsibility' focussed on how governments, industry, unions, and child rights groups could prevent 'inappropriate' child labour and ensure respect for child workers' rights.[45] The conference considered social support and services, and assistance to migrant and impoverished families, which needed children to contribute to family incomes. It also addressed strategies to inform children of their rights and legal protections and to ensure that exploitative practices were eliminated. The conference concluded that governments and social partners shared responsibility and recommended a 'long-term, concerted effort to end exploitative child labour' with government leadership as a 'voice for children'.[46]

Despite Mexican efforts to make school hours consistent with work, many families withdrew children to work full time in the fields or migrated to other regions,

---

42 US Department of Labor, *Foreign Labor Trends: Mexico*, 2002, 12.

43 US department of Labor, ILAB, NAO Cooperative Activities, 1994–2005.

44 'Conference Report: Protecting Working Children in North America: a Shared Responsibility' Ottawa, Canada October 15–16, 1997 [cited April 26, 2005]. Available at http://www.dol.gov/ilab/media/reports/nao/childlabor2.htm.

45 'Conference Report: Protecting Working Children in North America': a Shared Responsibility' Ottawa, Canada October 15–16, 1997 [cited April 26, 2005]. Available at http://www.dol.gov/ilab/media/reports/nao/childlabor2.htm.

46 Conference Proceedings, *Protecting Working Children in North America: a Shared Responsibility* Ottawa, Canada October 15–16, 1997. [cited April 26, 2005]. Available at http://www.dol.gov/ilab/media/reports/nao/childlabor2.htm.

disrupting children's educational and social development. Law enforcement was limited by attitudes and resources. Mexican unions argued that 'inspectors who have the responsibility for spotting underage employees are overworked and underpaid, and the government allows favored companies and industries to get away with prohibited labor practices'.[47] The conferences developed an ambitious agenda for government and community actors to address inappropriate child labour, including community reporting of violations, and regulation of child labour not currently governed by laws, such as family business, domestic labour, farm work, and small contractors.[48] The community should use 'local initiatives', including children's representation via unions, to promote protection, encourage workplace safety, and inform consumers about how their purchases affect children.

Child labour was potentially open to an ECE, arbitration and sanctions. Some observers predicted that, given the scale of the problem in Mexico, where children could be widely seen working in agriculture, child labour could prompt a NAALC challenge leading to millions of dollars in fines. Evidence of children as young as 6 working in agriculture in border regions indicates how deep and intractable the problem remains.[49] Though the problem has persisted, no such challenge has emerged since the abandoned Florida Tomato submission, though the legal grounds improved when Mexico ratified ILO Convention 182 in 2000. Instead, the 3 countries decided to use NAALC to search for best practices, collect data, promote education and continue dialogue. While the NAOs could act 'as a catalyst by bringing together representatives of the key interest groups in each country' the responsibility to act as shared with 'all social partners'.[50]

Violence and Labour Trafficking

In 2001 a session on Violence in the Workplace addressed an issue raised in submissions respecting intimidation and harassment. The conference brought together stakeholders to discuss psychological and physical aspects of violence. The sessions sought to raise awareness of violence, examine its extent, explain its impact on firms and workers, and compare approaches to resolving or reducing the threat. Compensation to victims, treatment for offenders, and roles for public and private insurance were also discussed. Mexico was just beginning to assess violence and hoped NAALC forums could help to develop statistical methods. The high costs of

---

47 S.L. Bachman, 'Young workers in Mexico's economy: NAFTA aims at curbing child labor, but it's rampant south of the border' *U.S. News & World Report*, 123, 8 Sept 1, 1997, 40.

48 *'Conference Report: Protecting Working Children in North America'*.

49 David Bacon *Children of NAFTA: Labor Wars on the US/Mexico Border* Berkeley, University of California Press, 2004.

50 *Conference Report: Protecting Working Children in North America*.

violence in the US versus Europe in worker absenteeism were notable. Globalization, competitiveness, workplace hierarchy, and rapid change led to stressful, conflict-ridden work environments; 'strategic' harassment and violence was sometimes used by superiors to force out contentious workers or to act out racial or gender bias.[51]
Criminal acts by outsiders, violence by clients, customers, suppliers, patients or inmates, employee conflicts or past grievances, and personal relationships led to varied, but frequent, violence. Case studies from different sectors – medicine, construction, retail sales, banking, taxis, public transit, fast food, libraries, and education – illustrated the ubiquitous nature of violence. The threat could be decreased by empowering workers, defusing grievances, and managing aggression; hazard analysis, early warning, surveillance and security, preventative equipment (alarms, locks, or monitors), incident reports, sensitivity and diversity training, and education were also useful. Victims required compensation and counselling, but often did not receive it, especially after recent cutbacks.[52]

Most recently, the 3 countries held a 'Conference on Trafficking in Persons', which focussed on trafficking for labour purposes, and considered anti-trafficking strategies. The countries faced different issues, but the trans-border nature of trafficking made cooperation essential. This complex issue involved immigration, law enforcement, health, labour and human services, so the attendees were diverse. The conference reviewed a recent increase in trafficking including illegal migration, sweat shopping, and the sex trade. Officials shared data, though it was incomplete owing to the illicit nature of trafficking. Transnational cooperation to thwart trafficking included governments, international agencies and NGOs on sex tourism, forced labour and migrant smuggling. There was no dissent from Secretary Chao's declaration that the 'worldwide incidence of men, women and children being enslaved demands a vigorous and sustained international effort to rescue victims and protect future generations.'[53].

Labour Market Development

Finally, several cooperative activities addressed transnational collaboration to encourage development of labour markets, improve employment services, and upgrade skills. These activities focussed on economic promotion as opposed to social protection or enhancement of labour rights. At first, the countries shared information and coordinated standards and terminology to allow more effective collaboration.

---

51 North American Agreement on Labour Cooperation, Cooperative Activities Program *Trinational Conference on Violence as a Workplace Risk* Montreal, November 29–30, 2001 [cited April 12, 2004]. Available at http://www.dol.gov/ILAB/media/reports/nao/violenceworkrisk.htm#002.

52 *Trinational Conference on Violence as a Workplace Risk.*

53 '800,000 People Trafficked Yearly, U.S. Labor Secretary Says' *Weekly Special Report* December 9, 2004 [cited April 22, 2005]. Available at http://usembassy.state.gov/ethiopia/wwwh4216.html.

A June, 1994 'Technical Seminar on Microenterprises and the Informal Sector' provided information about the US underground economy and Mexico's informal sector. An October 1994 'Workshop on Productivity Trends and Indicators' allowed officials to compare statistical methods and interpretations of labour market trends. Canada sponsored a trinational meeting on 'Workshop on Continuous Learning and Development in the Workplace' to discuss current practices and improvements in workforce training programs. The certification of transnational workers and professionals was raised as an area for collaboration.[54]

Ottawa hosted a 1996 'Workshop on Income Security Programs' which compared national approaches on unemployment insurance, retirement pensions, mothers and family supports, worker compensation and health and injury benefits. Canada's capital was also the venue for a 'Tripartite Seminar on Responding to the Growth of Non-Standard Work and Changing Work Time Patterns and Practices'. The meeting sought common definitions and regulations for such non-standard work. Positive features like flexible hours and telework were balanced against the low pay and benefits and job insecurity of contract and on-call employment.[55]

The Secretariat published *North American Labor Markets. A Comparative Profile* which assessed labour market trends in each country from 1984 to 1995. The report presented statistical information to highlight trends including unemployment, worker skills, non-standard contracts, hours of work, union density, productivity, wages and benefits, and income inequality. Mexico hosted a 'Seminar on Labor Market Trends and the Role of Governments' to share information on training and placement services. The conference sought to inspire short-term thinkers in government to consider effective long-term strategies for tooling workers and matching them with jobs.[56]

The Secretariat organized seminars on 'Incomes and Productivity in North America' which considered whether wages had kept pace with productivity.[57] Papers from the 2000 seminar, which comprised two roundtable sessions on macro and micro-economic dimensions of incomes and productivity, were made available as a downloadable e-book on the NAALC website as a resource for policy makers.[58] The Secretariat study on *'Standard' and 'Advanced' Practices in the North American Garment Industry* recommended government-business collaboration to encourage firms to enforce labour standards while investing in technology, to increase productivity and profitability.[59]

---

54 US department of Labor, ILAB, NAO Cooperative Activities, 1994–2005.

55 US department of Labor, ILAB, NAO Cooperative Activities, 1994–2005.

56 US department of Labor, ILAB, NAO Cooperative Activities, 1994–2005.

57 Commission for Labor Cooperation, *'Seminar Proceedings'* [cited April 28, 2005]. Available at http://www.naalc.org/english/seminar.shtml.

58 Commission for Labor Cooperation, *Incomes and Productivity in North America. Papers from the 2000 Seminar* Washington: NAALC Secretariat, 2001. [cited April 28, 2005]. Available at http://www.naalc.org/english/pdfs1.shtml.

59 Commission for Labor Cooperation, *'Standard' and 'Advanced' Practices in the North American Garment Industry* Washington: NAALC Secretariat, 2000. [cited April 12, 2005].

Mexican officials visited US cities to study job classification, online information and 'one-stop' job banks. US officials visited Mexico to help develop its internet job 'bank'.[60] At the 2003 'Workshop on Standard Occupational Classification", US Labor officials provided technical advice on Mexico's job classification system. This multi-agency event brought officials from the US Labor Department and the Bureau of Labor Statistics together with Mexican labour and statistical officials. The secretariat published *The Rights of Nonstandard Workers: A North American Guide* which surveyed workers in situations not dealt with in labour and social security laws. Contract workers, home workers, domestics the self employed and part-time workers were excluded from many protections enjoyed by unionized colleagues in standard employment. Canadian temporary and part-time workers had less protection from severance or dismissal and were not covered by laws on hours, holidays, vacations, unemployment and other benefits. In Mexico's informal sector, labour rights, social security, life and retirement benefits were officially protected. But intermittent workers may not be eligible and *indigenas* lack language skills or registered status. Informal sector workers cannot secure social security unless they can pay premiums, so coverage is not universal.[61] Also in 2003, the NAALC organized a 'Seminar on Linking Job Skills and Education in North America'. The conference addressed the demand for rapidly evolving skills and considered how to bridge the divide between public and private sectors in training and human resource development. Participants discussed standardized professional certification, quality assurance, vocational orientation and job placement.[62]

Another major publication was *North American Labor Markets: Main Changes Since NAFTA* which assessed labour market transformations, including the aging of the population, participation of women, education levels, sectoral distribution of employment, occupational composition, working hours, unemployment rates, and non-standard forms of employment. Wage and benefit inequality were noted based on age, years of service, occupation, economic sector, and education levels. Also surveyed were minimum wages and the relationship between wages and productivity, a conundrum in Mexico where real wages declined while productivity rose. Packed with statistical details, the report indicated that the economies of all three countries benefited from the trade and investment stimulus of NAFTA though employment gains were not as high as in earlier decades. Mexican job creation remained inadequate to employ the large population of young adults, as its population

Available at http://www.naalc.org/english/pdf/study3.pdf.

60 Commission for Labor Cooperation, *Annual Report, 2002* Washington: NAALC Secretariat, 2003, 17. [cited April 21 2005]. Available at http://www.naalc.org/english/pdf/AR02_eng_web.pdf.

61 Commission for Labour Cooperation, *The Rights of Nonstandard Workers: A North American Guide* Washington: NAALC Secretariat, 2003. [cited April 16, 2005]. Available at http://www.naalc.org/english/pdf/study1.pdf.

62 US Department of Labor, ILAB, NAO, 'Linking Job Skills and Education in North America' [cited February 17, 2004]. Available at http://www.dol.gov/ilab/programs/nao/agendamex.htm.

aged more slowly than its neighbours; hence informal employment remained critical creating regulatory and policy challenges.[63] In the same year, there was extensive collaboration between US and Mexican officials on information management and statistical analysis of productivity and employment.

A Conference on Labor Market Information Statistics was held in July 2004, which addressed projections of employment and skills requirements. Officials shared information on statistical methods, evaluation techniques and training opportunities.[64] The NAALC secretariat co-sponsored a session on incomes and productivity with the Carnegie Endowment for International Peace which examined the transformation of economic activity, particularly manufacturing, and considered NAFTA's impact on productivity and incomes. Canadian manufacturing employment recovered to pre-NAFTA levels after an earlier decline, but productivity gains outpaced job creation. Mexico concentrated even more on maquila activities, with little Mexican content in products; wages in export industries lagged behind despite productivity and efficiency gains, and incomes stayed below pre-NAFTA levels. The US coped with declines in textiles with losses to both Mexico and China.[65]

The 'Workshop on Supporting Economic Growth Through Effective Employment Services' linked NAALC and the Inter-American Conference of Ministers of Labor, in anticipation of future hemispheric cooperation on labour and trade. The focus was on means of linking workers and jobs (via phone, Internet, job fairs, or walk-in job exchanges) to improve the utilization of the workforce. The workshop looked at existing cooperation, assessed their transferability to other Latin American and Caribbean states, and considered international cooperation to promote growth and efficiency, with input from hemispheric unions, and the Inter-American Development Bank.[66]

Assessment of Cooperative Activities

This chapter has briefly surveyed the substantial cooperation and consultation on labour affairs among the 3 NAFTA states. It has been a selective reading of this

---

63 Commission for Labour Cooperation, *North American Labor Markets Main Changes Since NAFTA* Washington, NAALC Secretariat, 2003 [cited April 22, 2005]. Available at http://www.naalc.org/english/pdf/labor_markets_en_1.pdf.

64 US department of Labor, ILAB, NAO Cooperative Activities, 1994–2005.

65 'North American Incomes and Productivity in the Global Context: Industry Challenges Seminar in Washington, DC Carnegie Endowment for International Peace and the North American Commission for Labor Cooperation', October 22, 2004 (summaries by Jennifer Maul, [cited April 12, 2005,]. Available at http://www.carnegieendowment.org/pdf/nafta_conference_summaries.pdf.

66 'Preliminary Agenda, Workshop on Supporting Economic Growth Through Effective Employment Services' NAALC – IACML September 29–30, 2004 Cancun, Quintana Roo, Mexico, [cited April 23, 2005]. Available at www.oas.org/udse/english/ documentos/updatedagendaaugust31.doc.

complex field, which has resulted in numerous studies, seminar proceedings, conference reports, and briefing notes. The NAALC Secretariat has maintained a wide-ranging research agenda above and beyond these core themes. For instance, the Secretariat has published a comprehensive guide to *Income Security Programs for Workers in North America*, which covered unemployment payments, illness and injury benefits, maternity leave, wages and salaries, income support for the poor and disabled, and income tax credits.[67] Its research Briefs include short, timely publications on union density, work stoppages, productivity, employment rates, demographics, education, illness and injuries, and benefits.[68] A working paper series was inaugurated in December 2004 with a study of integration's effects on labour markets.[69] While several substantial projects have resulted in publications, some of the Secretariat's work remains confidential for what insiders deem 'political reasons'.[70]

Cooperative activities, research studies and seminars were praised for increasing understanding of labour practices and facilitating stakeholder interaction across the three countries. Even those disappointed with the disputes resolution process expressed some positive reaction to these activities, which focussed on labour matters meriting particular concern and on issues raised in the submissions. Cooperation provided technical training and shared expertise, and created mechanisms for exchange of best practices. As cases were processed by the NAO's, cooperative activities emerged from controversial issues of freedom of association, right to organize and bargain, gender discrimination, child labour, labour market adjustment, farm workers and migrant labour. Publicity about lax law enforcement via these cooperative activities can bring pressure to bear on governments to live up to their commitments to protect workers.

But interviews and feedback from stakeholders reveal a divide on the efficacy of the cooperative activities. Business representatives welcome these activities, which should take precedence over submissions and disputes resolution. Business claims an ability to draw on the information exchanged in these activities to adjust behaviours in an efficacious way, consistent with freedom from government regulation or infringements on national sovereignty. Business groups suggested that valuable cooperation and information exchange had been overshadowed by the undue

67 Commission for Labor Cooperation, *Income Security Programs for Workers in North America: A Reference Manual for Workers and Employers* Washington: NAALC Secretariat, 2000. [cited April 20, 2005]. Available at http://www.naalc.org/english/other2.shtml.

68 Commission for Labour Cooperations, 'Briefs' [cited April 22, 2005]. Available at http://www.naalc.org/english/briefs.shtml. Downloadable versions of all briefs are available at this web address.

69 Commission for Labour Cooperation, *The Impacts of Integration and Trade on Labor Markets: Methodological Challenges and Consensus Findings in the NAFTA Context* Working Paper Series No. 1 Dec., 2004 [cited April 22, 2005]. Available at http://www.naalc. org/english/pdf/WP_Eng.pdf.

70 American Center for International Labor Solidarity (AFL-CIO) *Justice for All: The Struggle for Worker Rights in Mexico* Washington: ACILS, 2003, 37.

submissions process.[71] The cooperative activities and publications had been useful in standardizing measurements of labour market trends, incomes and productivity, providing comparative information on laws and regulations and income support, occupational health and safety and job skills and education. Businesses expressed concerns about 'political' activities arising from the submissions, some of which led to biased reports.[72]

Government officials, especially in Mexico and Canada, regard the cooperative agenda as the core of the side agreement. Mexico's advisory committee suggested that the partners place 'greater emphasis on cooperation as opposed to confrontation' and disputes resolution; the countries should focus on common ground not on contention or difference. Mexico believed that cooperative activities had been relegated to the backburner by the US NAO as it assumed the role of a 'moral tribunal' on Mexican affairs. Cooperation must respect differences in national practices and should not be aimed at creating common or homogenous trinational standards.[73] Canadian advisors told the author that they found the cooperative elements preferable to a confrontational strategy and felt the research agenda would prove more substantive and important than submissions and disputes resolution. Only in the US under President Clinton did officials appear to emphasize the public submissions process, though that may have altered with the Bush administration.

Union and human rights advocates concede that the cooperative agenda has produced substantial research and useful interchanges among officials and actors. They welcomed the transnational collaboration among unions and worker rights advocates and labour analysts which have been spawned by some cooperative activities and conferences. Nonetheless, this does not compensate for the deficiencies in the public submissions process or the failure of the actors to even attempt to follow through on evaluation committees or arbitration, disputes resolution and sanctions. As an AFL-CIO study suggested, 'the consultation method has only demonstrated a limited power to embarrass'.[74]

Even those closely associated with the process have lamented that the NAALC process had produced mainly conferences and studies which, while producing 'significant findings and recommendations ... have not directly addressed or resolved worker rights violations documented and proven in NAALC proceedings'.[75] Some

---

71 'USCIB Letter on NAFTA Labor Side Agreement' December 17, 1997 [cited November 30, 2001]. Available at http://www.uscib.org/index.asp?documentID=1362.

72 'Comments by the U.S. Chamber of Commerce on the Operation and Effectiveness of the North American Agreement on Labor Co-operation' Feb. 4, 2004. [cited April 23, 2005]. Available at http://www.uschamber.com/NR/rdonlyres/erpzeassnd7gdoojppmv7rb3kape5kflcg3wqmwhs4rmsolemthei77vkiuxz5nzzizjr2sik74tkh/ChamberNAFTAComments2404.pdf.

73 Mexico, STPS, General Coordination for International Affairs *Report of the Mexican National Advisory Committee on the First Four Years of the Operation of the NAALC* [cited April 16, 2005]. Available at http://www.stps.gob.mx/01_oficina/03_cgai/ingles/report.htm.

74 *Justice for All*, 106.

75 *Justice for All*, 45.

labour advocates concede that 'the net effect of measures taken under NAALC so far has been increased acceptance of the duty to respect worker rights, including the rights of women workers, and a greater appreciation by employers and officials of the member governments of the need to enforce such rights.'[76] But they stress NAALC's limited potential for enforcement and its lack of clear transnational standards as shortcomings which limits it to publicity and awareness, a far cry from stringent enforcement on trade and investment matters.[77]

The Mexicans objected to portrayals of NAALC as a social clause but agreed that it should be 'better utilized to enhance trilateral cooperation in responding to 'the emerging challenges presented by the changing nature of the workplace.'[78] Few would deny that these initiatives have been of some value. It will take years and detailed analyses to evaluate the effects of cooperation. For instance, how will migrants fare under NAALC-led innovations like the Guide for Migrant Workers, Mexican consular outreach and NGO engagement? Will public pressure and informed workers and advocates reduce gender discrimination such as pregnancy testing? According to those close to the process, cooperative activities, especially those responsive to submissions, can contribute to the NAALC objective of improving conditions and living standards in each country. NAALC cooperation may foster improvements if backed by committed engagement by transnational and domestic social actors and by political will and resources.

A survey of the participants involved in these cooperative ventures reveals the breadth of potential for transborder networking and social interaction. The cooperation began largely on a government to government level, with US, Mexican and Canadian labour officials meeting to share information on laws and practices related to health and safety or labour organization and bargaining rights. The role of social movements escalated in subsequent activities, with increased trilateral involvement of union activists, state and federal officials and business representatives. Academic and social movement participation was notable in many of the activities. The session on gender relations helped mobilize transnational coalitions in the women's movement; and child labour advocates gained a common forum in the cooperative activities undertaken by the NAALC secretariat and NGOs. Because Mexico was the venue for so many cooperative activities, there also was a potential demonstration effect which could contribute to civic activism and reduce deference to state actors by many non-governmental entities.

How significant is the regionalization wrought by these interactions? In some of the core areas identified above, activity has been constant and frequent enough to potential lead to ongoing transnationalization of practices (for instance on

---

76 Jane Dwasi 'Kenya: a Study in International Labor Standards and Their Effect on Working Women in Developing Countries: the Case for Integration of Enforcement Issues in the World Bank's Policies' *Wisconsin International Law Journal* 347, (Summer, 1999), 30.

77 Dwasi, 30.

78 Rod Dobell, 'A Social Charter for a North American Community' *Isuma* 1, 2000, 4; [cited April 16, 2005]. Available at http://www.isuma.net/v01n01/dobell1/dobell1_e.pdf.

labour force development, statistical standards etc. Some participants suggest that the connections forged in these venues contributed to a more genuinely regional, transborder discourse on these core issue areas and other themes. Others are more sceptical, noted the infrequency of such contacts and the disparate views represented; it was often not easy to bridge the gulf between national norms and traditions to secure any commonality of position on some intractable issues, such as union rights, child labour and other contentious issues across the North-South divide. It is notable that one of the most active research streams has been on labour market development issues focussed on efficiency and productivity rather than worker rights and protections.

Clearly some of the technical exchanges and sharing of skills and technology can help improve commonality in workplace safety, inspections and operations in beneficial directions for workers. Technical training for Mexico's workplace inspectors should help upgrade skills and improve enforcement, by overcoming the deficiencies which are unavoidable for this cash-strapped nation. The practical collaboration among agencies and consulates on migrant issues, and between government officials and non-governmental activists groups on outreach to women workers set positive precedents which can hopefully be sustained and expanded; similarly the community based approaches to child workers rights and educational opportunities also provide useful models for improvements.

Nonetheless, the liberalizing effects of free trade and capital flows have also augmented the threats faced by these vulnerable workers. Critics argue that the NAALC is 'ineffectual in stopping the abuse of women and children in Mexico' because it reinforces 'existing domestic laws rather than providing meaningful international oversight'.[79] Sharing of expertise and values is hard to measure and its impact may remain gradual and subtle. NAALC' cooperative element provided an opportunity for labour practices to evolve in constructive directions. However, as Pierre Verge warned in one of the earliest cooperative activities, because of the 'profound transformation' towards 'individualization' and 'internationalization', worker rights may be hard to protect in a transnational capital market without emergence of strong transborder social movements.[80] Whether the networks spawned by cooperation will become engrained and serve to change practice towards a regional labour culture of sufficient strength to balance the liberalizing pressures of global and continental economic forces remain uncertain.

---

79 Joshua Briones. "Paying the Price for NAFTA: NAFTA's Effect on Women and Children Laborers in Mexico' *UCLA Women's Law Journal* 9 (1998–99), 304.

80 Pierre Verge, 'Les modes canadiens de régulation juridique du travail: disparition ou adaptation au changement?' in Commission for Labor Cooperation, *Industrial Relations for the 21ˢᵗ. Century: Canada-United States-Mexico Tripartite Conference, Proceedings* Montreal, March 18–20, 1996, 23–31.

Chapter 10

Evaluating NAALC: The Potential For Transnational Regionalism

Introduction

An assessment of the cases submitted over the past 12 years, and the actions taken by the National Administrative Offices and North American Commission for Labour Cooperation Secretariat suggests limited direct benefits for workers in affected plants. Most efforts to secure independent union recognition using the NAALC have been transitory and subject to reversals. Workers fired for union activities have found themselves with little recourse, often forced to accept severance settlements. Agreements to improve recognition processes in Mexico have been disregarded, notably the accord on secret ballots for certification. Mexico has focussed its accepted cases narrowly on its ex-patriot migrant workers, creating some new networks to assist these vulnerable persons, but limiting the side agreement's application to other deficiencies in US standards. Canada's partial engagement means many important labour rights disputes cannot even be taken to NAALC processes, such as violations of ILO commitments by provinces which have not signed the accord. Yet there is also a record of publication of violations, and pressure via public hearings and cooperative activities which may balance these shortcomings in enforcement power.

It remains to assess the impact of the NAALC submissions process and cooperative activities on the deepening of regionalism in North America. Despite widespread scepticism, some observers still consider the NAALC a major and continuous source of transnational integration. In the style of European Union institutionalism, some argue that there is a similar functionalist logic at work which will continuously prod the three countries towards ever deeper levels of integration. For instance, H.W. Arthurs argues that

> As levels of trade rise, as economic integration of the regional economy broadens and deepens, as it is increasingly accepted as irreversible, as it begins to generate non-economic side effects in diverse realms from politics to the environment to popular culture to law enforcement, the logic of systematizing and institutionalizing the relationship becomes more and more compelling. This logic is ultimately re-ordering the normative hierarchies of the three NAFTA countries, though not in identical or even commensurate fashion.[1]

---

1   H.W. Arthurs, cited in John N. McDougall 'National differences and the NAFTA' *International Journal* 55, (2000), 281.

This chapter will survey the impact of the NAALC on such transnational regionalism by examining the impact of NAALC institutions and processes on transborder unions and social movements, on transnational bureaucracies and labour practices, and the potential for expansion to hemispheric dimensions. While these new institutions have inevitably affected the institutional and social configuration of North American regionalism, it remains unclear if they have significantly compensated for the liberalizing emphasis of NAFTA itself.

Most positive assessments focus on the NAALC's new mechanisms for publicizing concerns about labour standards and its generation of transnational awareness of how trade and economic integration affect labour rights and working conditions. The NAALC created a more transparent climate for the discussion of labour issues in North America and brought the trade-labour linkage into the mainstream of debates on free trade in the hemisphere and beyond.[2] Cooperative activities and research by the NAALC secretariat have enhanced knowledge about labour conditions, regulations and legislation in the three countries, contributing to mutual understanding and providing the basis for a more effective social dimension to trade relations.[3]

The NAALC has important limitations, but represents an innovative compromise, acknowledging concerns about sovereignty and yet encouraging transnational scrutiny, broadening of labour principles beyond the ILO's core, engaging civil society actors and encouraging transborder union and NGO collaboration.[4] The NAALC struck a balance by setting forth standards but allowing these very different partners the flexibility to implement these in a manner and tempo suited for their unique histories, cultures and development levels.[5] Thus, if the immediate results have been limited, there may be long-term, gradual and less visible potential effects. The creation of the NAALC submission processes, which requires transnational engagements among social actors, unions and officials, could have more transformative effects than are immediately apparent.

NAALC has generated unprecedented transnational interaction and integration among labour advocates, analysts and bureaucracies, stimulated by cooperative activities and the transnational character of the submissions process.[6] Even those

---

2   Joseph A. McKinney, *Created from NAFTA – the structure, function, and significance of the treaty's related institutions* (New York: M.E. Sharpe, 2000), Chapter 4.

3   Lance Compa, 'NAFTA's labour side agreement five years on: progress and prospects for the NAALC' *Canadian Labour and Employment Law Journal*, 7, (1999), 2–30.

4   Lance Compa, 'The North American Free Trade Agreement (NAFTA) and the North American Agreement on Labor Cooperation (NAALC)' In R. Blanpain (ed.) *International encyclopaedia for labour law and industrial relations*, (The Hague: Kluwer Law International, Suppl. 2001).

5   James Mercury and Bryan Schwartz 'Creating the Free Trade Area of the Americas: linking labour, the environment, and human rights to the FTAA' *Asper Review of International Business and Trade Law*, 1 (2001), 37–65.

6   Lance Compa, 'The North American Agreement on Labor Cooperation and international labor solidarity' *Memorias del Encuentro Trinacional de Laboralistas*

who see the agreement as weak do consider the increase in labour interaction across national borders to be an important development, spurred in part by the NAALC. Gagnon notes that free trade debates have brought American and Canadian unionists closer than ever; while obstacles remain to cooperation with the very different Mexican unions, NAALC has created a context in which labour will interact in mutually beneficial ways across the North-South divide. [7] Bolle speaks of the 'creation of a labour communications superhighway between labour movements and sectors in the three countries' [8] The analysis now reviews some of these potential avenues for the formation of a new regionalism in labour affairs.

NAALC and the Potential For Transnational Unionism

The submissions process, which requires bilateral cooperation to bring complaints about a country's practices to the NAO of another NAFTA state, contributed to trans-border contacts among unions and human rights networks. Canadian and American unions, and sympathetic associations for labour and human rights, established stronger ties with their Mexican counterparts.[9] Even though unions were disappointed with the resolution of submissions, they agreed that the NAALC gives them incentives to cooperate across boundaries. Increased cross-border activity by firms has created transnational labour forces with workers in all three countries sharing common interests in negotiations with the same multinational enterprises.[10] Workers forged closer links with unions in the other countries to bargain with transnational companies for the highest possible labour standards. Despite past protectionist and cultural aversions to cooperation with independent Mexican unions, American and Canadian unions have recognized the need to improve wages and conditions in Mexico, and have made efforts to forge connections, including financial support, information exchanges, fact-finding visits and reports on labour rights violations. Liaisons have developed in garment, food and agriculture and automobiles, among other sectors.[11]

Democráticos (México: Universidad Nacional Autónoma de México, 1999), 185–211.

7   Mona-Josée Gagnon, 'Trade union cooperation in the NAFTA area' *Transfer: European Review of Labour and Research*, 6, (2000), 43–57.

8   Mary Jane Bolle, *NAFTA labor side agreement: lessons for the worker rights and fast-track debate* (Washington, D.C.: Congressional Research Service, 2001).

9   'Mexican unionists find common ground in U.S.' *Working Together* 21 Nov.-Dec., 1996, 3.

10   Laura McClure, 'Workers of the World Unite!' *Dollars and Sense* Sept., 1992, 19; Kim Moody, 'NAFTA and the corporate redesign of North America' *Latin American Perspectives*. 22 (1995), 95–117; Albert Blum and Janet Tanski, 'Workers of the hemisphere, unite! Your wages depend on it!' *Commonweal* 121 (June 17, 1994), 18–21.

11   Robin Alexander and Peter Gilmore, 'The emergence of cross-border labor solidarity' *NACLA Report on the Americas* 28, 1 (July-August, 1994), 46.

Optimistic labour advocates predict that the continental economy produces transnational social movements with the power to affect global commerce; organization of transnational unions will be aided by 'continental deregulation and international production' which binds workers of all three countries into 'a labor movement without borders'.[12] Some analysts see American unionism shifting away from its past of economism and voluntarism towards a social movement orientation, linked to recognition of the need for transnational strategies.[13] This includes cross-border organizing among workers in the same firm or sector as unions seek to counter a high mobility of capital and jobs, but low mobility for labour.[14] AFL-CIO President John Sweeney suggested that labour cooperation in the Echlin case heralded a new era in which companies 'can run to other countries, but they cannot hide'.[15] Robert Kingsley of the United Electrical Workers testified: 'we cannot allow workers in our three countries to be pitted against one another in a race towards the lowest labor standards. Instead, we intend to use the strength of union solidarity across national borders to protect ourselves from corporate exploitation across those same national boundaries.'[16]

One of the reasons for NAALC's slow start was hostility from American and Canadian unions, which failed to take advantage of the accord's potential. But frustration with NAALC's weaknesses and NAFTA's negative effects simulated interactions among labour activists across national boundaries. Hanigan notes how 'battles to implement' NAALC 'encouraged Mexican and U.S. unionists to meet together, to target specific employers, and to exchange organizers.'[17] Later cases, like those involving migrant farm workers, show the potential for labour and human rights groups to partner to press longstanding concerns about America's treatment of migrants. American unions have taken the threat of downward wage pressures seriously, by initiating contact with Mexican labour, and supporting organizing campaigns of new unions which press vigorously for increased wages and benefits. Unions fear that trade with a country with limited union independence will reward companies who move operations from the US to benefit from low wages and benefits in Mexico. Hence stronger independent Mexican unions help American workers, by reducing the cost advantages for companies operating in Mexico.

---

12   Mary McGinn and Kim Moody, 'Labor goes global' *Progressive* 57 (March, 1993), 24–28.

13   Ian Robinson 'Neoliberal Restructuring and U.S. Unions: Toward Social Movement Unionism?' *Critical Sociology* 26, (2000), 109–138.

14   Fred Rosen, 'The underside of NAFTA: a budding cross-border resistance.' *NACLA Report on the Americas*, 32 (January/February 1999), 37–40.

15   'Action Signals New Era of Labor Cooperation Across Borders: AFL-CIO and National Labor Federations in Canada and Mexico Join Alliance NAFTA Complaint Against U.S. Firm' *Teamsters' Press Release*, March 18, 1998.

16   *Public Hearing on NAO Submission 9703, Before the US NAO* March 23, 1998, 9.

17   Michael P. Hanagan, 'Labor Internationalism: An Introduction' *Social Science History* 27, (2003), 491.

The NAALC may have helped spur development of Mexican independent unions. Several alternatives to the official CTM, CROC and CROM unions affiliated with the government emerged as major players in the early NAALC cases. The Frente Autentico de Trabajo (FAT) describes itself as a popular Mexican social and political movement and a national union central of workers, campesinos and cooperatives seeking to transform the capitalist system into a self-determining socialism based on endogenous Mexican ideas.[18] It developed relations with the AFL-CIO and with Canadian unions and supported their call for the defeat of NAFTA or for a treaty with a 'social charter' of labour rights. For the Frente, the NAFTA debate created a 'permanent' alliance among unions and social groups in the three countries.[19] The FAT was allied with the Red Mexicana de Accion Frente de el Tratado de Libre Comercio (RED), an alliance of labour, green, women, community and native groups concerned about NAFTA's impact, which promoted an alternative treaty based on sustainable development, worker rights, community decision-making, debt cancellation, improved trade terms for developing countries, 'green' land management, access to education, technology, health and scientific information and resources, and democratic institutions to regulate global markets.[20]

Several larger unions in public utilities formed the Federacion de Sindicatos de Bienes y Servicios (FESEBES), one of the most significant challengers to the official unions. This union describes itself as centrist to leftist. FESEBES supported free trade, because of the high cost to workers of the existing system of 'savage protectionism'. But it sought measures to protect workers from diminished standards from freer trade. The Federacion took the lead in the Sprint case to broaden the areas in which complaints could lead to sanctions, to include freedom of association and right to organize. Other public sector workers, notably teachers, sought independence from the PRI, but initially saw advantages in working from within the Congresso de Trabajo (CT), the government-sanctioned union central.[21] NAFTA has stimulated expansion of such groups partly through alliances using the NAALC to promote greater labour independence from state-linked unions.

There have been gains in membership and transnational linkages since NAFTA came into effect. A merger among independent unionists from FAT, FESEBES and their allies into the National Union of Workers (UNT), a rival to the official CT unions, promises a more active presence for independent unions. However, the decisions by teachers and other independents to reconcile with the CT were a disappointment and foreshadowed difficulties in uniting independent unions into a

---

18 Que es el FAT? (Mexico, D.F: Frente Autentico de Trabajo, n.d.).

19 Lineas Generales de Trabajo Aprobadas por el X Congresso Nacional de FAT Noviembre de 1993 (Mexico, FAT, 1993), 17–19.

20 Red Mexicana de Accio Frente al Libre Comercio, *Sustentable: Por un Comercio Justo* (Mexico, D.F.: Foundacio Friedrich Ebert, 1993), 35–33.

21 Interview with officials at the Sindicato Nacional des Trabajadores de Educacion, Mexico, March, 1995.

coherent rival to the official unions.[22] Nonetheless, the dynamics in Mexico's labour movement has been altered, with new unions and alliances with other social actors in response to political change, economic liberalization and privatization, driven in part by NAFTA. La Botz suggests that independent unions, though variegated in their political allegiances, constitute a progressive force in Mexican politics, which helped strengthen a leftist challenge in the 2006 Presidential elections. While NAFTA and its side accord have contributed to this dynamic, its roots go much deeper and constitute a response to liberalization, corporate dominance, increased inequalities and dependency on the United States.[23]

But the effects of cross-border liberalization under NAFTA alerted US unions to the problems regionalization and globalization posed to worker's welfare. Unions like the United Electrical, Radio and Machine Workers Union of America and the International Brotherhood of Teamsters formed links with FAT to help organize maquiladora workers. A UE representative, described the alliance:

> The objective of our alliance is to build concrete solidarity between the workers employed by the same corporations in the United States and Mexico, with the ultimate objective of coordinating our bargaining demands across borders and providing concrete assitant(sic) to each other in our struggles with a common employer[24]

These unions opened a worker's centre in Ciudad Juarez near the border to educate Mexican workers on the benefits of a democratic, representative trade union.[25] Unions expressed willingness to take actions including strikes to support workers in Mexico threatened with wage and benefits cuts. For example, the International Longshoreman and Warehousemen's Union protested against reductions in wages of Mexican dockworkers of up to $7 per hour under privatization.[26]

The Communication Workers of America and Communications and Electrical Workers of Canada formed a connection with the Telephonistas, a major actor in the FESEBES coalition which has become important since the privatization of the telephone industry. The United Auto Workers organized trinational conferences on adjustment and downsizing in the auto sector and aided workers at a Ford factory in Cuautitlan. The UAW organized a tour of border factories to inspect working conditions. Delegations to Mexico assisted in union organization. Displaced workers

---

22	Dan LaBotz, 'The Founding of The UNT: a Progressive Step for Mexican Labor' *Mexican Labor News and Analysis*, 2, Dec. 5, 1997.

23	Dan La Botz, 'Mexico's Labor Movement in Transition' *Monthly Review* 57 (2005) 62–71.

24	United States Department of Labor, Bureau of International Affairs, National Administrative Office, *Hearings*, September 12, 1994 (Washington, Bailey Recording Service, 1993), 15.

25	'UE, FAT Plan Border Workers' Center' *BorderLines* 21 (1996) Found at http://www.zianet.com/irc1/bordline/bl21brie.html.

26	Bill Mongelluzzo, 'ILWU Vows to Fight for Rights of Mexican, Asian Workers,' *Journal of Commerce*, April 15, 1994.

from a Green Giant factory went to Iraputo to inform the workers there of the need for effective organization to prevent the company from depressing wages and benefits by shifting jobs to low wage locations. John Hovis, president of the United Electrical Workers, argued that 'Strong Mexican unions stop job flight.'[27]

So far the Mexican unions which have developed the most transnational affiliations, like the FAT and UNT represent fewer workers.[28] Some larger unions are increasing transborder linkages, notably the Telephonistas, who collaborated with the CWA in the Sprint case.[29] But these trends do not herald an immediate transformation of the labour movement in Mexico. Changes in the attitudes and activities of the majority unions, with changes in their leadership, will be more significant and problematic. The leader of the CTM was skeptical in his response to American support for unionists at Han Young: 'With all due respect, I think that my U.S. labor comrades are mistaken in involving themselves in an affair that does not involve their homes, their jobs or their factory'.[30] While the independent unions have developed increased visibility and in some cases improved representation for the rank and file, they still have fewer members than their established rivals; even the strongest of these have suffered significant reversals lately.[31]

Major unions like the AFL-CIO and Mexico's official unions remained aloof from such contacts at the outset, though joining in later submissions.[32] Most skeptical was the Canadian Labour Congress, which referred to the 'marginal impacts' of NAALC which should be replaced by an enforceable mechanism which can provide redress to workers suffering from lax standards.[33] The Teamsters, though joining some submissions, have been opposed to opening borders to Mexican truckers, with a campaign that some consider somewhat stereotypical of Mexicans, notably an advertisement which played on fears of poorly trained Mexican truckers, driving unsafe vehicles, and smuggling narcotics into the United States.[34] Despite the

---

27 John Ross, 'On the Offensive,' *El Financiero International*, March 14–20, 1994.

28 The leaders of the FAT argued that they represented 100,000 workers in their own affiliates and in allied unions and peasant organizations, a far cry from the membership in the largest unions. Interview with officials at FAT, March, 1995.

29 Interview with officials at the, Sindicato de Telephonistas, March, 1995.

30 'After 4 Years of NAFTA, Labor Is Forging Cross-Border Ties' *New York Times*, Dec. 20, 1997, A1.

31 'Unreformed, unrepresentative; Mexico's trade unions' *The Economist* Nov. 12, 2005, 61; Dan La Botz, 'Mexican Health Care Workers Lose Big Fight on Pensions as Union Foregoes Planned Strike' *Labor Notes* 321, Dec 2005, 6.

32 Russell E. Smith, 'An Early Assessment of the NAFTA Labor Side Accords' in *Industrial Relations Research Association, Proceedings of the Forty-Ninth Annual Meeting* (New Orleans, Jan. 4–6, 1997), 234–35.

33 CLC, 'Chapter 5 The Social Dimension of NAFTA: A Work in Progress' *NAFTA: The Social Dimensions of North American Economic Integration* http://www.clc-ctc.ca/policy/trade/nafta5.html April 4, 2002.

34 'Internal restructuring, domestic politics take front seat: Post-NAFTA Labor Solidarity Advances Shakily' *BorderLines* 25 (1996) http://www.zianet.com/irc1/bordline/bl25fta.html

promising signs, many unionists in North America and Mexico have had difficulty adjusting to the prospects and possibilities for transnational collaboration.

Some labour activists charge that NAFTA liberalization has exceeded their worst fears. For instance, even companies lauded for good practices have been forced by competitive pressures to seek avoidance of labour regulations and diminished standards. North American employers have also used the NAFTA to coerce workers into rejecting unionization, with the strong threat to relocate to Mexico. The Mexican government forbids foreign unions to actively recruit members in Mexico, and has harassed or deported some trans-border activists, a possible hindrance to these efforts.[35] There are many challenges to overcome, as northern unions and those in developing states may have many interests which are in conflict. Restructuring caused by liberalization can pit unions against one another in competition for employment. The liberalization project creates pitfalls as well as possibilities for labour organization transnationally, and employers seeking to decrease wages, benefits and regulations can use intra-class, cross-national conflicts to their benefit if labour does not learn to coordinate its approach.

Many 'unions have spent more time criticizing the agreement than strategizing about how to use it for limited purposes or how to improve it in future years'.[36] It has been difficult to persuade unionists used to focussing on short-term economistic self-interest to accept the need for long-term, transnational collaboration to promote social goals, such as upward levelling of labour standards and generation of high wage employment. As Clark Reynolds warned, if Mexican development leads to 'downward convergence of productivity, wages, and income for its northern partners' political polarization could intensify.[37] A fall in North American wages and employment could cause at least a weakening of NAFTA, through 'petty protectionism' – frivolous trade limitations in vulnerable sectors, which will hurt all the North American partners. This could be heightened if Mexico faces another devaluation crisis and decline in real wages as in 1995, which made Mexican goods more competitive and reduced its purchasing power. In these conditions, U.S. unions may retreat to protectionism rather than cross-border unionism or international labour standards. Hence, the path to transborder cooperation is not smooth.

---

35   Geri Smith, and John Pearson, 'Which side (of the border) are you on? Well, both' *Business Week*, April 4, 1994, 50.

36   'Does Anybody Care? Labor Commission Quietly Gets to Work' *BorderLines* 18 (November 1995) Found at http://www.zianet.com/irc1/bordline/bl18naclc.html.

37   Clark W. Reynolds, 'Power Value and Distribution in the NAFTA' in Riordan Roett (ed.) *Political and Economic Liberalization in Mexico: At a Critical Juncture?* (Boulder, Col., Lynne Reinner, 1993), 90.

Transnational Social Movements and the NAALC

Transborder labour regionalism has been assisted by new social movements and transnational advocacy groups which have augmented, or substituted for, union actions. Activism surrounding the trade-labor connection in NAFTA, in part utilizing the NAALC, reveals an evolution in the contemporary context of political alliances. Elements of the old social movements, based on class (especially labour) have become allied with new social movements based on new political and cultural identifications and power relations not strictly connected to economics. Coalitions of activists have featured diverse new social movements. Trans-border collaboration has emerged even as unions are weakened by restructuring, declining wages and decreased membership. Partly to compensate for union decline, 'activists on both sides of the border increasingly have turned to broad-based fronts or coalitions to further their goals and compensate for lost political ground'.[38] Evans suggests that transnational social networks, though overmatched by those in finance, trade and investment, are mounting challenges to the globalized economy, even if with only marginal impacts overall.[39] The collaborative networks in the submissions process documented above illustrate this trend. Groups like the Coalition for Justice in the Maquiladoras, civil and human rights groups, and migrant support movements have used NAALC and other forms of transnational cooperation to help bolster worker rights.

Stillerman argues that NAALC stimulated cross border labour and NGO collaboration, by providing new forums for transnational interactions.[40] As the submissions moved beyond freedom of association and the right to organize to health, safety, gender discrimination, child labour and other human rights themes, collaboration among social constituencies increased. A diverse array of submitters brought the elaborate submissions on health and safety and migrant rights. Some submissions were joined by several dozen supporting groups, illustrating the emerging alliances. Compa argues that NAALC helped stimulate such collaborations. most notably in those cases involving migrant workers.[41]

Graubert concurs that the submissions which have achieved the most required elaborate networks of actors from unions and social constituencies.[42] Even sceptics in the AFL-CIO recognized that NAALC could help generate the social movement

---

38   Heather L. Williams, 'Mobile capital and transborder labor rights mobilization.' *Politics and Society*, 27, 1 (March 1999), 152.

39   Peter Evans 'Fighting Marginalization with Transnational Networks: Counter-hegemonic Globalization.' *Contemporary Sociology*, 29 (2000) 230–41.

40   Joel Stillerman 'Transnational Activist Networks and the Emergence of Labor Internationalism in the NAFTA Countries' *Social Science History* 27, (2003), 579.

41   Lance Compa,. 'NAFTA's labor side agreement and international labor solidarity.' *Antipode*, 33 (2001), 451–467.

42   Jonathan Graubart, 'Giving teeth to NAFTA's Labour Side Agreement.' in John Kirton and Virginia Maclaren (eds.) *Linking Trade, Environment, and Social Cohesion – NAFTA Experiences, Global Challenges* (Aldershot: Ashgate, 2002), 215–216.

228 *The Limits of Regionalism*

alliances needed for labour to challenge liberalizing arrangements like NAFTA effectively.[43] Gender advocates likewise saw the NAALC process as one tool which could be employed to address issues of employment discrimination specific to women workers.[44] Stevenson notes the effective collaboration which has emerged around gender and pregnancy discrimination, which helped invigorate a transnational women's movement in the NAFTA region.[45]

Others claim that NAALC, which allows only government enforcement, not corporate practices, to be challenged, is marginal to social coalition's efforts to challenge adverse effects of free trade. Although the USAW did employ NAALC in the Puebla case, much of its success did not rely on the side agreement. 'Organizers had to operate outside of the legislative realm of any established trade agreement'[46] to bring together consumers, students and activists to challenge corporations. Despite these problems, NAALC can serve as a tool for transnational networks to mobilize support and challenge corporate practices. Cases such as Han Young illustrate the potential role for NAALC as transnational activist networks combine in a variety of arenas to challenge undesirable working conditions.[47] Graubert concurs that the NAALC framework provides one avenue to address these issues, which social networks must use effectively in conjunction with other tactics.[48]

NAALC's cooperative activities also created an institutional context which spurred development or extension of transnational social movements and advocacy networks. Keck and Sikkink note how conferences, seminars, information exchanges of the kind generated by NAALC contribute to network formation and deepening. And the unresponsiveness of a state such as Mexico to human and labour rights can instill a search for transnational 'triangulation' by bringing external NGOs into the political mix.[49] The question remains whether such collaborations will be durable. Williams discerns a decrease in collaboration via the Coalition for Justice

43 Stanley Gacek, 'The political context for the NAALC – the viewpoint of the AFL-CIO and the U.S. labor movement.' *Memorias del Encuentro Trinacional de Laboralistas Democráticos* (México: Universidad Nacional Autónoma de México, 1999) 213–219.

44 Shareen Hertel, 'Campaigns to protect human rights in Mexico's maquiladoras: current research findings.' *Newsletter, Institute of Latin American Studies*, Columbia University, (Spring 2002), 1–10.

45 Linda S. Stevenson 'Confronting gender discrimination in the Mexican workplace: Women and labor facing NAFTA with transnational contention' *Women and Politics* 26, (2004), 71.

46 Victoria Carty, 'New Social Movements and the Struggle for Workers' Rights in the Maquila Industry' *Theory and Science* 4, (2003), found June 12, 2005 at http://theoryandscience.icaap.org/content/vol004.002/02_carty.html.

47 David Trubek, Jim Mosher, and Jeffrey S. Rothstein, 'Transnationalism in the regulation of labor relations: international regimes and transnational advocacy networks.' *Law and Social Inquiry*, 25, 3–4 (2000) 1187–1211.

48 Graubert, 2002, 220.

49 Margaret E. Keck and Kathryn Sikkink 'Transnational advocacy networks in international and regional politics' *International Social Science Journal* 51, (1999), 93.

in the Maquiladoras after 1997. Hertel notes that women's activists are relying on individual legal challenges, and have not pursued additional NAALC actions despite their success in the Gender Discrimination case.[50]

The limited accomplishments available through NAALC affect how much labour-based activists will use this process, since limited rewards make the efforts of collaboration less desirable. Asymmetry comes into play here, as US (and Canadian) NGOs have resources which outweigh their Mexican counterparts; if the submissions return few discernable benefits for their constituencies, then their pursuit of NAALC-driven interactions across the border may decline. Disillusionment of NGOs may explain why some have limited their use of the NAALC. Similarly, activists complained of exclusion from consultations, lengthy bureaucratic processes, and lack of political will to fully implement NAALC. Delp et al concluded, 'The NAALC is no longer a viable tool under the current political climate and is in danger of fading into oblivion if lessons learned are not applied to improve the NAALC and future agreements'.[51] NSMs like greens and workers remain problematic allies on some aspects of the social dimension of regionalism and globalism in international trade, though they have been able to mobilize effectively in opposition to the WTO and FTAA in Seattle and Quebec City.[52]

But collaboration by varied social movements, including human rights, indigenous rights, women, environmental and trade unions is a major accomplishment, given the very diverse, often conflicting nature of the interests of each of these constituencies within individual states let alone across a diverse hemisphere. Such solidarity has remained a constant through the opposition to the FTAA which as yet remains incomplete.[53] Social activism at the consumer level could also be a successful stategy, as the United Students Against Sweatshops campaigns in Puebla indicated. Transnational enterprises are going to continue to seek advantageous market conditions including child and cheap labour if so permitted by developing states. Multinational firms have only implemented 'minimalist labor rights standards after consumer groups have drawn attention to abuses such as child labor, low wages, and unhealthy labor practices.'[54] Firms cannot be relied upon to adopt standards consistently given the fluctuations in consumer pressure which are inevitable in a

---

50   Williams, 1999, 150; Hertel, 2002.

51   Linda Delp, et. al., *NAFTA's Labor Side Agreement: Fading into Oblivion? An Assessment of Workplace Health & Safety Cases* (Los Angeles: UCLA Center for Labor Research and Education, 2004), viii.

52   Kenneth A. Gould, Tammy L. Lewis and J. Timmons Roberts 'Blue-Green Coalitions: Constraints and Possibilities in the Post 9–11 Political Environment' *Journal of World-Systems Research,* 10 (2004), 91–116.

53   Marcelo I. Saguier 'Convergence in the Making: Transnational Civil Society and the Free Trade Area of the Americas' *CSGR Working Paper* No. 137/04, 2004, 3 [cited Dec. 16, 2005]. Available at http://www2.warwick.ac.uk/fac/soc/csgr/research/workingpapers/2004/wp13704.pdf.

54   Jackie G. Smith et. al., 'Human Rights and the Global Economy: A Response to Meyer' *Human Rights Quarterly* 21 (1999), 208–9.

global economy, especially since the costs of mobilizing boycotts is high, and many nations willingly offer lax labour laws and repression of worker rights to secure investment.[55]

But the potential contribution of transnational advocacy to Mexican activists should not be underrated. As Stillerman suggests, 'The emergence of these networks is particularly important for movement actors in resource-poor settings with closed political opportunity structures. Actors in these contexts can appeal to resource – and information rich members of principled networks for international advocacy as well as pressure on governments and international institutions to strengthen activists' hands against local governments.' Hence NAALC may create a 'boomerang effect'[56] benefiting advocacy in Mexico even if the initial results for particular workers appear marginal. It is encouraging that the pace of submissions, having dropped off, resumed in 2004–2005, with innovative new cases again seeking to expand the purview of NAALC.

NAALC and the Creation of a Trinational Bureaucracy

The NAALC created new institutions which could foster transnational networks of officials, and perhaps even shared norms or a shared labour culture. Most commentators noted that the new institutions were successfully established and that they did bring together innovative trinational teams of officials and experts. Officials at the Mexican NAO suggested that the new institutions would create a generation of officials open to influences form other nations, and bring pressure on governments and industries to improves in worker protection and union rights.[57] The NAOs organized National Advisory Committees comprised of business, labour, academic and public representatives to advise on how to implement the principles of the NAALC. So the constituency of individuals contributing to new norms in labour relations expanded.

The NAALC has relatively modest objectives, of promoting public understanding of each countries' labour laws, and increasing the transparency of law enforcement. But the creation of institutions with these goals increased transnational communication on labour matters. As Joaquin Otero of the U.S. Department of Labor wrote,

> Dialogue and information exchange among the labor ministries of the three countries has been very intense. Our overall level of common understanding and appreciation of labor laws, enforcement and labor market conditions in all three countries had grown by leaps and bounds.[58]

55   Smith et. al., 1999, 209–11.
56   Stillerman, 2003, 581.
57   Interview with Mexican NAO official, Feb. 13, 1995.
58   Joaquin F. Otero, 'The North American Agreement on Labor Cooperation: Overview and Status of Implementation' *Labor Law Developments*, 1995 (Southwestern Legal Foundation, 41st. Annual Institute on Labor Law, 1995), 11–10.

The Hispanic heritage of the first head of the American NAO facilitated communication between the two nations. Officials noted the regular discussions among officials and senior executive officers, though meetings of ministers have been infrequent and irregular.

The trinational North American Commission for Labour Cooperation secretariat brings together labour experts and officials from all three states sharing expertise and insights and developing an institutional loyalty to the NACLC. Cooperative activities produce meetings to share perspectives on numerous themes which integrated knowledge and disseminate ideas among a growing community of administrators, interest group activists and scholars. Although as yet unused, the evaluation committees of experts could also become a mechanism for integration of norms and practices at the elite institutional level. Officials involved in the implementation of the NAALC argued that engagement with nationals of the other states in hearings, meetings and cooperative activities created networks of labour, business, state officials, academics and activists. This increased the willingness to exchange information, and fostered integration and transparency among civil societies and state agencies.

As the bureaucracies themselves developed, they introduced new priorities into the discourse of labour relations, for instance on child labour, part-time and contracted work. As conferences and symposiums were held on issues of plant closings, women labourers, associational and bargaining rights and health and safety, changes occurred to the values and outlook of labour relations specialists in all three states, through mutual learning.[59] Transnational interactions could foster a new institutional mentality which could contribute to new labour practices in all three states. This process may be less direct or immediate than Europe's imposition of common standards, with transnational judicial enforcement, but cannot be discounted as a route to 'enforcement of parallel measures' over time.[60]

Article 11 of NAALC calls for cooperative activities, research studies and seminars, which were praised for increasing understanding of labour practices across borders. This contributed to mutual understanding and facilitated the improvement of relationships among actors. Even those disappointed with the disputes resolution process expressed some positive reaction to these activities. As demonstrated above, cooperation focussed on issues that are viewed as meriting particular concern and on issues raised in submissions. Some activities provided technical training and expertise, or created mediums for exchange of best practices, to produce 'information that will facilitate better understanding of each country's labour laws, policies and practices'[61]. Initially, studies were commissioned on technical issues like accidents, inspections, health and safety, hygiene, bio-hazards, ergonomics, labour law and productivity. These started the cooperation process while providing for a practical

---

59   Interview with Canadian NAO official, January 30, 1998.

60   James A. Smith, in 'Panel Discussion: the Challenges and Opportunities under the NAFTA Labor Cooperation Agreement', *United States-Mexico Law Journal*, 1995, 150.

61   North American Agreement on Labour Cooperation, Article 11.

exchange on issues where deficient practices were evident. As cases were processed by the NAO's, cooperative activities turned to controversial issues of association, right to organize and bargain, gender discrimination, child labour, contracting out, farm workers and migrant labour.

It is unlikely the bureaucratic interactions initiated by the NAALC will create transnational institutions on the scale seen in Europe. One key problem has been the limited resources provided to the NAALC secretariat and the national administrative offices. NAALC is restricted by its small budgets compared to the trade enforcement dimensions of NAFTA. Some suggest that this budget shortfall limits the visibility of NAALC proceedings, and investigations, which conclude with 'symbolic' measures.[62] Verge notes that the agreement is really tri-national and depends on collaboration between the three labour ministers acting as the governing council of the NAALC. The Secretariat does not have the authority or capacity to develop more transnational regimes and norms. Core elements of the NAALC remain domestic, notably the NAOs and their national advisory committees, which steer the consideration of submissions into a bilateral or trinational, not supranational, format.[63]

This has been heightened by a lack of continuity in personnel, with frequent changes in Mexico in particular, and long delays in appointments to the secretariat. This author found the early optimism about integration of bureaucracies dissipated after 6 or 7 years because of discontinuities in personnel. As Singh and Adams warned, the coming to office of anti-labour administrations may lead states to devote less resources to the NAALC and NAOs, further weakening the integrative potential.[64] This appears to have been the case since Bush and Fox took office with slow appointments to NAALC and NAO offices, a reduction in funds, and gaps in consultations for instance. US international labour affairs budgets have been cut from initial Clinton era allotments, though remaining steady recently.

But the effects of the new institutions should not be underestimated, whatever the constraints against homogenization of standards. The NAALC has the potential, in conjunction with ILO and WTO provisions, to balance fundamental labour rights – association, organization, bargaining non-discrimination, freedom from forced labour – and those which remain dependent on a country's economic performance, like wages and benefits, working conditions).[65] If cooperative activities and information exchanges point the way to a consensus among officials, then integration

---

62 Alan B. Simmons,'NAFTA, international migration and labour rights.' *Labour, Capital and Society*, 31, (1998), 10–43.

63 Pierre Verge, 'Analytical Presentation of the North-American Agreement on Labour Cooperation (NAALC)' *ILO, research in support of the Inter-American Conference of Ministers of Labor*, 14; found Feb. 23, 2004 at http://www.oit.org.pe/cimt/documetospdf/146eng.pdf.

64 Parbudyal Singh, and Roy J. Adams,'Neither a gem nor a scam: the progress of the North American Agreement on Labor Cooperation.' *Labor Studies Journal*, 26, (2001), 1–16.

65 Lance Compa, 'Labor Rights and Labor Standards in International Trade' *Law and Policy in International Business* 25 (1993), 189–90.

and harmonization of labour policy might accomplish more than mere liberalization. Such integration could also be encouraged if transnational union and social activism remains elevated.

Emergence of a Regional Labour Culture?

Some optimistically suggest that the NAALC, by bridging transnational deficiencies in awareness and mutual understanding, could help generate, if not common standards, a shared North American labour culture. Summers suggests that 'the very articulation of the Labor Principles in a formal agreement gives these labor standards a definiteness and salience with a moral clam to be observed' with violations highlighted via submissions.[66] Trubek et. al. note how NAALC has helped create common approaches and links across borders.[67] NAALC served as a mechanism for publicizing workers'concerns and has given voice to groups which had formerly had no means of influence, notably migrant workers in the US and women workers in Mexico. It allowed workers in unrepresented service sectors to bring attention to their situation, as in the fast food industry in Quebec. The NAALC enhanced these possibilities by giving social actors and public officials the right to challenge and questions action or inaction by authorities in the other states.[68] This combination of publicity and investigation may create pressure for change: 'Clearly, the very presence of the NAALC has helped stimulate the social policy debate in its member countries surrounding core labour practices.'[69]

NAALC is credited by some authors with generating new pressure on Mexican officials to enforce and improve labour standards. The publicity given to issues of freedom of association and rights of minority unions to fair process have also generated alternatives and created challenges, spurring changes in approach by Mexico's entrenched unions [70] Singh and Adams suggest the NAOs have been receptive to the submissions, and adopted an expansive approach, gradually broadening the issues considered. Cooperative activities and complaints procedures have built pressure on labour authorities. Examples include US concessions over migrant labour, in addition to pressure on Mexico on freedom of association, union

---

66   Clyde Summers, 'NAFTA's Labor Side Agreement and international labor standards.' *The Journal of Small and Emerging Business Law*, 3, (1999), 187.

67   Trubek et. al., 1187–1211.

68   Marie-Ange Moreau et Gilles Trudeau. 'Le droit du travail face à la mondialisation de l'économie.' *Relations industrielles/Industrial Relations*, 53 (1998), 55–89.

69   Michael Abbott 'Labour-side Agreements Involving Canada: Current Practices and Comparative Effectiveness' (Ottawa, Canada Industrial Relations Board, 2004) [cited Sept. 12 2004]. Available at http://www.cira-acri.ca/IIRA%20CIRA%20docs/Abbott,%20Michael. pdf.

70   Victoria Hottenrott, and Stephen Blank *Assessing NAFTA – Part II – The impact of NAFTA on jobs, wages, and income inequality*, Pan-American Partnership for Business Education, Working Paper no. 178 December 1998.

recognition and gender issues.[71] Even highly sceptical players such as the CLC acknowledge that the submissions could 'be utilized for fact-finding purposes and to expose problems in order to generate a broader public awareness' of the need for reform.[72] Hence, there appears to be potential for NAALC to generate transformation in policy, attitudes and practices. Moreover, if tensions between labour movements in the US and Mexico are overcome, there is greater potential for them to promote long-term homogenization of labour standards and practices.[73]

It was significant that early cases proceeded to ministerial consultations, to the chagrin of Mexican officials and business leaders. Perez-Lopez stressed how ministerial consultations increased the profile of basic labour rights like freedom of association and union registration. Though limited, new trinational, channels of communication should eventually work to the benefit of workers in all three nations.[74] Though NAALC did not provide for sanctions to enforce standards, it did permit different approaches to be reconciled via cooperative forums.[75] Most promisingly, while Mexico's legal system did note effectively prevent violations, the side agreement gave labour advocates a new route to challenge government indifference and to expose corporate practices via the 'intrusive sunshine' of the submissions.[76] Mexican lawyers noted that the complaints provided 'a mechanism for denouncing... the Mexican government's past unnoticed abuses of workers' rights'.[77] The NAALC exposed problems in Mexican plants and in law enforcement, and created a venue for independent unions to express their concerns and press for change. Some American worker advocates felt that the use of NAALC processes to draw attention to the conditions in Mexican industries could 'bring tremendous leverage' for unions.[78] NAALC activities could raise worker awareness of existing and desired legal protections, generating a cultural shift enhancing the defense of worker rights in that country.

But the sunshine capabilities of the NAALC do not produce immediate benefits for workers or independent unions in Mexico, or alleviate the concerns of northern unions and workers about 'social dumping'. This reflected in part the character of the first cases selected which dealt with issues of freedom of association, right to organize

---

71   Singh and Adams, 1–16.

72   CLC, 'Chapter 5 The Social Dimension of NAFTA: A Work in Progress'.

73   Claudia Franco Hijuelos, 'Normas laborales en el comercio internacional: el ACLAN.' *Foro Internacional,* 51 (2001), 309–323.

74   Jorge F. Perez-Lopez, 'Conflict and Cooperation in US-Mexican Labor Relations: The North American Agreement on Labor Cooperation' *Journal of Borderlands Studies* 11 (1996), 57.

75   Perez-Lopez, 1996, 56.

76   Reed J. Slogoff, 'Mexico: Living with the NAFTA Labor Laws', *Trade and Culture Magazine* March/April 1995.

77   Dora Delgado, 'Side Accord Seen As a Mechanism for Change in Mexico, Groups Say' *Daily Labor Report* 156, August 13, 1996, CC-1.

78   Sam Dillon, 'Union Vote in Mexico Illustrates Abuses' *New York Times*, Oct. 13, 1997.

and collective bargaining rights. These matters, important to independent unions, were exempted from sanctions and expert evaluations, and therefore ministerial consultations were the limit of possible action. Consultations have failed to rectify the problems raised in submissions, as governments have been unwilling to use the process to make strong condemnations of the other parties.[79] Hence no common level of enforcement has emerged, and independent unions still find it difficult to register and bargain in Mexico.

The Maquiladora Health and Safety Network credited the NAALC with exposing the limits and deficiencies in Mexico's enforcement of labour regulations. But the agreement failed to prevent transnational companies from taking advantage of Mexico's lax system and putting workers health at risk for the sake of profit. This was attributed to NAALC's weaknesses and the dearth of political will. But notably it also reflected 'economic disincentives for Mexico in enforcement of labor rights that would 'discourage foreign investment.'"[80] Thus, NAALC did not result in worker reinstatement, creation of independent unions or correction of plant-level health and safety problems.

This reflected a failure to understand the political economy of Mexico, which created limited political will, administrative resources and enforcement capability and encouraged corruption. This was heightened by the secrecy, limited public particpation and lack of accountability in NAALC processes. For instance, in the Han Young and Custom Trim cases, Mexican workplace inspections were shown to be secretive, at times held without worker participation and knowledge. Workers were not kept abreast of the nature or direction of ministerial consultations. They were not consulted on remedies or asked if they accepted the conclusions reached or the closure of their submissions. Under Bush and Fox, creation of a Tri-National Working Group on health and safety sidestepped the NAALC and continued a pattern of 'secrecy' and 'exclusion' of workers.[81] Limited advances in health and safety in the maquiladoras were obtained outside NAALC by workers and NGOs using the publicity and revelations of the submissions to generate political pressure for change.

The reliance on domestic labour standards has also been assailed. The presumption that national standards in the three countries adequately meet the NAALC principles is debatable. Mexican labour laws contains serious deficiencies which limit the ability of unions to secure recognition or access due process, and serious reforms to the labour code are required to rectify this. However, current labour law reforms are moving to weaken, not strengthen union rights and prospects. In particular, the

---

79 Barry LaSala, 'NAFTA and worker rights: an analysis of the Labor Side Accord after five years of operation and suggested improvements' *Labor Lawyer*, 6 (2001), 319–347.

80 Garrett D. Brown, 'NAFTA's 10 Year Failure to Protect Mexican Workers' Health and Safety' (Berkely, CA: Maquiladora Health and Safety Support Network, December 2004).

81 Brown, 2004, 1; the NAALC website later reported the Secretariats unspecified participation in the working group's activities. 'Stay Tuned for 2006' [cited March 20, 2006]. Available at http://www.naalc.org/english/sept2005.shtml.

state must not interfere with union democracy, must improve transparency about collective agreements and improve procedures for union organizing, recognition and registration. Using domestic laws as the standard for NAALC inherently limits the ability to generate a significant cross-border culture supportive of labour rights. Critics argue that Mexico's existing laws are inadequate to implement NAALC principles even if properly enforced; a mechanism is needed which promotes reforms to better protect workers.[82] But as the Mexican NAO cases illustrate, the same could also be said of laws in particular American states and laws applied to migrant labour. While many Canadian practices remain outside NAALC's purview, deficiencies in treatment of rural postal contractors and franchise workers illustrate the challenges that remain in that society as well.

One author notes that the political nature of the complaints process, with NAOs tied explicitly to the executive branch in each country, inserts political criteria into the process, limiting its potential effectiveness.[83] Hence the US government has been criticized for not insisting on stronger measure by Mexico to promote compliance with NAALC principles, which produces disappointing results from ministerial consultations.[84] Even though NAALC allowed the exploration of important issues in labour affairs, unions and their supporters were distressed over the narrowness of the NAO's willingness to consider innovative complaints; as Human Rights Watch concluded:

> two cases that the U.S. NAO rejected for review—relating to the national security rationale cited by the Mexican government for its intervention in a strike in Mexico and the exclusion of rural postal workers from the safeguards provided under federal labor legislation in Canada—could surely have added to important discussions of the NAALC.[85]

Despite the potential for sanctions in the health and safety cases, action was always terminated at ministerial consultations. The MHSSN noted that 'no significant changes have occurred in the functioning of health and safety inspectors in the maquiladoras, or in the U.S. workplaces where complaints have been filed, as a result of the NAFTA complaint process'.[86]

---

82   Russell E. Smith, 'NAFTA and industrial relations in Mexico: what's important now?' *Perspectives on Work*, 6 (2002), 25–27.

83   Bobbi-Lee Meloro, 'Balancing the goals of free trade with workers' rights in a hemispheric economy.' *University of Miami Inter-American Law Review*, 30, (1999), 433–460.

84   Justine Nolan and Michael Posner. 'International standards to promote labor rights: the role of the United States government.' *Columbia Business Law Review*, 3 (2000), 529–543.

85   HRW, *Trading Away Rights The Unfulfilled Promise of NAFTA's Labor Side Agreement* (New York, Human Rights Watch 2001), 23.

86   *Maquiladora Health & Safety Support Network Newsletter* 3 September 17, 2001 [cited Feb. 22, 2003]. Available at http://www.igc.org/mhssn/news16.htm.

Hence, the limits to political will to seek higher levels of enforcement restricted the NAALC's usefulness in challenging differences in labour standards and practices and generating more common approaches and values. If the momentum of transnational social networks builds, this could produce an interaction of ideas which will create cultural change not around common global labour standards, but rather around a North American labour culture articulated gradually via experiences both inside and outside the NAALC. Some evidence of this potential has emerged in decisions by state and corporate actors partly in response to NAALC-inspired activism.

Anticipated Reactions and Policy Change

While evidence of integration of cultural norms and standards is limited, there are signs that the NAALC introduced new parameters to policy which could lead to significant adjustments. The accord has potential to embarrass Mexican authorities and corporations into improvements.[87] Its publicity approach prompted some reversals (evidenced by withdrawn or settled complaints) by business and governments seeking to avoid negative fallout over their labour practices.[88] Some companies avoided adverse publicity and potential consumer backlash by resolving issues before they became targets for NAALC investigations. Similarly, Mexican authorities adjusted their behaviours to avoid confrontation and seek resolutions with unions and their supporters.[89]

The evidence discovered in the case studies examined here suggests some potentially important anticipatory effects, as business and state actors adjusted their behaviours to take account of the scrutiny and embarrassment of the NAALC. In the Maxi-Switch case, the Mexican government agreed to certification on the eve of hearings by the US NAO. In a potential case involving Canada, a coalition of labour law associations and human rights advocates planned to lay a complaint with the US NAO respecting the Alberta government's plans to contract out enforcement of basic labour standards in that province. The case was problematic, as it involved predictions of the possible effects of privatization on law enforcement, not an actual situation of non-enforcement. However, Alberta withdrew its proposal, perhaps in response to the prospect of NAO investigation.[90]

---

87   Diana Chew and Richard Posthuma. 'International employment dispute resolution under NAFTA's side agreement on labor.' *Labor Law Journal*, 53 (2002), 38–45.

88   A.L.C. de Mestral, 'The significance of the NAFTA side agreements on environmental and labor cooperation.' *Arizona Journal of International and Comparative Law*, 15 (1998), 169–185.

89   Williams, 1999, 150.

90   Compa, 1997, p. 20; 'Border Briefs: NAFTA Labor Challenge Likely in Canada' *BorderLines* 30 (1996) [cited June 14, 1999]. Available at http://www.zianet.com/irc1/bordline/bl30bb.html.

Quebec resolved the St. Hubert's McDonald's case before an NAO hearing was required; the Yale case was also resolved before Canadian hearings, with the US Labor department agreeing to cease submitting information on illegal migrants to the INS. But Maxi-Switch reveals the potential for corporate deviousness to avoid strong application of the NAALC, with the reincorporation and renaming of the company forcing unions to restart certification procedures. Similarly, in the Sprint and Han Young cases, initial successes were reversed on appeal, or negated through local state resistance.[91]

Publicity about lax law enforcement via cooperative activities can pressure governments to live up to their commitments to protect workers. Polaski notes how cooperative programs driven by submissions, especially where trade penalties are possible, have had an impact. In her words, 'Discussions (whether through hearings, workshops or other fora) that are linked to allegations of existing problems – and that could lead to adverse consequences such as sanctions – appear to elicit more attention from key actors and are more likely to change their behavior than activities that are seen as purely informative.'[92] Examples include the outreach efforts in the migrant workers' cases, where the dissemination of information about worker rights and collaboration between agencies and consulates may improve implementation of labour protections for this vulnerable group. The gender case created pressures to reconsider gender discrimination in Mexican law, and outreach may have 'played a role in ameliorating some of the problems'.[93]

However, the evidence of influence on domestic laws and enforcement is limited so far. Cases on freedom of association are hampered by the mild remedies allowed.[94] Little will be conceded on labour rights, given the competitive continental market, and few changes will occur to domestic practices without significant efforts by labour, government and transnational institutions. For critics, deficiencies in the NAALC's design and implementation limit its ability to generate pressure. Unions complain that the lengthy complex NAALC process is too cumbersome, time consuming and expensive, in terms of finances, manpower and other resources, to make it worthwhile. The sunshine effects produced few concrete results, and the omission of the core rights from the sanctions process made the efforts to use the process of dubious value.[95] Knowing that the process can be extended and can produce few concrete results can lead policy makers and firms to ignore adverse publicity and to pursue practices harmful to workers in search of profit.

---

91   Jacqueline McFadyen NAFTA Supplemental Agreements: Four Year Review , Institute For International Economics Working Paper 98-4 [cited April 1, 1999]. Available at http://www.iie.com/CATALOG/WP/1998/98-4.htm.

92   Sandra Polaski, 'Protecting Labor Rights Through Trade Agreements: an Analytical Guide' *Journal of International Law and Policy*, 10 (2004), 24.

93   Polaski, 2004, 24.

94   McFadyen, 1999.

95   Jeff Faux, 'The fast track to globalization: can labor slow it down?' *WorkingUSA*, (March-April 1998), 10–22.

These deficiencies may be inherent in the design of the NAALC. Although it incorporated civil society participants, it did not provide sufficient return for their efforts as fews cases had a significant, visible impact. The limited effectiveness of the investigatory and publication functions of NAALC led many major union and rights constituencies to diminish their commitment to the process, as deficient practices became apparent and the NAALC had limited effects on labour laws and regulations. For Dombois and his colleagues, the problem was not weaknesses in the institutions themselves, since significant sections of the NAALC have never been implemented in practice. Rather, 'divergent understandings and strategies of the actors, whose contradictory interests and expectations and reluctance to cooperate left the NAALC no room to develop dynamically'.[96] Hence the potential of NAALC elements like ECE's and sanctions have never been tried, as none of the nations has the political will or desire to deepen the processes into a genuine supra-national arrangement.

The failure to maximize the NAALC's potential is highlighted by a review of submissions targeting occupational health and safety by the UCLA Center for Labor Research and Education. NAALC revealed numerous violations of domestic labour laws and international commitments respecting health and safety, especially but not exclusively in Mexico's maquiladoras and among Mexican immigrant workers in the United States. But it failed to provide effective remedies for the problems exposed partly because of the its deficient mechanisms, which only targeted poor law enforcement, not inadequate laws or company practices. The lack of sanctions prevented NAALC from compelling enforcement agencies to act more effectively.

NAALC processes were drawn out, bureaucratic and draining on plaintiffs and workers, who could not afford to wait for limited remedies. Mexican workers were particularly vulnerable to retaliation or violence for seeking to protect their health and safety. They often had to yield their rights to accept severance pay, needed for subsistence. Most importantly, the signatory governments showed no 'political will' to fully employ the NAALC via ECEs, disputes resolutions and sanctions even in egregious cases of health and safety violations. The countries feared destabilizing the broader trilateral relationship and sought to avoid confrontational processes even where permitted under NAALC.

The Accord also gives little meaningful role to workers and their representatives in processes to alleviate or eliminate health and safety violations and threats. Workers are not included in ministerial consultations directly and only invited into cooperative activities on some occasions; cases like Autotrim-Customtrim were dealt with strictly on a government to government basis. The UCLA review concludes that

> The political, historic moment for using the NAALC as leverage to improve workers' conditions appears to have passed. The limited positive outcomes from previous NAALC cases – the sunshine effect and cross-border dialogue – have been undermined by a lack

---

96   Rainer Dombois and Jens Winter, *A Matter of Deficient Design? Observations on Interaction and Cooperation problems in the NAALC* (Bremen: University of Bremen, Institut Arbeit und Wirtshaft, 2003) 2.

of political will to resolve the problems identified and by a refusal to include workers in government dialogue to resolve those problems.[97]

The NAALC process needs to be expedited and made credible by pursuit of evaluation committees and sanctions on health and safety matters; however, the report suggested the 'current political climate' of neo-liberalism meant NAALC was no longer 'viable'.[98]

The potential for success in such creative uses of the NAALC rests on the degree of vigour which labour and their allies employ in pursuing innovative cases.[99] Other authors agree that the potential of NAALC will only be realized if social constituencies seek to maximize its potential uses to encourage protection of standards and to promote transnational connections.[100] In particular, North American unions must adopt a more constructive attitude and make full use of the accord, which should also be ratified by all Canadian provinces to extend its reach.[101]

Broadening Regionalism: NAALC as a Model for the Hemisphere?

Canada and the US have championed labour and environmental provisions in a broader Free Trade Agreement of the Americas (FTAA). The initial summit in Miami in 1994 articulated a vision which placed labour rights at the forefront of negotiations. In the early stages of the FTAA talks, the Clinton administration pressed for inclusion of a labour agenda, and secured agreement for improvements and fulfilment of labour rights in accordance with ILO conventions. The US called for a hemispheric study group, whose work would be reviewed by ministers of labour and trade as the negotiations proceeded.

But most countries in the hemisphere resisted even these limited measures, insisting that the ILO was the proper forum for labour advancement. Many developing and newly industrializing states regard flexibility in wages and labour regulations as trade advantages. The declaration after the Summit of the Americas in San Jose in 1998 only included the following general statement:

---

97   Delp, et. al., 2004, vii.

98   Delp, et. al., 2004, vii.

99   Roy Adams, 'Using the North American Agreement on Labour Cooperation to Achieve Industrial Relations Reform.' *Canadian Labour and Employment Law Journal*, 7 (1999), 31–44.

100 Rodrigue Blouin and May Morpaw. 'L'Accord nord-américain de coopération dans le domaine du travail.' in Rodrigue Blouin and Anthony Giles (eds.) *L'intégration économique en Amérique du Nord et les relations industrielles* (Québec: Les Presses de l'Université Laval, 1998), 177–199; Constance Phelps, 'Social work and labor: a look at the North American Agreement on Labor Cooperation.' *Journal of Sociology and Social Welfare*, 28 (2001), 23–41.

101 Parbudyal Singh, 'NAFTA and labor: a Canadian perspective.' *Journal of Labor Research*, 23 (2002), 433–446.

To further secure, in accordance with our respective laws and regulations, the observance and promotion of worker rights, renewing our commitment to the observance of internationally recognized core labour standards, and acknowledging that the International Labour Organization is the competent body to set and deal with those core labour standards.[102]

Thus the commitments at the San Jose summit were vague, but called on countries in the hemisphere to foster compliance, consistent with domestic laws, with international conventions and ILO core standards. As in the WTO Singapore formula, this shifted responsibility for labour protection to the ILO and limits incorporation of labour rights in the FTAA. A later declaration at the Quito summit in 2002 clearly stated that labour and environmental concerns should not be backed by threat of withdrawal of trade privileges.[103]

While Congress moved ahead on fast track authorization, the Bush administration did not vigorously pursue a labour component. Some Republicans 'wanted new fast-track legislation to specifically forbid the U.S. Trade Representative from negotiating *any* type of labor or environmental standards in any trade deals reached under fast track authority'.[104] Despite this, the 2002 trade negotiating authority required labour issues to be taken into account. The Americans' official position remained committed to pushing labour issues in the FTAA forums, with the goal of preventing the use of low labour standards as a means to attract investment or subsidize exports. The US Labor department still asserts a desire to 'improve observance of international labor standards' in the FTAA, and has committed funds for technical assistance and bilateral initiatives to promote labour law enforcement.[105]

However, indicating disillusionment with even the weak compromise of the NAALC, Mexico took a lead role in opposing the extension of the NAALC or inclusion of any alternative labour accord in the FTAA. It was joined by other major states as well. The most that has been accomplished is a parallel process for consideration of 'civil society' views on very general issues on the FTAA agenda, grouping together labour, environment, and other so-called 'academic' issues. Thus has given unions, NGOs and other interested parties the opportunity to provide comments on these dimensions of hemispheric integration, but amounted to a 'harmless repository' for

---

102 'Ministerial Declaration of San José' Fourth Western Hemisphere Trade Ministerial Meeting of the Free Trade Area of the Americas San José, Costa Rica March 19, 1998. [cited June 24 1998]. Available at www.ftaa-alca.org.

103 'Ministerial Declaration of Quito', Seventh Western Hemisphere Trade Ministerial Meeting of the Free Trade Area of the Americas, Quito Ecuador, Nov. 1, 2002 . [cited Dec. 13, 2003]. Available at www.ftaa-alca.org.

104 'Free trade onslaught expected early in new Congress' *Working Together* 21 Nov.-Dec., 1996, 1.

105 Bruce Jay, Commentary, 'US Department of Labor Active in FTAA' Summit of the Americas Website, [cited Feb. 2, 2004]. Available at http://www.americasnet.net/Commentators/Bruce_Jay/COMMENTARY_MARCH.pdf.

these contentious matters, which only appeared to balance direct corporate input for political reasons.[106]

Canada trumpeted the NAALC compromise as a pattern for the FTAA. But with the Bush administration's disinterest in labour matters, Canada cannot expect to achieve too much in the near future. This reflects the reluctance of Latin American states to surrender sovereignty over such matters to an organization which they expect to be dominated by the Americans. The costs of making enforcement work are great for these states as they adjust to liberalized global economics. As Mehmet and Daudelin suggest

> Canada should ... be sensitive to the fact that agreements such as NAALC are likely to involve significant efforts and costs to Latin American countries, and significantly less to the two rich members of the hemispheric community. The choice to include a social charter in an FTAA, or the design of one, should involve a generous consideration of this situation.[107]

Canada has some regional allies in fostering a greater presence for civil society issues.[108] However, resistance from Mexico and disinterest in Washington likely doom the prospects for a labour dimension in the FTAA. This would in turn reduce pressure for enhancing the NAALC as it would open up the competition for 'social dumping' to many new states.

Not surprisingly, union leaders in North America, referring to NAFTA precedents, argue that the FTAA is a bad idea without enforceable labour rights. Workers groups denounced the FTAA in general, citing experience with NAFTA, which they claimed had led to net job losses. As Thea Lee testified, 'Integration has to be about more than just protecting corporate rights and raising profits. Trade agreements must include, in their core, enforceable protections for fundamental workers' rights, human rights and the environment.'[109] But AFL leaders expected the FTAA to repeat the 'mistakes' of NAALC, or exclude reference to labour rights, as the countries of the hemisphere press for liberalization without a social dimension. 'No negotiating group, no study group, not even an official discussion on labor issues has occurred within the FTAA negotiating process. Only one provision relating to labor has even been

---

106 Sandra Polaski 'Labor Provisions in the FTAA? A Continuing Controversy' For presentation at the Yale Conference on Hemispheric Trade New Haven, Connecticut, April 2–4, 2003.

107 Ozay Mehmet and Jean Daudelin, *Labour Mobility, Labour Standards and Hemispheric Integration: Mercosur, NAFTA, the Caribbean and the FTAA* (Ottawa: FOCAL, 1998).

108 *'Civil Society and the Summit Process' Summit 2001: Going Beyond Trade* (Canadian Foundation for the Americas [FOCAL] and Summit of the Americas Centre, Florida International University, 1999), p. 4.

109 Thea M. Lee, Assistant Director for International Economics, American Federation of Labor and Congress of Industrial Organizations (AFL-CIO) 'Testimony on the Free Trade Area of the Americas' September 9, 2002, [cited Feb. 6, 2004]. Available at http://www. citizenstrade.org/pdf/afl_ftaa_comments.pdf.

proposed in the FTAA, and even this provision would be non-binding.'[110] The CLC also considered another NAALC insufficient and decried the FTAA process for its undemocratic exclusion of labour and other civil society elements.[111] The CLC and allied organizations pressed 'fair trade', which addressed the effects of integration on poverty, social exclusion and job creation. This model was articulated at the alternative 'Peoples Summit of the Americas' such as that held at Belo Horizonte, Brazil in 1997, and subsequently in Santiago and Rio de Janeiro.

The issue has been kept alive despite staunch opposition from Mexico and Brazil, and indifference by other hemispheric states. Because of the close partisan alignments in Congress, trade negotiating authority was only passed with explicit requirement that the president seek attention to labour issues. The declaration of Nuevo Leon in 2004 repeated the partners' commitment to fundamental ILO principles and their determination to work to eliminate the worst forms of abuse, such as child labour and human trafficking. Yet there was no substance to the declaration on worker and human rights, nor any mechanism linking labour standards to changes in level of development with further hemispheric integration.[112] Contention between the parties on other issues may indeed restrict the prospects for early completion of FTAA negotiations; the Americans appear prepared to negotiate a series of bilateral agreements with states in different positions, providing access to American markets to small, non-threatening states or those willing to make concessions, while excluding troublesome competitors like Brazil.

A Hemispheric Social Alliance of New Social Movements also emerged, linking labour, environmental, women, human and indigenous rights groups to present alternatives to the FTAA. The Summit of the Americas process presented an important opportunity for transnational mobilization, which drew upon the failure of neo-liberal reforms, the decline of corporatist politics and union power and the emergence of new communications systems to produce innovative social constituencies across formal borders. These groups acted not only to promote common opposition to the FTAA, but to promote alternative understandings, interpretations and approaches to hemispheric integration.[113] Such labour advocates suggest that the flawed NAALC would be a poor model for the FTAA labour regime. Dickey argued that the NAALC's lack of enforcement mechanisms renders it useless for advancing human and labour rights; those using it have faced repression and violence. NAFTA's has been a largely liberalizing and negative deal for labour, which encouraged the emergence

---

110 Thea Lee, Testimony, Sept. 9, 2002.

111 CLC – FTAA: Working Families Want 'Fair Trade' found at http://www.clc-ctc.ca/campaigns/ftaa_2001.html Jan 22, 2004.

112 Special Summit of the Americas, 'Declaration of Nuevo León' Monterrey, Mexico January 13, 2004.

113 Marcelo I. Saguier Convergence in the Making: Transnational Civil Society and the Free Trade Area of the Americas Center for the Study of Globalisation and Regionalisation Working Paper No. 137/04, Warwick University, June 2004.

of sweatshops but provided limited protections. An FTAA must include mechanisms for enforcement and gradual harmonization of labour standards.[114]

Bilateral Alternatives to the FTAA

The willingness of developing states to commit to such arrangements appears to be remote, given their concerns about competitiveness and protectionism. This is only deepened by the emergence of China, now protected by WTO provisions, which allow it to compete with its huge, low cost labour force. Hence, suspicions of North America aside, Latin American leaders may find it inopportune to negotiate any side agreement at the moment, assuming the FTAA proceeds. But the social constituencies opposed to a neo-liberal FTAA without strong social guarantees remain vibrant.[115] So the two North American states are turning to bilateral deals with hemispheric (and extra-hemispheric) trade partners, which include some labour dimensions loosely modelled on NAALC but in some respects possibly weaker in application.

Canada first adopted a free trade agreement with Chile in 1997, when the US Congress stalled Chilean accession to NAFTA. The agreement incorporated labour and environmental side agreements modelled on the NAALC and NACEC. The negotiators sought to make the accord compatible with the NAALC, as they expected Chile to join NAFTA. So many NAALC features were replicated, despite labour complaints that these were inadequate. Hence, the Chile-Canada Agreement on Labour Cooperation adopted a focus on cooperation and consultations with a similar (though untested) complaints and submissions process. It also followed the NAALC in dividing labour principles into the three tiers, and allowing disputes resolutions and sanctions only in the case of child or forced labour, minimum wages and health and safety.[116] However, the negotiators weakened the sanctions by limiting them to monetary fines and excluding the possibility of trade penalties. Less transnational bureaucracy was established; the ministerial council is assisted by national Secretariats responsible for conducting cooperative activities, combined with the NAOs in a CCALC centre in each government. Unlike NAALC the agreement invoked the possibility of enforcement of CCALC rulings by courts.[117]

While trade between the two remains modest, Canadian investments in Chilean mining is significant, and union activists in the mining sector have established

---

114 Sheryl Dickey, 'The Free Trade Area of the Americas and human rights concerns.' *Human Rights Brief*, 8 (Spring 2001), 26–28.

115 Frederick W. Mayer, Negotiating NAFTA: Political Lessons for the FTAA Working Papers Series SAN01-17, Terry Sanford Institute of Public Policy, Duke University, July 2001, 25.

116 Adolfo Ciudad Reynaud, *Labour Standards and the Integration Process in the Americas* (Geneva: International Labour Organization, 2001) 244–45.

117 Agreement on Labour Cooperation Between the Government of Canada and the Government of the Republic of Chile Ottawa and Santiago February, 1997, 22–24.

collaborative ties.[118] There was evidence that at least one local at a new mine secured a better collective agreement because of experience and advice shared by their Canadian counterparts. But even though the gains have been limited and the costs for Chilean competitiveness marginal, Chile joined with other leading developing nation's to oppose any further linkage of trade and labour standards. Hence Canada's expressed goal of extending a NAALC style arrangement to the hemisphere and beyond did not take off from the Chilean example.

Starting with Costa Rica (and then extending to other Central American states) Canada again entered bilateral trade negotiations using the NAALC model to promote some attention to labour issues. It quickly conceded that the NAALC approach would not work for these small developing economies. So a limited version was crafted which did not commit these states to the bureaucratic elements of the national administrative offices or submissions. Evaluation committees were excluded, as were any trade sanctions or fines for unresolved, persistent violations. This meant the process for rectification of problems could be indeterminate and depend on Costa Rica's willingness to reform. While the 1998 ILO declaration on core rights was directly included, with most NAALC principles, migrant workers were excluded from the CCRALC.[119]

Canada's agreement with other Central American states, still pending, would also be weaker than NAALC since Canadian officials promised it would be based on the Costa Rica model. A limited effort has been made to open dialogue with other Latin American states, like a Memorandum of Understanding with Brazil covering, labour laws, inspections, labour relations and pay equity, and other issues; the memorandum focuses on cooperative activities with no complaints procedure. Whether Canada will continue to promote labour dimension in trade accords under a new Conservative government remains doubtful, as North and South America appear to drift further apart on trade, and neo-liberal approaches, unpopular in the South, remain dominant in North American visions of regionalization and globalization.

The US has also proceeded with bilateral free trade agreements with varying labour dimensions. An agreement with Jordan looked promising, since it went beyond NAALC in incorporating ILO core principles as a guiding force. But this was not translated into stronger commitments with hemispheric partners. The US agreement with Chile only required enforcement of existing national laws, even if these deviated from core ILO principles; any fines levied would be redirected back to the offending country to undertake remedies in future (though with no guarantees the revenue would not be shifted to other purposes).[120]

---

118 Christopher McLaughlin 'Chilean miners dig Canada' *Alternatives Journal* 24 (Fall, 1998), 29; Judith Marshall, 'Worker exchanges between Chilean and Canadian miners' *Canadian Dimension* 32 (March, 1998), 37–9.

119 American Centre for International Labor Solidarity, *Justice for All: A Guide to Worker Rights in the Global Economy* (Washington: AFL-CIO, 2003), 141.

120 Elizabeth Drake, 'Worker Rights in the FTAA' [cited June 20, 2005]. Available at http://www.unimep.br/alca/www/textos/drake.pdf, 3–4.

The Bush administration took a similar weak approach in the recent Central American Free Trade Agreement negotiations. Again, the fines would be payable to the country itself, with no means to ensure the funds would enhance worker rights. While some elements of the NAALC were restored, these provisions remained completely unenforceable. Exclusion of employment discrimination meant that the CAFTA would not protect women against pregnancy discrimination or other harassment. Drafts of CAFTA also excluded elements of NAALC which required prompt and effective domestic remedies for law violations, and had no means to ensure that labour standards would be sustained or would approximate ILO norms.[121]

AFL-CIO critics concluded the CAFTA was weaker than NAALC by requiring respect for sovereignty in cooperative activities, so that improved labour standards might not be eligible topics for such activities.[122] While the USTR insisted that the agreement included provisions for funding to strengthen labor law enforcement, critics suggested funds were being diverted from labour rights to market and productivity initiatives. In the past, the US had successfully pressured Central American states to improve labour laws via threat of loss of trade access under the general system of preferences, but the new CAFTA would weaken this leverage over future policy, since it guaranteed trade access above GSP levels. After 'CAFTA, employers and governments will actually enjoy more freedom to deny workers their fundamental human rights than they currently have under our trade preference programs.'[123]

Therefore, there is little likelihood of any hemispheric or global agreement on trade and labour in the near future. Opposition to labour's inclusion in the WTO remains high while the resolve of the US and EU to press for it has diminished. In the Western Hemisphere, the FTAA has stalled with Brazil's inability to reach accord with the Americans on anti-dumping and agricultural subsidies, among other issues. For the moment, Northern pressure for a stronger labour dimension would further limit the willingness of many South Americans states to continue negotiating the FTAA. While the alternatives pressed by the Hemispheric Social Alliance hold eventual promise, the focus for now will remain regional with occasional bilateral extensions. And most of the bilateral labour accords will be weaker than the NAALC. The NAALC model remains important as a regional exemplar, and may well influence subsequent trade agreements elsewhere. But it is unlikely to be completely emulated in other developing regions, given resistance there and the undermining effects of

---

121 Office of the United States Trade Representative 'CAFTA – Labor and Environment Capacity Building' CAFTA Policy Brief, July 2005 [cited August 17, 2005]. Available at http://www.ustr.gov/assets/Trade_Agreements/Bilateral/CAFTA/Briefing_Book/asset_upload_file758_7871.pdf?ht=central%20america.

122 'USTR Misleads Congress on CAFTA Labor Provisions', *AFL CIO Global Fairness 2004* [cited June 21, 2005]. Available at http://www.citizen.org/documents/CAFTAandLaborIssues(AFL-CIO).pdf.

123 AFL-CIO 'Fair Trade or Free Trade? *Understanding CAFTA (Labor Rights Provisions in CAFTA are Inadequate)* [cited June 21, 2005]. Available at www.wola.org/economic/brief_cafta_labor_april04.pdf.

China and India's emergence as global economic players. These same factors may well hinder any efforts to strengthen the NAALC regime itself in future.

A Final Test? Labour Law Reform in Mexico

Finally, one of the most recent cases illustrates the limits of the NAALC's ability to influence the direction of labour relations in the North American region. This case merits attention because of its highly contentious, political character, which cuts directly to the liberalizing tendencies in recent Mexican policy. In early 2005, a wide range of unions from all three NAFTA parties submitted US NAO 2005-01 and an identical submission, CANA 2005-01, which challenged Mexico's proposed labour law reforms. Designed by President Fox's minister of Labour, Carlos Abascal Carranza, former head of a business association, the reforms aimed at increasing the flexibility available to employers to deal with labour matters, without the formal constraints, however poorly enforced, of Mexico' legal, constitutional and treaty obligations to trade unions. These measures had been proposed by Abascal as a business lobbyist and came to fruition as legislation when he joined Fox's administration, after lengthy negotiations with unions on adjustments proved fruitless.[124] Formally introduced in 2002, and pushed despite the lack of consensus among the parties, the bill could secure passage, though it stalled in the Congress in the run-up to the 2006 elections.

The proposal reflected a longstanding desire of business associations to secure liberalization of the labour market and removal of some of the statutory benefits and constitutional guarantees which Mexican workers had enjoyed on paper. The measure was part of a larger project of liberalization, which transformed the character of Mexican labour relations, which evolved slowly through the corporatist period.[125] The measure had not been adopted earlier despite constant business pressures, because government apparently considered the corporatist system and statutory benefits as a minimal obstacle to increased flexibility and adjustment in the labour market.[126] In addition, corporatism was difficult to alter, as the dominant PRI had come to rely on the established unions and secured their loyalty by protecting, however minimally, their statutory benefits. The passing of the long-serving leader of the CTM, Fidel Velasquez Sanchez, and the political instability in the mid-1990s made the PRI reluctant to undertake fundamental changes in their relationship with a core partner, which had helped sustain stability for 70 years. After the PRI lost its majority in Congress in 1997, the novelty of power sharing also had a restraining effect.

---

124 Michael O'Boyle, 'Union blues' *Business Mexico*, 12, Nov. 2002, 53–5.

125 Ian T. MacDonald, 'Negotiating Mexico's labour law reform: corporatism, neoliberalism and democratic opening' *Studies in Political Economy* 73 (2004), 139–.

126 Viviana Patroni 'The decline and fall of corporatism? Labour legislation reform in Mexico and Argentina during the 1990s' *Canadian Journal of Political Science* 34 (2001), 249 .

As the proposals evolved, unionists occasionally had reason for optimism; Canadian steelworkers opined that many of the elements in the Dana submission would be addressed via the reforms, including secret ballots and health and safety measures. Also positive were bans on discrimination against workers in different categories, and guarantees for freedom of association, though the reforms had to be tested in practice.[127] But as the measures took shape, it seemed clear that business associations held more sway over their content. Labour advocates feared that it would be even harder to register independent union, as the law required supporters to identify themselves, risking dismissal or retaliation, and might allow dummy union petitions to thwart genuine organizing campaigns. It also gave employers more freedom to hire temporary workers, shift hours and dismiss employees without cause.[128] Despite negotiations with unions and a promise to present legislation only when consensus was reached, the bill was presented to Congress in Dec. 2002, though it stalled in the gridlock which characterised executive-legislative relations in the Fox era.[129]

The measure was supported by business associations and established unions. It would increase state control over union formation and impose restrictions on the nature of bargaining units, the constituencies they could unionize and the conditions for union recognition. The proposal was seen to break an accord President Fox had signed when he was campaigning for office, in which he pledged to further the rights of independent unions. The reforms ignored independent union concerns respecting the openness of the process and worker access to information about union certification and collective agreements; the government accepted the business position that these should remain corporate secrets even though this veil of ignorance protected phantom unions. Compa suggested the 'effect would be to 'lock in' bargaining monopoly by incumbent official unions and insulate them against challenges from independent unions.'[130]

Human Rights Watch noted that the proposal would reverse the limited gains made in the NAALC era:

> The Abascal Project not only fails to remedy key shortcomings in Mexican labor law, but it weakens existing protections. In doing so, the proposal also violates Mexico's obligations under international law to protect and promote workers' human rights. The proposed changes would make it virtually impossible for most workers to exercise their rights to strike, bargain collectively, and join a union of their choosing. The proposal also

---

127 'Four Years After NAFTA Complaint: Mexico Labour Reforms Only a First Step Say Steelworkers' *Canada NewsWire*. Ottawa: Jan 30, 2003.

128 'The Abascal Plan: Codifying Employer Control' *NACLA Report on the Americas* 39, Jul/Aug 2005, 21–2.

129 LaBotz, 2005, 69.

130 Lance Compa, *Justice for All : The Struggle for Workers Rights in Mexico*, Washington: AFL-CIO Solidarity Center 2003, p. 18, [cited April 11, 2004]. Available at http://www.solidaritycenter.org/docUploads/Solidarity%20Mexico%20final%20pdf%2011-17-03.pdf?CFID=1165299&CFTOKEN=82992828.

fails to provide sufficient protections for workers facing pregnancy-based discrimination in hiring.[131]

Most ominously, in a bid to ensure that union certification drives were above board, the measure called for full disclosure of personal and contact information for all workers joining registration drives or signing union cards. In the recent past, cases of intimidation against union organizers had a chilling effect on independent union activity. Extending this disclosure requirement to all workers would increase the threat to the membership, undermining the supposed benefits of a secret certification ballot. 'Requiring every worker's name and address and making this information immediately available to management and to an incumbent official puts all workers at the risk of reprisals and would have a chilling effect on workers' freedom of association.'[132]

Critics feared the bill, which imposed new requirements for documents and certification from local conciliation boards before bargaining and strikes, might weaken the opportunity for successful negotiations by independent unions, stimulated by NAALC and by transnational collaborations. The conditions for holding a secret ballot vote to challenge an existing union were so onerous that such ballots would be rare. It also allowed established unions to file a bogus application for a vote on a new union, perhaps tying up the process for months, since only one such application could be considered at a time.[133] And finally the measure placed the burden on workers to prove that dismissals were in retaliation for union activism or union membership, making such retaliation more likely.[134]

Critics opposed the proposal which they believed would strengthen the position of official, established unions and minimize the potential for new independent unions to make serious challenges. This would allow business greater flexibility to deal with unions and workers, erode statutory protection and not give workers any additional means to protect themselves. Business claimed that they needed the changes to meet competition from China and other states, which had eroded Mexico's market share using their unregulated labour markets, and disenfranchised, unprotected workers. But the unions regarded the reforms as an affront to the spirit of the NAALC, which ostensibly aimed at the improvement of labour standards, not their further degradation. The submission cited the NAALC's obligations to 'provide high labor standards' and to 'strive to improve those standards.'[135]

---

131 Human Rights Watch, 'Mexico: Fox's Labor Reform Proposal Would Deal Serious Blow to Workers' Rights' (Letter to Mexico's Chamber of Deputies) Feb. 9, 2005 [cited August 19 2005]. Available at http://hrw.org/english/docs/2005/02/09/mexico10156_txt.htm.

132 Compa, 2003, 18.

133 Human Rights Watch 'Mexico: Workers' Rights at Risk Under Fox Plan' Dec. 9, 2004, [cited July 28, 2005] Available at http://hrw.org/english/docs/2004/12/09/mexico9814_txt.htm.

134 Compa, 2003, 18.

135 Washington Office on Latin America (WOLA), et. al., *Public Communication to the U.S. National Administrative Office under the North American Agreement on Labor*

This tri-national collaboration demonstrated how NAALC brought workers together across the 3 countries. It also had implications for the future usefulness of NAALC, which only required the parties to enforce their own laws; critics suggested the Abascal bill would eliminate the NAALC as a means to challenge barriers to independent unions, such as a lack of secret ballots:

> Labour law reform can stifle these complaints. Simply stated, enacting labour laws tailored to the needs of capital will allow the Mexican government to enforce them without discouraging new investment. NAFTA's critics would no longer be able to use the labour side agreement to put pressure on the Mexican government.[136]

However, the political nature of the complaint, which challenged the liberalization of Mexican labour markets, reaffirmed NAALC's limits. In February 2006, the US NAO rejected this case for review, since it deals with Mexico's domestic reforms of labour laws and does not promote the intentions of the NAALC. Canada's NAO rejected an identical submission in January 2006. Thus the NAOs restricted their interventions to the non-enforcement of Mexican laws even if new Mexican laws deviated significantly from NAALC objectives or undermined NAALC's potential to challenge deficient labour standards in future. The fate of the reforms will depend on elections in Mexico in August 2006, which could significantly shift the balance between President and Congress, and left and right political forces.

Conclusions

NAFTA's labour accord has provided some impetus for increased transnational interactions among unions, allied social movements, government agencies and trinational bureaucracies. The public submissions process stimulated some cooperation among social actors across borders, motivated by the need to collaborate on complaints; the nexus of union and human rights groups, generated initially by opposition to NAFTA, was sustained at least in part by these NAALC interactions. It would not be accurate to suggest that the side agreement played a causal role in creating this transnational nexus, and the limited results from submissions caused some groups to turn to other forms of collaboration.

Creation of trinational bureaucracies linked official and experts with common interests in labour rights and workplace standards together. This has produced a degree of mutual learning, sharing of best practices and standardization of measures and concepts which has contributed to common understandings of the challenges to

---

Cooperation (NAALC) Concerning the Introduction of Reforms to the Federal Labor Code of Mexico (Abascal Project), Which Would Seriously Diminish Current Labor Standards, including the Right to Freely Associate, to Organize and to Bargain Collectively, in Violation of the Mexican Constitution, ILO Conventions Adopted By Mexico, and the NAALC, February 17, 2005.

136 Bruce Allen, 'Tightening the belt: labour law 'reform' in Mexico' *Briar Patch* 27 (Dec 1998/Jan 1999), 25.

labour from trade liberalization. Labour relations practices may have been modified by shared learning, training and outreach opportunities as both officials and social actors learned new ways of protecting labour rights or measuring and interpreting labour standards. A few examples of 'anticipated reactions' and adjustment of practices are evident. Again, the limited resources, lack of continuity and cultural divisions on key issues reduce these regionalizing effects.

Therfore, there is limited evidence that the NAFTA labour accord has stimulated regionalization of labour relations, via a common cognitive construct or a new social nexus across borders. Certainly, it would be premature to declare the existence of a common labour culture across the three states. Within Mexico itself, competing neo-liberal flexibilization and social democratic visions of labour law reform remain hotly contested[137]; the political strength of conservative regimes in the US and Canada do not bode well for vigorous promotion of a labour rights agenda. Reliance on national labour laws and domestic institutions in the NAOs also limits the prospects for a genuine transnational culture to emerge. Such integration occurred over half a century in Europe and NAFTA is barely 12 years old. Yet early trends provide limited evidence only of significant deepening of regionalization in response to NAFTA's labour accord. And the western hemisphere as a whole has proven no more hospitable to a trade-labour linkage than global institutions. Indeed, if the Mexican labour reforms are indicative, liberalization and flexibilization are more likely than deepened transnational labour standards.

---

137 'Origins of Mexico's Labor Law Reform' *NACLA Report on the Americas,* 39 (Jul/Aug 2005), 18–19.

Conclusions

The Limits of Regionalism
in Labour Affairs

Evaluating NAALC: Persistent Divisions

This book has presented an evaluation of the impact of the NAFTA labour accord and the submissions and cooperative activities it has spawned. NAALC falls short of the demands of organized labour in Canada and the U.S. for a transnational regulatory regime. Its provisions for consultation and cooperation and its complaints process provide a limited opportunity for generation of new transnational norms and practices in labour relations. For its supporters, the NAALC has been a creative addition to trade law, with an innovative dispute settlement mechanism which will allow for consideration of social issues and political efforts to encourage compliance with national labour laws. Individuals and labour organizations have been empowered to bring their concerns into the process and initiate efforts at improvement of labour practices.[1] New alliances of officials, unions and interested corporations also developed from the many bilateral activities of the NAALC and its central institutions. Neo-institutional analysts might predict that this integration will generate a transformation over time of labour practices in the three societies, as a new transborder, regional labour culture develops among societal and government actors.

Establishment of NAFTA with even a half-hearted labour side agreement could change the system of institutional incentives for industrial relations. This transformation has particular potential in Mexico, where the labour relations system is constrained by the post-revolution corporatist compromise. So far, domestic labour relations systems and union and corporate organizations have not been significantly altered. Entrenched practices and regulations will be hard to transform, particularly where affected interests like established unions and bureaucracies resist change. At least the NAALC creates new openings for Mexican workers and independent unions to exert their legal rights to organization and collective bargaining. These new opportunities may not sufficiently strengthen independent unions so that they can counter the threats to workers' welfare and rights in transnational economics and domestic political instability. The evidence so far from Han Young and elsewhere is

---

1   Jack I. Garvey, 'Trade law and quality of life – dispute resolution under the NAFTA side accords on labor and the environment' *American Journal of International Law*. 89 (1995), 439–453.

not encouraging. But potential for change does exist, even if it is gradual, and beset with setbacks from labour's viewpoint.

As the cases and precedents accumulate, the limitations and possibilities of the NAALC become apparent. The NAALC will not provide a transnational regulatory or judicial regime ensuring enforcement of ILO standards. However, it may produce greater transparency which will pressure the three partners to enforce their own labour laws and to move towards high standards of protection for workers and unions. Supporters like Compa are realistic about the limitations, but nonetheless still see potential for the NAALC:

> The NAALC does not create a supranational tribunal to take evidence and decide the guilt or innocence of alleged labor rights violators. It does not provide specific remedies like union certification, reinstatement, back wages, or punitive damages for workers whose rights are violated. Nor does it set up an international labor appeals court that can overrule domestic authorities. However, the NAALC does provide an accessible, flexible forum for transnational action by unions and human rights groups.[2]

NAALC's enforcement mechanisms are limited but some US unions have recognized their potential, and pressed innovative cases to try to make the side agreement effective. Canadian unions have also seen the advantages of participation. So far, Canadian participation remains limited owing to the hostility of labour and to federal-provincial jurisdictional complications, but Canada has been active in cooperative programs.

Interactions generated by the new institutions have forged new connections and promoted awareness of labour practices and laws across borders. Cooperation programs have provided opportunities for the sharing of information on a growing range of topics. The NACLC secretariat has brought together a transnational bureaucracy (albeit modest in size) and its consultation activities will generate further transnational dialogue. Submissions have not led to sanctions or evaluation committees of experts, but have spawned numerous cooperative activities, exchanges of information and ministerial consultations on labour rights violations. Interchange has been encouraged at the highest decision making levels in labour matters in North America, the Council of Ministers of Labour. The placement of the NAOs within national labour departments put them in position to influence government responses to labour complaints, as in the ministerial acceptance of NAO recommendations in Mexico and the United States. This political role is a double-edged sword; the NAOs are also shy of political controversy and diplomatic offense, possibly limiting their willingness to strengthen enforcement via evaluation committees or arbitration and sanctions.

NAALC's provisions on expert investigation, arbitration, disputes settlement, sanctions or trade penalties remain untested. As Human Rights Watch concludes,

---

2   Lance Compa 'International Labor Rights and NAFTA's Labor Side Agreement' *LASA Forum*, Summer 1999, [cited April 4, 2002]. Available at http://lasa.international.pitt.edu/Compa.htm.

'The governments themselves have not publicly discussed, clarified, or challenged each other's positions related to the NAALC, with the result that the NAALC's potential as a means to effect broad improvements in the labor rights situation in the signatory countries has remained severely under-utilized.'[3] The key problem appears to be a lack of political will, which has not been improved by the election of the anti-labour Bush, Fox and Harper. For instance, the US labour secretary has shown less interest in international labour venues and did not appear at the interhemispheric ministerial meetings in Ottawa in 2001. According to a Mexican analyst, 'To win votes, Fox made the famous '20 commitments,' which included union democracy ... But he's made no effort to live up to the promise.'[4] Canada's Liberals did little to promote NAALC's application nationwide, let alone strengthen its mechanisms. In 2006, Canada elected a Conservative government not known for its ties to labour.

Some supporters of free trade consider the linking of labour and trade formally through the NAFTA or WTO to be unachievable and undesirable. The best approach to securing improvements for labour is for developed states to open their borders to the developing world to encourage growth and support ILO efforts to improve compliance with its conventions.[5] To assist workers, governments should extend adjustment assistance and retraining programs for workers to limit any erosion of domestic political support for the free trading system. Governments should adopt policies to encourage investment in high value added service and technological industries, while generating sufficient employment.[6] For neo-liberals, such measures will produce trickle down benefits to workers which would make stronger unions or guaranteed rights less necessary.

Yet others consider action to improve the regional and social distribution of economic growth related to integration between the NAFTA nations is crucial if development is to diffuse throughout the entire region.[7] Measures of importance include distributive social security initiatives, backed by genuinely diffused economic growth. Investments in infrastructure, and active labor market policies to promote worker adjustment must be at the core of the strategy, replacing the reliance on passive income maintenance programs. Given the laissez faire views of the US Congress, the anti-deficit cautiousness of Canadian decision makers, and the scale of necessary investment in infrastructures and human resources in Mexico, the prospects for such innovative, expensive government intervention remain minimal. Indeed some recent Canadian and American governments have acted against such

---

3   Human Rights Watch, *Trading Away Rights The Unfulfilled Promise of NAFTA's Labor Side Agreement* (New York: Human Rights Watch 2001), 23.

4   David Bacon 'Border Labor War Defies Mexico's Fox Administration' Oct. 21, 2001. http://www.maquilasolidarity.org/resources/maquilas/bacon2001.htm.

5   Drusilla K. Brown, Alan V. Deardorff and Robert M. Stern, 'Trade and Labor Standards' *Open Economies Review* 9 (1998), 171–194.

6   Mary E. Burfisher, Sherman Robinson and Karen Thierfelder 'The Impact of NAFTA on the United States' *Journal of Economic Perspectives* 15 (2001), 142.

7   Robert Pastor, *Towards and North American Community* (Washington: Institute for International Economics, 2001).

needed expenditures in the name of deficit reduction or ideological preference for small government. Labor representatives accuse US administrations of undermining already weak training initiatives by budget restrictions.[8]

A few authors suggest that NAALC has already exceeded expectations. For instance, Abbott argues that

> The NAO complaint procedure has been more robust than might have been expected. Labor unions of Canada, Mexico and the United States have initiated a number of complaints that have resulted in negotiations among Labor Ministers of the Parties, and in several cases have produced concrete results in terms of remedial action by employers or government administrative reform.[9]

The basic NAALC formula can succeed only if organized labour maximizes its collaboration across borders.[10] Rod Dobell is optimistic that the labour and environmental side agreements can become the basis for a more effective 'social charter' for North America. But as Dobell notes, the parties to the agreement show different visions of cooperation based on domestic traditions and standards. In his words,

> the second generation challenge for the North American community and the NAFTA institutions is to achieve effective cooperative management without unilateralism and without any forced convergence or harmonization of standards accomplished by suppressing cultural differences in favour of technical uniformity based on ostensibly objective technical standards or rulings.[11]

Such a socially sensitive approach forms an essential element of North America's future and is necessary to ensure cultural survival and economic sustainablity.

Critics of the side agreement assert that it does nothing to offset the neo-liberal character of NAFTA as a whole and the overall effects of the NAFTA are costly for labour. An ILO study argued that NAFTA is a 'cornerstone' of neo-liberal policies in North America, designed to force restructuring of these societies in line with a

---

8   Sheldon Freidman, 'Trade Adjustment Assistance: No Cure for a Bad NAFTA, but Badly Needed to Help NAFTA's Victims' in Raphael Fernadez de Castro, Monica Verea Campos and Sydney Weintraub, (eds.) *Sectoral Labor effects of North American Free Trade* (Austin: U.S. Mexican Polcy Studies Program, University of Texas, 1993), 73.

9   Frederick M. Abbott 'The NAFTA and the Political Economy of Regionalism' *The North American Integration Regime and its Implications for the World Trading System* Harvard Law School Jean Monnet Chair Working Papers, http://www.jeanmonnetprogram. org/papers/99/990200.html.

10   Paul Teague 'Labour-standard setting and regional trading blocs: Lesson drawing from the NAFTA experience' *Employee Relations*, 25 (2003), 428–452.

11   Rod Dobell, 'A Social Charter for a North American Community' *Isuma* 1, 1 Spring 2000, 1 [cited April 16, 2005]. Available at http://www.isuma.net/v01n01/dobell1/dobell1_ e.pdf.

corporate agenda. It concludes that NAFTA has worked with liberalizing policies against the interests of workers throughout the NAFTA region.

> Over time, these have had a generally adverse effect on employment and income conditions of a majority of working people and their families in all three NAFTA countries. It is our contention that this is not an unintended consequence of these policies. Underlying these policies are relations of power and its redistribution: from workers to corporations, from low and median income to high income earners, from wages to profits, from governments to the market.[12]

Studies of the effects in Mexico suggest that workers living conditions have declined, arguably because of NAFTA. Even where more jobs exist, intolerable social conditions remain common, which is a result of putting trade liberalization before social protections.[13]

For critics, the side agreements are too weak to significantly alter NAFTA's neo-liberal character. 'NAFTA's labour and environmental side agreements have not and were never meant to alter the basic character of the treaty. Nor will they ever do so because they are weak and ineffectual.'[14] Opponents of free trade continue to suggest that the 'anaemic' NAALC left the undesirable Mexican industrial relations regime intact, and 'sent a signal that the 'status quo' in the labor area would not impede an expanded trading relationship.'[15] Some analyses note limited gains which have been made; union votes at Han Young and Kuk Dong, and transnational education and worker exchanges, for instance. But actual victories by Mexican independent unions like FAT have remained few. And much of the limited success involves domestic and transnational activism outside of or marginally connected to the NAALC, such as cross border union networks and the USAW campaigns in Puebla.[16]

This situation is compounded by the simultaneous movement towards liberalization in Mexico which weakens the prospects for strong, effective labour organizations. Overall, job growth in Mexico has been disappointing, with recent reversals. By 2001, economic expansion since NAFTA trailed pre-NAFTA trends by some estimates.[17] This trend worsened with the US recession after the terrorist

---

12 Bruce Campbell, Andrew Jackson, Mehrene Larudee, and Teresa Gutierrez Haces *Labour market effects under CUFTA/NAFTA* ILO, Employment and Training Papers, 29. (Geneva: International Labour Organization, 1999), 1.

13 Linda Diebel, 'Mexicans Paying Big Price for NAFTA' *Toronto Star* April 15, 2001.

14 Bruce Allen 'CLC Left Opposition: Work Reorganization and NAFTA' [cited Jan. 21, 2004]. Available at http://www.geocities.com/RainForest/Vines/7731/clc-lo/dox/work_reorganization_n_nafta.html.

15 Harley Shaiken 'The New Global Economy: Trade and Production under NAFTA' *Journal für Entwicklungspolitik* 17 (2001), 243.

16 Dale A. Hathaway 'Mexico's Frente Autentico del Trabajo and the Problem of Unionizing Maquiladoras' *Labor History*, 43 (2002), 434–35.

17 Daniel Drache, Trade, *Development and the Doha Round: A Sure Bet or a Train Wreck?* Centre for International Governance Innovation, Working Paper No. 5, March 2006. [cited March 28, 2006] Available at http://www.cigionline.ca/publications/docs/Trade_Dev_Drache.pdf.

attacks in 2001. NAFTA has been disappointing for Mexico as expected gains from low-wage, low-regulation competition have not materialized. Instead Mexican producers find themselves fighting competition from Asia, and especially from China, which have invaded Mexico's home market, and secured a competitive share of North American markets overall. Pessimism among business is increasing on this issue.[18] Greider refers to this "treadmill' that ensnares developing countries'[19] forced to compete with lower wages and standards. This causes employers to seek flexible labour legislation, which could weaken labour rights and independent unions, further sapping prospects for transnational collaboration to enhance standards.

The security situation after 9/11 has also tilted the regional dialogue unfavourably. First, the prospects for enhanced labour mobility across the Rio Grande – essential if North America is to become a fully functional labour market instead of a one-sided arrangement favouring capital – were swept aside by US security concerns. Since then disquiet over China's role in undermining the US manufacturing sector, plus the continued flow of illegal migrants across the border has enhanced a climate approaching 'nativism' in US views of Mexican immigration. Also, neo-liberal forces in the corporate and security sectors have used the terrorist threat as an opportunity not to enhance security, but to promote deeper, liberalizing integration among the three states in search of profit. The proposals by the Independent Task Force on the Future of North America, *Creating a North American Community* focus on creating a security perimeter to prevent terrorism and crime, common tariffs versus other trading blocs, and enhanced competitiveness via reduced differences in standards, regulations and rules of origins.

There is limited discussion of the need to produce 'balanced development' in Mexico, though even here the goal is to upgrade infrastructure to integrate Mexico more effectively. There is no mention of the social costs of adjustment to this enhanced liberalized integration.[20] A trinational summit in Cancun planned to revive talk of a 'security and prosperity partnership' included participation by CEO's but not by any union or social actors.[21] It led to creation of a 'North American Competitiveness Council' composed only of business leaders to make recommendations on trade policy.[22] Given the influence of such actors and ideas in policy circles in all three states, deepened neo-liberalism is a more likely blueprint for future integration than enhanced labour and social standards; the 'free trade model' has trumped the

---

18 Interview with business association executive, Mexico City, July 2003.

19 William Greider 'A New Giant Sucking Sound', *The Nation* Dec. 31. 2001, [cited Feb. 3, 2004]. Available at http://www.thenation.com/doc.mhtml?i=20011231&s=greider,

20 Independent Task Force on the Future of North America, *Creating a North American Community* New York: Council on Foreign Relations, 2005.

21 Stephen Chace 'Move over politicians – it's the CEOs turn to talk' *Globe and Mail* Mar. 22, 2006 [cited Mar. 28, 2006]. Available at http://www.globeinvestor.com/servlet/story/GAM.20060322.RNAFTA22/GIStory/.

22 'Leaders Note Progress on the Security and Prosperity Partnership of North America' Leaders' Joint Statement, Cancun, Mexico March 31, 2006 [cited March 31, 2006] Available at http://pm.gc.ca/eng/media.asp?id=1085.

'fair trade model' for now though the balance of partisan forces in Mexico after presidential and congressional elections in 2006 could alter the dynamics.

Proposals to Improve the NAALC

If the climate did become more favourable, what improvements should be made to the NAALC? Some critics like the International Labour Rights Fund have long argued: 'In order for workers to benefit from NAFTA, labor unions and their partners must insist that a labor clause, reflecting the need to improve enforcement of labor laws in North America, be a central part of the NAFTA agreement' not 'relegated to the uncertain status of a 'side agreement'.[23] Early supporters of the NAALC like Compa now advocate sanctions:

> Trade-labor links should start with dialogue, oversight, publicity, technical assistance, diplomatic chiding and other 'soft' measures to promote respect for worker's rights. But at the end of the day, a social dimension in trade must be backed by hitting hard at the pocketbooks of governments and corporations that abuse workers'.[24]

Suggestions to meet this objective include enforceable remedies for labour violations to allow unions and workers and supportive groups to bring legal actions against corporations for violations of NAALC principles.

There is no single reform proposal on the table, as different societal actors promote various aspects of the 'fair trade' agenda. Many agree that the NAALC must be amended to end the three-tier hierarchy of rights, to allow for trade sanctions on all NAALC principles. Also proposed are an 'enforceable Code of Conduct for businesses' operating in more than one NAFTA country; and 'an annual Labor Information Audit' for businesses including information on employment conditions, contracts, and company operations.[25] The AFL-CIO calls for 'enforceable worker's rights and environmental standards in NAFTA's core; workers must be able to enforce core ILO rights such as freedom of associations, collective bargaining, freedom from child labour, labour discrimination or forced labour.[26]

The Maquiladora Health and Safety Network suggests any future trade deals need to promote 'upward leveling' of labour rights and standards, from a transnational 'floor' set by ILO conventions using 'best practices' for health and safety matters for instance. ILO and OECD declarations on labour rights and social responsibility of transnational companies might also be invoked, backed by enforcement using sanctions to secure compliance, directed at negligent governments and companies.

---

23 Economic Policy Institute, et. al. *The Failed Experiment: NAFTA at Three Years* (Washington: Economic Policy Institute, 1997), 19.

24 Lance Compa, 'Ensuring a Decent Global Workplace: Labor Rights belong in trade agreements'*Washington Post*, Aug. 1, 2001, A17.

25 'The Failed Experiment: NAFTA at Three Years' June 26, 1997, 19–20.

26 AFL-CIO Public Policy Department, 'NAFTA's Seven-Year Itch: Promised Benefits Not Delivered to Workers', 8.

Workers rights and health and safety deserve 'at least the same level of rapid, enforceable sanctions against employers and governments that the protection of copyrights and patents always enjoy'.[27]

Proponents of improved labour rights like HRW are skeptical of NAALC because of the lack of political will to make it work more effectively. Thus the 'NAFTA experience demonstrates that it is unrealistic to expect governments to police each other when it comes to protection of labor rights.' While NAALC includes provisions for arbitration panels and financial and trade penalties, the governments have been politically reluctant to use this mechanism to credibly act on issue of health and safety, child labour, etc.

> The potential of the NAFTA side agreement and of future efforts to protect labor rights in trade agreements can be realized only through an independent oversight body. That is the only way to take the enforcement of labor rights, and indeed, of other provisions of trade agreements, out of the realm of politics and into the realm of objective law enforcement.[28]

Human Rights Watch advocates fines for labour law violations which would be enforced by an independent body. Penalties would be imposed on the governments which failed to live up to their commitments on labour rights and could not become broad sanctions which would encourage protectionism or discourage trade and jobs.[29] A Canadian Postal Workers spokesperson suggested that there is 'a real imbalance of rights under NAFTA. .... On the one hand, there are weak provisions and conferences to deal with people's basic rights. On the other hand, there is a real enforcement mechanism for corporations with complaints.'[30] Equivalent enforcement for labour and human rights versus unfair trade practices, intellectual property rights and other business concerns should be instituted.

Obstacles to Improving NAALC

Given the North-South divide, the great asymmetry in North American trade relations and the rigidity of domestic institutions, and the balance of transnational social forces favouring corporate interests, the prospects for strengthening the NAALC into an effective supranational institution appear slim. The asymmetrical character of regionalism in NAFTA, with one dominant partner and two trade-dependent peripheral countries, is a significant barrier. On the one hand, the American hegemon

---

27 Garrett D. Brown, 'NAFTA's 10 Year Failure to Protect Mexican Workers' Health and Safety' Berkeley, CA: Maquiladora Health and Safety Support Network, December 2004, www.igc.org/mhssn, 2.

28 'Human Rights Watch Letter to Robert B. Zoellick, U.S. Trade Representative' http://www.hrw.org/press/2001/04/tradelet.htm accessed Apr. 4, 2002.

29 'Human Rights Watch Letter to Robert B. Zoellick, U.S. Trade Representative', April 25, 2001, http://www.hrw.org/press/2001/04/tradelet.htm, April 4, 2002.

30 'Conference On NAFTA Side Accord' *CUPW Communique*, Feb. 2, 2001, http://www.cupw-sttp.org/pages/document_eng.php?Doc_ID=11 April 4, 2002.

is unwilling to cede sovereignty to a transnational body, while on the other Mexico and Canada fear more enforceable standards backed by trade or financial penalties would work mostly against them. Secondly domestic political institutions mitigate against approval of strong measures. America's neo-liberal polity, and its effective congressional blocking mechanisms have marginalized labour's political clout. Mexico's transitional corporatism is evolving into congressionalism, and its president must deal with both entrenched corporate interests and a fractious newly empowered legislature. Meanwhile, Mexico's newly independent state and local authorities are often willing to thwart national measures designed to protect workers, as evident in local resistance to recognition of independent unions. Canada's decentralized federalism means only a few provinces have been willing to participate in NAALC, let alone strengthen it. And recent governments in Canada's contested minority parliaments have shown a preference for liberal integration models.

Transnational alliances of unions and social movements, albeit strengthened by the response to NAFTA and the use of NAALC, may be insufficient to overcome these obstacles. The best that can be expected will be increased pressures from civil society actors on the three nations to improve labour protections, against threats from liberalized, flexibilized labour markets. As Carty concludes

> grassroots efforts have proven far more effective than alternative 'top-down' mechanisms such as corporate codes of conduct or supranational initiatives such as NAFTA or the WTO. However, they have succeeded only when the state has been forced to play a proactive role in protecting worker rights. Thus, the goal should be to ensure workers have a democratic space to pressure their governments to enforce their rights. In lieu of any supranational enforcement policy, for the time being both a stronger governmental role and increased organization in civil society are needed to ensure workers' rights are upheld.[31]

The NAALC has potential to encourage this type of alternative to supranational enforcement of labour standards, though imperfectly, by strengthening the social groups pressing for sympathetic state action.

But such a social movement would have to overcome increasing weakness and fragmentation in organized labour itself. NAFTA itself has done little to strengthen the position of labour domestically. Research done by the NAALC secretariat indicates the trend towards a decline in union density, which is evident in all three NAFTA signatories. Many observers explain this trend with reference to structural characteristics of the economy, in which many new jobs are non-unionized personal services or part-time contractual employment. Canada has higher union density than its trading partners, owing primarily to the continued vigour of public sector unions, notwithstanding some weakening due to privatization, restraint policies, and provincial laws which have undermined unions over the past 25 years. Canada's union density has been constant recently after slow declines in the previous two decades.

---

31 Victoria Carty, 'New Social Movements and the Struggle for Workers' Rights in the Maquila Industry' *Theory and Science* 4, 3 (Winter, 2003).

The most notable weakening has been in the United States, where union density, always comparatively low, has decreased dramatically from 25% to just 13% of the workforce since the early 1970s. Mexican unionism, which was as high as 25% in the late 1980s decreased suddenly in the early 1990s to 16% before levelling off again, doubtless as a reflection of liberalizing trends which weakened the old economy based on corporatist unions in state owned industrial and resource sectors.[32] Hence, the economic and political strength of labour has been undermined most notably in the asymmetrical hegemon, whose interests dictate the broad parameters for NAFTA and NAALC. This sector was able to press for some attention to labour rights in the original side agreement but may not be well placed politically to demand a more powerful NAALC.

Social movement actions could create some pressure to for improvements, as the overall impact of NAFTA 'will be determined by the nature and character of resistance from below'. [33] The asymmetrical character of North American regionalism and the weak position of labour within domestic political institutions in all three states make any dramatic movement towards strengthening of the accord unlikely. There are also pronounced barriers to cooperation among workers across the North-South divide, which are difficult to overcome even with effective transnational mobilization. Whether this will generate the political momentum to strengthen NAALC remains to be seen. North America will not approach Europe for transnational integration but it could become a different place for workers in the post NAFTA era, if there is no retreat to protectionism, and the NAALC is not further diluted in the FTAA. But problems in reconciling the interests of civil societies and unions across the North-South divide, and the declining power of labour in post-Fordist economies in all three countries still limit these prospects.

There are critics of the NAALC who suggest that, as an unsuccessful political compromise which failed to broker support from organized labour, it may be prudent to eliminate it as a form of 'mercy killing' or 'prune' it back to a few tasks. For instance, a study for the Institute for International Economics advocates increased funding for the NAALC secretariat but with a reduced mandate to facilitate more effective implementation. This report suggests trimming the NAALC's to core policy areas – preventing discrimination, enforcing child and forced labour protections, and improving workplace health and safety. This would allow the NAALC to focus its efforts on important, but achievable objectives, rather than wasting resources on areas where no mutual agreement is likely, such as rights to association, collective bargaining and strikes.[34] Labour unions would surely resist the removal of rights of

---

32 Martin Dumas, *Recent Trends in Union Density in North America* Briefing Note Commission for Labour Cooperation August 2003. [cited July 22, 2004]. Available at http://www.naalc.org/english/pdf/april_03_english.pdf.

33 Walt Vanderbush 'Mexican Labor in the Era of Economic Restructuring and NAFTA: Working to create a Favorable Investment Climate' *Labor Studies Journal* 20 no. 4 (Winter, 1996), 58.

34 Gary Clyde Hufbauer and Jeffrey J. Schott, (assisted by Diana Orejas, Ben Goodrich and Yee Wong) 'North American Labor under NAFTA' Washington: Institute for International

association and collective bargaining from the mandate. Even if NAALC achievements in these areas has been limited, it has at least highlighted the deficiencies of labour law enforcement in all three NAFTA states and generated awareness of these issues, if not political pressure to rectify them.

Regionalism in a Global Context

The interaction of the North American region with the global economy has produced greater complications for the trade-labour nexus. While Mexican wages have evolved to average $1.50 an hour, highly competitive with North America, those in China range only from $.22 to $.25 per hour. Workers in border factories, who struggled for years to see wages rise to around $200 per week now see factories and jobs moving to China and elsewhere in Asia, where wages of $15 per week are common. Jobs which had migrated from the US South to Mexico in the past 15 years, have now relocated to China, especially in smaller consumer goods where shipping costs are low, though Mexico retains an advantage respecting larger items which are more expensive to ship.[35] Some estimates place job losses in the maquiladoras at up to 200,000 over two years prior to 2003.[36] Mexico fell behind China into third place as an exporter to the United States, despite its tremendous geographic advantage. And the rapid rise of unemployment escalated social problems like crime, pollution and poor health in already beleaguered border communities.[37]

The growth of globalization alongside regionalization has imposed new constraints on the NAFTA region which may make deepening or strengthening of social accords like the NAALC even more unlikely. The global market place has put a premium on restraint of labour costs, both in wages and expensive measures to protect worker rights. Competition from emerging economic powers like India and China and Southeast Asia makes upward leveling of labour rights untenable for developing countries. China's willingness to avoid even the minimal of global labour requirements (by using child labour for instance[38]) makes it harder for newly industrialized competitors like Mexico to enforce such rights.

This presents a dilemma for those seeking to promote labour standards within a regional trade arrangement like the NAFTA. This may be a difficult and elusive goal, as long as mobile capital can continue to move to alternative production sites outside

---

Economics, February, 2005 [cited April 16, 2004]. Available at www.iie.com/publications/papers/nafta-labor.pdf.

35 Mary Jordan 'Mexican border factories move to Asia' *Washington Post*, Jun. 21, 2002 [cited Jan 29, 2004]. Available at http://www.montereyherald.com/mld/mcherald/2002/06/21/business/3516040.htm.

36 Labor News Association, Exporting the Blame for Job Loss in the United States (Oct. 1, 2003) [cited at Jan. 27, 2004]. Available at http://www.laborresearch.org/print.php?id=321.

37 Leif Utne 'Giant sucking sound rises in the East' *Utne 116* 2003, 22–.

38 Ching-Ching Ni 'China's Use of Child Labor Emerges from the Shadows' *Los Angeles Times* May 13, 2005.

the region. This demonstrates a real limitation to regionalism in promoting a social dimension to trade, suggesting that global organizations like the WTO and ILO may be required to enforce labour rights. Notably, the WTO has insisted that the ILO provides the appropriate forum for defining and enforcing worker rights, and will not use its superior capacity to impose trade penalties to this end. One observer suggested that the WTO ministerial declaration at Singapore had explicitly 'rejected the use of labour standards for protectionist purposes and gave formal recognition to low wage labour as a comparative advantage for developing countries, while indicating that any future work on the issue must not question the legitimacy of this advantage or work to undermine it.'[39] However, the ILO has demonstrated an inability to act on violations of its standards and relies on self-policing by member states; the 'issue of labor rights, therefore, has been left in the hands of an organization structurally incapable of enforcing its own provisions and mandate'.[40]

Advocates of global labour standards have sought a middle ground, promoting a basic set of guarantees modeled on those core elements of the ILO charter which most states have ratified. These include basic rights to freedom of association and organization for workers, rights to collective bargaining, non-discrimination in employment on gender or ethnic lines, and prevention of the abuses of child or forced labour and slavery. Some effort to promote minimum working conditions, including wages and protections for health and safety in the workplace are advocated, though with recognition of the need to allow for wide differences in national levels of development and capacities to promote these standards. But developing world opposition to labour standards as protection and a lack of sufficient political will in the north make global or WTO action unlikely. Advocates concede, 'Pursuing a global social clause in the WTO appears, at least for the near future, to be an impractical prospect', and regional action may be all that can be expected.[41]

While it remains true that the China card is strategically overplayed by those seeking to keep labor rights and wages limited, the competitive forces at work on a global scale and MNCs advantages of mobility and unity will make regional labour arrangements limited in effectiveness for some time to come. But that presents a dismal prospect, given the difficulties in securing a social dimension in the Western hemisphere between developing and developed states. It seems unlikely that NAALC can be strengthened or enforced more effectively even if transnational

---

39 Nigel Haworth and Stephen Hughes, 'Death of a Social Clause? Reconstructing the trade and labour standards debate in the Asia-pacific' Paper to the International Conference on Labour Standards and Human Rights University of California, Berkeley, January 1998. [cited Feb 4, 2004]. Available at http://www.iir.berkeley.edu/clre/publications/death.html#intro.

40 Pharis J. Harvey, Terry Collingsworth, and Bama Athreya 'Summary: A Plan of Action for Including a Social Clause in U.S. Trade Policy as Outlined in Developing Effective Mechanisms for Implementing Labor Rights in the Global Economy' International Labor Rights Fund, [cited Jan. 26, 2004]. Available at http://www.laborrights.org/projects/globalecon/ilrf/intro.html.

41 Harvey, Collingsworth, and Athreya, 2004.

union and social movement pressure mounts, and transborder bureaucratic and cultural integration proceeds.

Limits of Regionalism in Labour Affairs

Hence the prospects for augmenting the NAALC arrangements do not seem propitious. Essentially, the asymmetrical regionalism of North America, which crosses the divide between the developed and developing world, creates states with very different interests and orientations towards enforceable labor standards. The limited power of labour and social movements coupled with strong transnational integration of capital via MNCs and modern capital markets puts unions in a weak position to secure support from national states for a stronger side agreement with enforceable standards. In addition, the immersion of this regional system in a hemispheric and global context, where competitive capitalism provides exit strategies for investors and firms dissatisfied with what they consider inflated labour protections and standards, makes the task of elevating those standards highly difficult. This situation is ripe for the 'race to the bottom' feared by proponents of labour rights. This scenario clearly illustrates the limits of regionalism as a means for social protection in an increasingly integrated global economy.

Ultimately, the global may trump the regional on the labour dimension of trade for the forseeable future. There are reasons for disillusion with many aspects of NAFTA, as the US insists on the primacy of its trade laws on contentious issues like softwood lumber. Indeed NAFTA as a whole must be regarded as having exacerbated inequalities, with Mexico and Canada more dependent than ever on US markets and economic decisions.

> In contrast to the conscious effort made during the long decades that went into the EU's institutional development to mitigate economic and political disparities among its member states, NAFTA was carefully conceived so as to prevent, rather than promote, continental political integration. As a result it arguably serves to exacerbate, rather than attenuate, the extreme power asymmetry between its peripheral members, Canada and Mexico, and its hegemon, the USA.[42]

Both the hegemon and its smaller partners were responsible for the limits to this integration and the weak governing structures created under the NAALC. The smaller partners were jealous of their sovereignty and fearful of the disproportionate penalties they would face as dependent traders targeted for labour violations by their larger partner. And the US treats its constitutional order and congressional autonomy as inviolable limiting a willingness to commit to supranational institutions (as evident in the current spate of unilateralism in many areas, from global warming

---

42 Stephen Clarkson, 'Democratic Deficit or Democratic Vacuum? The North American Variant of the New Regionalism' International Political Science Association, Special Session: Critical Political Economy and New Regionalisms August 2000 http://www.chass.utoronto. ca/~clarkson/manuscripts/IPSA%20DemVac%20July26.html.

and nuclear disarmament to trading relations). Abrogation of NAFTA now seems prohibitively costly for Mexico or Canada, as critics of the accord warned. Therefore, North American regionalism may persist or deepen with increased talk of a security perimeter, and immigration coordination. But the unequal results of NAFTA may prevent its development into a broader regionalism of the kind found in Europe. In particular, the failure of Mexico to prosper and the continued impoverishment of many of its citizens will act as a constraint on full regionalization or deepened institutionalization of NAFTA; tensions over migration, drug trafficking and other trans-border concerns have pushed the two partners farther apart, stalling further discussion of integrating labour markets or creating more powerful transnational institutions. Pastor and Poitras suggest that NAFTA's future evolution depends on finding mechanisms to deal with these inequalities, such as social fund based on the European model, or an immigration regime that allows smoother adjustment of labour markets to the new transnational regional economy. Only through such measures can further deepening of the NAFTA region and fuller institutionalization of the regional space ultimately occur. As Carranza argues, these authors acknowledge a political dimension to the new regionalism, which cannot be assumed to have an inexorable logic based on continental economic integration.[43] Such resolutions may take acts of political will which at the moment appear distant in the neo-liberal security emphasis in trilateral relations.

While the new regionalism appears pronounced in trade, finance, investor rights and intellectual property in North America, the NAALC experience indicates the limits of regionalism in labour relations, working conditions, and social standards. But regional integration is not confined to formal transnational institutions such as the NAALC. Hence the nature of the new regionalism in labour affairs may not hinge on the effectiveness of state-to-state and transnational arrangements such as the NAALC, but rather is a more complicated and variegated phenomenon. As Soderbaum argues, 'the new regionalism is characterized by its multi-dimensionality, complexity, fluidity and non-conformity, and by the fact that it involves a variety of state and non-state actors, who often come together in rather informal multi-actor coalitions'.[44] Chase Dunn agrees that transnational movements from below have the potential to challenge liberalizing projects like the NAFTA.[45] It may be the potential and limits to the intervention by non-state actors, such as transnational unions, human rights NGOs, consumer groups, anti-sweatshop campaigners etc. which ultimately determine if a labour element to North American regionalism deepens or atrophies.

---

43 Mario E. Carranza, 'Neighbors or Partners? NAFA and the Politics of Regional Economic Integration in North America' *Latin American Politics and Society* 44 (2004) 145–49.

44 Frederick Soderbaum, 'Introduction: Theories of New Regionalism' in Soderbaum and Timothy Shaw (eds.) *Theories of new regionalism: a Palgrave reader* (London: Palgrave, 2003), 1–21.

45 Christopher Chase-Dunn 'Globalization from below: Toward a collectively rational and democratic global commonwealth' *Annals of the American Academy of Political and Social Science* 581, (2002), 48.

Frundt is generally pessimistic respecting union advances in light of global restructuring, privatization and government reductions of worker protections. However, he sees hope for collaborations with a wider social constituency of NGOs including those attentive to women and indigenous peoples.[46] Furthermore, the use of corporate codes of conduct provide a tool for transnational collaboration which can directly benefit workers in the developing world and forge cooperation between unions and consumer groups as well. If these codes are effective in securing empowerment rights for workers to countervail MNC power, and are based on sustained transnational collaboration and advocacy, they may have an appreciable and sustainable effect on working conditions.

> Codes of conduct, therefore, must be viewed as part of an emerging transnational field of labor regulation that crucially includes other types of labor standards – national state laws, international treaties, unilateral sanctions, and social clauses in trade agreements – as well as the TANs that exert the requisite leverage for the formulation and enforcement of such standards.[47]

While side agreements may not be sufficient, such social clauses could remain part of a larger picture of devices to limit or challenge abuses under liberalization.

Hence it is possible that transnational progress and resistance will proceed largely outside the established labour movement, and certainly outside the NAALC, but possibly in ways supportive of workers rights. As O'Brien asserts, labour activism has moved outside international union organizations to include actions by 'grassroots union locals' and supportive social groups. Using new information technologies, 'labor activism is now feasible via networks of concerned people rather than reliant on hierarchical, bureaucratic internationals'.[48] But unions have a stronger institutional base and a disciplined, distinct membership occasionally capable of effective collective action backed by work disruptions, which makes labour an indispensable element in any such transnational coalition. It remains important for unions to take the lead among social movements in seeking human and worker rights guarantees in whatever form as the global economy progresses. The coalitions seeking such social alternatives to neo-liberalism will be 'janus-like' as diverse social movements emerge in the regional and global economy.[49]

---

46 Henry J Frundt, 'Central American unions in the era of globalization' *Latin American Research Review* 37 (2002), 7–53.

47 Cesar A Rodriguez-Garavito, 'Global Governance and Labor Rights: Codes of Conduct and Anti-Sweatshop Struggles in Global Apparel Factories in Mexico and Guatemala' *Politics and Society* 33 (2005), 206.

48 Robert O'Brien, 'The Agency of Labour in a Changing Global Order' in Richard Stubbs and Geoffrey R.D. Underhill (eds.) *Political economy and the Global Order* (3rd. Ed.) (Don Mills, Ont.: Oxford, 2005), 229.

49 Owen Worth, 'The Janus-like Character of Counter-hegemony: Progressive and Nationalist Responses to Neoliberalism' *Global Society*, 16 (2002).

Robinson believes that the initial struggle against NAFTA encouraged trans-national activism among unions and a broad coalition of sympathetic interests which provides a basis for a counter strategy to neo-liberalism in North America. In his words,

> the fight against the NAFTA – despite its outcome – has already had a positive impact on the labour movements of the two countries. Above all, it has been an important catalyst to creative, constructive thinking about what a superior alternative to the neoliberal agenda might be in a post-Cold War world. In the United States, the struggle created the first prototype of the alliance of social movements that is arguably necessary to realize politically such an alternative.[50]

Throughout the cases studies, evidence has been provided to indicate that these links have persisted and proliferated over the past 12 years, induced in part by the NAFTA labour accord. The submissions and cooperative activities reveal the successes and limits of such coalitions across national boundaries and the North-South divide, as NAFTA induced integration accentuates the challenges facing workers. If integration continues to impose costs on labour and its allies, then perhaps the motivation for activism may increase[51]. But the structural conditions for successful mobilization may also diminish with declining labour unity, union density, and increased competition between workers in the three nations.

The question remains whether social constituencies can coalesce across such different national and economic circumstances sufficiently to generate a meaningful regionalization in labour affairs, despite the limits imposed by North-South divisions, asymmetry and rigid domestic institutions, neo-liberalism and corporate dominance. The sad reality for the near term may be that the strength of the liberalizing agenda makes it unmoveable, and millions of workers, in this region and others, will suffer the consequences – diminished rights, decreased wages, unsafe workplaces, occupational illnesses, gender discrimination, abusive child labour, displacement of indigenous communities, mistreatment of migrants, and poverty for the majority who remain outside the protection of unions and social programs. As the submissions and cooperative activities reveal, NAFTA's labour accord can make us aware of the deep desperation caused by inequitable liberalizing integration; but it has limited ability to promote improvements or generate countervailing regional coalitions which can challenge this neo-liberal consensus. Whether the NAALC eventually promotes effective regional coalitions which can seek higher labour standards remains uncertain – so far its limited effects have revealed the limits of regionalism in labour affairs.

---

50 Ian Robinson, 'NAFTA, social unionism, and labour movement power in Canada and the United States' *Relations Industrielles* 49, (1994), 668.

51 S. Babson, 'Cross-border Trade with Mexico and the Prospect for Worker Solidarity: the Case of Mexico' *Critical Sociology*, 26 (2000), 13–35.

Bibliography

Abbott, Michael 'Labour-side Agreements Involving Canada: Current Practices and Comparative Effectiveness' Ottawa: Canada Industrial Relations Board, 2004 [cited Sept. 12 2004]. Available at http://www.cira-acri.ca/IIRA%20CIRA%20docs/ Abbott,%20Michael.pdf.

Abbott, Frederick M. 'The NAFTA and the Political Economy of Regionalism' *The North American Integration Regime and its Implications for the World Trading System* Harvard Law School Jean Monnet Chair Working Papers, Available at http://www.jeanmonnetprogram.org/papers/99/990200.html.

Adams, Roy 'Using the North American Agreement on Labour Cooperation to Achieve Industrial Relations Reform.' *Canadian Labour and Employment Law Journal*, 7 (1999), 31–44.

AFL-CIO 'Fair Trade or Free Trade? *Understanding CAFTA (Labor Rights Provisions in CAFTA are Inadequate)* [cited June 21, 2005]. Available at www. wola.org/economic/brief_cafta_labor_april04.pdf.

AFL-CIO, 'Taste of Victory' *AFL-CIO Work in Progress* September 20, 1999 http:// www.aflcio.org/publ/wip1999/wip0920.htm

Alexander, Robin and Gilmore, Peter 'The emergence of cross-border labor solidarity' NACLA *Report on the Americas* 28, (1994), 42–48.

Allen, Bruce 'Tightening the belt: labour law 'reform' in Mexico' *Briar Patch* 27 (Dec 1998/Jan 1999), 25–6.

Alston, Philip 'Labor Rights Provisions in U.S. Trade Law: Aggressive Unilateralism?' in Lance A Compa and Stephen F Diamond eds. *Human rights, labor rights, and international trade* Philadelphia: University of Pennsylvania Press, 1996, 71–97.

Amarillo Globe-News Nov. 25, 1999.

American Center for International Labor Solidarity (AFL-CIO) *Justice for All: A Guide to Worker Rights in the Global Economy* Washington: ACILS, 2003.

Andersen, Sarah, Cavanagh, John, and Smith, Dan, '1st. Anniversary Report: Clinton's NAFTA Promises to Congress and Workers' Alliance for Responsible Trade/Citizen's Trade Campaign, Nov. 17, 1994.

Babson, S. 'Cross-border Trade with Mexico and the Prospect for Worker Solidarity: the Case of Mexico' *Critical Sociology*, 26 (2000), 13–35.

Bachman, S.L. 'Young workers in Mexico's economy: NAFTA aims at curbing child labor, but it's rampant south of the border' *U.S. News & World Report*, 123, Sept 1, 1997, 40–.

Bacon, David 'Just south of Texas, democracy faces its hardest test' *Canadian Dimension* 34 (2000), 25–7.

270 *The Limits of Regionalism*

Bacon, David *Children of NAFTA: Labor Wars on the US/Mexico Border* Berkeley: University of California Press, 2004.

Bacon, David 'Unions Without Borders' *The Nation* Jan. 22, 2001 [cited October 12 2003]. Available at http://www.thenation.com/docPrint.mhtml?i=20010122&s=bacon.

Bailey, Norman 'The Economic Effects of NOT Passing the NAFTA,' in Amber H. Moss, ed. *Assessments of the North American Free Trade Agreement* New Brunswick, N.J.: Transaction Books, 1993, 1–18.

Bartlett, Steve 'Teamwork: The illegal management tool' *Management Review* 85 Apr 1996, 7.

Bartow, Ann M. 'The Rights of Workers in Mexico' *Comparative Labor Law Journal* 11, 1990, 182–202.

Befort, Stephen F. and Cornett, Virgina E. 'Beyond the Rhetoric of the NAFTA Treaty Debate: A Comparative Analysis of Labor and Employment Law in Mexico and the United States' *Comparative Labor Law Journal*, 17 (1996), 269–313.

Bensusán, Graciela 'Integración regional y cambio institucional: la reforma laboral en el norte del continente.' in Graciela Bensusán ed., *Estándares laborales después del TLCAN* México: FLACSO/Fundación, 1999, 177–209.

Bhagwati, Jagdish 'Free Trade, 'Fairness' and the New Protectionism: Reflections on an Agenda for the World Trade Organisation' *24th Wincott Memorial Lecture,* Westminster, Oct. 25, 1994 London: Institute of Economic Affairs/Wincott Foundation, 1995.

Bhagwati, Jagdish 'The Demands to Reduce Domestic Diversity Among Trading Nations' in Bhagwati, J. and Hudec, Robert E. eds. *Fair Trade and Harmonization: Prerequisites for Free Trade?* Cambridge: MIT Press, 1996, 9–40.

Bhagwati, Jagdish 'After Seattle: Free Trade and the WTO,' *International Affairs* 77, (2001), 15–29.

Block, Richard N and Karen Roberts, 'A comparison of labour standards in the United States and Canada,' *Industrial Relations* 55, (2000), 273–307.

Block, Richard N. Karen Roberts, Cynthia Ozeki and Myron J. Roomkin, 'Models of international labor standards,' *Industrial Relations* 40 (2001), 258–93.

Blouin, Rodrigue and May Morpaw, 'L'Accord nord-américain de coopération dans le domaine du travail.' in Rodrigue Blouin and Anthony Giles eds. *L'intégration économique en Amérique du Nord et les relations industrielles* Québec: Les Presses de l'Université Laval, 1998, 177–199.

Blum, Albert and Tanski,, Janet 'Workers of the hemisphere, unite! Your wages depend on it!' *Commonweal* 121 (June 17, 1994), 18–21.

Bolle, Mary Jane *NAFTA labor side agreement: lessons for the worker rights and fast-track debate* Washington, D.C.: Congressional Research Service, 2001.

Bourque, Deborah 'Denial of Basic Rights – The Situation of Rural and Suburban Mail Couriers' Presented to the Workshop on the Right to Organize and Bargain Collectively in Canada and the United States Toronto, February 1–2, 2001.

Brennan, Barry 'Canadian Labor Today: Partial Successes, Real Challenges,' *Monthly Review* 57 (2005), 46–61.

Briones, Joshua 'Paying the Price for NAFTA: NAFTA's Effect on Women and Children Laborers in Mexico' *UCLA Women's Law Journal* 9 (1998–99), 301–27.

Brown, Drusilla K. 'Labor Standards: Where Do They Belong on the International Trade Agenda?' *Journal of Economic Perspectives* 15 (2001), 89–112.

Brown, Garrett D. 'NAFTA's 10 Year Failure to Protect Mexican Workers' Health and Safety' Berkeley, CA: Maquiladora Health and Safety Support Network, December 2004, www.igc.org/mhssn.

Brown, Drusilla K. Deardorff, Alan V. and Robert M. Stern 'Trade and Labor Standards' *Open Economies Review* 9 (1998), 171–194.

Brown, Drusilla K. Deardoff, Alan V. and Stern, Robert M. 'International Labor Standards and Trade: A Theoretical Analysis' Bhagwati, J. and Hudec, Robert E. eds. *Fair Trade and Harmonization: Prerequisites for Free Trade?* Cambridge: MIT Press, 1996, 123–167.

Burfisher, Mary E. Robinson, Sherman and Thierfelder, Karen 'The Impact of NAFTA on the United States' *Journal of Economic Perspectives* 15 (2001), 125–144.

Business Week Jan 25, 1993, April 4, 1994.

Cameron, Maxwell A. 'North American Free Trade, Public Goods and Asymmetrical Bargaining: The Strategic Choices for Canada,' *Frontera Norte* 3, 6, (1992), 47–64.

Cameron, Maxwell A. and Brian W. Tomlin, *The Making of NAFTA: How the Deal Was Done* Ithaca: Cornell University Press, 2000.

Camp, Roderic Ai *Politics in Mexico* (2nd. Ed.) New York: Oxford, 1996.

Campaign for Labor Rights, *Workers in the Global Economy Report on a Labor Rights-Immigrant Worker Advocacy Dialogue: Labor Rights, Migrant Workers' Rights and Immigration Policy in an International Economy*, June 1999 [cited June 18, 2002]. Available at http://www.laborrights.org/projects/globalecon/immigrant/index.html.

Campbell, Bruce 'A Canadan Labour Perspective on the North American Free Trade Agreement' Raphael Fernadez de Castro, Monica Verea Campos and Sydney Weintraub, eds. *Sectoral Labor effects of North American Free Trade* Austin: U.S. Mexican Policy Studies Program, University of Texas, 1993, 65–72.

Campbell, Bruce, Andrew Jackson, Mehrene Larudee, and Teresa Gutierrez Haces *Labour market effects under CUFTA/NAFTA* ILO, Employment and Training Papers, 29. Geneva: International Labour Organization, 1999.

Canada, Department of Human Resources (Labour), numerous documents in text or electronic format.

Canadian Dimension, 32, 5 Sept-Oct 1998.

Canadian Foundation for the Americas *'Civil Society and the Summit Process' Summit 2001: Going Beyond Trade* Ottawa: FOCAL and Summit of the Americas Centre, Florida International University, 1999.

Canadian Labour Congress, 'Chapter 5 The Social Dimension of NAFTA: A Work in Progress' *NAFTA: The Social Dimensions of North American Economic*

Integration http://www.clc-ctc.ca/policy/trade/nafta5.html April 4, 2002.

Canadian Labour Congress *CLC – What's New: The Morning NAFTA* June 1997 No. 9. http://www.clc-ctc.com/news/m-nafta2.html.

Canadian News Digest Tuesday, Feb. 17, 1998.

Canadian-Press-Newswire April 6, 1998.

Canadian Union of Postal Workers *Your Public Post Service: More than Just the Mail More than Just the Quebec-Windsor Corridor (Submission to the Canadian Government on Public Postal Services and the World Trade Organization's General Agreement on Trade in Services)* Ottawa: CUPW, 2000.

Cappyuns, E. 'Linking Labor Standards and Trade Sanctions: An Analysis of their Current Relationship' *Columbia Journal of Transactional Law* 36, (1998), 659–86.

Carr, Barry, 'Globalization from Below: labour internationalism under NAFTA' *International Social Science Journal* 51 (1999), 49–59.

Carranza, Mario E. 'Neighbors or Partners? NAFTA and the Politics of Regional Economic Integration in North America' *Latin American Politics and Society* 44 (2004), 141–157.

Carty, Victoria 'New Social Movements and the Struggle for Workers' Rights in the Maquila Industry' *Theory and Science* 4, (2003), http://theoryandscience.icaap. org/content/vol004.002/02_carty.html.

Centro de Reflexión y Acción Laboral de Fomento Cultural y Educativo, A.C., *Derechos Humanos Laborales en México: entre la imagen protectora y una política de represión, Informe de violación de los Derechos Humanos Laborales en México, durante 1997*, Mexico: Centro, 1998.

Cetré Castillo, Moisés. 'Comercio internacional y normas laborales: el debate actual.' *Comercio Exterior* 48, (1998), 797–803.

Chan, Anita and Ross, Robert J.S. 'Racing to the bottom: international trade without a social clause' *Third World Quarterly* 24, (2003), 1011–28.

Charnovitz, Steve 'The Influence of International Labour Standards on the World Trading Regime' *International Labour Review* 126, (1987), 565–584.

Chase-Dunn, Christopher 'Globalization from below: Toward a collectively rational and democratic global commonwealth' *Annals of the American Academy of Political and Social Science* 581, (2002), 48–61.

Chew, Diana and Posthuma, Richard, 'International employment dispute resolution under NAFTA's side agreement on labor.' *Labor Law Journal*, 53 (2002), 38–45.

Chin, David, *A Social Clause for Labour's Cause: Global Trade and Labour Standards – A Challenge for the New Millennium* London: Institute of Employment Rights, 1998.

Clarkson, Stephen 'Democratic Deficit or Democratic Vacuum? The North American Variant of the New Regionalism' International Political Science Association, Special Session: Critical Political Economy and New Regionalisms August 2000 http:// www.chass.utoronto.ca/~clarkson/manuscripts/IPSA%20DemVac%20July26. html.

Cobián, Felipe and Salvador Corro, 'Desde 1998, las autoridades conocían la inseguridad en TAESA' *Proceso* Nov, 1999.

Cohen, Larry and Early, Steve 'Defending Workers' Rights in the Global Economy: The CWA Experience,' in Nissen, Bruce, ed. *Which Direction for Organized Labor? Essays on Organizing, Outreach, and Internal Transformations* Detroit, MI: Wayne State University Press, 1999, 143–164.

Collier, Ruth *The Contradictory Alliance* Cambridge: Cambridge University Press, 1995.

'Comisiones trilaterales, sin caracter supranational: Mexico y Canada' *El Dia* (Apr. 15, 1993).

Commission for Labour Cooperation: numerous documents in text and Internet format.

Compa, Lance 'International Labour Rights and the Sovereignty Question: NAFTA and Guatemala, Two Case Studies,' *Journal of International Law and Policy* 9, 1 (1993), 117–150.

Compa, Lance 'International Labor Rights and NAFTA's Labor Side Agreement' *LASA Forum*, Summer 1999, [cited April 4, 2002]. Available at http://lasa. international.pitt.edu/Compa.htm.

Compa, Lance 'NAFTA's Labor Side Accord: A Thee-Year Accounting' *NAFTA: Law and Business Review of the Americas* (1997), 6–23.

Compa, Lance 'NAFTA's labour side agreement five years on: progress and prospects for the NAALC' *Canadian Labour and Employment Law Journal*, 7, (1999), 2–30.

Compa, Lance 'The First NAFTA Labor Cases: A New International Labor Rights Regime Takes Shape' *U.S.-Mexico Labor Law Journal* 3, (1995), 155–81.

Compa, Lance 'The North American Agreement on Labor Cooperation and international labor solidarity' *Memorias del Encuentro Trinacional de Laboralistas Democráticos* México: Universidad Nacional Autónoma de México, 1999, 185–211.

Compa, Lance 'NAFTA's labor side agreement and international labor solidarity.' *Antipode*, 33 (2001), 451–467.

Compa, Lance 'Labor Rights and Labor Standards in International Trade' *Law and Policy in International Business* 25 (1993), 165–192.

Compa, Lance 'The North American Free Trade Agreement (NAFTA) and the North American Agreement on Labor Cooperation (NAALC)' In R. Blanpain ed. *International encyclopaedia for labour law and industrial relations*, The Hague: Kluwer Law International, Suppl. 2001.

Compa, Lance, *Justice for All: The Struggle for Workers Rights in Mexico*, Washington: AFL-CIO Solidarity Center 2003, p. 18, [cited April 11, 2004]. Available at http://www.solidaritycenter.org/docUploads/Solidarity%20Mexico %20final%20pdf%2011-17-03.pdf?CFID=1165299&CFTOKEN=82992828.

Cooper, Andrew F. 'NAFTA and the politics of regional trade,' in Brian Hocking, and Steven McGuire eds. *Trade Politics: International, Domestic and Regional Responses* New York: Routledge, 1999, 229–45.

Daily Labor Report Feb. 10, 1995, June 27, 1995, July 27, 1995, Sept. 11, 1995, Sept. 18, 1995, August 13, 1996, Nov. 13, 1996, Feb. 10, 1998, April 29, 1998, Feb. 3, 1999, Sept. 8, 1999, Feb. 15, 2000, Nov. 30, 2000, June 12, 2002.

Davis, Diane E. 'Mexico's New Politics: Changing Perspectives on Free Trade' *World Policy Journal,* 9, (1992), 655–671.

de Wet, Erika 'Labor Standards in the Globalized Economy: The Inclusion of a Social Clause in the General Agreement On Tariff and Trade/ World Trade Organization,' *Human Rights Quarterly* 17, (1995), 443–462.

de Buen, Néstor 'A cinco años del Acuerdo de Cooperación Laboral anexo al Tratado de Libre Comercio.' *Memorias del Encuentro Trinacional de Laboralistas Democráticos.* México: Universidad Nacional Autónoma de México, 1999, 81–93.

de Buen, Néstor. 'El Acuerdo de Cooperación Laboral de América del Norte.' *El Cotidiano,* 15, (March/April 1999), 5–12.

De Mestral, A.L.C. 'The significance of the NAFTA side agreements on environmental and labor cooperation.' *Arizona Journal of International and Comparative Law,* 15 (1998), 169–185.

Delp, Linda et. al., *NAFTA's Labor Side Agreement: Fading into Oblivion? An Assessment of Workplace Health & Safety Cases* Los Angeles: UCLA Center for Labor Research and Education, 2004.

Diaz, Luis Miguel 'Private Rights Under the Environmental and Labor Agreements' *U.S. Mexico Law Journal.* 2, 1994. 11–24.

Dickey, Sheryl 'The Free Trade Area of the Americas and human rights concerns.' *Human Rights Brief,* 8 (Spring 2001), 26–28.

DiMaggio, Paul J. and Walter W. Powell, The *New Institutionalism in Organizational Analysis* Chicago: University of Chicago Press, 1991.

Dobell, Rod 'A Social Charter for a North American Community' *Isuma* 1, 2000, 4; [cited April 16, 2005]. Available at http://www.isuma.net/v01n01/dobell1/dobell1_e.pdf.

Dombois, Rainer and Winter, Jens *A Matter of Deficient Design? Observations on Interaction and Cooperation problems in the NAALC* Bremen: University of Bremen, Institut Arbeit und Wirtshaft, 2003.

Doran, Charles F. 'Building a North American community' *Current History* 94 (1995), 97–101.

Drache, Daniel *Trade, Development and the Doha Round: A Sure Bet or a Train Wreck?* Centre for International Governance Innovation, Working Paper No. 5, March 2006. [cited March 28, 2006] Available at http://www.cigionline.ca/publications/docs/Trade_Dev_Drache.pdf.

Dumas, Martin *Recent Trends in Union Density in North America* Briefing Note Commission for Labour Cooperation August 2003. http://www.naalc.org/english/pdf/april_03_english.pdf.

Durand Ponte, Victor Manuel, 'The Confederation of Mexican Workers, the Labor Congress and the Crisis of Mexico's Social Pact', in Kevin Middlebook, ed.

Unions, Workers and the State in Mexico San Diego: Centre for U.S.-Mexican Studies, University of California, 85–104.

Dwasi, Jane 'Kenya: a Study in International Labor Standards and Their Effect on Working Women in Developing Countries: the Case for Integration of Enforcement Issues in the World Bank's Policies' *Wisconsin International Law Journal* 347, (Summer, 1999), 347–60.

Economic Policy Institute, et. al. *The Failed Experiment: NAFTA at Three Years* Washington: Economic Policy Institute, 1997.

Economist Nov. 12, 2005.

'EFCO's Illegal Four: Committees that went astray' *Personnel Journal* Feb., 1996, 87.

Ehrenberg, Daniel S. 'From Intention to Action: an ILO-GATT/WTO Enforcement Regime for International Labor Rights' in Lance Compa and S. Diamond eds. *Human Rights, Labor Rights and International Trade* Philadelphia: University of Pennsylvania Press, 1996, 163–80.

El Financiero International, March 14–20, May 9–15, 1994, May 4–10, 1998, March 23, 1999.

New York Times, March 19, 21, 1994, Feb. 28, 1996, Oct. 13 1997, Dec. 6, 20, 1997, Aug. 5, 1998.

Elliot, Kimberley and, Richard Freeman *Can Labor Standards Improve Under Globalization?* Washington: Institute for International Economics, 2003.

Elliott, Kimberly A. 'International Labor Standards and Trade: What Should Be Done? In Jeffrey J. Schott ed. *Launching New Global Trade Talks* Washington DC: Institute for International Economics, 1998, 165–177.

El Universal, Dec. 3, 1998, Nov. 13, 1999.

Elwell, Christine *Human Rights, Labour Standards and the New World Trade Organization: Opportunities for a Linkage* Montreal: International Centre for Human Rights and Democratic Development, 1995.

Englehart, Frederick 'Withered Giants: Mexican and US Organized Labor and the North American Agreement on Labor Cooperation' *Case Western Reserve Journal of International Law* 29 (1997), 321–88.

Ethier, Wilfred J. 'The new regionalism in the Americas: A theoretical framework,' *North American Journal of Economics and Finance* 12, 2 (2001), 159–172.

Evans, Peter 'Fighting Marginalization with Transnational Networks: Counter-hegemonic Globalization.' *Contemporary Sociology*, 29 (2000), 230–41.

Faulkner, Gerda 'The EU's social dimension' in Cini, Michelle ed. *European Union Politics* New York, Oxford, 2003, 264–77.

Faux, Jeff 'The fast track to globalization: can labor slow it down?' *WorkingUSA*, (March-April 1998), 10–22.

Favilla-Solano, Teresa R. 'Legal Mechanisms for Enforcing Labor Rights Under NAFTA' *University of Hawaii Law Review* 18 (1996), 293–338.

Federal Register Nov. 10, 1994, September 7, 2000.

Flanagan, Robert J. 'Labor Standards and International Competitive Advantage' in Robert J. Flanagan and Gould, William B. IV eds. *International Labor Standards:*

Globalization, Trade and Public Policy Palo Alto CA: Stanford University Press, 2003, 13–40.

Fredericton Daily Gleaner Oct. 17, 2001.

Freeman, Richard B. 'International Labor Standards and World Trade: Friends or Foes' in Schott, Jeffrey J. ed. *The World Trading System: Challenges Ahead* Washington, D.C.: Institute for International Economics, 1996, 87–114.

Freidman, Sheldon 'Trade Adjustment Assistance: No Cure for a Bad NAFTA, but Badly Needed to Help NAFTA's Victims' in Raphael Fernadez de Castro, Monica Verea Campos and Sydney Weintraub, eds. *Sectoral Labor effects of North American Free Trade* Austin: U.S. Mexican Polcy Studies Program, University of Texas, 1993, 73–86.

Frundt, Henry J 'Central American unions in the era of globalization' *Latin American Research Review* 37 (2002), 7–53.

Gacek, Stanley 'The political context for the NAALC – the viewpoint of the AFL-CIO and the U.S. labor movement.' *Memorias del Encuentro Trinacional de Laboralistas Democráticos* México: Universidad Nacional Autónoma de México, 1999, 213–219.

Gagnon, Mona-Josée 'Trade union cooperation in the NAFTA area' *Transfer: European Review of Labour and Research*, 6, (2000), 43–57.

Garvey, Jack I. 'Trade law and quality of life – dispute resolution under the NAFTA side accords on labor and the environment' *American Journal of International Law*. 89 (1995), 439–453.

Guardian April 30, 2003.

General Accounting Office, *North American Free Trade Agreement: Structure and Status of Implementing Organizations* Washington: GAO, Oct. 1994.

Globe and Mail Feb. 8, 1995, March 6, 1997, August, 21, 1998, March 16, 1999, April 14, 1999, March 22, 2006.

Goldin, Amy H. 'Collective Bargaining in Mexico: Stifled by the Lack of Democracy in Trade Unions' *Comparative Labor Law Journal* 11, 1990, 206–11.

Golub, Stephen S. 'Are International Standards Needed to Prevent Social Dumping?' *Finance and Development* December, 1997, 21 [cited Dec. 15, 2002]. Available at http://www.worldbank.org/fandd/english/1297/articles/041297.htm.

Gotbaum, Victor 'American Labor Looks at the U.S.– Mexico Free Trade Agreement' in Raphael Fernandez de Castro, Monica Verea Campos and Sidney Weintraub eds. *Sectoral Labor Effects of North American Free Trade* Austin: University of Texas, 1993. 103–107.

Gould, Kenneth A., Tammy L. Lewis and J. Timmons Roberts 'Blue-Green Coalitions: Constraints and Possibilities in the Post 9–11 Political Environment' *Journal of World-Systems Research,* 10 (2004), 91–116.

Grace, Brewster 'WTO Trade and Labour Standards' *Foreign Policy in Focus* 5, (2000), 1–4.

Graubart, Jonathan 'Giving teeth to NAFTA's Labour Side Agreement.' in John Kirton and Virginia Maclaren eds. *Linking Trade, Environment, and Social*

Cohesion – NAFTA Experiences, Global Challenges Aldershot: Ashgate, 2002, 203–22.

Greider, William 'A New Giant Sucking Sound', *The Nation* Dec. 31. 2001, [cited Feb. 3, 2004]. Available at http://www.thenation.com/doc.mhtml?i=20011231&s =greider.

Grinspun, Ricardo and, Maxwell Cameron, 'The Political Economy of North American Integration,' in Grinspun and Cameron eds. *The Political Economy of North American Free Trade* Montreal/Kingston: McGill-Queen's University Press, 1993, 3–25.

Grugel, Jean and Wil Hout, 'Regions, regionalism and the South,' in Hout and Grugel eds. *Regionalism Across the North–South Divide: State strategies and Globalization* London: Routledge, 1999, 3–13.

Guerra, Maria Teresa and Anna L. Torriente, 'The NAALC and the Labor Laws of Mexico and the United States' *Arizona Journal of International and Comparative Law* 14 (1997), 503–526.

Gunderson, Morley 'Harmonization of Labour Policies Under Trade Liberalization' *Relations Industrial Relations*, 53, (1998), 24–52.

Hall, Peter A. and Rosemary C.R. Taylor, Political Science and the Three New Institutionalisms' *Political Studies* 44,(1996), 936–957.

Hamilton Spectator Nov. 26, 1991, March 5, 2001.

Hanagan, Michael P. 'Labor Internationalism: An Introduction' *Social Science History* 27, (2003), 485–499.

Harrison, Bennett 'Averting a race to the bottom' *Technology–Review.* 98 (1995) p. 74.

Harvey, Pharis 'Trade and Labor' *Foreign Policy In Focus* 2, 15 January 1997 [cited Dec. 16, 2003]. Available at http://www.foreignpolicy-infocus.org/briefs/vol2/ v2n15trd.html.

Harvey, Pharis J., Collingsworth, Terry, and Athreya, Bama 'Summary: A Plan of Action for Including a Social Clause in U.S. Trade Policy as Outlined in Developing Effective Mechanisms for Implementing Labor Rights in the Global Economy' International Labor Rights Fund [cited Feb 4, 2004]. Available at http://www.laborrights.org/projects/globalecon/ilrf/intro.html.

Hathaway, Dale A. 'Mexico's Frente Autentico del Trabajo and the Problem of Unionizing Maquiladoras' *Labor History*, 43 (2002), 427–438.

Haworth, Nigel and Hughes, Stephen 'Death of a Social Clause? Reconstructing the trade and labour standards debate in the Asia-pacific' Paper to the International Conference on Labour Standards and Human Rights University of California, Berkeley, January 1998. [cited Feb 4, 2004]. Available at http://www.iir.berkeley. edu/clre/publications/death.html#intro.

Hayes, Daniel 'Mexico to probe N.Y. workers' comp board' *National Underwriter* 105, 51, Dec. 17, 2001, 20.

Hayes, Daniel 'N.Y. governor pushes WC reform proposal' *National Underwriter* 103, 21, May 24, 1999, 1.

Henwood, Doug 'Clinton's Trade Policy' in Fred Rosen and Dierdre McFayden eds. *Free Trade and Restructuring in Latin America: A NACLA Reader* New York: Monthly Review Press, 1995), 27–38.

Hertel, Shareen 'Campaigns to protect human rights in Mexico's maquiladoras: current research findings.' *Newsletter, Institute of Latin American Studies,* Columbia University, (Spring 2002), 1–10.

Herzenberg, Stephen 'Calling Maggie's Bluff: The NAFTA Labor Agreement and the Development of an Alternative to Neoliberalism' *Canadian American Public Policy* 28, (1996).

Hettne, Björn and Söderbaum, Frederik 'Theorising the Rise of Regions,' *New Political Economy* 5 (2000), 457–73.

Hijuelos, Claudia Franco 'Normas laborales en el comercio internacional: el ACLAN.' *Foro Internacional,* 51 (2001), 309–323.

Hoberg, George, 'Canada and North American Integration,' *Canadian Public Policy* 26, (2000), 35–50.

Holloway, Gary 'Solec Workers Win First Contract!' *The Organizer* (OCAW Local 1–675), 3, 1 September , 1998, http://www.pace8-675.org/articles/organizer0998. html.

Hottenrott, Victoria and Stephen Blank, *Assessing NAFTA – Part II – The impact of NAFTA on jobs, wages, and income inequality*, Pan-American Partnership for Business Education, Working Paper no. 178 December 1998.

Housman, Robert F. and Paul M Orbuch, 'Integrating Labor and Environmental Concerns into the North American Free Trade Agreement' *American University Journal of International Law and Policy.* 8 (1993), 719–816.

Hout, Wil 'Theories of International Relations and the New Regionalism,' in W. Hout and J. Grugel eds. *Regionalism Across the North–South Divide: State strategies and Globalization* London: Routledge, 1999, 14–28.

Howard, James and Winston Gereluk, 'Core Labour Standards and Human Rights in the Workplace' *Opinion 2001* International Institute for Environment and Development, World Summit on Sustainable Development, [cited April 23, 2005]. Available at http://www.iied.org/docs/wssd/bp_corelabor.pdf.

Hufbauer, Gary Clyde and Jeffrey J. Schott, (with Diana Orejas, Ben Goodrich and Yee Wong) 'North American Labor under NAFTA' Washington: Institute for International Economics, February, 2005 [cited April 16, 2004]. Available at www.iie.com/publications/papers/nafta-labor.pdf.

Human Rights Watch *A Job or Your Rights: Continued Sex Discrimination in Mexico's Maquiladora Sector* December 1998 [cited June 12, 2002]. Available at http://www.hrw.org/reports98/women2/Maqui98d.htm.

Human Rights Watch, *Trading Away Rights The Unfulfilled Promise of NAFTA's Labor Side Agreement* New York: Human Rights Watch 2001.

Human Rights Watch World Report, *Mexico: The Role of the International Community* [cited July 27, 2000]. Available at http://www.hrw.org/worldreport99/americas/ mexico3.html.

Hurrell, Andrew 'Regionalism in Theoretical Perspective' in Andrew Hurrell and Louise Fawcett eds), *Regionalism in World Politics: Regional Order and International Order* New York: Oxford University Press, 1995, 37–73.

Immergut, Ellen M., 'The Theoretical Core of the New Institutionalism.' *Politics and Society* 26, (1998), 5–34.

Independent Task Force on the Future of North America, *Creating a North American Community* New York: Council on Foreign Relations, 2005.

Inter Press Service May 27, 1998, June 2, 1998.

International Labour Organization, 'Declaration on Fundamental Principles and Rights at Work' ILO 86th Session, Geneva, June 1998 [cited Dec. 11, 2003]. Available at http://www.ilo.org/dyn/declaris/DECLARATIONWEB.static_ jump?var_language=EN&var_pagename=DECLARATIONTEXT.

International Labour Organization, *World Labour Report 1997–98: Industrial relations, democracy and social stability* Table 1.2. [cited Jan. 23, 2004]. Available at http://www.ilo.org/public/english/dialogue/ifpdial/publ/wlr97/annex/ tab12.htm.

International Confederation of Free Trade Unions. 1999. *Building Workers' Human Rights into the Global Trading System* Brussels: ICFTU, 1999.

Janero, Kenneth A. and Schreiber, Phillip M. 'Revisiting the Legality of Employee Participation Programs under the NLRA' *Employee Relations Law Journal* 25, 1 (Summer, 1999), 119–28.

Jay, Bruce Commentary, 'US Department of Labor Active in FTAA' Summit of the Americas Website, [cited Feb. 2, 2004]. Available at http://www.americasnet.net/ Commentators/Bruce_Jay/COMMENTARY_MARCH.pdf.

Journal of Commerce, April 15, 1994, Feb. 29, 1996, May 29, 1996, April 18, 1997, Nov. 19, 1997, Aug. 6, 1998, Nov 30, 1999.

Karson, Tom 'Confronting Houston's Demographic Shift: the Harris County AFL-CIO' *WorkingUSA* 8, (2004) 213–14.

Keck, Margaret E and Sikkink, Kathryn 'Transnational advocacy networks in international and regional politics' *International Social Science Journal* 51, (1999), 9–101.

Kleinman, Ronald W. and Shapiro, Joel M. 'NAFTA's Proposed Tri-Lateral Commissions on the Environment and Labor' *U.S. Mexico Law Journal* 2 (1994), 25–36.

Kreklewich, Robert 'North American Integration and Industrial Relations: Neoconservativism and Neo-Fordism?' in Ricardo Grinspun and Maxwell A. Cameron, eds. *The Political Economy of North American Free Trade* Montreal: McGill-Queen's University Press, 1993, 261–70.

Krugman, Paul 'What should trade negotiators negotiate about?' *Journal of Economic Literature* 35, (1997), 113–120.

Krugman, Paul 'The uncomfortable truth about NAFTA: it's foreign policy, stupid,' *Foreign Affairs* 72, 5 (1993), 13–20.

Labor Relations Weekly Sept. 1995, March 2002.

La Botz, Dan 'Mexican Health Care Workers Lose Big Fight on Pensions as Union Foregoes Planned Strike' *Labor Notes* 321, Dec 2005.

LaBotz, Dan 'Mexico's Labor Movement in Transition' *Monthly Review* 57 (2005) 62–71.

Langille, Brian A. 'Labour Standards in the Globalized Economy and the FreeTrade/ Fair Trade Debate,' in W. Sengenberger and D. Campbell eds., *International Labour Standards and Economic Interdependence* Geneva: International Institute for Labour Studies, 1994, 329–38.

LaSala, Barry 'NAFTA and worker rights: an analysis of the Labor Side Accord after five years of operation and suggested improvements' *Labor Lawyer*, 6 (2001), 319–347.

Lavelle, Marianne 'NAFTA jars labor laws; U.S., Mexico to discuss criticisms of Sprint's firing of employees' *National Law Journal* 17 (1995), A9.

La Voz de La Fronterra April 20, 1999.

Leary, Virginia 'Worker's Rights and International Trade: The Social Clause, in Bhagwati, J. and Hudec, R. eds. *Fair Trade and Harmonization, Vol. 2* Cambridge, MA: MIT Press, 1997, 177–230.

Leary, Virginia A. 'The WTO and the Social Clause: Post-Singapore,' *European Journal of International Law*, 8, 118 (1997), 118–123.

Leibfried, Stephan and Piersen, Paul 'Social Policy' in Wallace, Helen and Wallace, William eds. *Policy-Making in the European Union* New York: Oxford, 2000, 268–93.

Levinson, Jerome *NAFTA's Labor Side Agreement: Lessons from the First Three Years* Washington: Institute for Policy Studies and International Labor Rights Fund, 1996.

Levinson, Jerome *The Labor Side Accord to the North American Free Trade Agreement: An endorsement of the Abuse of Worker Rights in Mexico* Washington: Economic Policy Institute, 1993.

Li Wai Suen, Rachel 'You sure know how to pick 'em: human rights and migrant farm workers in Canada.' *Georgetown Immigration Law Journal* 15 (2000), 199–227.

Linas, Jesus Campos 'la primer audiencia pública en el marco del tlc' *Evidencias*, Fall, 1994.

Lineas Generales de Trabajo Aprobadas por el X Congresso Nacional de FAT Noviembre de 1993 Mexico: FAT, 1993.

Los Angeles Times August 20, 1999, May 13, 2005.

MacDonald, Ian T. 'Negotiating Mexico's labour law reform: corporatism, neoliberalism and democratic opening' *Studies in Political Economy* 73 (2004), 139–158.

Mansfield, Edward D. and Helen V. Milner 'The New Wave of Regionalism,' in Paul F. Diehl ed. *The Politics of Global Governance: International Organizations in an Interdependent World*, 2d ed. Boulder: Lynne Rienner, 2001, 313–25.

Manuel Godinez Zuniga, Victor, Testimony to the *Foro Permanente de Informacion, Opinion y Dialogo Sobre los Negociaciones del Tratado Trliateral de Libre Comercio entre Mexico, los Estados Unidos y Canada*, Senado de la Republica, March 14, 1991, Mexico: Senado de la Republica, 1991.

Maquiladora Health & Safety Support Network Alerts January 2002.
Maquiladora Health & Safety Support Network Newsletter, September 17, 2001.
March, James G. and Johan P. Olsen. 'The New Institutionalism: Organizational Factors in Political Life.' *The American Political Science Review* 78, (1984), 734–749.
Marchand, Marianne H., Morten Boas and Timothy M. Shaw, 'The political economy of new regionalisms,' *Third World Quarterly* 20, 5 (1999), 897–910.
Marshall, Ray 'The North American Free Trade Agreement: Implications for Workers' in Raphael Fernadez de Castro, Monica Verea Campos and Sydney Weintraub, eds. *Sectoral Labor effects of North American Free Trade* Austin: U.S. Mexican Polcy Studies Program, University of Texas, 1993, 3–33.
Marshall, Judith 'Worker exchanges between Chilean and Canadian miners' *Canadian Dimension* 32 (March, 1998), 37–9.
Martin, Philip 'Immigration and Farm Labor: An Overview' University of California, Davis August 31, 1999, 9; www.farmfoundation.org/1999NPPEC/martin.pdf June 11, 2002.
Martin, Andrew 'Labour, the Keynesian Welfare State and the Changing Global Economy,' in Richard Stubbs and Geoffrey R.D. Underhill eds. *Political Economy and the Changing Global Order* Toronto: McClelland and Stewart, 1994, 60–74.
Martin, Richard 'Canadian Labour and North American Integration' in Stephen J. Randall ed. *North America Without Borders*? Calgary: University of Calgary Press, 1992, 181–90.
Maskus, Keith *Should Core Labor Standards be Imposed Through International Tade Policy?* World Bank Working Paper 1817, 1997 [cited May 11, 2005]. Available at http://www-wds.worldbank.org/servlet/WDSContentServer/WDSP/IB/2000/02/24/000009265_3971110141359/Rendered/PDF/multi_page.pdf., 1997.
Mayer, Frederick W. Negotiating NAFTA: Political Lessons for the FTAA Working Papers Series SAN01-17, Terry Sanford Institute of Public Policy, Duke University, July 2001.
McCaffrey, Shellyn G. 'North American Free Trade and Labor Issues: Accomplishments and Challenges' *Hofstra Labor Law Journal* 10, (1993), 449–.
McClure, Laura 'Workers of the World Unite!' *Dollars and Sense* Sept., 1992, 19.
McCrudden, Christopher and Anne Davies, 'A perspective on trade and labor rights' *Journal of International Economic Law* 3, (2000), 43–62.
McDougall, John N. 'National differences and the NAFTA' *International Journal* 55, (2000), 281–90.
McDowell, Manfred 'NAFTA and the EC `Social Dimension'' *Labor Studies Journal* 20 (1995), 39–47.
McFadyen, Jacqueline NAFTA Supplemental Agreements: Four Year Review , Institute For International Economics Working Paper 98-4 [cited April 1, 1999]. Available at http://www.iie.com/CATALOG/WP/1998/98-4.htm.
McGinn, Mary and, Kim Moody 'Labor goes global' *Progressive* 57 (March, 1993), 24–28.

The Limits of Regionalism

McGuckin, Gene 'Rio Bravo union loses to guns, drugs, intimidation' *CEP Journal* 9, 2 Spring, 2001, 2–.

McKinney, Joseph A. *Created from NAFTA – the structure, function, and significance of the treaty's related institutions* New York: M.E. Sharpe, 2000.

McLaughlin, Christopher 'Chilean miners dig Canada' *Alternatives Journal*, 24 (Fall, 1998).

McShane, Denis 'Human Rights and Labor Rights: A European Perspective' in Lance Compa and S. Diamond eds. *Human Rights, Labor Rights and International Trade* Philadelphia: University of Pennsylvania Press, 1996, 48–70.

Mehmet, Ozay and Daudelin, Jean *Labour Mobility, Labour Standards and Hemispheric Integration: Mercosur, NAFTA, the Caribbean and the FTAA* Ottawa: Canadian Foundation for the Americas, 1998.

Meloro, Bobbi-Lee 'Balancing the goals of free trade with workers' rights in a hemispheric economy.' *University of Miami Inter-American Law Review*, 30, (1999), 433–460.

Mercury, James and Schwartz, Bryan 'Creating the Free Trade Area of the Americas: linking labour, the environment, and human rights to the FTAA' *Asper Review of International Business and Trade Law*, 1 (2001), 37–65.

Mexican Labor News and Analysis, Oct. 16, 1996, Dec. 5, 1997, June 16, 1998, March 1, 2001.

Mexico, Secretaria de Trabajo y Prevision Sociale, (STPS) numerous documents in text and electronic formats.

Mizrahi, Yemile , 'Will Vicente Fox be able to breathe new life into Mexican federalism?,' *Federations* 1, 1, (2000).

Montgomery, David 'Labor Rights and Human Rights: A Historical Perspective,' in Lance A Compa and Stephen F Diamond eds. *Human rights, labor rights, and international trade* Philadelphia : University of Pennsylvania Press, 1996, 13–21.

Moody, Kim 'NAFTA and the corporate redesign of North America' *Latin American Perspectives*. 22 (1995), 95–117.

Moreau, Marie-Ange and Gilles Trudeau 'Le droit du travail face à la mondialisation de l'économie.' *Industrial Relations*, 53 (1998), 55–89.

Morpaw, May 'The North American Agreement on Labour Cooperation: Highlights, Implementation and Significance' Closing Address at the 1995 Conference of the Canadian Industrial Relations Association, Montreal, May 29, 1995.

'NAFTA Labor Side Deal: From Useless to Dangerous' *Working Together: Labor Report on the Americas* 39 Fall, 2000, 1–.

National Radio Project 'Empty Promises: NAFTA and the Workforce' [cited June 12, 2002]. Available at http://www.radioproject.org/transcripts/9840.html.

National Law Journal Sept 19, 1994, 1995.

National Post March 16, 1999

Newsday July 24, 2001.

Nolan, Justine and Posner., Michael 'International standards to promote labor rights: the role of the United States government.' *Columbia Business Law Review*, 3 (2000), 529–543.

Norte de Ciudad Juarez Sept. 6, 1994, July 4, 1996.

North American Free Trade Agreement (NAFTA) Policy Documents National Administrative Offices [cited Dec. 11, 2002]. Available at http://www.ilo.org/public/english/employment/gems/eeo/nafta/nao.htm.

O'Boyle, Michael 'Union blues' *Business Mexico,* 12, Nov. 2002, 53–5.

O'Brien, Robert, 'The Agency of Labour in a Changing Global Order,' in Richard Stubbs and Geoffrey R.D. Underhill eds. *Political Economy and the Changing Global Order (3rd. ed.)* Toronto: Oxford, 2005, 222–32.

OECD, *International Trade and Core Labour Standards* Paris: OECD, 2000 [cited April 12, 2004]. Available at http://www.oecdbookshop.org/oecd/get-it.asp?REF=2200041E.PDF.

Office of the United States Trade Representative 'CAFTA – Labor and Environment Capacity Building' CAFTA Policy Brief, July 2005 [cited August 17, 2005]. Available at http://www.ustr.gov/assets/Trade_Agreements/Bilateral/CAFTA/Briefing_Book/asset_upload_file758_7871.pdf?ht=central%20america.

'Origins of Mexico's Labor Law Reform' *NACLA Report on the Americas,* 39 (Jul/Aug 2005), 18–19.

Otero, Joaquin F. 'The North American Agreement on Labor Cooperation: Overview and Status of Implementation' *Labor Law Developments*, 1995 (Southwestern Legal Foundation, 41st. Annual Institute on Labor Law, 1995).

Panitch, Leo 'Changing Gears: Democratizing the Welfare State' in Andrew Johnson, Stephen McBride and Patrick Smith eds. *Continuities and Discontinuities: The Political Economy of Social Welfare and Labour Market Policy in Canada* Toronto, University of Toronto Press, 1994, 36–43.

Pascual Moncayo, Pablo and Trejo Delarbe, Raul, *Los Sindicatos Mexicanos Ante el TLC* Mexico: Instituto de Estudios para la Transición Democrática, 1993.

Pasquero, J. 2000. 'Regional Market Integration in North America and Corporate Social Management. Emerging Governance Frameworks for Business and Public Policy'. *Business and Society*, 39: 6–23.

Pastor, Robert *Towards a North American Community* Washington: Institute for International Economics, 2001.

Patroni, Viviana 'The decline and fall of corporatism? Labour legislation reform in Mexico and Argentina during the 1990s' *Canadian Journal of Political Science* 34 (2001), 249–274.

Pearson, Carole 'A case of apples: Mexican farm workers in Washington' *Our Times,* 20, 6 Dec. 2001/Jan. 2002, 21–28.

Perez-Lopez, Jorge F. 'Conflict and Cooperation in US–Mexican Labor Relations: The North American Agreement on Labor Cooperation' *Journal of Borderlands Studies* XI, (1996), 43–58.

Peters, Susanna 'Labor Law for the Maquiladoras: Choosing Between Workers Rights and Foreign Investment', *Comparative Labor Law Journal* 11, 1990, 226–248.

Phelps, Constance 'Social work and labor: a look at the North American Agreement on Labor Cooperation.' *Journal of Sociology and Social Welfare*, 28 (2001), 23–41.

Polaski, Sandra 'Labor Provisions in the FTAA? A Continuing Controversy' For presentation at the Yale Conference on Hemispheric Trade New Haven, Connecticut, April 2–4, 2003.

Polaski, Sandra 'Protecting Labor Rights Through Trade Agreements: an Analytical Guide' *Journal of International Law and Policy*, 10 (2004), 13–25.

Pomeroy, Laura Okin 'The Labor Side Agreement under the NAFTA: Analysis of its Failure to Include Strong Enforcement Provisions and Recommendations for Future Labor Agreements Negotiated with Developing Countries' *George Washington Journal of International Law and Economics* 29, (1996), 769–800.

Poppe, David 'Tomato pasting: Florida tomato farmers say dumping by Mexico threatens to destroy them' *Florida Trend* 38, 1 Aug 1, 1995.

Press and Sun Bulletin, Mar. 3, 2002.

Proceso Nov, 1999.

Que es el FAT? Mexico, D.F: Frente Autentico de Trabajo, n.d.

Quinn, Kelly 'Stand And Deliver: The Solec Unit Organizing Campaign' *The Organizer* (OCAW Local 1–675) 3 July 1998 http://www.pace8-675.org/articles/organizer0/98.html.

'Rechaza la CTM crear una Comisión que supervise cumplir los paralelos' *Economía* June 3, 1993, 30.

Red Mexicana de Accio Frente al Libre Comercio, *Sustentable: Por un Comercio Justo* Mexico, D.F.: Foundacio Friedrich Ebert, 1993.

Reforma April 22, 1999, Nov. 10, 1999.

Reygades, Luis 'Libertad laboral y Tratado de Libre Comercio' *El Cotidiano* 7, (Sept.–Oct., 1991), 19.

Reynaud, Adolfo Ciudad *Labour Standards and the Integration Process in the Americas* Geneva: International Labour Organization, 2001.

Reynolds, Clark W. 'Power, Value and Distribution in the NAFTA' in Riordan Roett ed. *Political and Economic Liberalization in Mexico: At a Critical Juncture?* Boulder, Col., Lynne Reinner, 1993, 69–86.

Robinson, Ian 'NAFTA, social unionism, and labour movement power in Canada and the United States' *Industrial Relations* 49 (1994), 357–93.

Robinson, Ian 'Neoliberal Restructuring and U.S. Unions: Toward Social Movement Unionism?' *Critical Sociology* 26, (2000), 109–138.

Rodriguez-Garavito, Cesar A 'Global Governance and Labor Rights: Codes of Conduct and Anti-Sweatshop Struggles in Global Apparel Factories in Mexico and Guatemala' *Politics and Society* 33 (2005), 203–333.

Rosen, Howard 'Adjustment and Transition Mechanisms for a U.S.–Mexico Free Trade Agreement,' in M. Delal Baer and Sidney Weintraub eds. *The NAFTA Debate: Grappling With Unconventional Trade Issues* Boulder, Col.: Lynne Reiner, 1994, 35–52.

Rosen, Fred 'The underside of NAFTA: a budding cross-border resistance.' *NACLA Report on the Americas*, 32 (January/February 1999), 37–40.

Ross, Robert J.S. and Chan, Anita 'From North–South to South–South' *Foreign Affairs* 81, (2002), 8–13.

Rozwood, Benjamin and Walker, Andrew R. 'Side Agreements, Sidesteps and Sideshows: Protecting Labor from Free Trade in North America' *Harvard International Law Review* 34 (1993), 333–55.

Rubio, Luis 'Economic Reform and Political Change in Mexico'in Riordan Roett ed. *Political and Economic Liberalization in Mexico: At a Critical Juncture?* Boulder, Col.: Lynne Reinner, 1993, 35–50.

Saguier, Marcelo I. 'Convergence in the Making: Transnational Civil Society and the Free Trade Area of the Americas' *CSGR Working Paper* No. 137/04, 2004, 3 [cited Dec. 16, 2005]. Available at http://www2.warwick.ac.uk/fac/soc/csgr/research/workingpapers/2004/wp13704.pdf.

San Antonio Business Journal August 11, 2000.

San Antonio Express News April 9, 2002.

San Diego Telegraph March 10, 1996.

San Diego Union Tribune February 19, 1998, April 29, 1998, May 23, 1998, Jan.19, 2002.

San Francisco Chronicle Sept. 10, 1997, Nov. 28, 199, June 2, 1998.

San Francisco Examiner June 29, 1995

Sauber, James 'Continental Divide: Collective Bargaining Rights and Rural Letter Carrier Compensation in the United States and Canada' Prepared by Union Network International for the NAALC Workshop on the Right to Organize and Bargain Collectively in Canada and the United States Toronto, Feb. 1–2, 2001

Scheuerman, William E. 'False humanitarianism? US advocacy of transnational labour protections,' *Review of International Political Economy* 8, (2001), 359–88.

Scott, James Wesley 'European and North American Contexts for Cross-border Regionalism' *Regional Studies* 33, (1999), 605–617.

Seattle Times August 2, 1998.

Sefton-MacDowell, Laura 'The International Confederation of Free Trade Unions,' *Labour/Le Travaileur* 49, 1 (2002), 345–46.

Shaiken, Harley 'The NAFTA, A Social Charter and Economic Growth' in Belous, Richard S. and Lemco, Jonathan eds. *NAFTA As a Model of Development: The Benefits and Costs of Merging High–And Low–Wage Areas* Albany: SUNY Press, 1995, 27–36.

Shaiken, Harley 'The New Global Economy: Trade and Production under NAFTA' *Journal für Entwicklungspolitik* 17 (2001), 241–54.

Shields, James ''Social dumping' in Mexico under NAFTA' *Multinational Monitor* 16 (April, 1995), 20–25.

Simmons,'NAFTA, Alan B. international migration and labour rights.' *Labour, Capital and Society*, 31, (1998), 10–43.

Singh, Parbudyal 'NAFTA and labor: a Canadian perspective.' *Journal of Labor Research*, 23 (2002), 433–446.

Singh, Parbudyal and Adams,'Neither, Roy J. a gem nor a scam: the progress of the North American Agreement on Labor Cooperation.' *Labor Studies Journal*, 26, (2001), 1–16.

Slogoff, Reed J. 'Mexico: Living with the NAFTA Labor Laws', *Trade and Culture Magazine* March/April 1995.

Smith, James A. 'Panel Discussion: the Challenges and Opportunities under the NAFTA Labor Cooperation Agreement', *United States–Mexico Law Journal*, 1995, 149–157.

Smith, Russell E. 'NAFTA and industrial relations in Mexico: what's important now?' *Perspectives on Work*, 6 (2002), 25–27.

Smith, Russell E. 'An Early Assessment of the NAFTA Labor Side Accords' in *Industrial Relations Research Association, Proceedings of the Forty-Ninth Annual Meeting* (New Orleans, Jan. 4–6, 1997) 230–236.

Smith, Jackie G. et. al., 'Human Rights and the Global Economy: A Response to Meyer' *Human Rights Quarterly* 21 (1999), 207–219.

Frederick Söderbaum, 'Introduction: Theories of New Regionalism' in Soderbaum and Timothy Shaw (eds.) *Theories of new regionalism: a Palgrave reader* (London: Palgrave, 2003), 1–21.

F. Söderbaum, 'Rethinking the New regionalism,' Paper for the XIII Nordic Political Science Association Meeting, Aalborg 15–17 August 2002. [cited July 9, 2004]. Available at http://www.naalc.org/french/pdf/labor_boards_scm_starkmant.pdf.

Solidarity May, 1998.

Spalding, Hobart A. 'The Two Latin American Foreign Policies of the U.S. Labor Movement: The AFL-CIO Top Brass vs. Rank and File,' *Science and Society* 56, 4 (1992–93), 421–39.

Special Summit of the Americas, 'Declaration of Nuevo León' Monterrey, Mexico January 13, 2004.

'Sprint Hangs Up on Workers' Multinational Monitor, 17, March 1996 [Cited Oct. 13, 1998]. http://multinationalmonitor.org/hyper/mm0396.03.html.

Starkman, Akivah 'The Structure and Role of Canadian Labour Boards,' presented to the NAALC Trilateral Seminar on Labour Boards in North America, March 2003. [cited August 16, 2004]. Available at http://www.naalc.org/french/pdf/labor_boards_sem_starkmant.pdf.

Statement of Ezequiel Garcia, (STIMAHCS), 'Organizing Workers in Mexico, A NAFTA Issue', *Hearing Before the Employment, Housing and Aviation Subcommittee of the Committee on Government Operations,* U.S. House of Representatives, 103rd. Congress, 1st. Session, July 15, 1993, 8–.

Steagall, Jeffrey W. and Ken Jennings, 'Unions, PAC Contributions and the NAFTA Vote' *Journal of Labour Research* 17, (1996), 515–21.

Stevenson, Linda S 'Confronting gender discrimination in the Mexican workplace: Women and labor facing NAFTA with transnational contention' *Women and Politics* 26, (2004), 71–98.

Stewart, Gordon T. 'Three Lessons for Mexico from Canadian–American Relations,' *Frontera Norte* 3, 6, (1992), 29–98.

Stillerman, Joel 'Transnational Activist Networks and the Emergence of Labor Internationalism in the NAFTA Countries' *Social Science History* 27, (2003), 577–601.

Summers, Clyde 'NAFTA's Labor Side Agreement and international labor standards.' *The Journal of Small and Emerging Business Law*, 3, (1999), 173–187.

Teague, Paul 'Labour-standard setting and regional trading blocs: Lesson drawing from the NAFTA experience' *Employee Relations*, 25 (2003), 428–452.

'The Abascal Plan: Codifying Employer Control' *NACLA Report on the Americas* 39, Jul/Aug 2005, 21–2.

The International Brotherhood of Teamsters *News Release* March 18, 1998, September 15, 1998.

Testimony of Ambassador Richard Fisher, Deputy United States Trade Representative Before the Senate Committee on Foreign Relations on the 'Economic Effects of NAFTA' Tuesday, April 13, 1999 http://usembassy-mexico.gov/et990419TLC.html.

Toronto Star Nov. 20, 1986, April 7, 1998, Sept. 15, 1998, December 7, 1998, April 15, 2001.

Toronto Sun February 13 1998, April 18, 2002.

Troy, Leo 'U.S. and Canadian Industrial Relations: Convergent or Divergent?,' *Industrial Relations* 39, 4 (2000), 695–713.

Trubek, David Jim Mosher, and Jeffrey S. Rothstein, 'Transnationalism in the regulation of labor relations: international regimes and transnational advocacy networks.' *Law and Social Inquiry*, 25, (2000) 1187–1211.

'UNICE Rejects WTO's Labour Standards Definition' *European Report* Jul 14, 1999, 1–.

United Electrical Workers International 'NAFTA Side Agreement Sidelined Labor Rights' [cited April 2004]. Available at http://www.ueinternational.org/WorldTrade/nafta.html.

United States–Canada–Mexico Tripartite Conference, U.S. National Administrative Office, U.S. Department of Labor, *Improving Children's Lives: Child and Youth Labor in North America,* 1997.

USA Today Mar 23, 1995.

US Department of Labor and U.S. Department of Justice 'Memorandum of Understanding Between the Immigration and Naturalization Service and the Employment Standards Administration Department of Labor', Washington, Nov. 23, 1998.

US Department of Labor, International Labour Affairs Bureau, *Foreign Labor Trends: Mexico*, Washington: ILAB, 2002.

US Department of Labor, International Labor Affairs Bureau National Administrative Office, numerous documents in text or electronic formats.

US Department of Labour, *Press Release*, Nov. 10, 1994, Dec. 17, 1995, Jan. 12, 1998, August 11, 1998, Nov. 23, 1998, Dec. 18, 1998, Apr.21, 1999, April 15, 2002, June 12, 2002.

US Department of State, Bureau of Western Hemisphere Affairs *U.S–Mexico Binational Commission Labor Working Group, Report* Washington, Nov. 12, 2003

288   *The Limits of Regionalism*

[cited May 12, 2005]. Available at http://www.state.gov/p/wha/rls/rpt/26212. htm.

US Equal Employment Opportunities Agency 'EEOC Expands Immigrant Rights Partnership to Include OSHA, DOJ and Latin American Consulates' *Press Release* Washington Sept. 27, 2002, [cited May 5, 2005]. Available at http://www.eeoc. gov/press/9-27-02.html.

US General Accounting Office, *U.S.–Mexico Trade: The Work Environment at Eight U.S.–Owned Maquiladora Auto Plants* Report to the Chairman, Committee on Commerce, Science, and Transportation, U.S. Senate, November, 1993.

U.S.–Mexico Free Trade Reporter, Sept. 30, 1994.

U.S.–Mexico *Joint Declaration on Ministerial Consultations*, June 11, 2002, [cited Oct. 24, 2002]. Available at http://www.dol.gov/ilab/media/reports/nao/ jointdeclar061102.htm.

US News and World Report, Sept 1, 1997, Jan 26, 1998.

Utne, Leif 'Giant sucking sound rises in the East' *Utne 116* 2003, 22–.

van Liemt, Gijsbert 'International trade and workers,' rights,', in Brian Hocking and Steven McGuire eds. *Trade Politics: International, Domestic and Regional Responses* New York: Routledge, 1999, 111–127.

Van Wezel Stone, Katherine 'Labor and the Global Economy: Four Approaches to Transnational Labor Regulation,' *Michigan Journal of International Law* 16, (1995), 987–1028.

Vanderbush, Walt 'Mexican Labor in the Era of Economic Restructuring and NAFTA: Working to create a Favorable Investment Climate,' *Labor Studies Journal* 20, 4 (1996) 58–86.

Verge, Pierre 'Les modes canadiens de régulation juridique du travail: disparition ou adaptation au changement?' in Commission for Labor Cooperation, *Industrial Relations for the 21ˢᵗ. Century: Canada–United States–Mexico Tripartite Conference, Proceedings* Montreal, March 18–20, 1996, 23–31.

Verge, Pierre 'Analytical Presentation of the North-American Agreement on Labour Cooperation (NAALC)' *ILO, research in support of the Inter-American Conference of Ministers of Labor*, 14; [cited Feb. 23, 2004]. Available at http:// www.oit.org.pe/cimt/documetospdf/146eng.pdf.

von Bertrab, Hermann, *Negotiating NAFTA: A Mexican Envoy's Account* Washington: Praeger, 1997.

Wall Street Journal Jun 3, 1994, Oct. 14, 1994, Jan 26, 1996, Feb 5, 1996, May 17, 1996, Jul 3, 1996, Oct 14, 1996, Feb 4, 1998.

Washington Post, Aug. 1, 2001, Jun. 21, 2002.

Watkins, Kevin *Globalisation and liberalisation: Implications for poverty, distribution and inequality* UNDP, Human Development Reports, Occasional Paper 32, 1997 [Cited Feb. 14, 2004]. Available at http://hdr.undp.org/docs/ publications/ocational_papers/oc32c.htm.

Watson, Rachel 'Maquiladora discrimination: 'A serious issue'' *Ms*, May/Jun 1998, 13.

Watts, Julie *Mexico–U.S. Migration and Labor Unions: Obstacles to Building Cross–Border Solidarity* University of Californa at San Diego, Center for Comparative Immigration Studies Working Paper #79 June, 2003 [cited April 23, 2005]. Available at http://www.ccis-ucsd.org/PUBLICATIONS/wrkg79.pdf, 27.

Weekly Special Report December 9, 2004.

Wheeler, Hoyt N. 'Viewpoint' Collective Bargaining is a Fundamental Human Right,' *Industrial Relations* 39 (2000), 535–39.

Wilkinson, Bruce 'NAFTA in the World Economy: Lessons and Issues for Latin America,' in Richard G. Lipsey, and Patricio Meller, eds., *Western Hemisphere Trade Integration: A Canadian–Latin American Dialogue* London: MacMillan, 1997, 30–57.

Williams, Heather L. 'Mobile capital and transborder labor rights mobilization' *Politics and Society*, 27 (1999) 139–166.

Working Together, July–August, 1996, Nov.–Dec., 1996, Jan.–Feb., 1998, March–April 1999.

Worth, Owen 'The Janus-like Character of Counter-hegemony: Progressive and Nationalist Responses to Neoliberalism' *Global Society*, 16 (2002), 297–315.

'WTO: Ministers Agree to Do Nothing on Labour Standards' *European Report* Dec. 14, 1996.

Index

Locators shown in *italics* refer to tables.